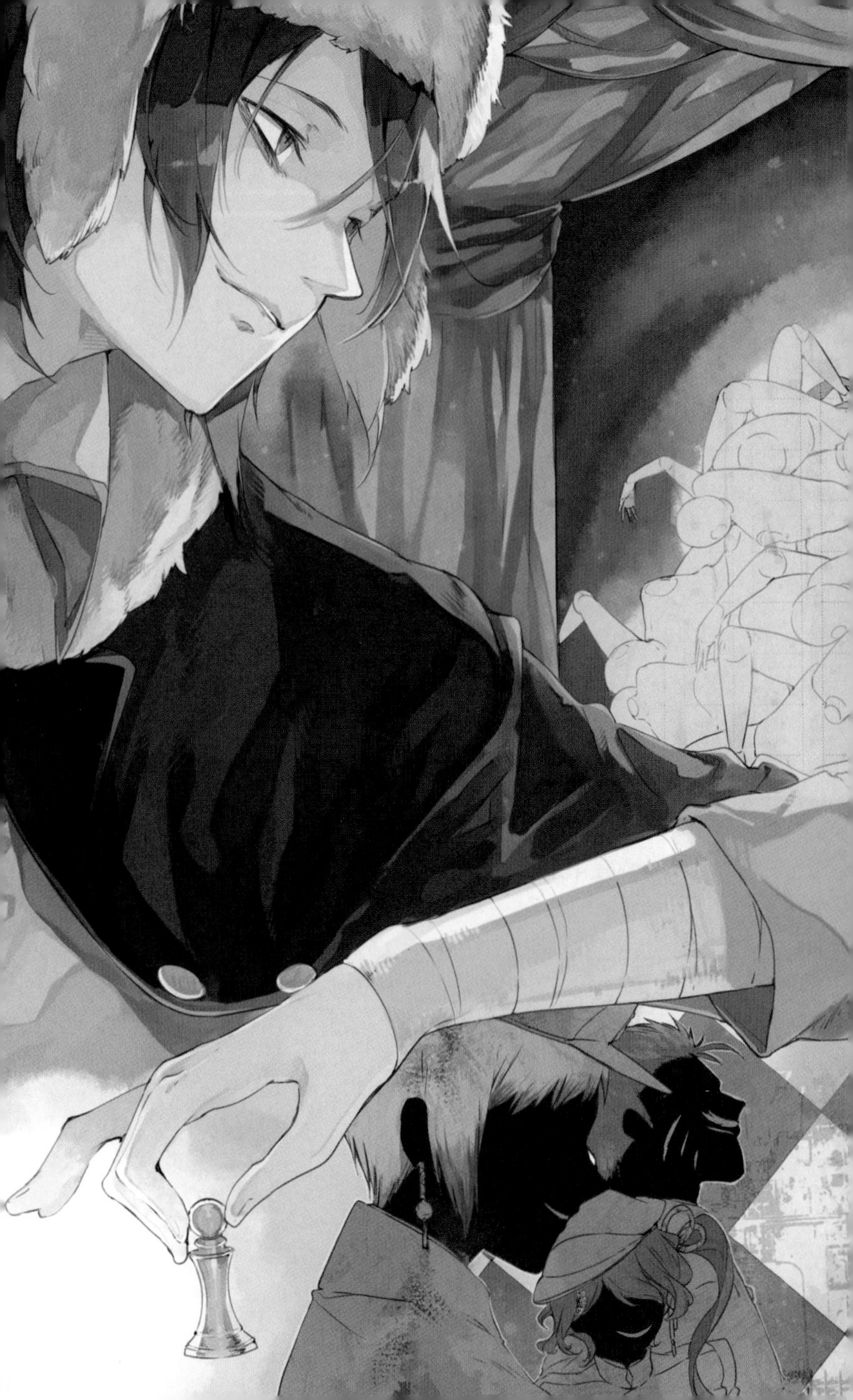

TABLE of CONTENTS

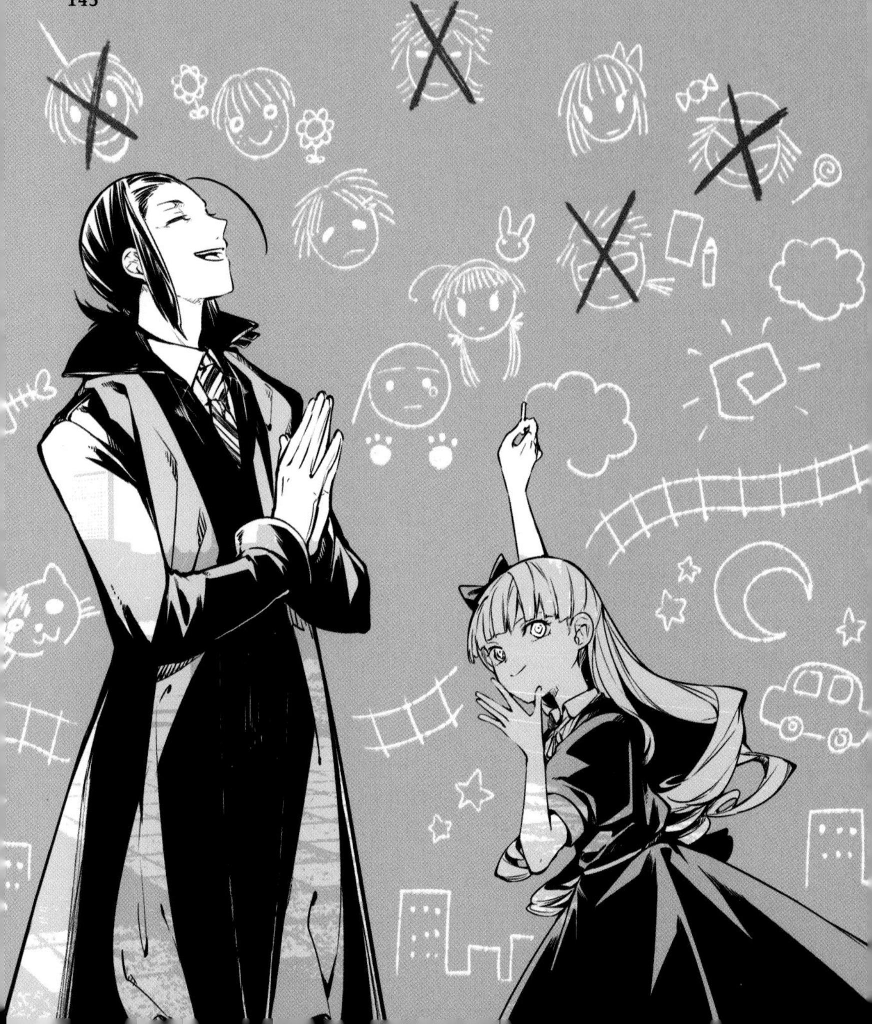

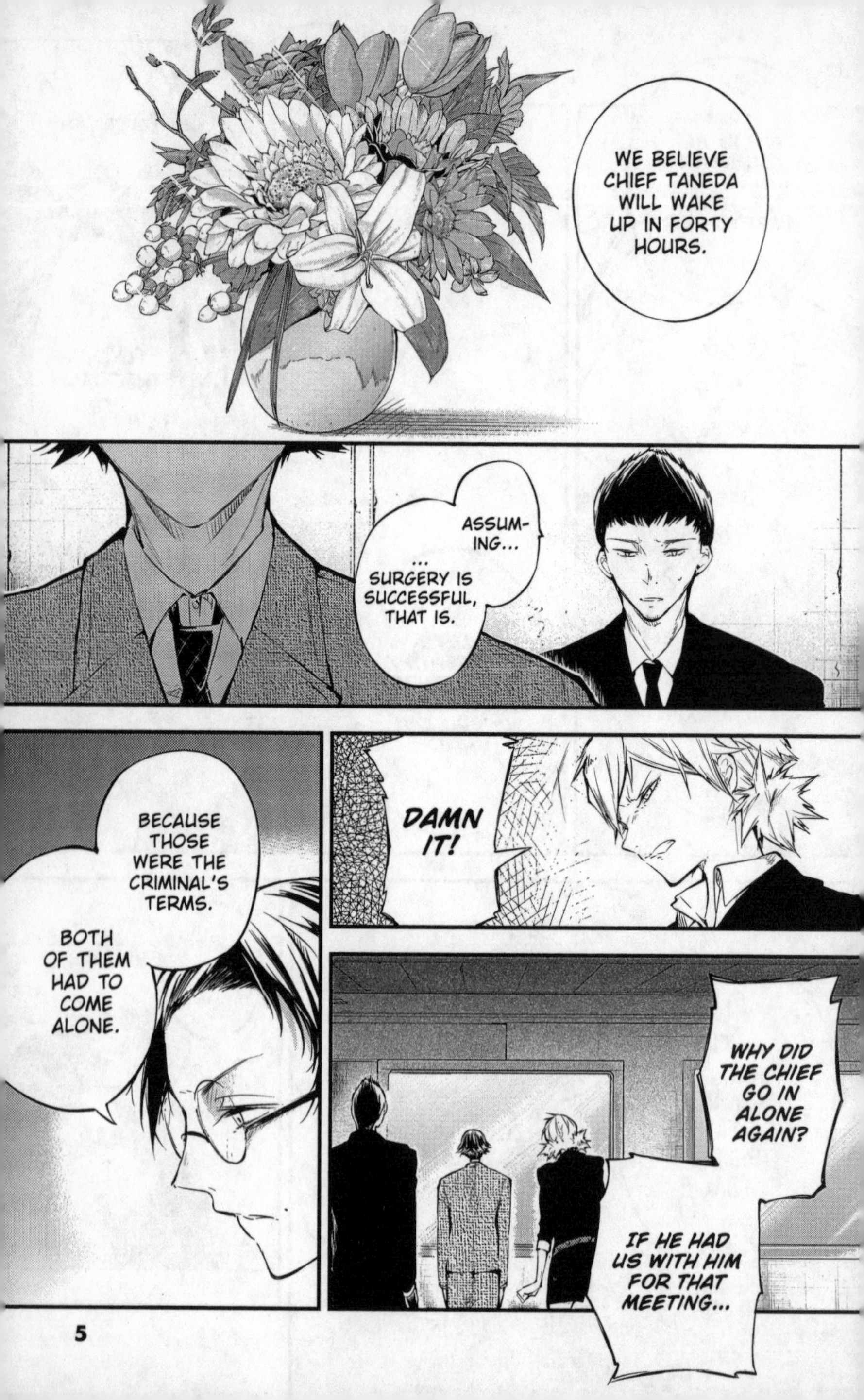
WE BELIEVE CHIEF TANEDA WILL WAKE UP IN FORTY HOURS.
ASSUMING...
...SURGERY IS SUCCESSFUL, THAT IS.
DAMN IT!
WHY DID THE CHIEF GO IN ALONE AGAIN?
IF HE HAD US WITH HIM FOR THAT MEETING...
BECAUSE THOSE WERE THE CRIMINAL'S TERMS.
BOTH OF THEM HAD TO COME ALONE.

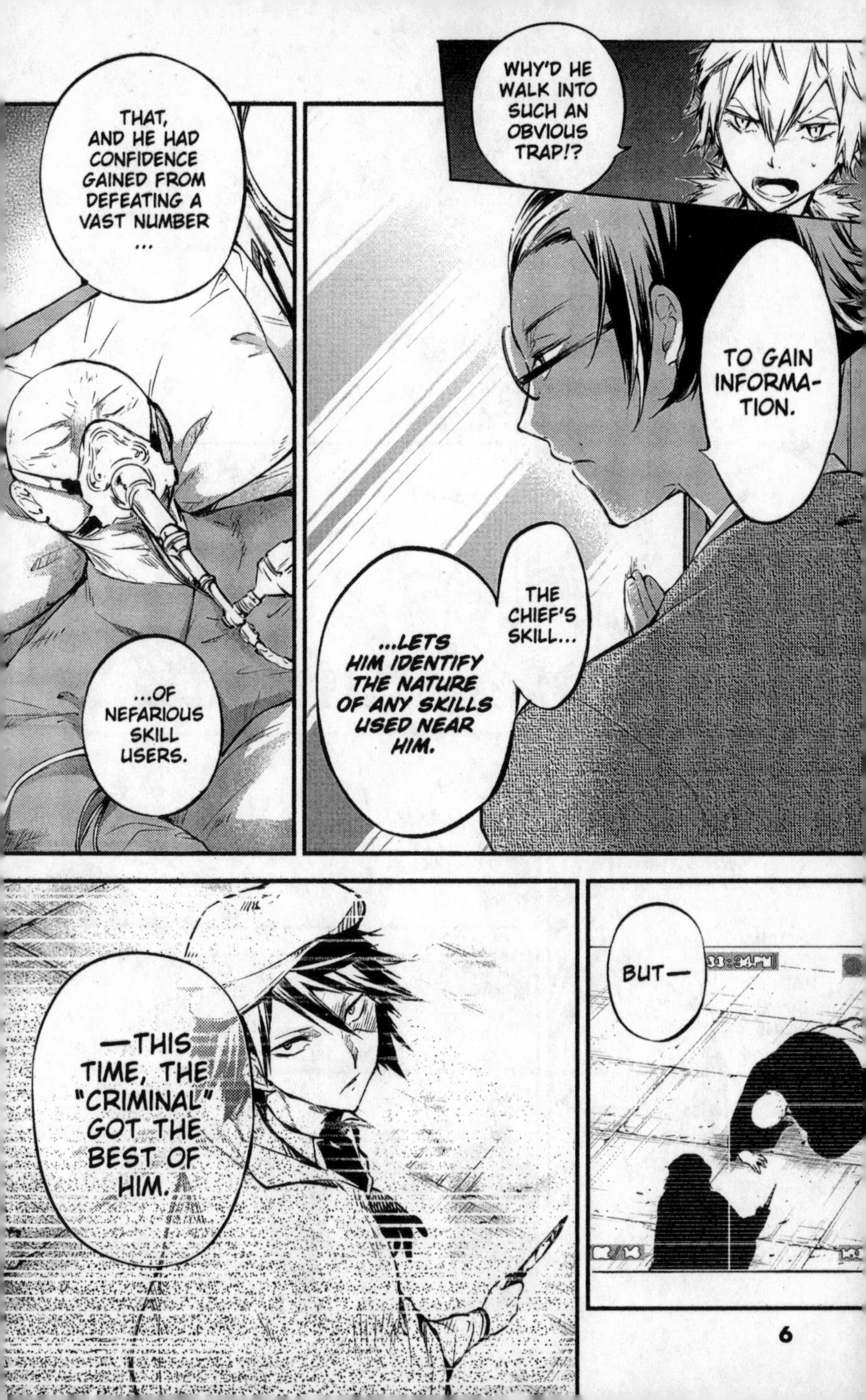
WHY'D HE WALK INTO SUCH AN OBVIOUS TRAP!?
TO GAIN INFORMATION.
THE CHIEF'S SKILL...
...LETS HIM IDENTIFY THE NATURE OF ANY SKILLS USED NEAR HIM.
THAT, AND HE HAD CONFIDENCE GAINED FROM DEFEATING A VAST NUMBER ...
...OF NEFARIOUS SKILL USERS.
BUT—
—THIS TIME, THE "CRIMINAL" GOT THE BEST OF HIM.

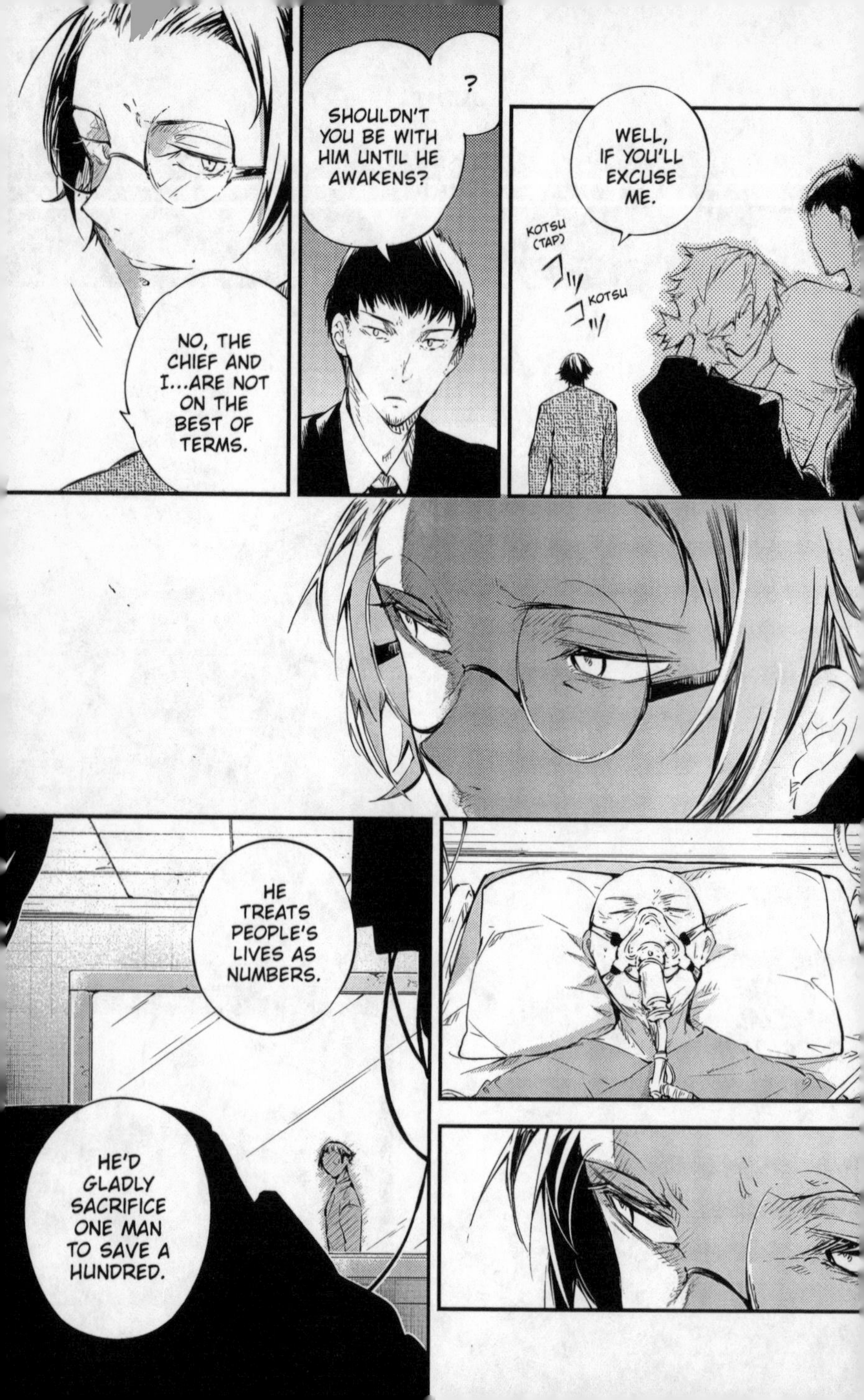
WELL, IF YOU'LL EXCUSE ME.
KOTSU (TAP)
KOTSU
?
SHOULDN'T YOU BE WITH HIM UNTIL HE AWAKENS?
NO, THE CHIEF AND I...ARE NOT ON THE BEST OF TERMS.
HE TREATS PEOPLE'S LIVES AS NUMBERS.
HE'D GLADLY SACRIFICE ONE MAN TO SAVE A HUNDRED.

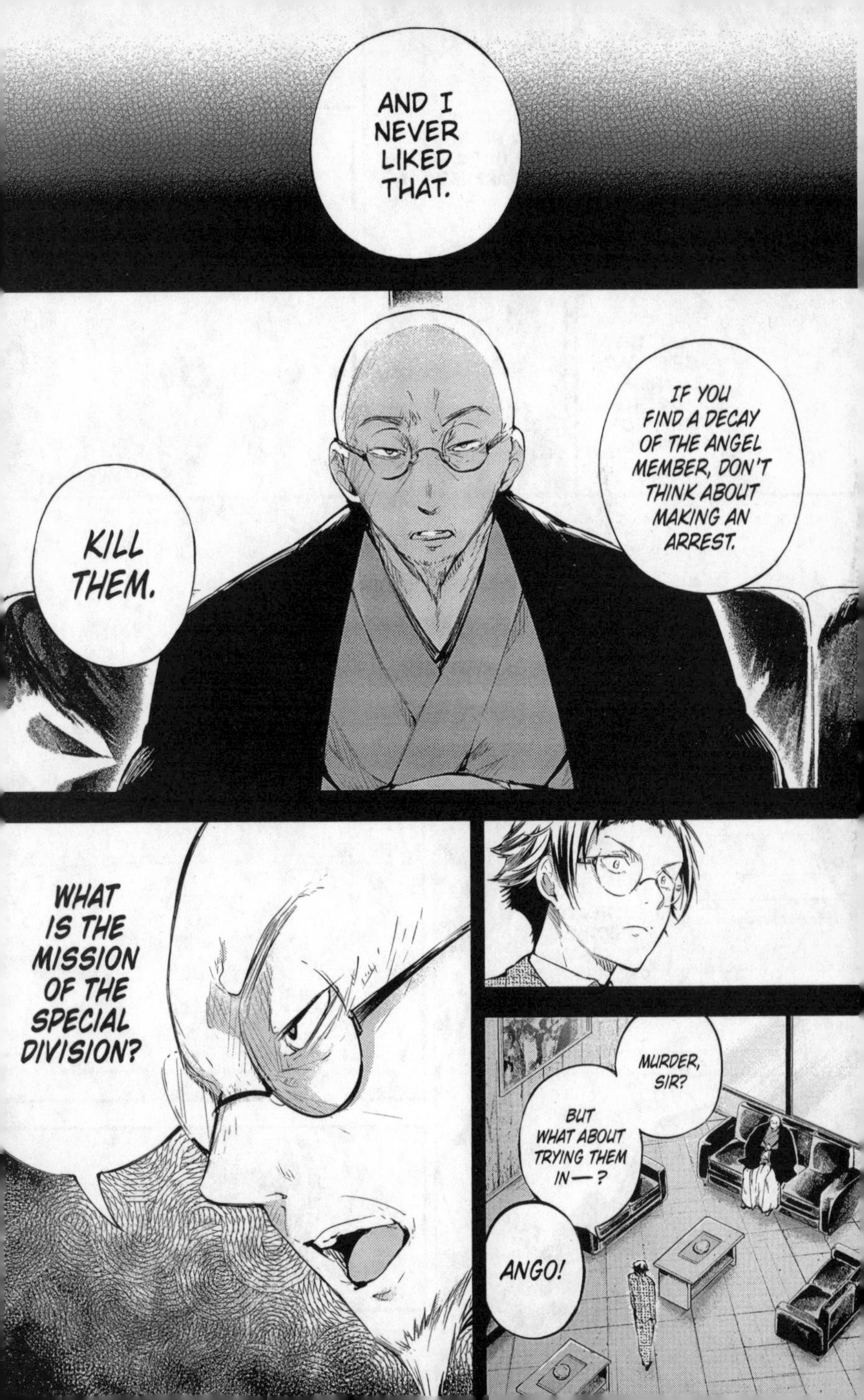
AND I NEVER LIKED THAT.
IF YOU FIND A DECAY OF THE ANGEL MEMBER, DON'T THINK ABOUT MAKING AN ARREST.
KILL THEM.
MURDER, SIR?
BUT WHAT ABOUT TRYING THEM IN—?
ANGO!
WHAT IS THE MISSION OF THE SPECIAL DIVISION?

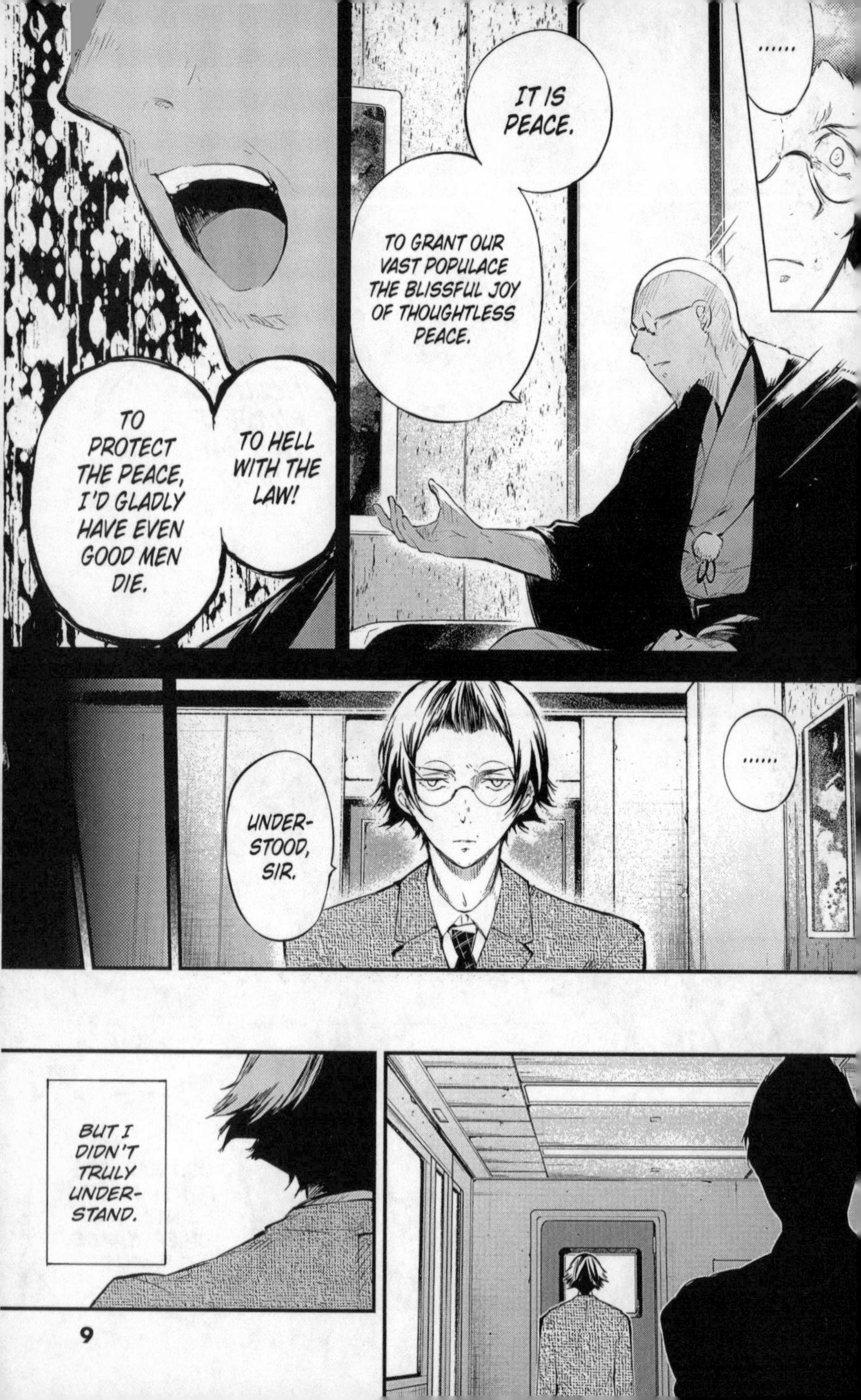
......
IT IS PEACE.
TO GRANT OUR VAST POPULACE THE BLISSFUL JOY OF THOUGHTLESS PEACE.
TO HELL WITH THE LAW!
TO PROTECT THE PEACE, I'D GLADLY HAVE EVEN GOOD MEN DIE.
......
UNDER-STOOD, SIR.
BUT I DIDN'T TRULY UNDER-STAND.

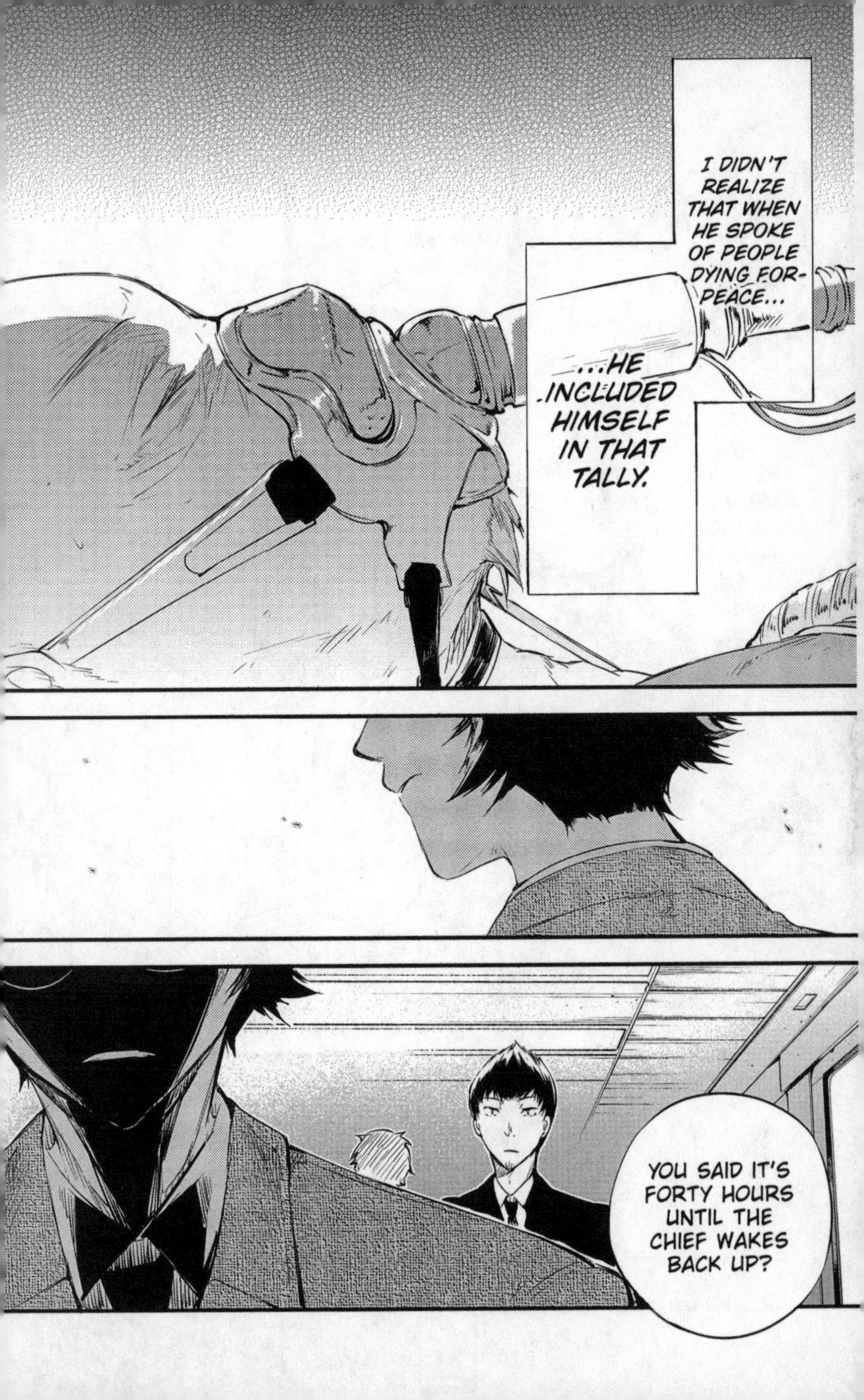

I DIDN'T REALIZE THAT WHEN HE SPOKE OF PEOPLE DYING FOR-PEACE...
...HE INCLUDED HIMSELF IN THAT TALLY.
YOU SAID IT'S FORTY HOURS UNTIL THE CHIEF WAKES BACK UP?

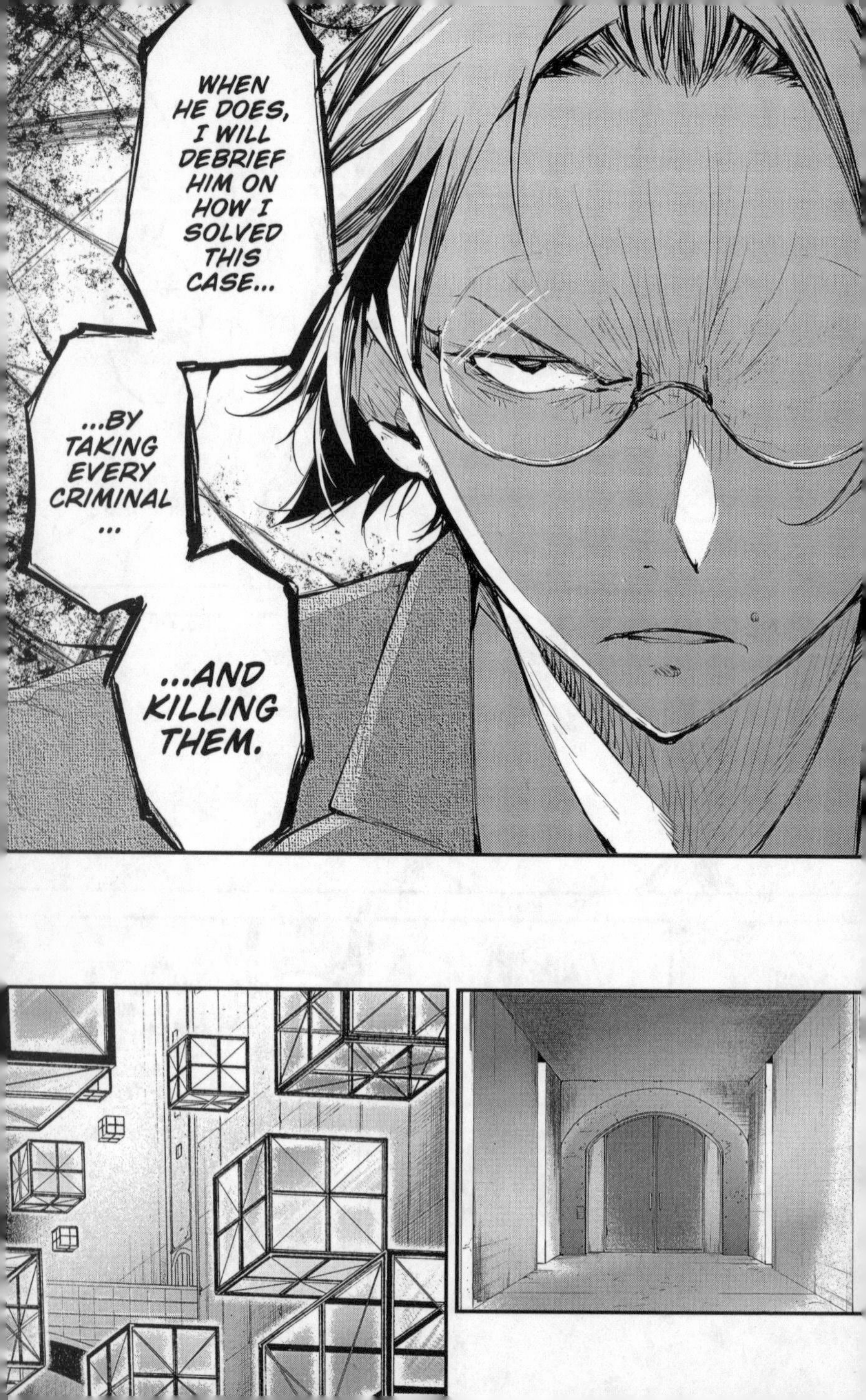
WHEN HE DOES, I WILL DEBRIEF HIM ON HOW I SOLVED THIS CASE...
...BY TAKING EVERY CRIMINAL ...
...AND KILLING THEM.

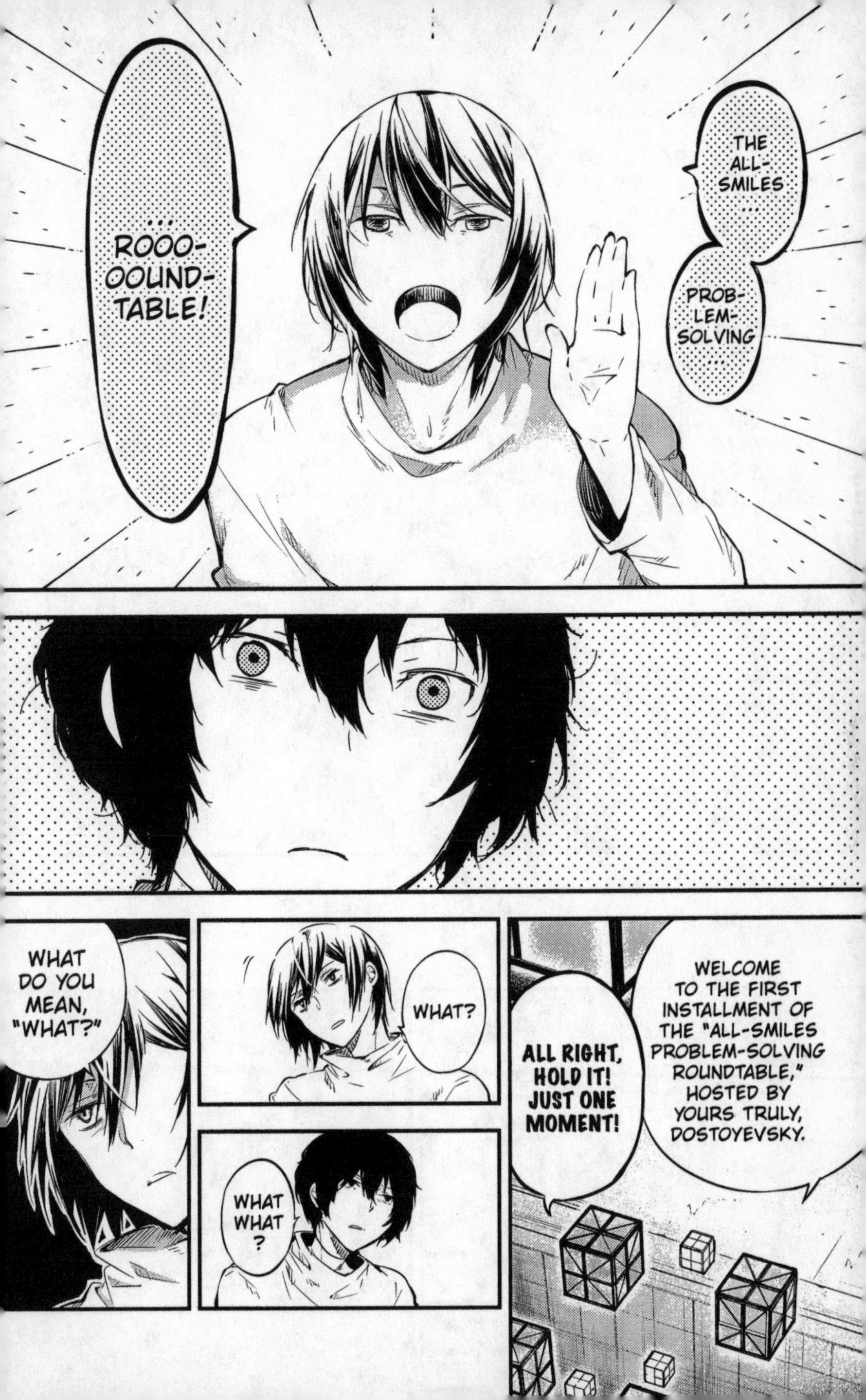
THE ALL-SMILES...
PROB-LEM-SOLVING...
...ROOOOOUND-TABLE!
WELCOME TO THE FIRST INSTALLMENT OF THE "ALL-SMILES PROBLEM-SOLVING ROUNDTABLE," HOSTED BY YOURS TRULY, DOSTOYEVSKY.
ALL RIGHT, HOLD IT! JUST ONE MOMENT!
WHAT?
WHAT WHAT?
WHAT DO YOU MEAN, "WHAT?"

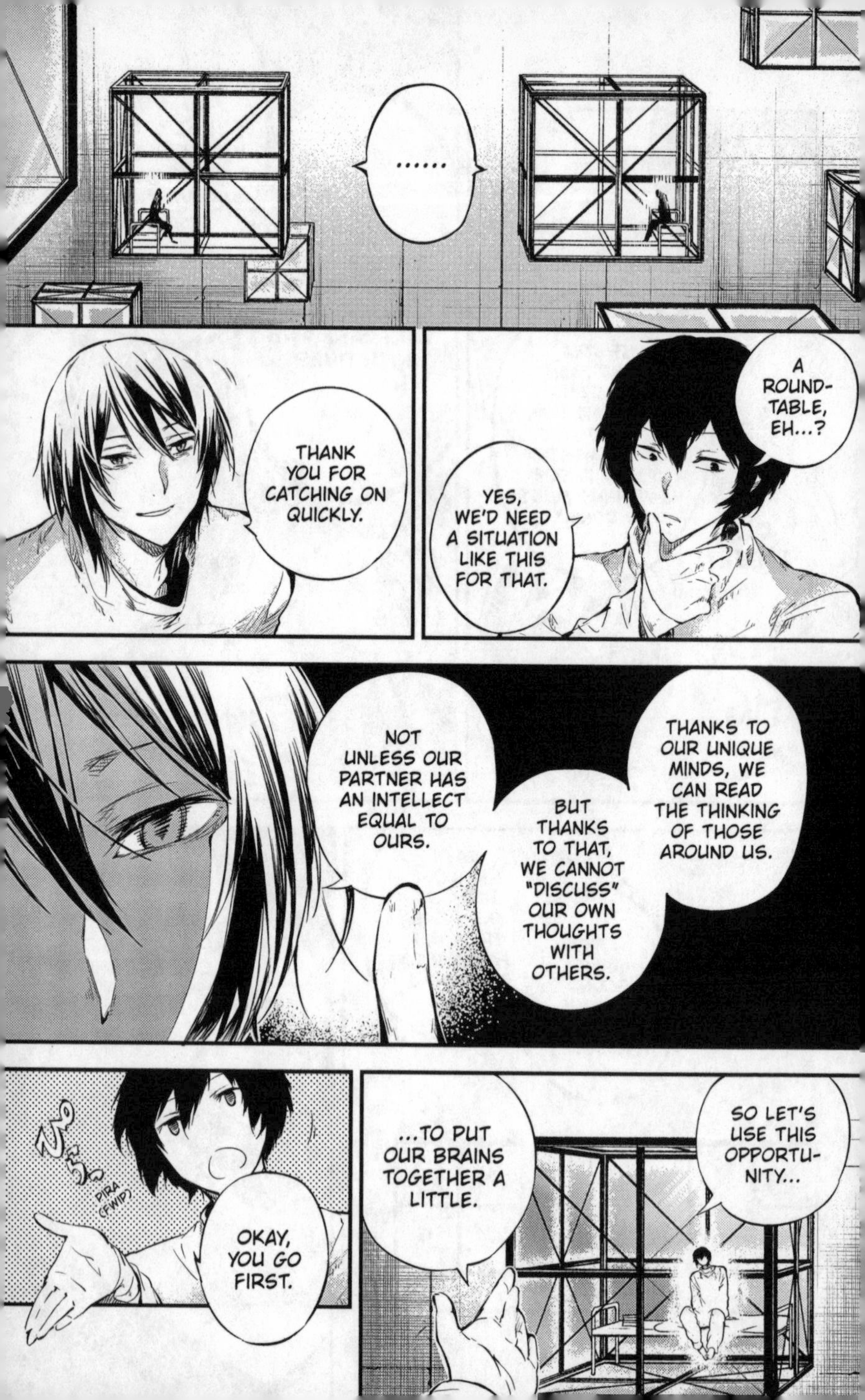
......
A ROUND-TABLE, EH...?
YES, WE'D NEED A SITUATION LIKE THIS FOR THAT.
THANK YOU FOR CATCHING ON QUICKLY.
THANKS TO OUR UNIQUE MINDS, WE CAN READ THE THINKING OF THOSE AROUND US.
BUT THANKS TO THAT, WE CANNOT "DISCUSS" OUR OWN THOUGHTS WITH OTHERS.
NOT UNLESS OUR PARTNER HAS AN INTELLECT EQUAL TO OURS.
SO LET'S USE THIS OPPORTU-NITY...
...TO PUT OUR BRAINS TOGETHER A LITTLE.
PIRA (FWIP)
OKAY, YOU GO FIRST.

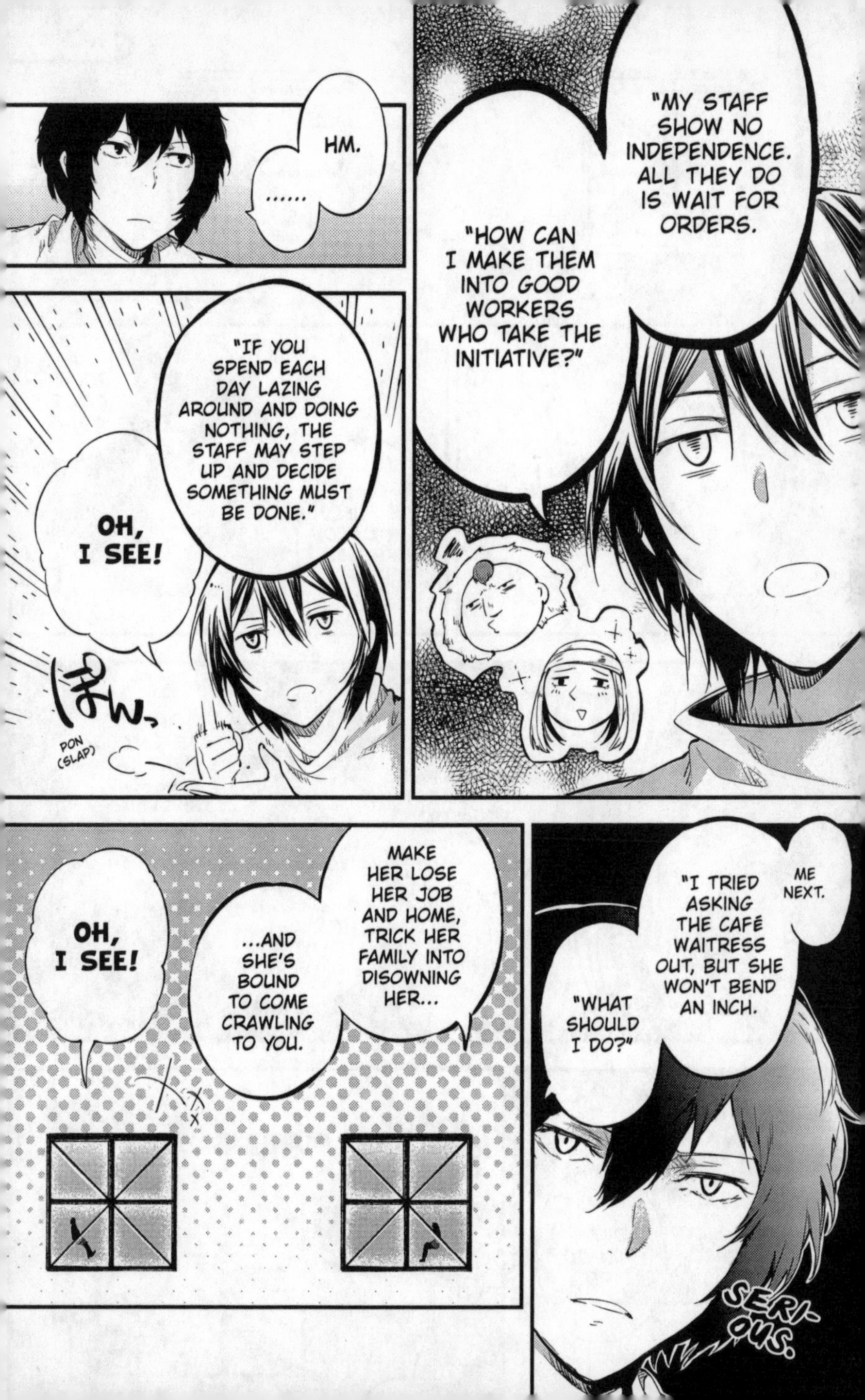
"MY STAFF SHOW NO INDEPENDENCE. ALL THEY DO IS WAIT FOR ORDERS.
"HOW CAN I MAKE THEM INTO GOOD WORKERS WHO TAKE THE INITIATIVE?"
HM.
......
"IF YOU SPEND EACH DAY LAZING AROUND AND DOING NOTHING, THE STAFF MAY STEP UP AND DECIDE SOMETHING MUST BE DONE."
OH, I SEE!
ぽん
PON (SLAP)
ME NEXT.
"I TRIED ASKING THE CAFÉ WAITRESS OUT, BUT SHE WON'T BEND AN INCH.
"WHAT SHOULD I DO?"
SERI-OUS.
MAKE HER LOSE HER JOB AND HOME, TRICK HER FAMILY INTO DISOWNING HER...
...AND SHE'S BOUND TO COME CRAWLING TO YOU.
OH, I SEE!

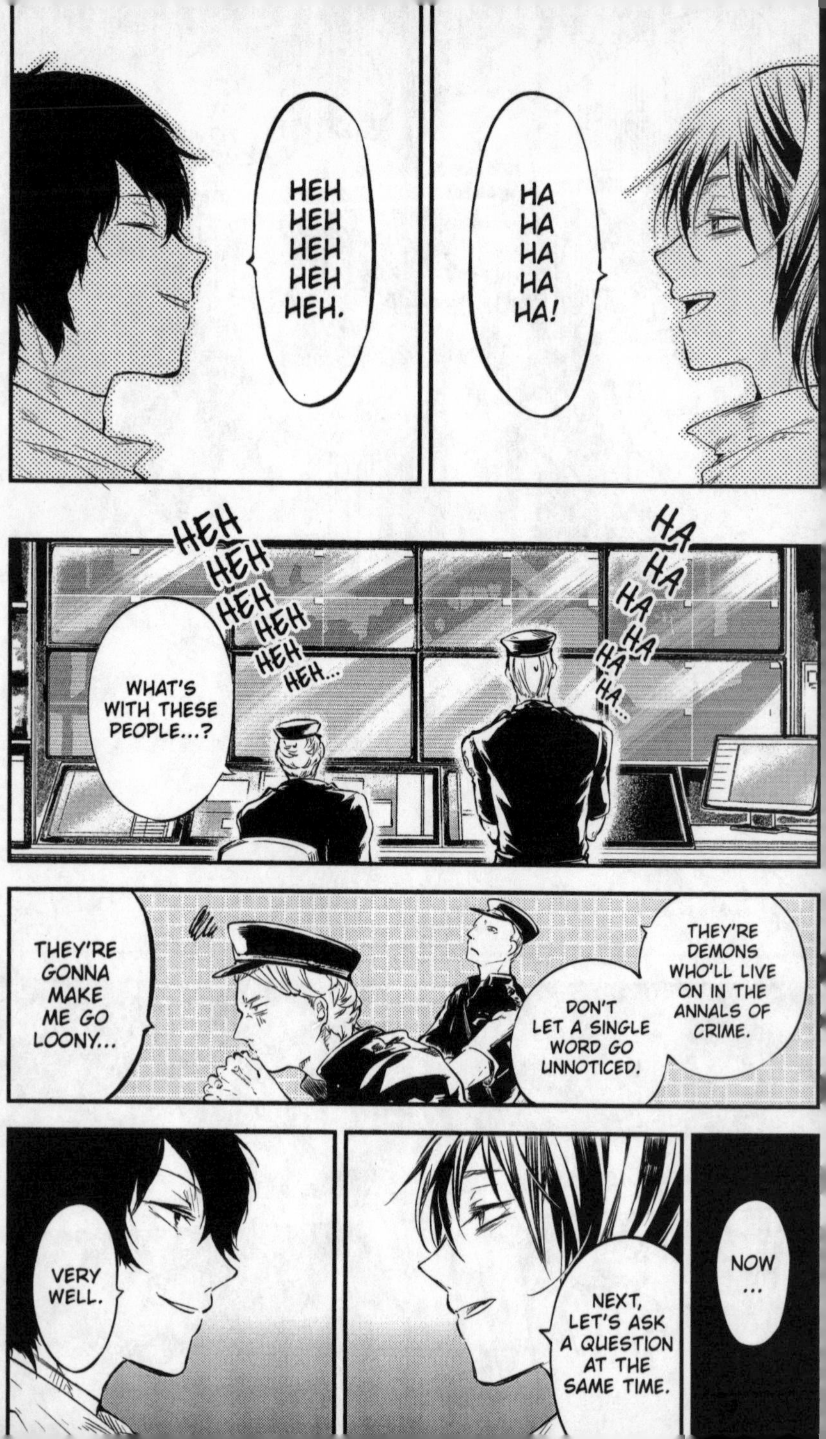
HA HA HA HA HA!
HEH HEH HEH HEH HEH.
HA HA HA HA HA HA...
HEH HEH HEH HEH HEH HEH...
WHAT'S WITH THESE PEOPLE...?
THEY'RE DEMONS WHO'LL LIVE ON IN THE ANNALS OF CRIME.
DON'T LET A SINGLE WORD GO UNNOTICED.
THEY'RE GONNA MAKE ME GO LOONY...
NOW ...
NEXT, LET'S ASK A QUESTION AT THE SAME TIME.
VERY WELL.

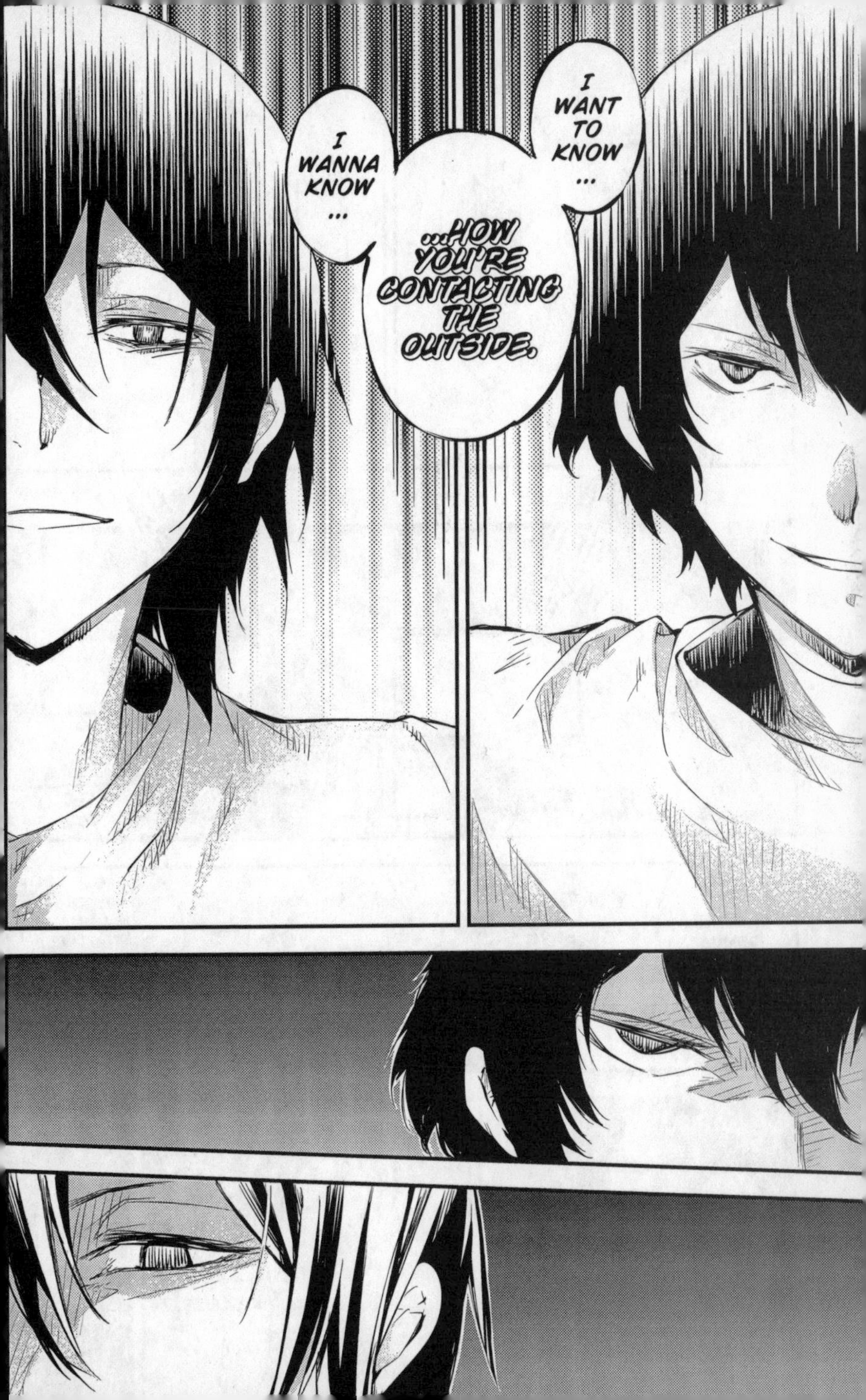
I WANT TO KNOW ...
I WANNA KNOW ...
...HOW YOU'RE CONTACTING THE OUTSIDE.

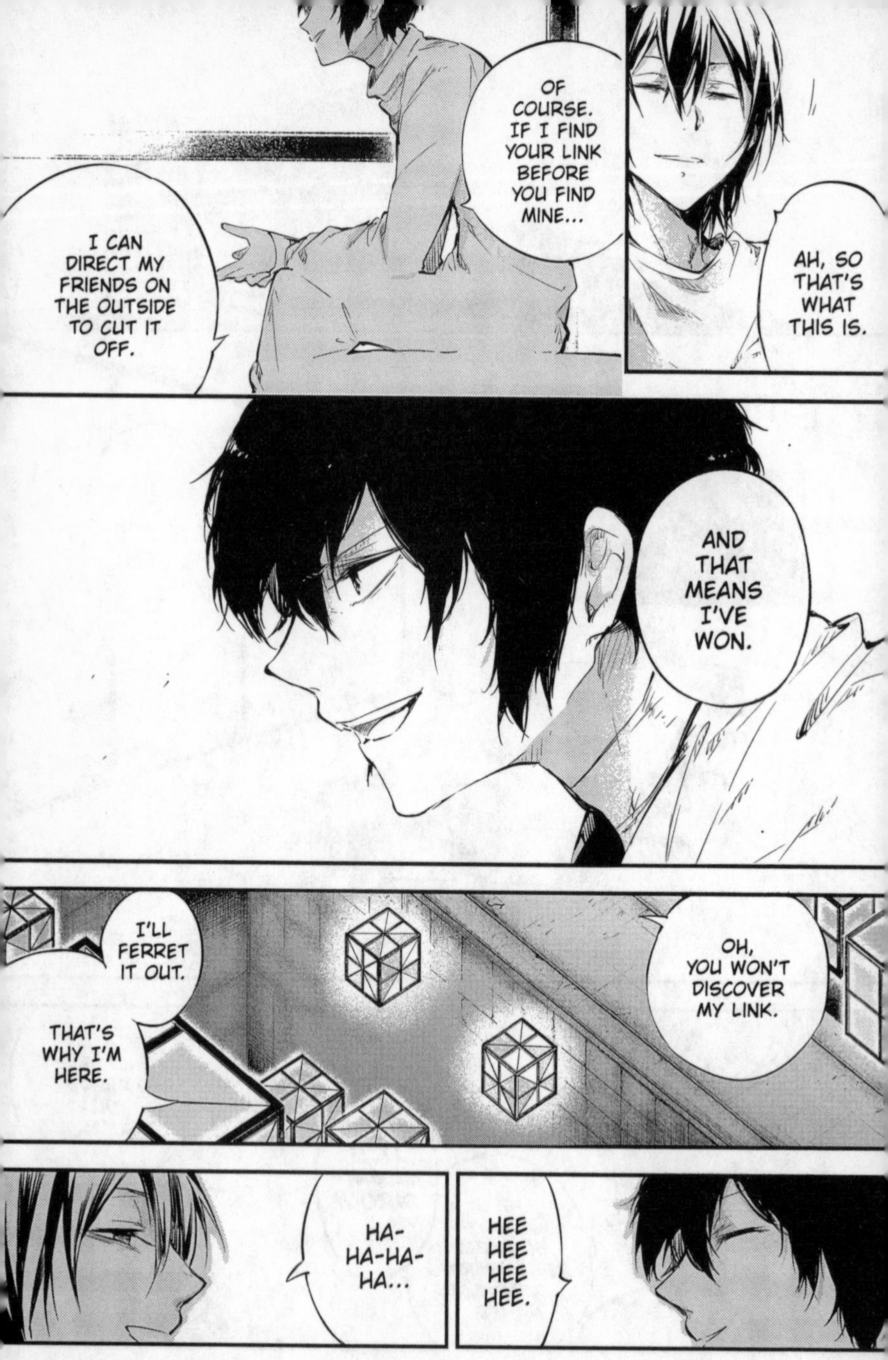
AH, SO THAT'S WHAT THIS IS.
OF COURSE. IF I FIND YOUR LINK BEFORE YOU FIND MINE...
I CAN DIRECT MY FRIENDS ON THE OUTSIDE TO CUT IT OFF.
AND THAT MEANS I'VE WON.
OH, YOU WON'T DISCOVER MY LINK.
I'LL FERRET IT OUT.
THAT'S WHY I'M HERE.
HEE HEE HEE HEE.
HA-HA-HA-HA...

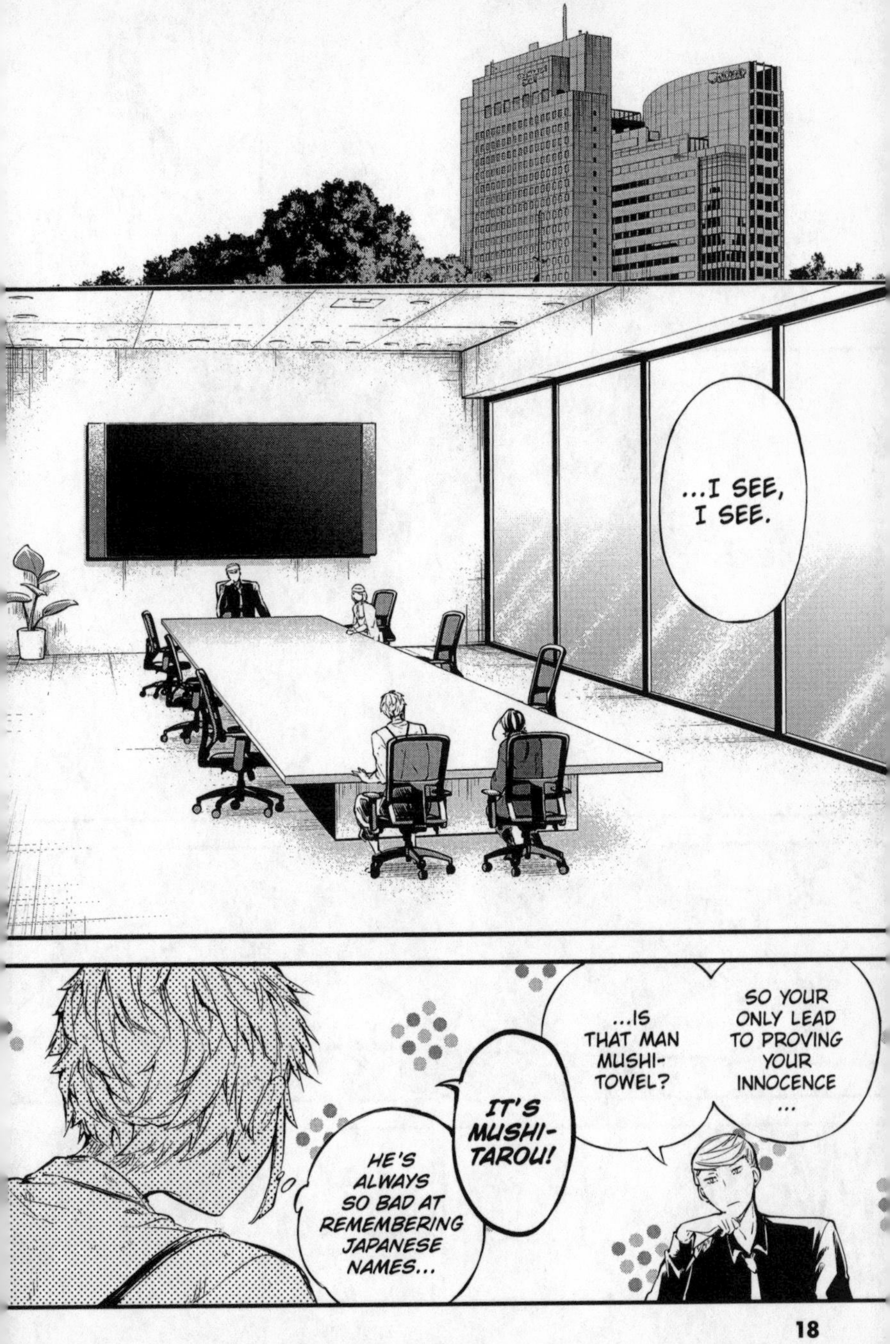
...I SEE, I SEE.
SO YOUR ONLY LEAD TO PROVING YOUR INNOCENCE ...
...IS THAT MAN MUSHI-TOWEL?
IT'S MUSHI-TAROU!
HE'S ALWAYS SO BAD AT REMEMBERING JAPANESE NAMES...

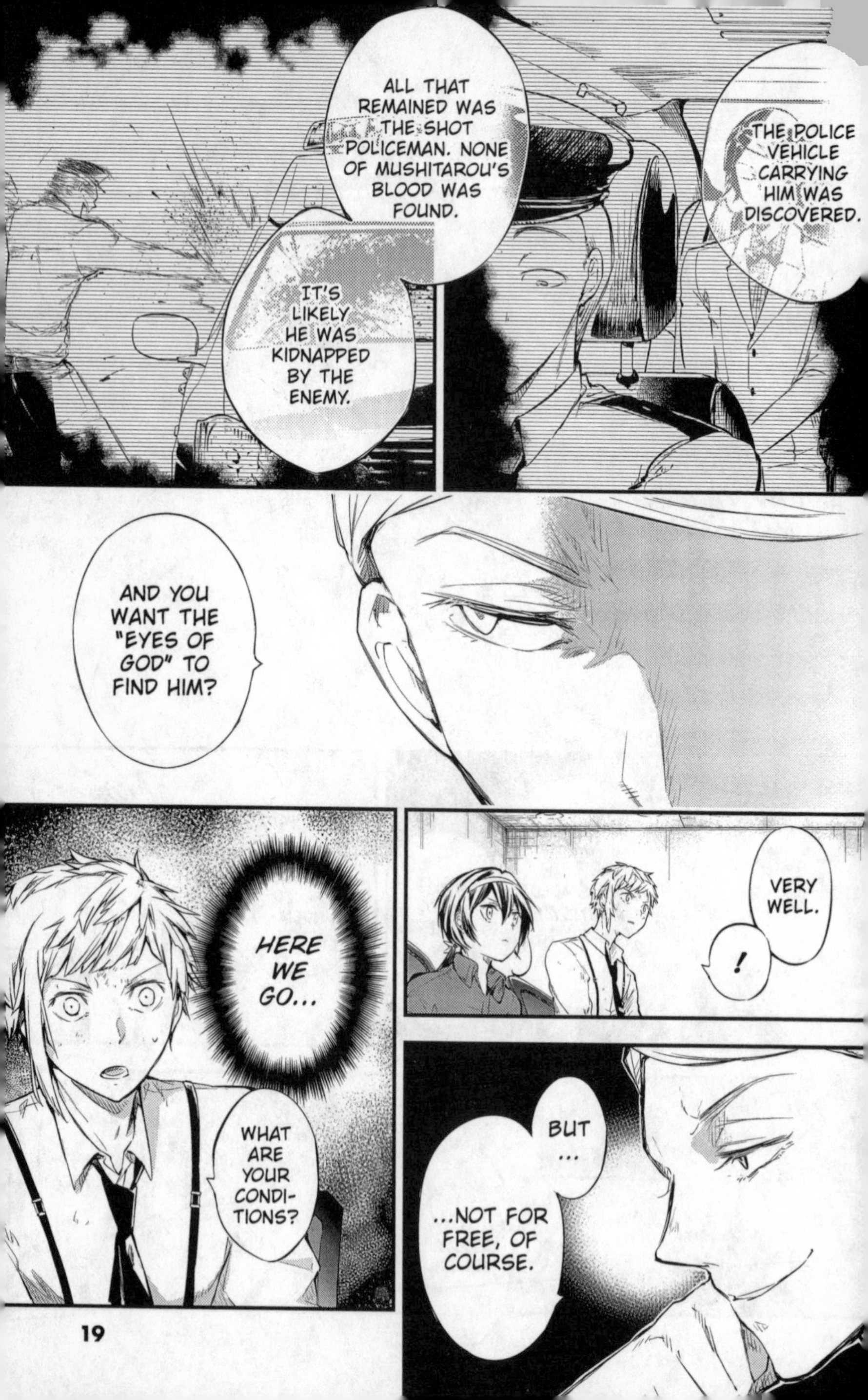
THE POLICE VEHICLE CARRYING HIM WAS DISCOVERED.
ALL THAT REMAINED WAS THE SHOT POLICEMAN. NONE OF MUSHITAROU'S BLOOD WAS FOUND.
IT'S LIKELY HE WAS KIDNAPPED BY THE ENEMY.
AND YOU WANT THE "EYES OF GOD" TO FIND HIM?
VERY WELL.
!
BUT ...
...NOT FOR FREE, OF COURSE.
HERE WE GO...
WHAT ARE YOUR CONDITIONS?

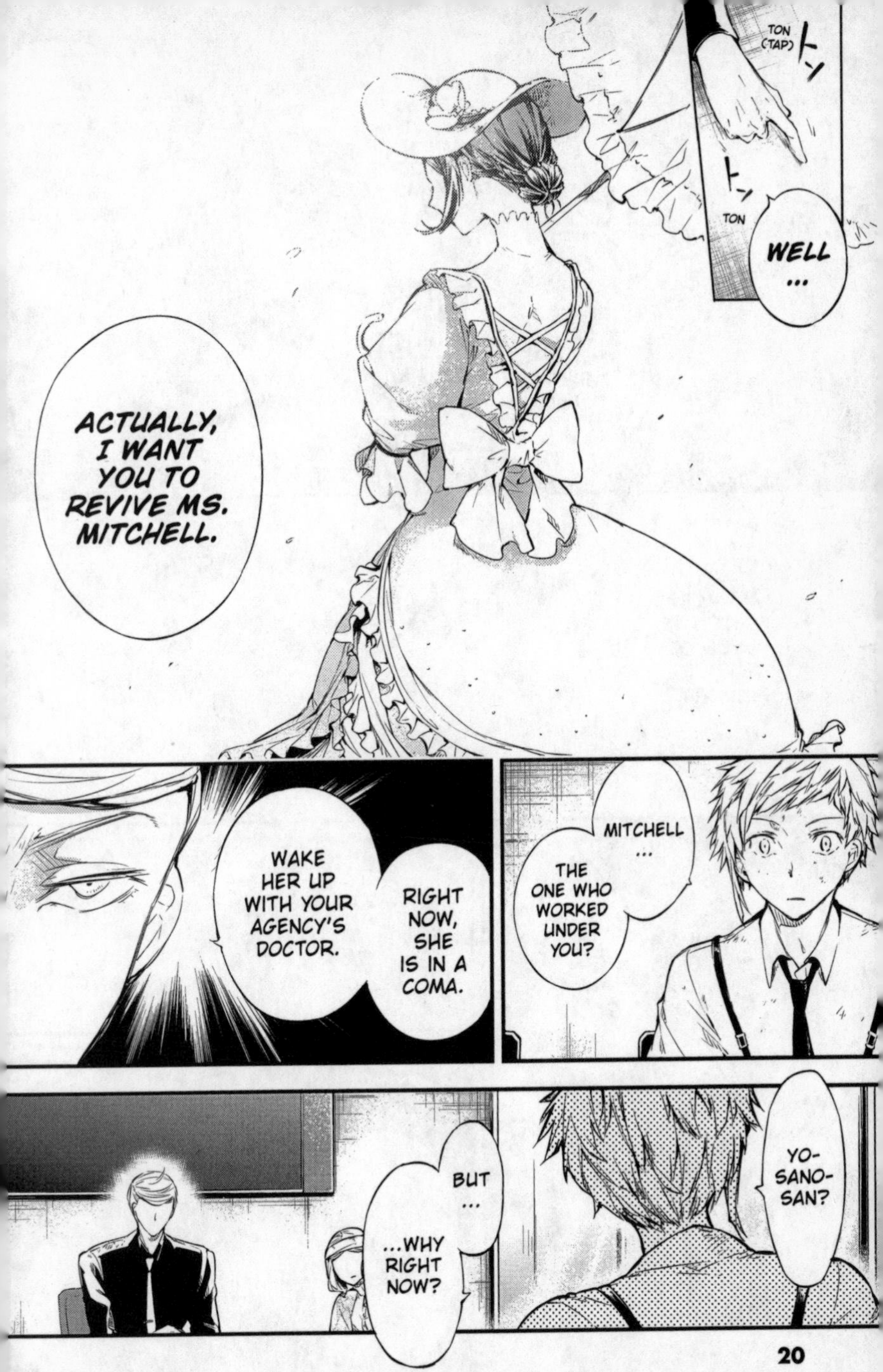
TON (TAP)
TON
WELL ...
ACTUALLY, I WANT YOU TO REVIVE MS. MITCHELL.
MITCHELL ...
THE ONE WHO WORKED UNDER YOU?
RIGHT NOW, SHE IS IN A COMA.
WAKE HER UP WITH YOUR AGENCY'S DOCTOR.
YO-SANO-SAN?
BUT ...
...WHY RIGHT NOW?

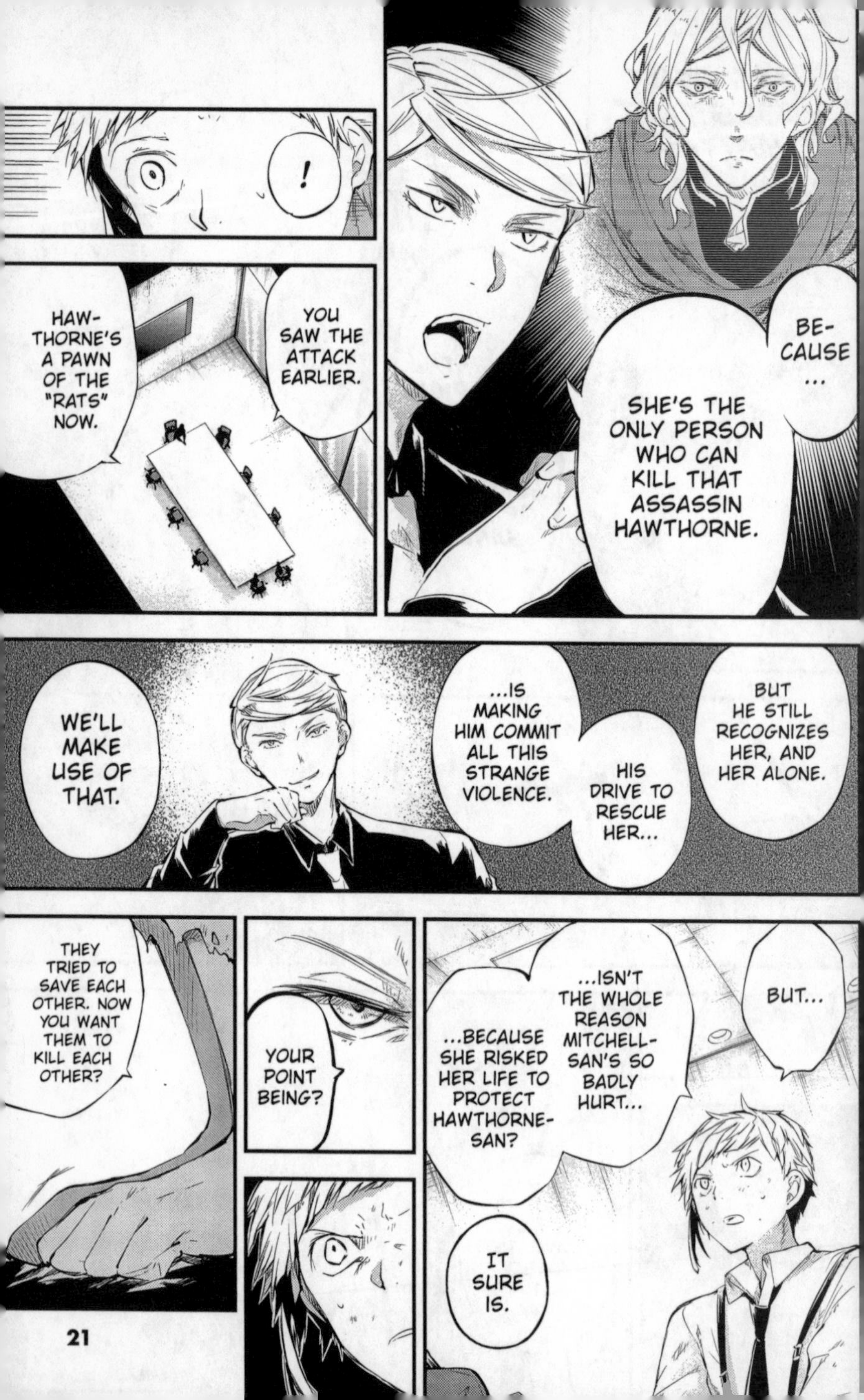
BE-CAUSE...
SHE'S THE ONLY PERSON WHO CAN KILL THAT ASSASSIN HAWTHORNE.
!
YOU SAW THE ATTACK EARLIER.
HAW-THORNE'S A PAWN OF THE "RATS" NOW.
BUT HE STILL RECOGNIZES HER, AND HER ALONE.
HIS DRIVE TO RESCUE HER...
...IS MAKING HIM COMMIT ALL THIS STRANGE VIOLENCE.
WE'LL MAKE USE OF THAT.
BUT...
...ISN'T THE WHOLE REASON MITCHELL-SAN'S SO BADLY HURT...
...BECAUSE SHE RISKED HER LIFE TO PROTECT HAWTHORNE-SAN?
IT SURE IS.
YOUR POINT BEING?
THEY TRIED TO SAVE EACH OTHER. NOW YOU WANT THEM TO KILL EACH OTHER?

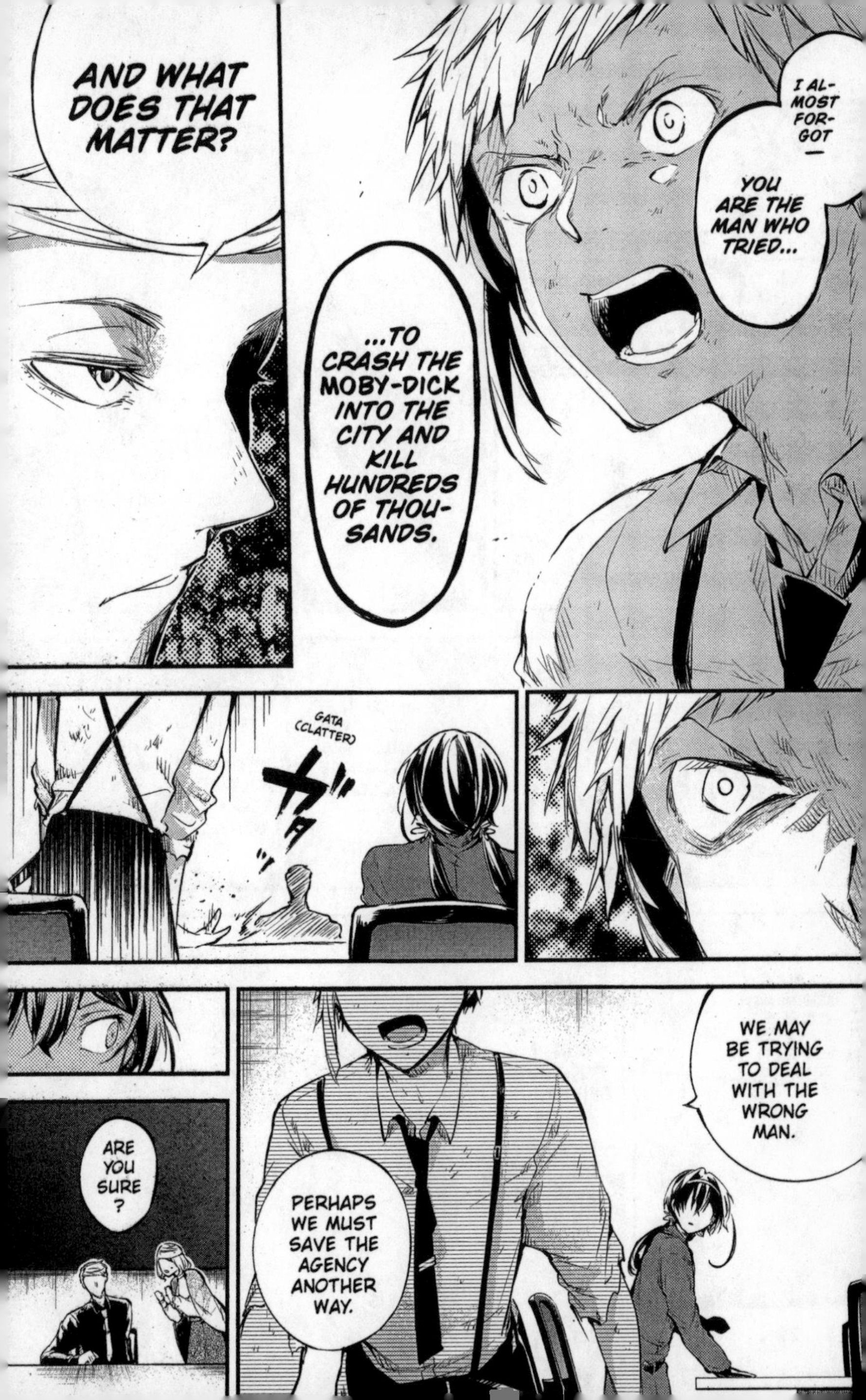
I ALMOST FORGOT—
YOU ARE THE MAN WHO TRIED...
...TO CRASH THE MOBY-DICK INTO THE CITY AND KILL HUNDREDS OF THOUSANDS.
AND WHAT DOES THAT MATTER?
GATA (CLATTER)
WE MAY BE TRYING TO DEAL WITH THE WRONG MAN.
PERHAPS WE MUST SAVE THE AGENCY ANOTHER WAY.
ARE YOU SURE?

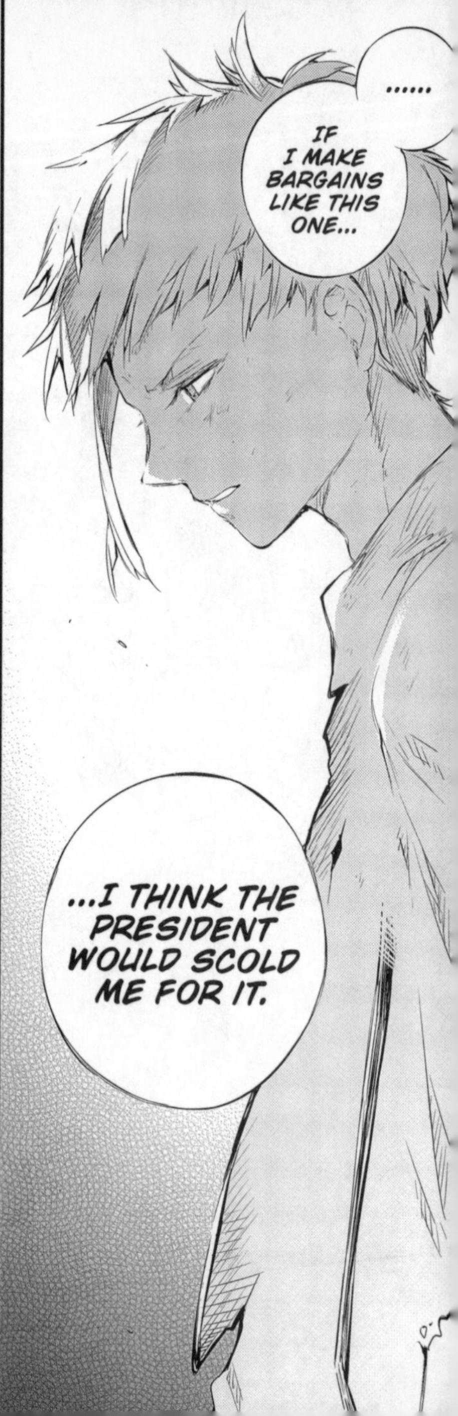
......
IF I MAKE BARGAINS LIKE THIS ONE...
...I THINK THE PRESIDENT WOULD SCOLD ME FOR IT.

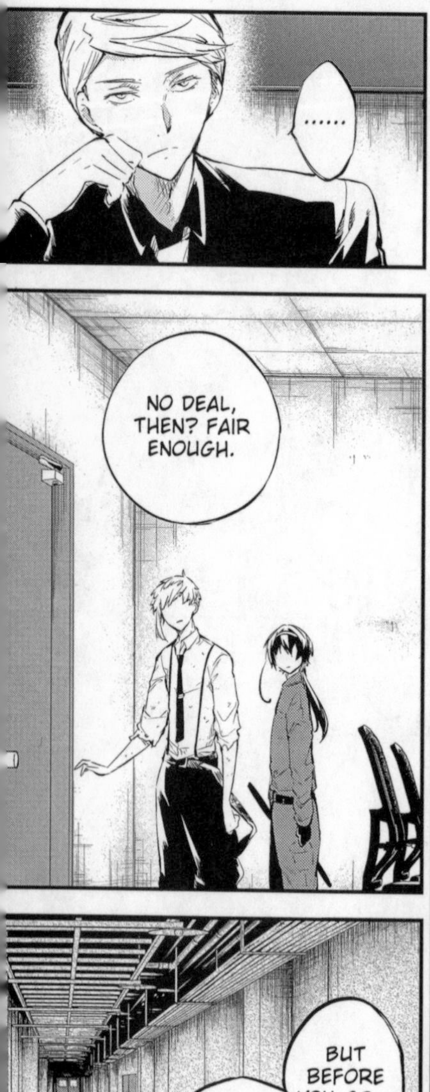
......
NO DEAL, THEN? FAIR ENOUGH.
BUT BEFORE YOU GO...
...I WANT TO SHOW YOU SOMETHING.

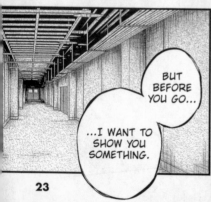

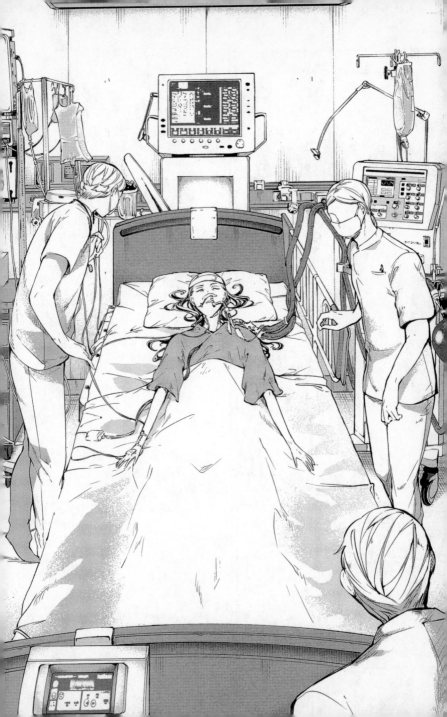

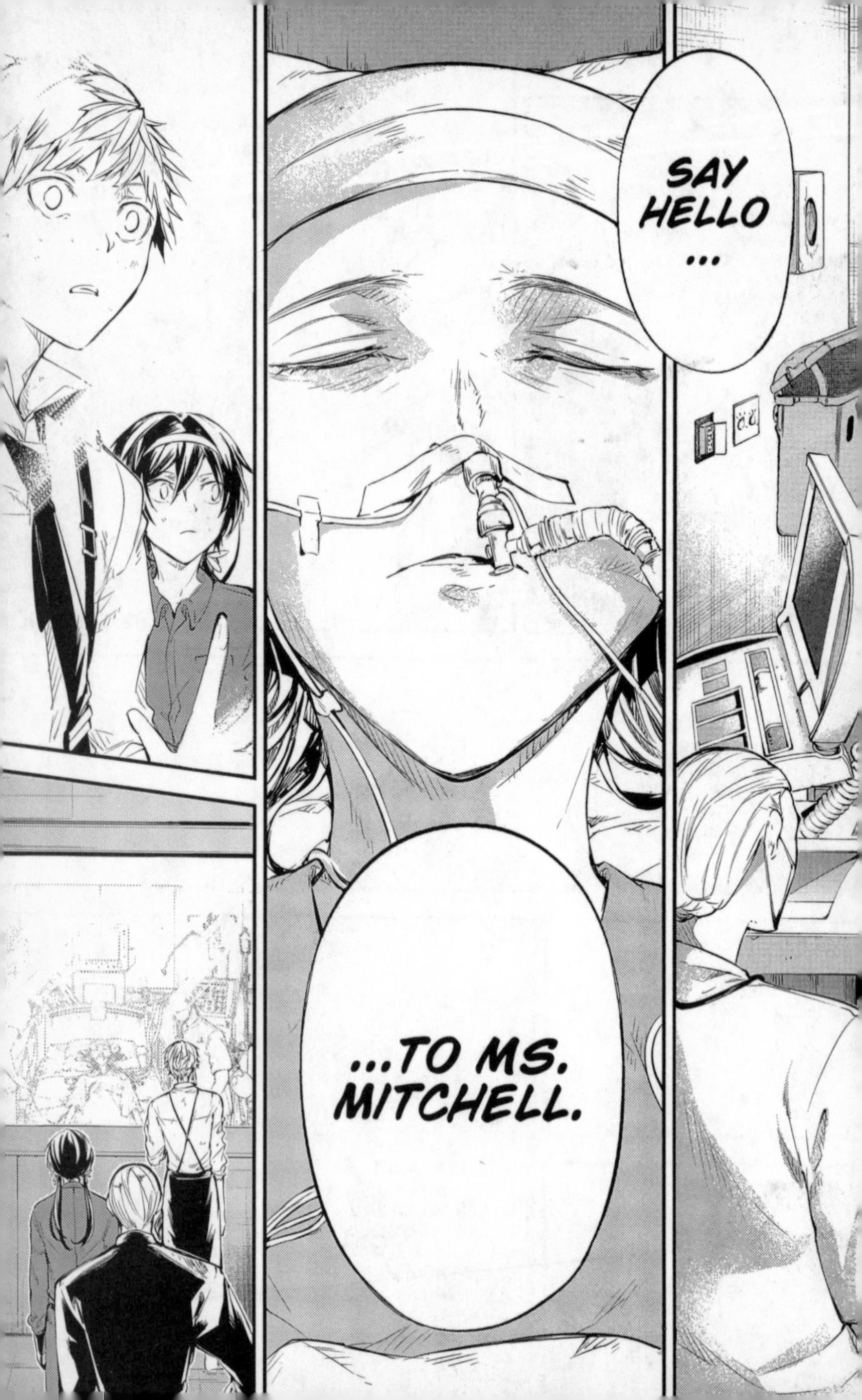
SAY HELLO ...
...TO MS. MITCHELL.

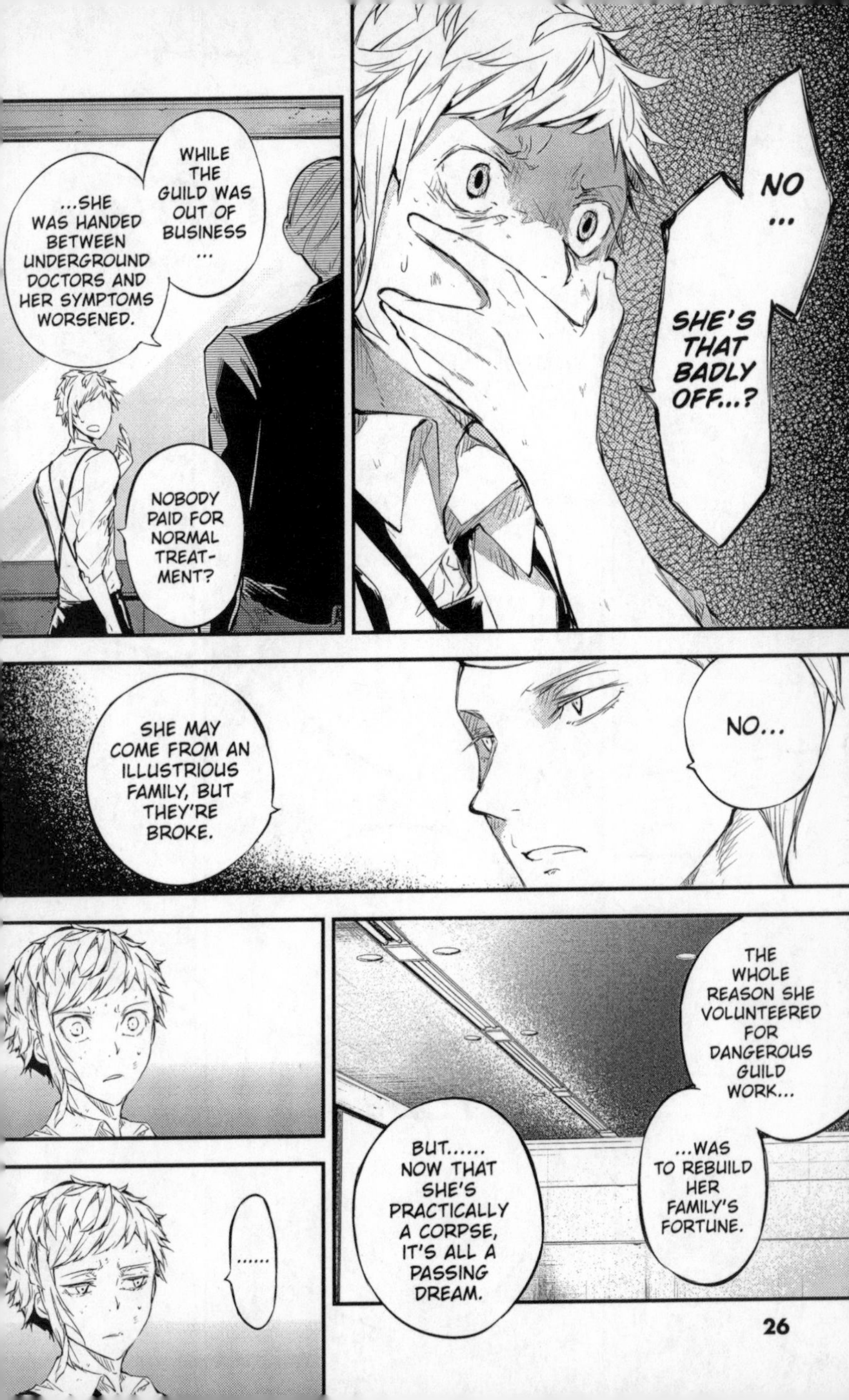
NO ...
SHE'S THAT BADLY OFF...?
WHILE THE GUILD WAS OUT OF BUSINESS ...
...SHE WAS HANDED BETWEEN UNDERGROUND DOCTORS AND HER SYMPTOMS WORSENED.
NOBODY PAID FOR NORMAL TREAT-MENT?
NO...
SHE MAY COME FROM AN ILLUSTRIOUS FAMILY, BUT THEY'RE BROKE.
THE WHOLE REASON SHE VOLUNTEERED FOR DANGEROUS GUILD WORK...
...WAS TO REBUILD HER FAMILY'S FORTUNE.
BUT...... NOW THAT SHE'S PRACTICALLY A CORPSE, IT'S ALL A PASSING DREAM.
......

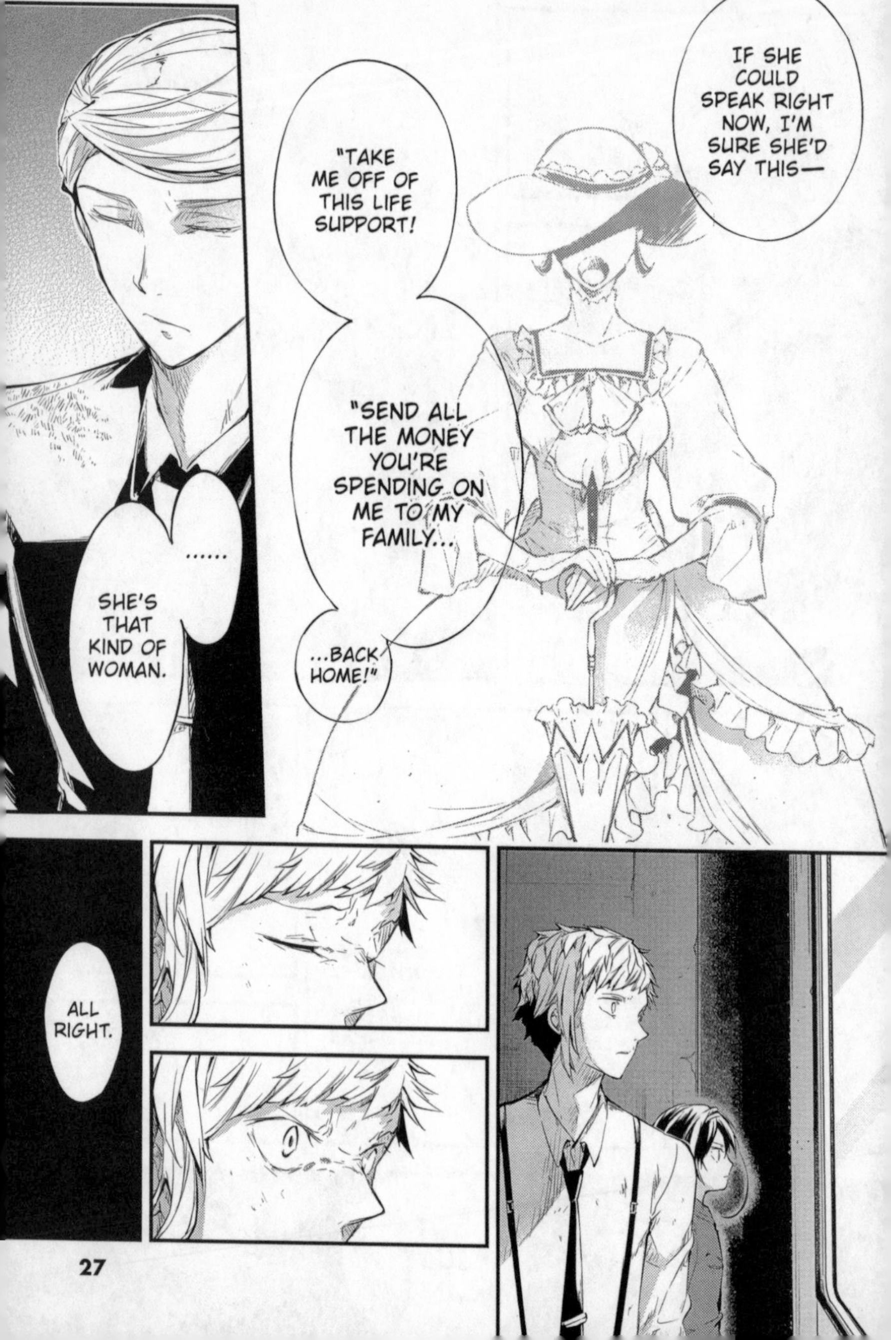
IF SHE COULD SPEAK RIGHT NOW, I'M SURE SHE'D SAY THIS—
"TAKE ME OFF OF THIS LIFE SUPPORT!
"SEND ALL THE MONEY YOU'RE SPENDING ON ME TO MY FAMILY...
...BACK HOME!"
......
SHE'S THAT KIND OF WOMAN.
ALL RIGHT.

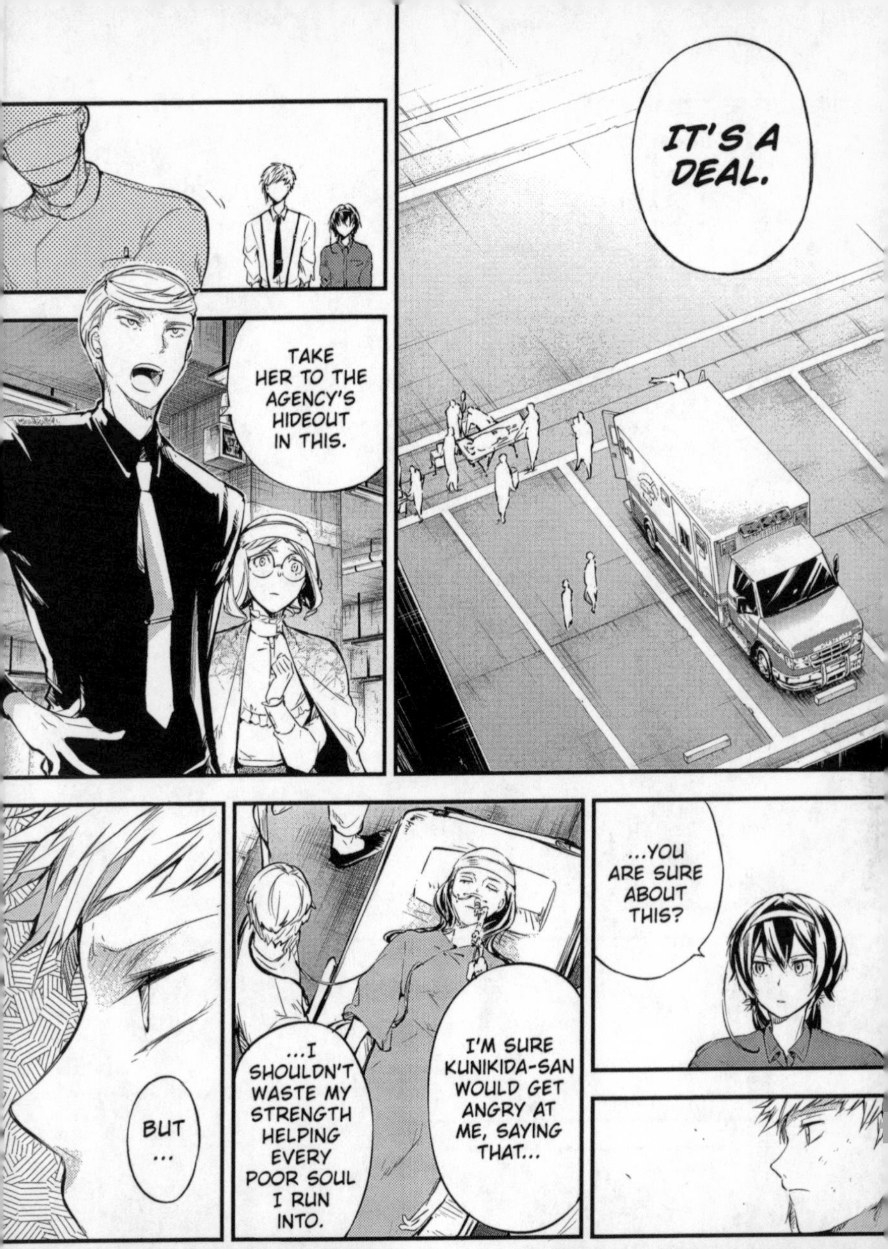
IT'S A DEAL.
TAKE HER TO THE AGENCY'S HIDEOUT IN THIS.
...YOU ARE SURE ABOUT THIS?
I'M SURE KUNIKIDA-SAN WOULD GET ANGRY AT ME, SAYING THAT...
...I SHOULDN'T WASTE MY STRENGTH HELPING EVERY POOR SOUL I RUN INTO.
BUT ...

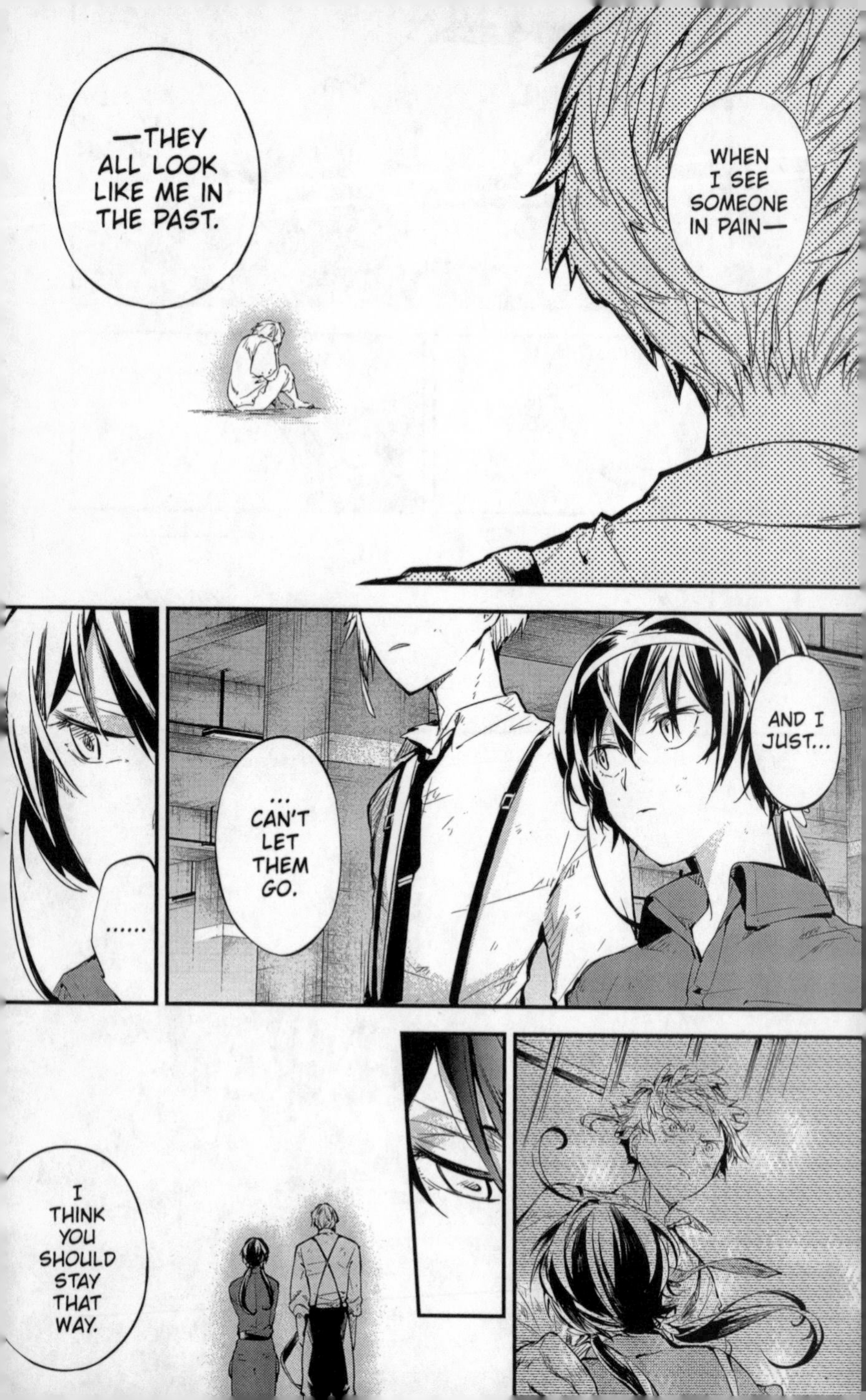
WHEN I SEE SOMEONE IN PAIN—
—THEY ALL LOOK LIKE ME IN THE PAST.
AND I JUST...
...CAN'T LET THEM GO.
......
I THINK YOU SHOULD STAY THAT WAY.

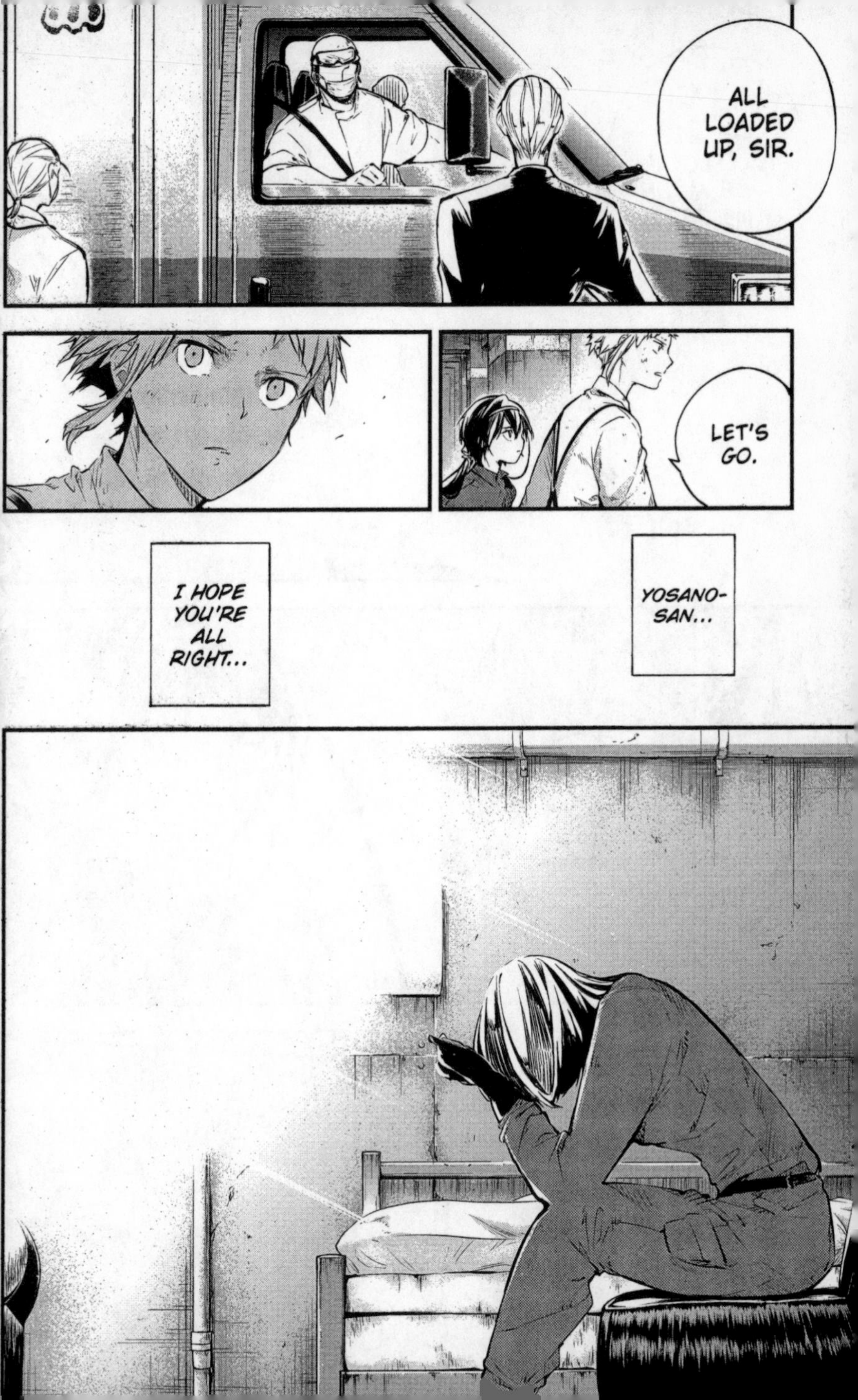
ALL LOADED UP, SIR.
LET'S GO.
YOSANO-SAN...
I HOPE YOU'RE ALL RIGHT...

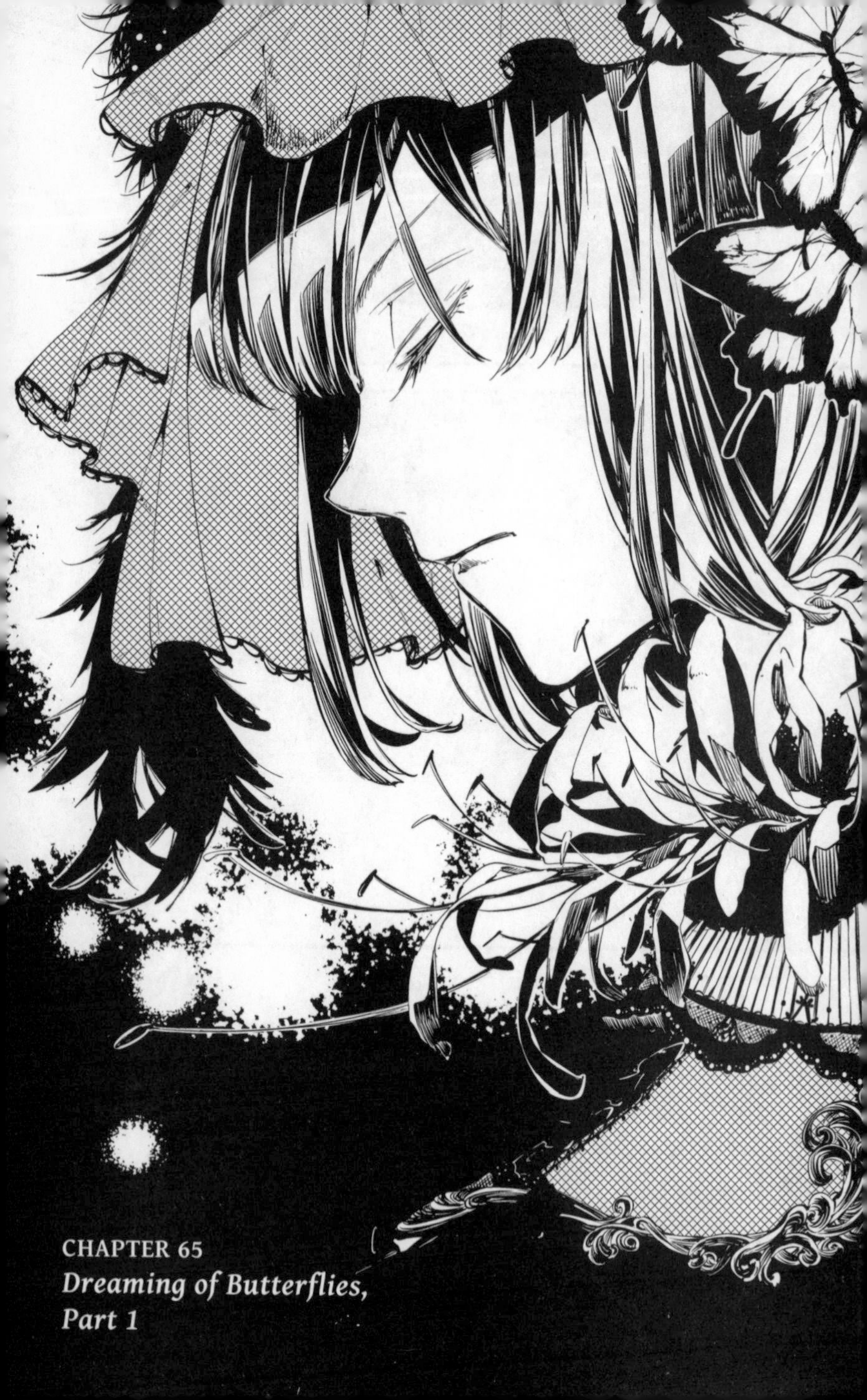

CHAPTER 65
Dreaming of Butterflies, Part 1

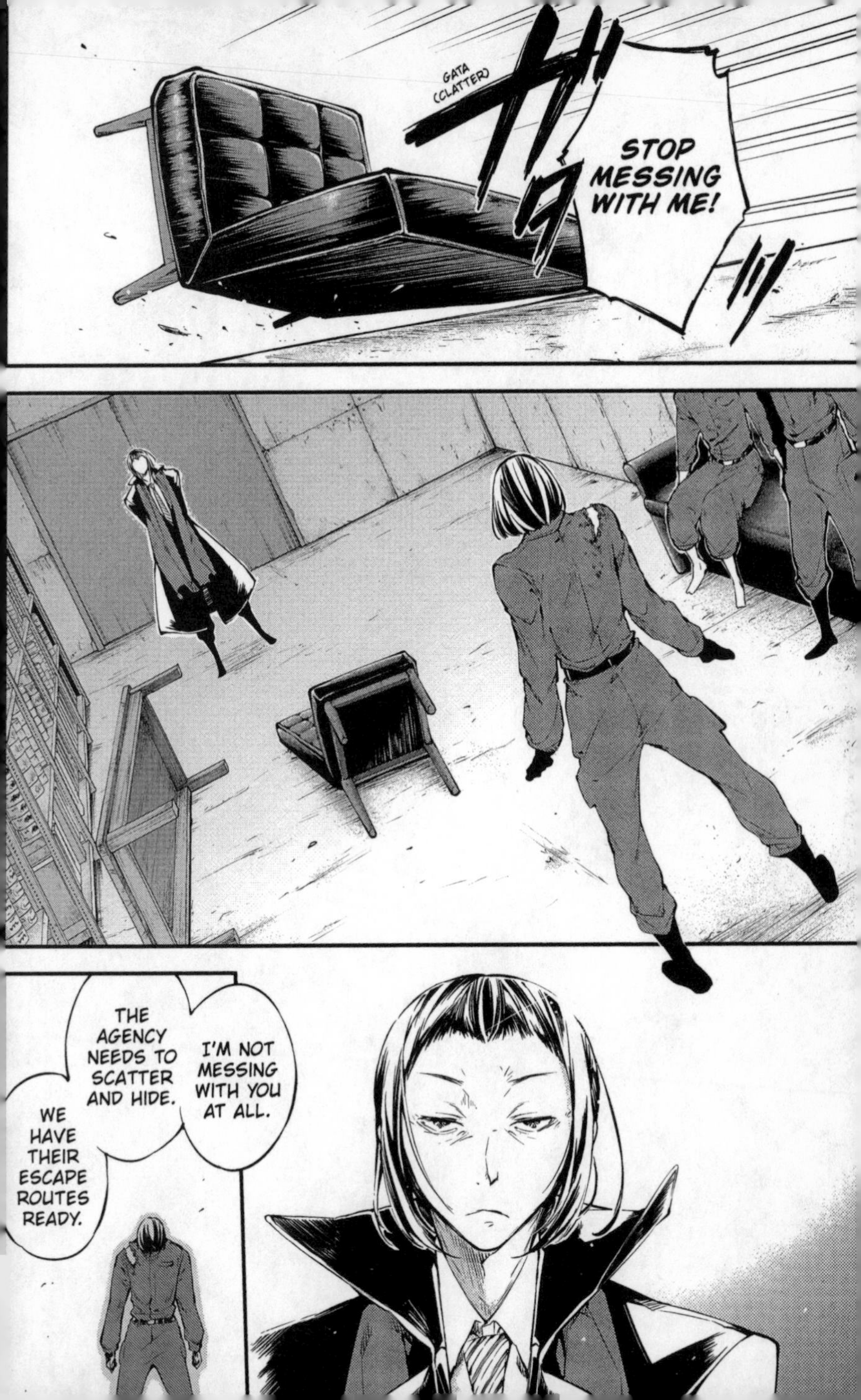
GATA (CLATTER)
STOP MESSING WITH ME!
I'M NOT MESSING WITH YOU AT ALL.
THE AGENCY NEEDS TO SCATTER AND HIDE.
WE HAVE THEIR ESCAPE ROUTES READY.

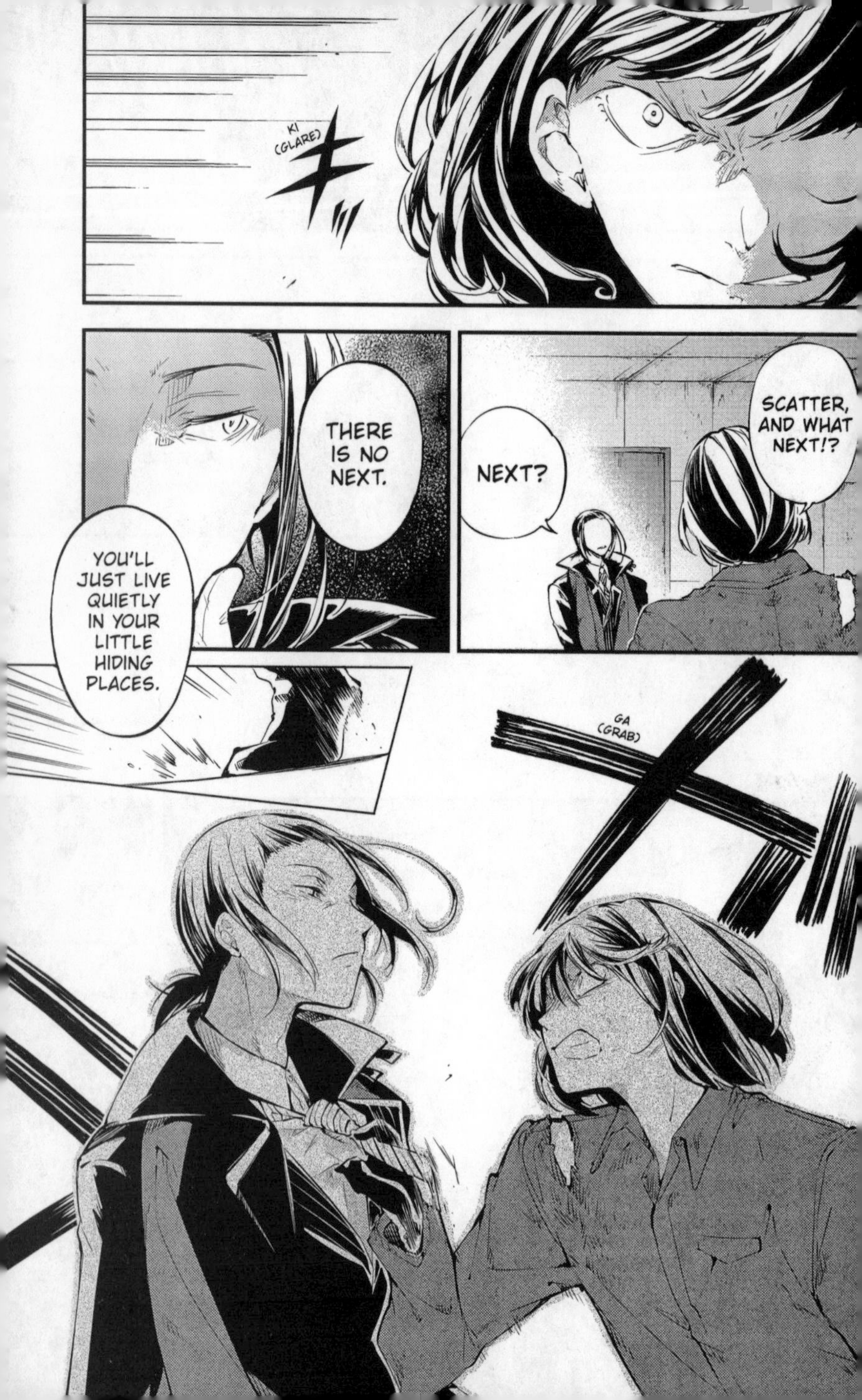
KI (GLARE)
SCATTER, AND WHAT NEXT!?
NEXT?
THERE IS NO NEXT.
YOU'LL JUST LIVE QUIETLY IN YOUR LITTLE HIDING PLACES.
GA (GRAB)

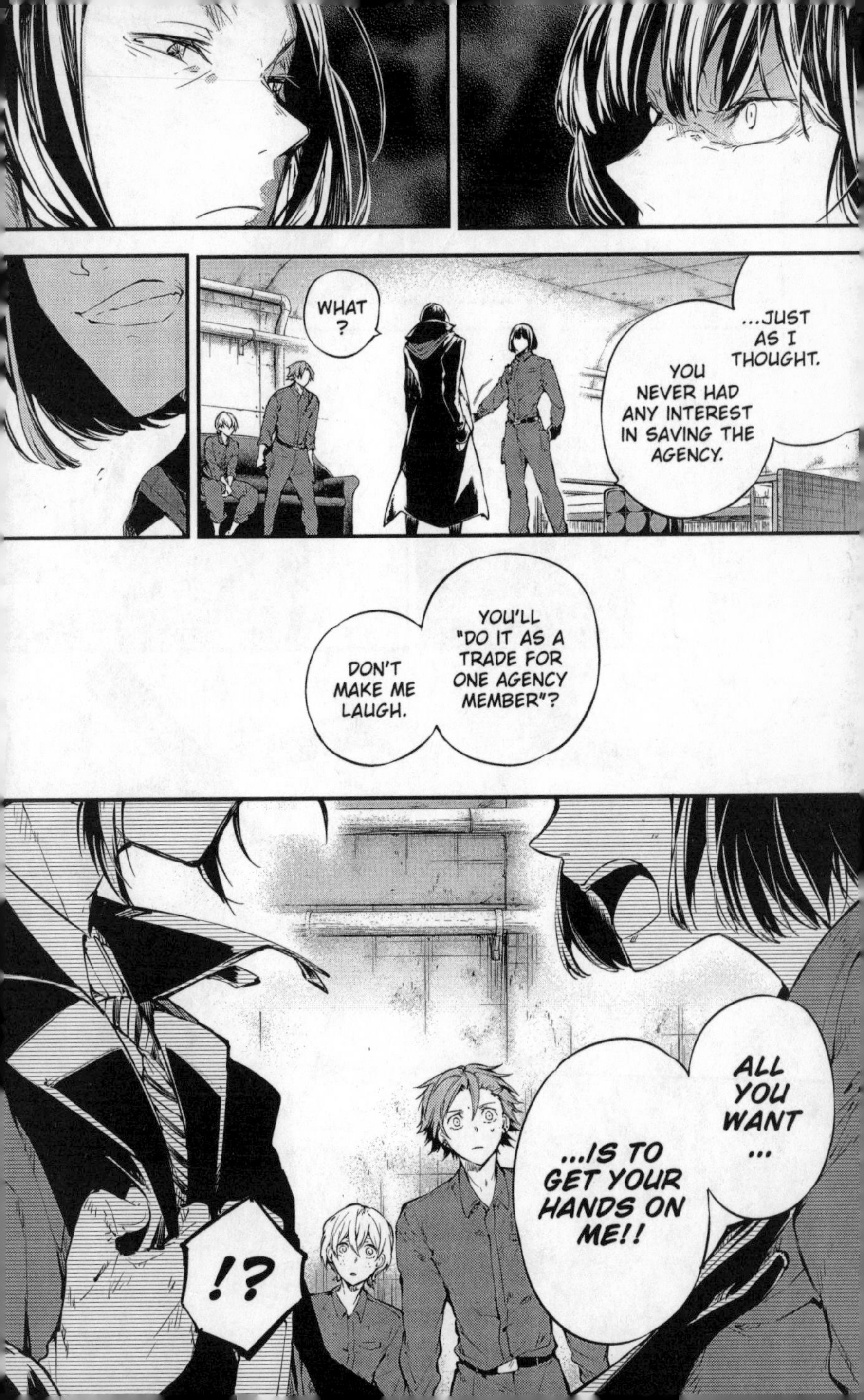
...JUST AS I THOUGHT.
YOU NEVER HAD ANY INTEREST IN SAVING THE AGENCY.
WHAT?
YOU'LL "DO IT AS A TRADE FOR ONE AGENCY MEMBER"?
DON'T MAKE ME LAUGH.
ALL YOU WANT...
...IS TO GET YOUR HANDS ON ME!!
!?

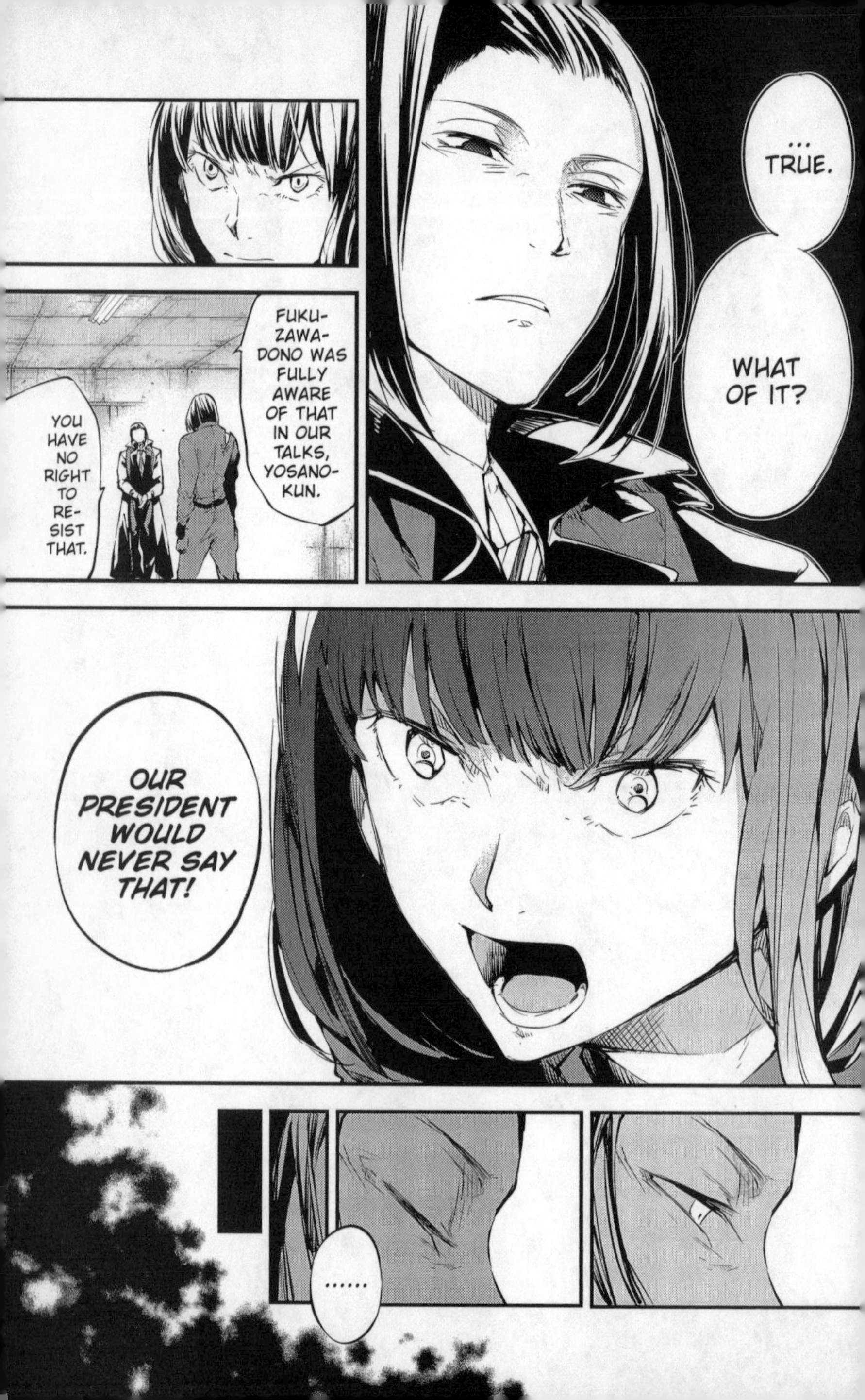

... TRUE.
WHAT OF IT?
FUKU-ZAWA-DONO WAS FULLY AWARE OF THAT IN OUR TALKS, YOSANO-KUN.
YOU HAVE NO RIGHT TO RE-SIST THAT.
OUR PRESIDENT WOULD NEVER SAY THAT!
......

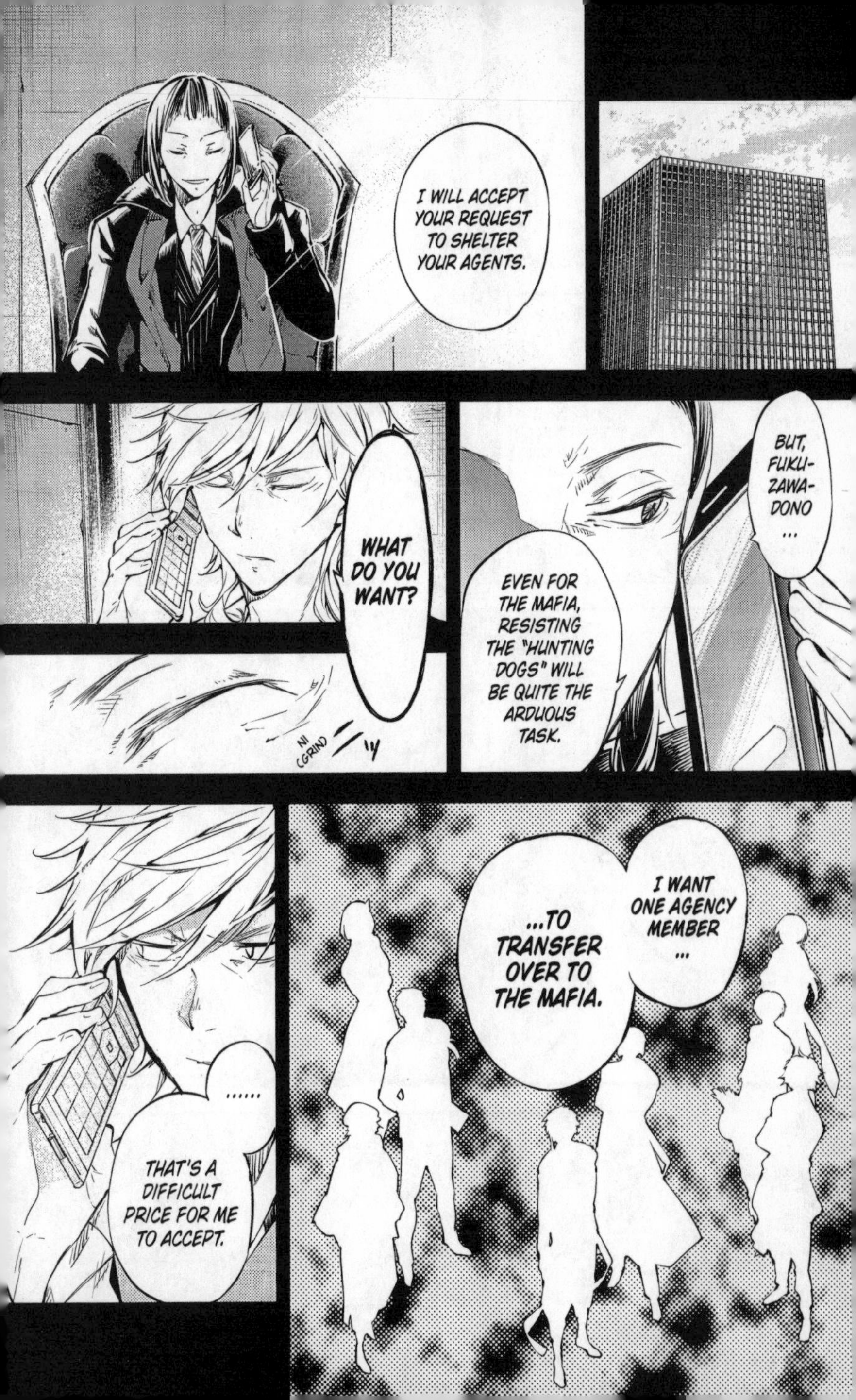
I WILL ACCEPT YOUR REQUEST TO SHELTER YOUR AGENTS.
BUT, FUKU-ZAWA-DONO...
EVEN FOR THE MAFIA, RESISTING THE "HUNTING DOGS" WILL BE QUITE THE ARDUOUS TASK.
WHAT DO YOU WANT?
NI (GRIN)
I WANT ONE AGENCY MEMBER...
...TO TRANSFER OVER TO THE MAFIA.
......
THAT'S A DIFFICULT PRICE FOR ME TO ACCEPT.

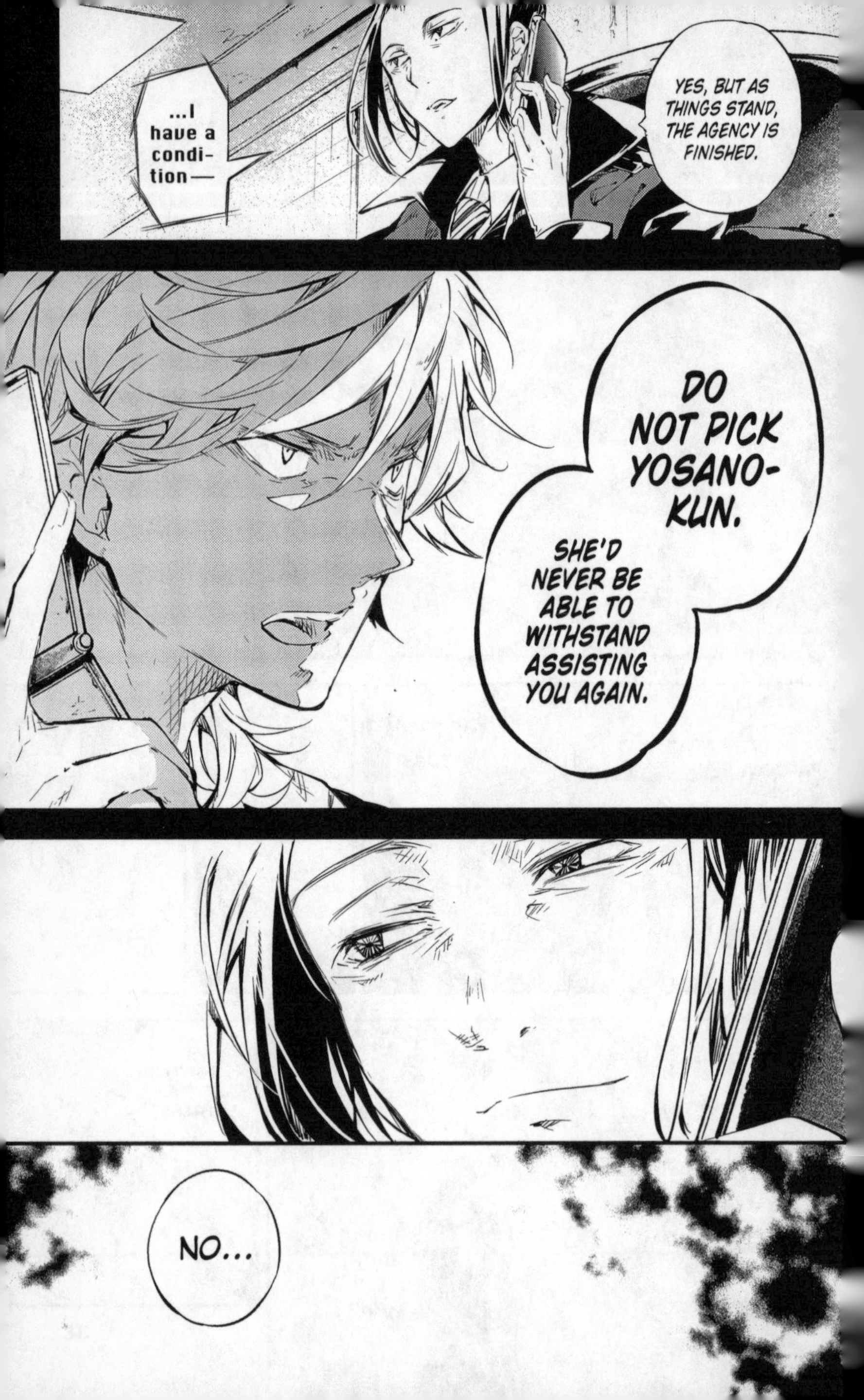
YES, BUT AS THINGS STAND, THE AGENCY IS FINISHED.
...I have a condition—
DO NOT PICK YOSANO-KUN.
SHE'D NEVER BE ABLE TO WITHSTAND ASSISTING YOU AGAIN.
NO...

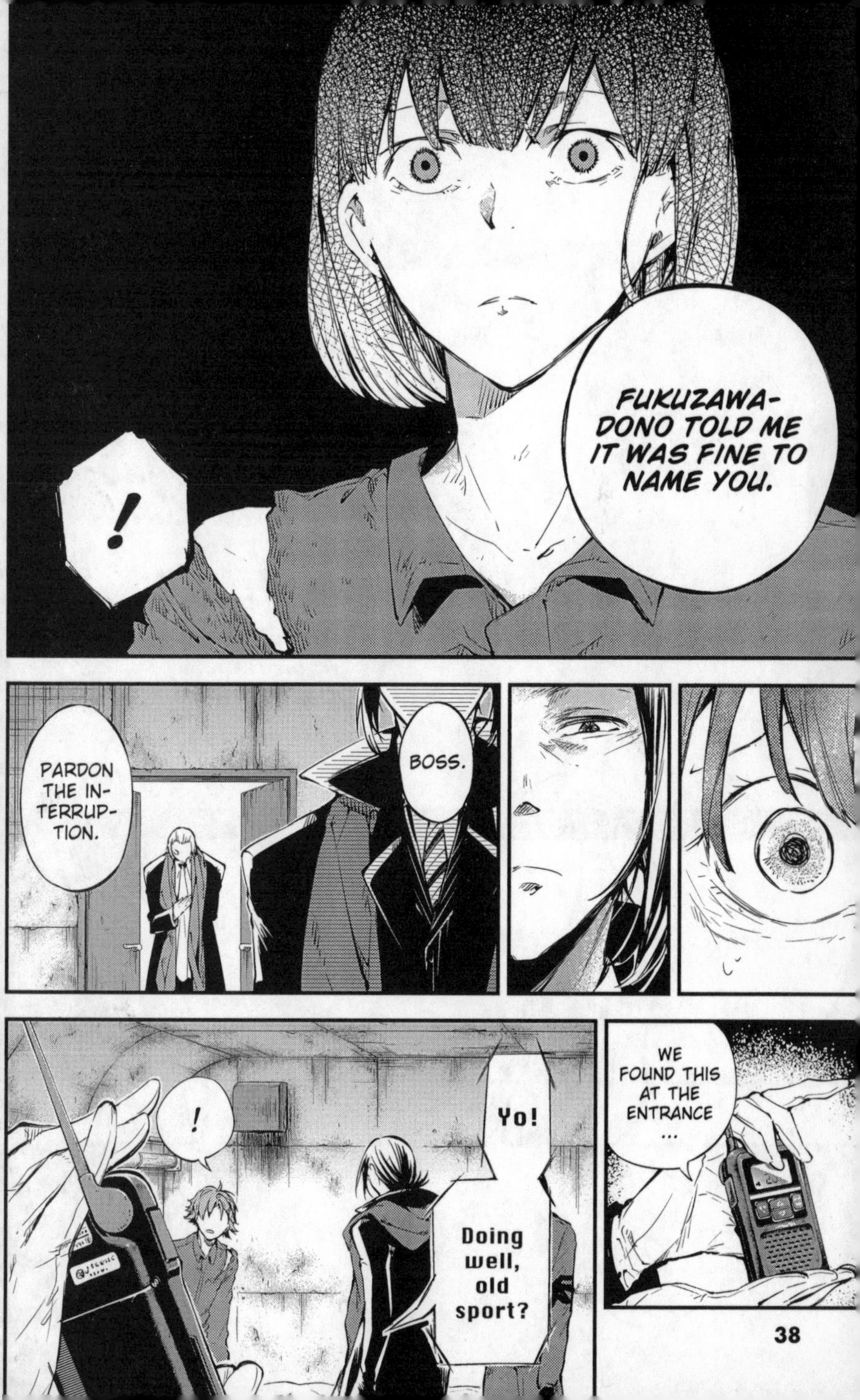
FUKUZAWA-DONO TOLD ME IT WAS FINE TO NAME YOU.
!
BOSS.
PARDON THE INTERRUPTION.
WE FOUND THIS AT THE ENTRANCE ...
Yo!
Doing well, old sport?
!

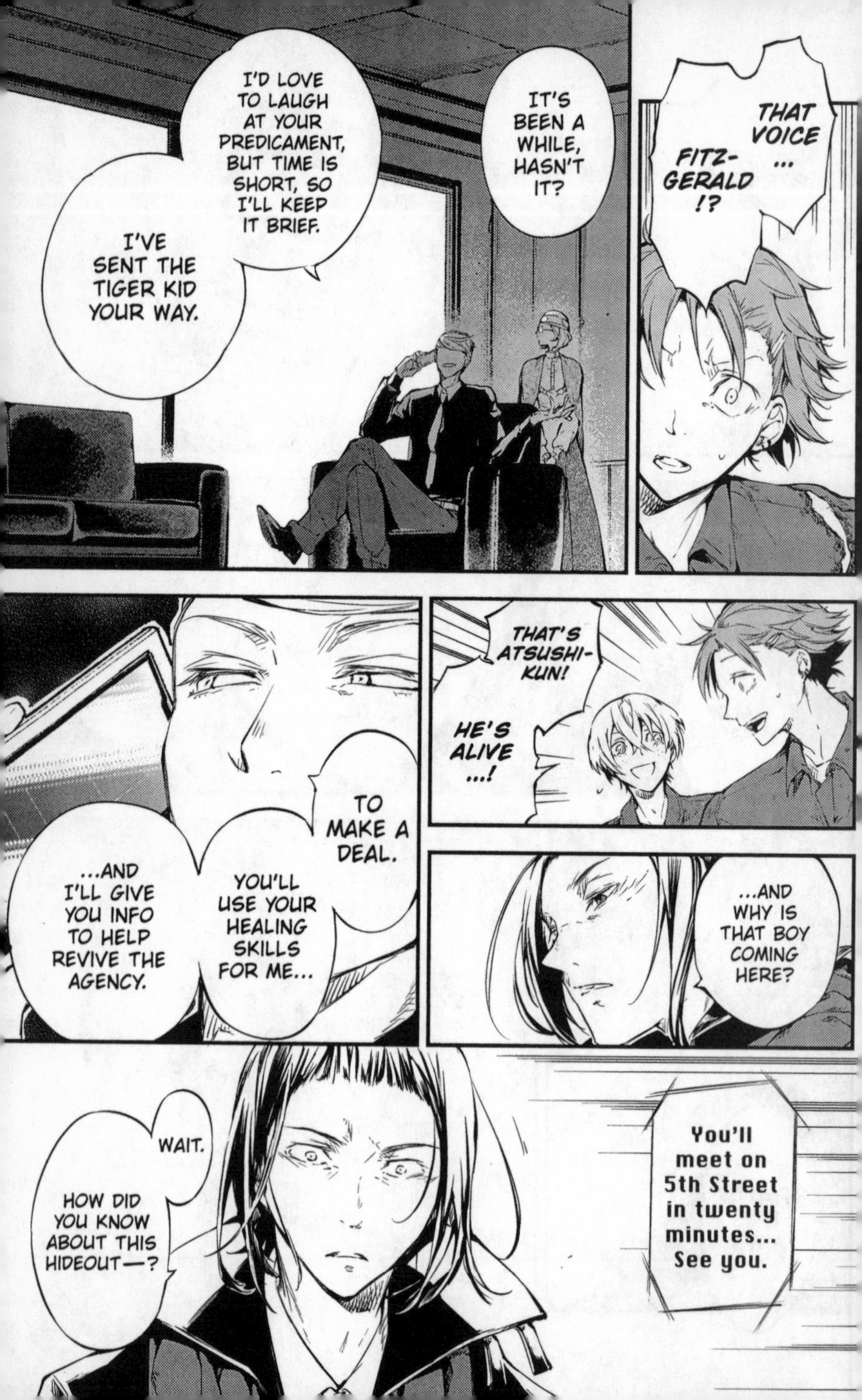
THAT VOICE ...
FITZ-GERALD !?
IT'S BEEN A WHILE, HASN'T IT?
I'D LOVE TO LAUGH AT YOUR PREDICAMENT, BUT TIME IS SHORT, SO I'LL KEEP IT BRIEF.
I'VE SENT THE TIGER KID YOUR WAY.
THAT'S ATSUSHI-KUN!
HE'S ALIVE ...!
...AND WHY IS THAT BOY COMING HERE?
TO MAKE A DEAL.
YOU'LL USE YOUR HEALING SKILLS FOR ME...
...AND I'LL GIVE YOU INFO TO HELP REVIVE THE AGENCY.
You'll meet on 5th Street in twenty minutes... See you.
WAIT.
HOW DID YOU KNOW ABOUT THIS HIDEOUT—?

PUTSU (CLICK)
......
INFO TO REVIVE THE AGENCY!
YEAH, NOW WE'VE GOT SOME HOPE!
......
HOW BIZARRE.
BI-ZARRE ...?
YES.
HOW DID HE DISCOVER THIS SECRET HIDEOUT?
?
WITH THE "EYES OF GOD," NO...?
THAT'S THE THING.

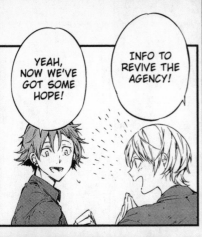

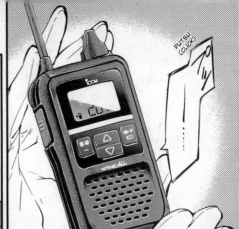

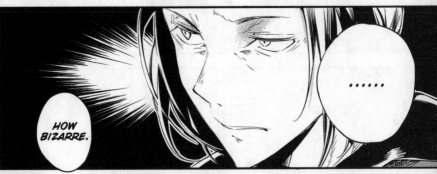

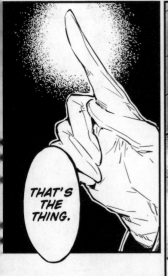

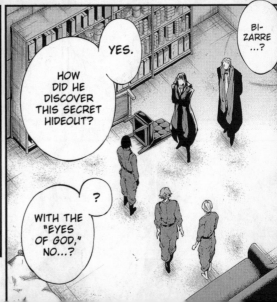

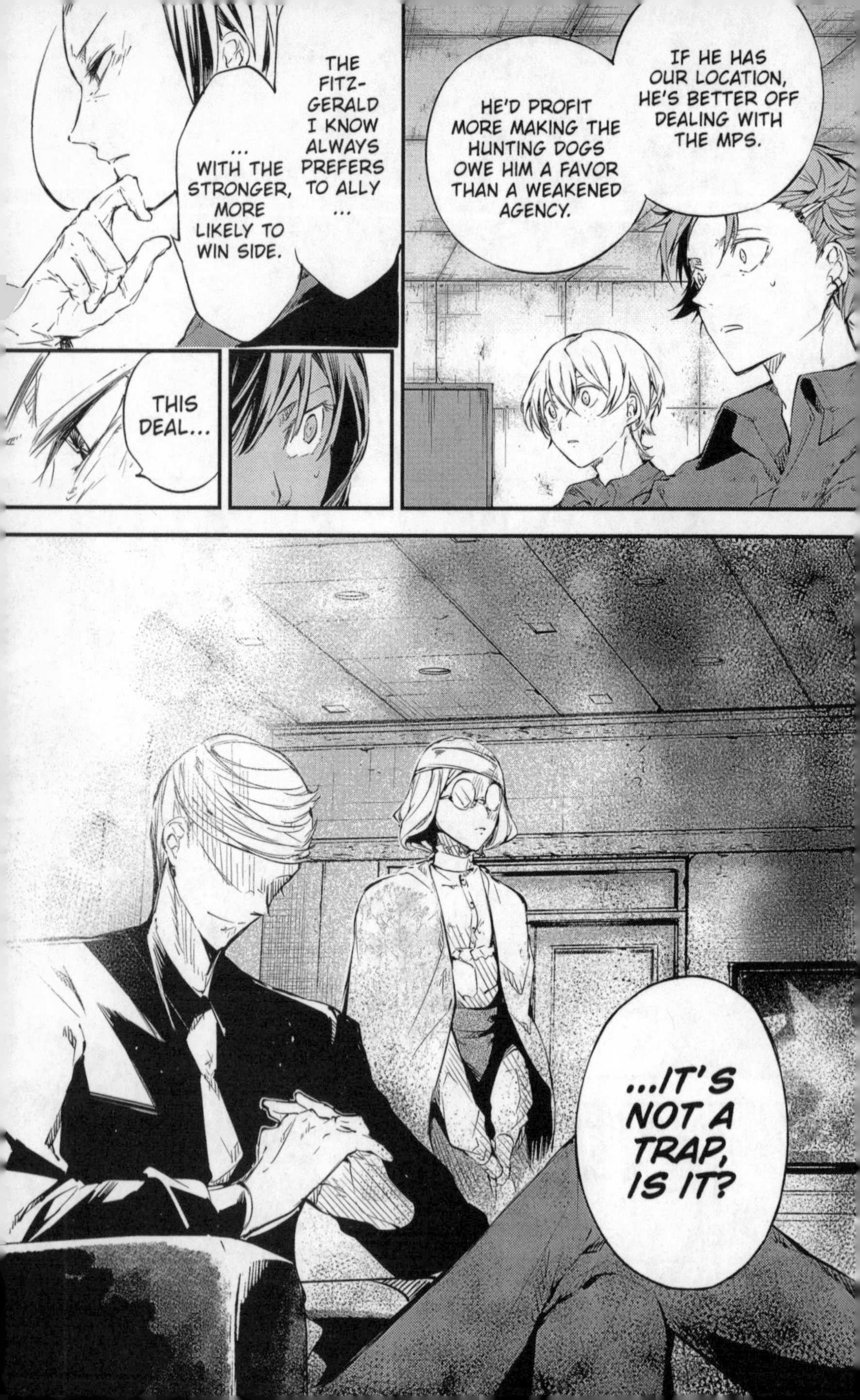
IF HE HAS OUR LOCATION, HE'S BETTER OFF DEALING WITH THE MPS.
HE'D PROFIT MORE MAKING THE HUNTING DOGS OWE HIM A FAVOR THAN A WEAKENED AGENCY.
THE FITZ-GERALD I KNOW ALWAYS PREFERS TO ALLY ...
... WITH THE STRONGER, MORE LIKELY TO WIN SIDE.
THIS DEAL...
...IT'S NOT A TRAP, IS IT?

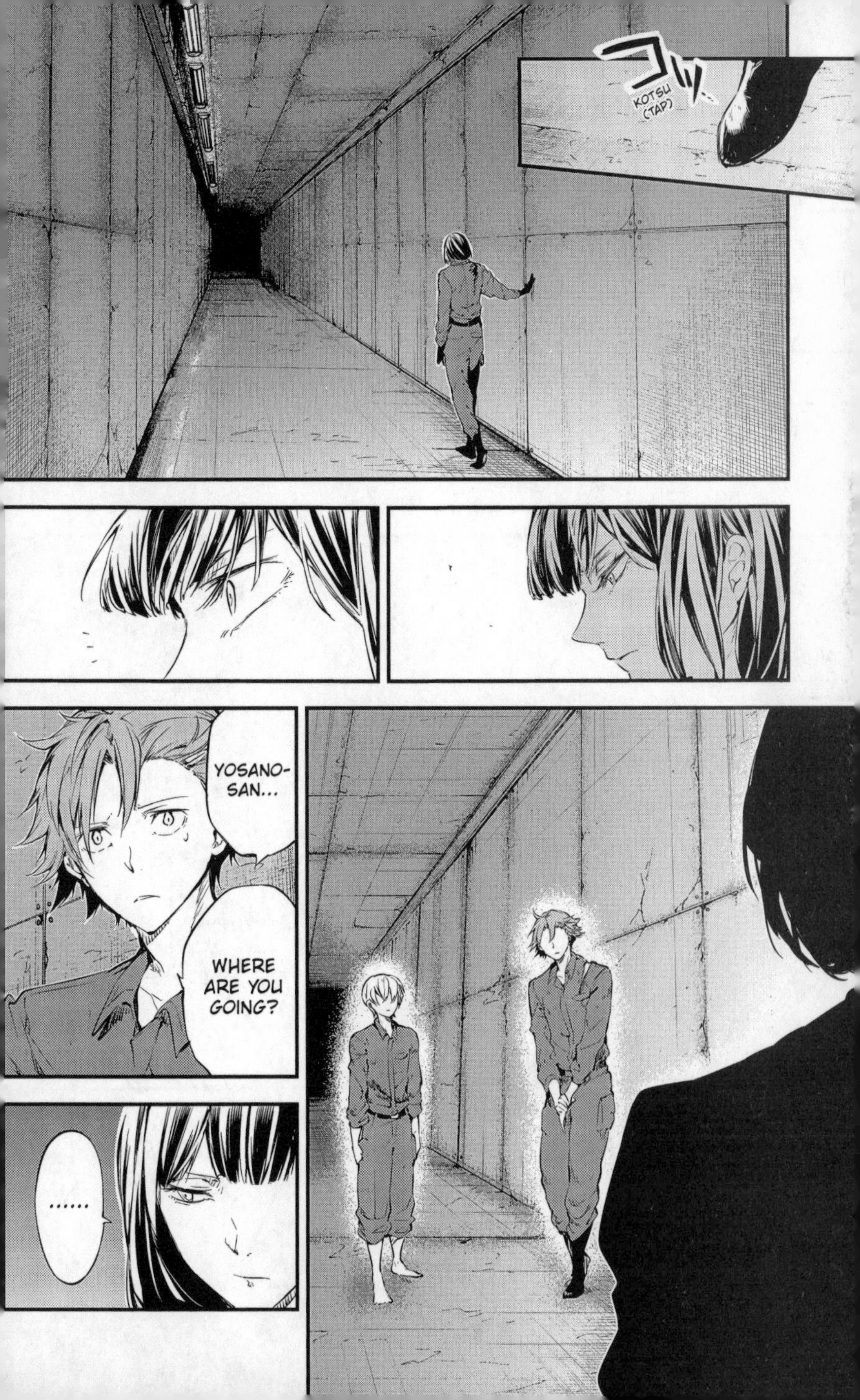
コツ…
KOTSU (TAP)
YOSANO-SAN...
WHERE ARE YOU GOING?
......

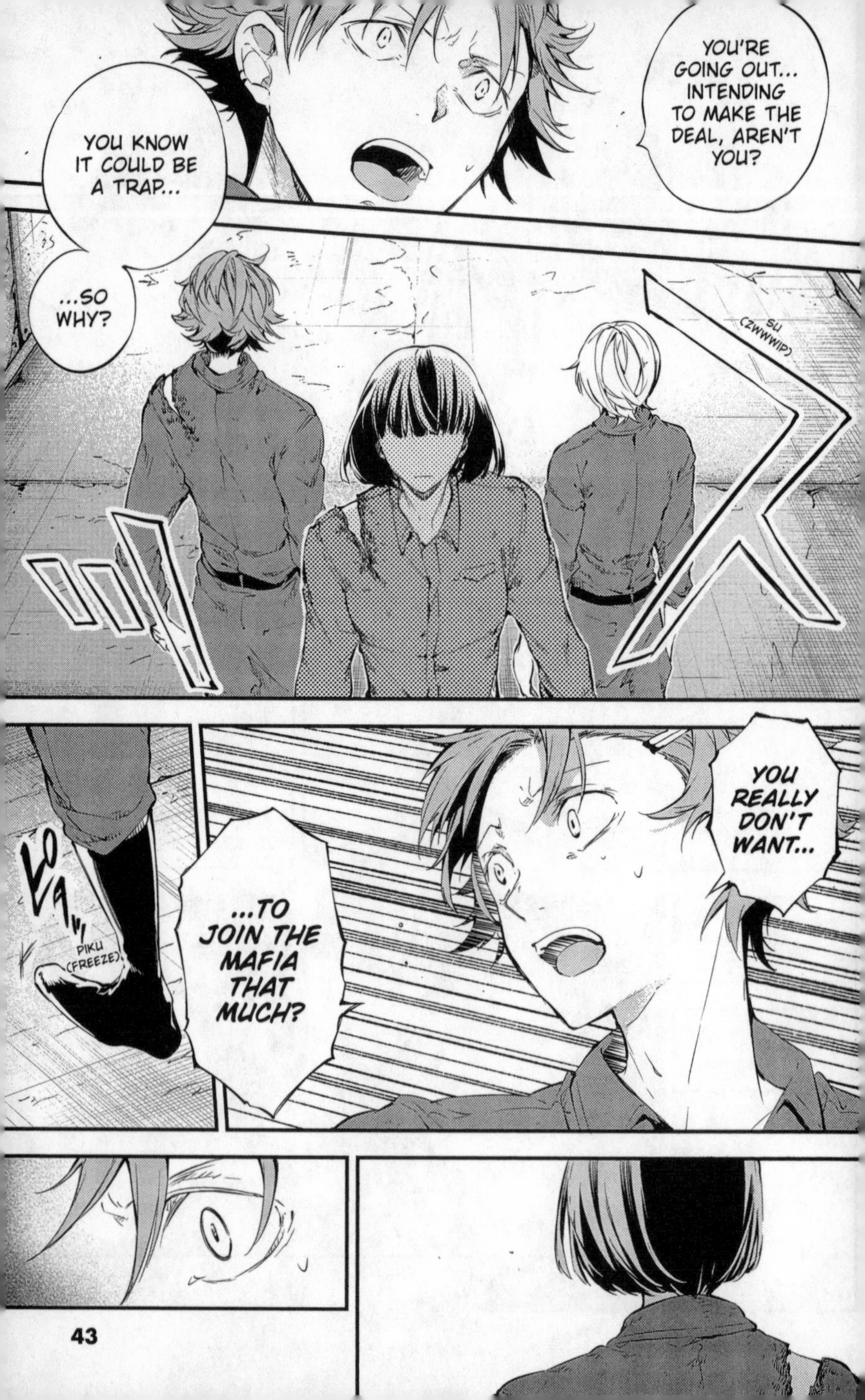
YOU'RE GOING OUT... INTENDING TO MAKE THE DEAL, AREN'T YOU?
YOU KNOW IT COULD BE A TRAP...
...SO WHY?
SU (ZWWWIP)
YOU REALLY DON'T WANT...
...TO JOIN THE MAFIA THAT MUCH?
PIKU (FREEZE)

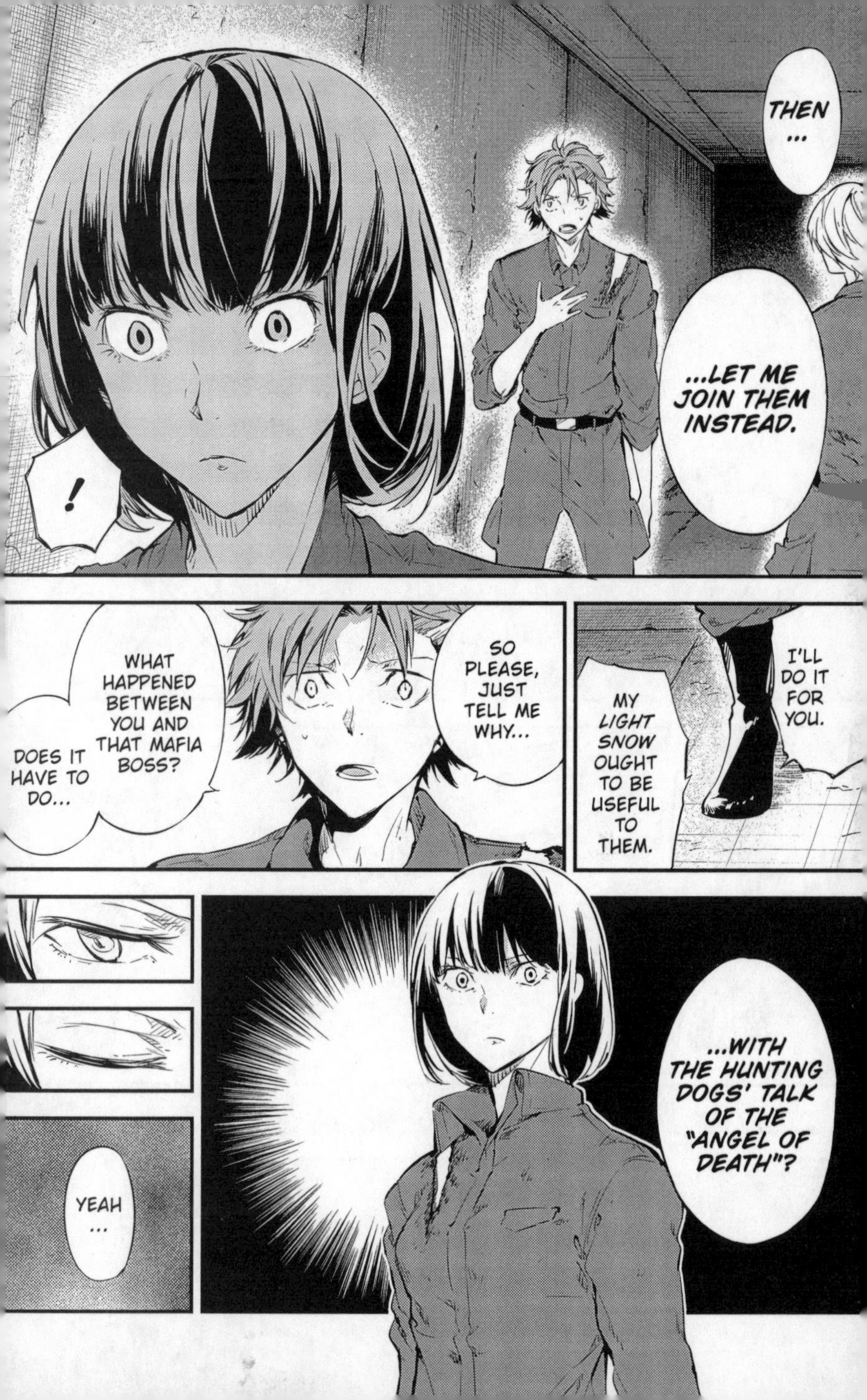
THEN ...
...LET ME JOIN THEM INSTEAD.
!
I'LL DO IT FOR YOU.
MY *LIGHT SNOW* OUGHT TO BE USEFUL TO THEM.
SO PLEASE, JUST TELL ME WHY...
WHAT HAPPENED BETWEEN YOU AND THAT MAFIA BOSS?
DOES IT HAVE TO DO...
...WITH THE HUNTING DOGS' TALK OF THE "ANGEL OF DEATH"?
YEAH ...

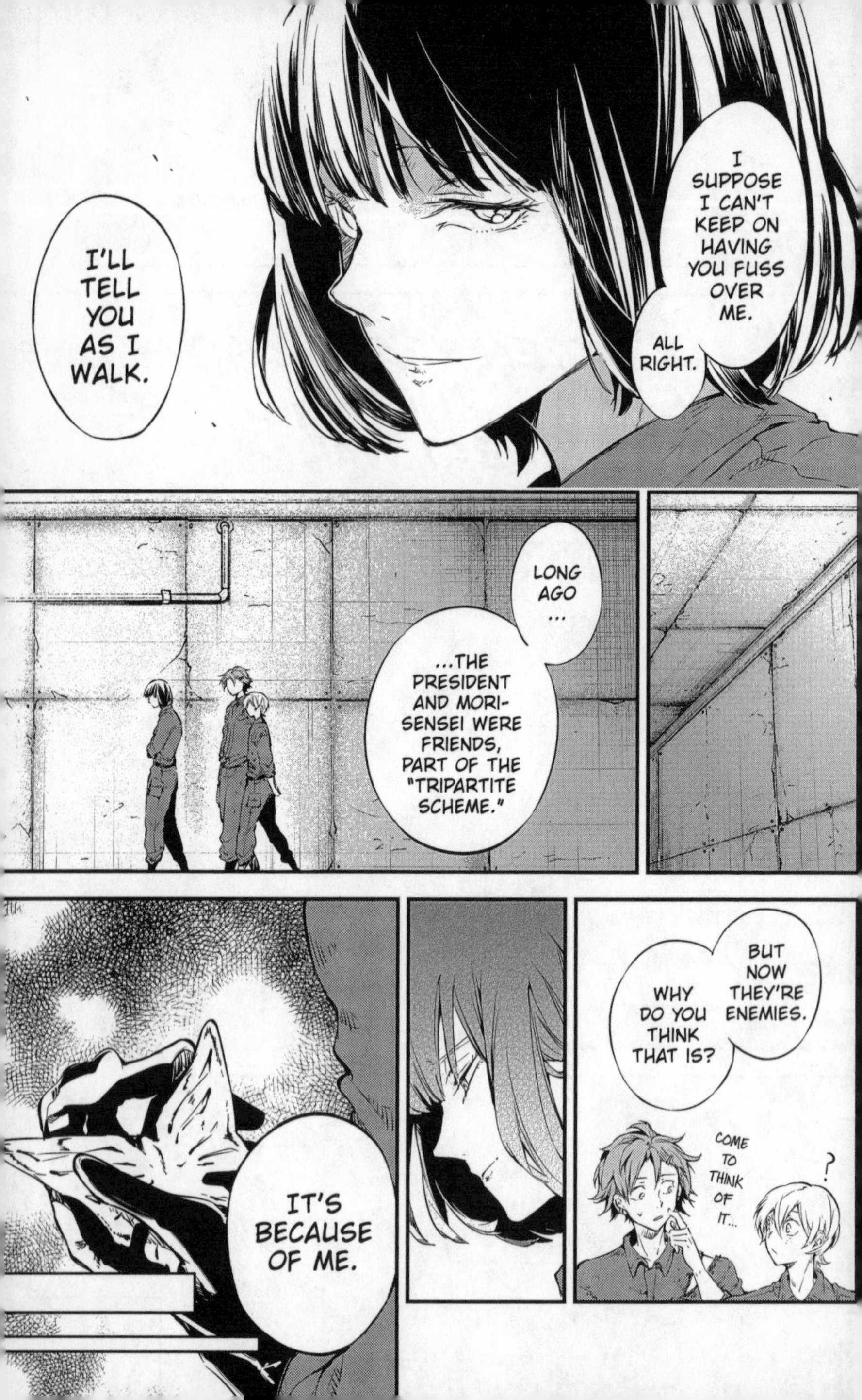
I SUPPOSE I CAN'T KEEP ON HAVING YOU FUSS OVER ME.
ALL RIGHT.
I'LL TELL YOU AS I WALK.
LONG AGO ...
...THE PRESIDENT AND MORI-SENSEI WERE FRIENDS, PART OF THE "TRIPARTITE SCHEME."
BUT NOW THEY'RE ENEMIES.
WHY DO YOU THINK THAT IS?
COME TO THINK OF IT...
?
IT'S BECAUSE OF ME.

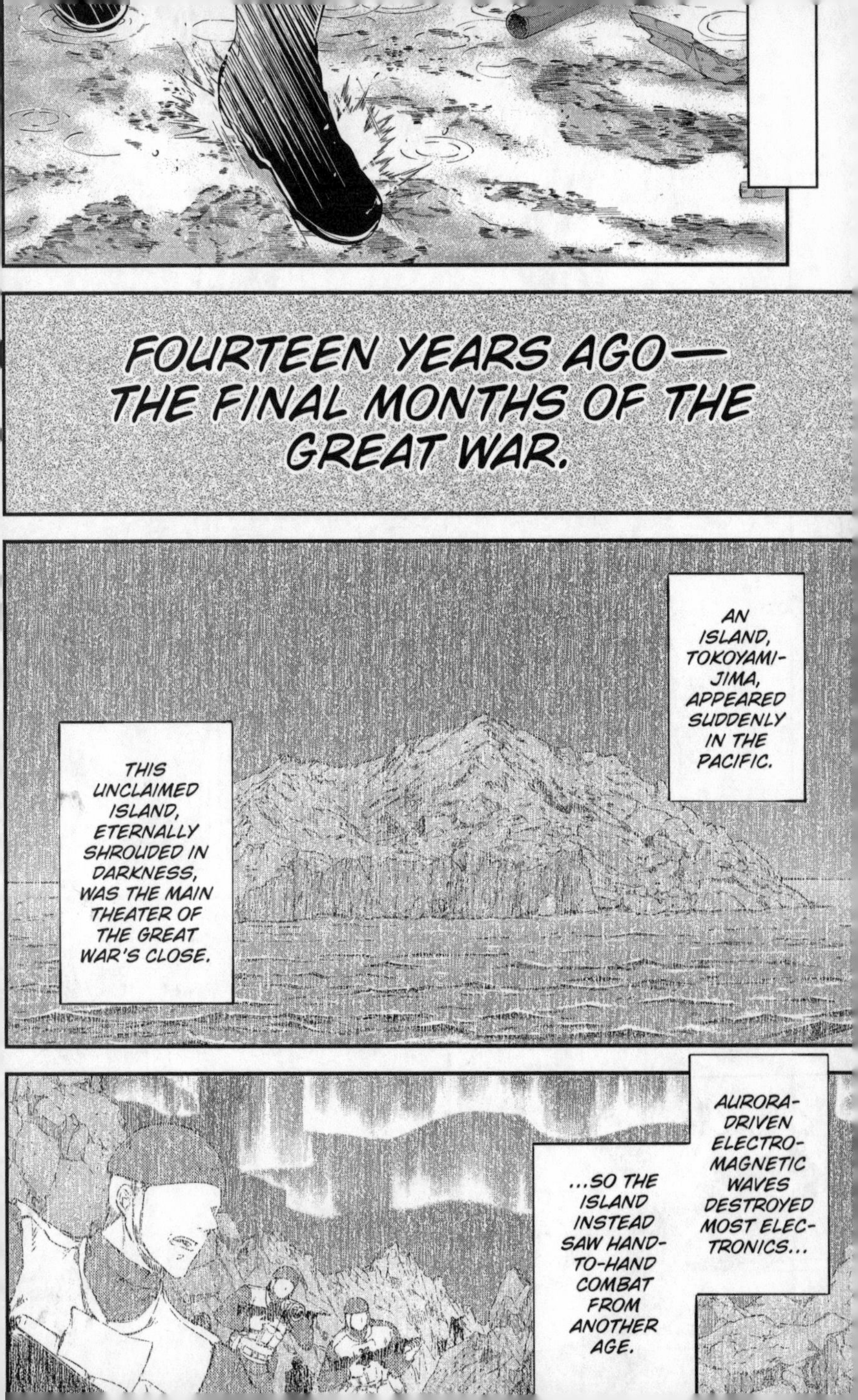
FOURTEEN YEARS AGO— THE FINAL MONTHS OF THE GREAT WAR.
AN ISLAND, TOKOYAMI-JIMA, APPEARED SUDDENLY IN THE PACIFIC.
THIS UNCLAIMED ISLAND, ETERNALLY SHROUDED IN DARKNESS, WAS THE MAIN THEATER OF THE GREAT WAR'S CLOSE.
AURORA-DRIVEN ELECTRO-MAGNETIC WAVES DESTROYED MOST ELEC-TRONICS...
...SO THE ISLAND INSTEAD SAW HAND-TO-HAND COMBAT FROM ANOTHER AGE.

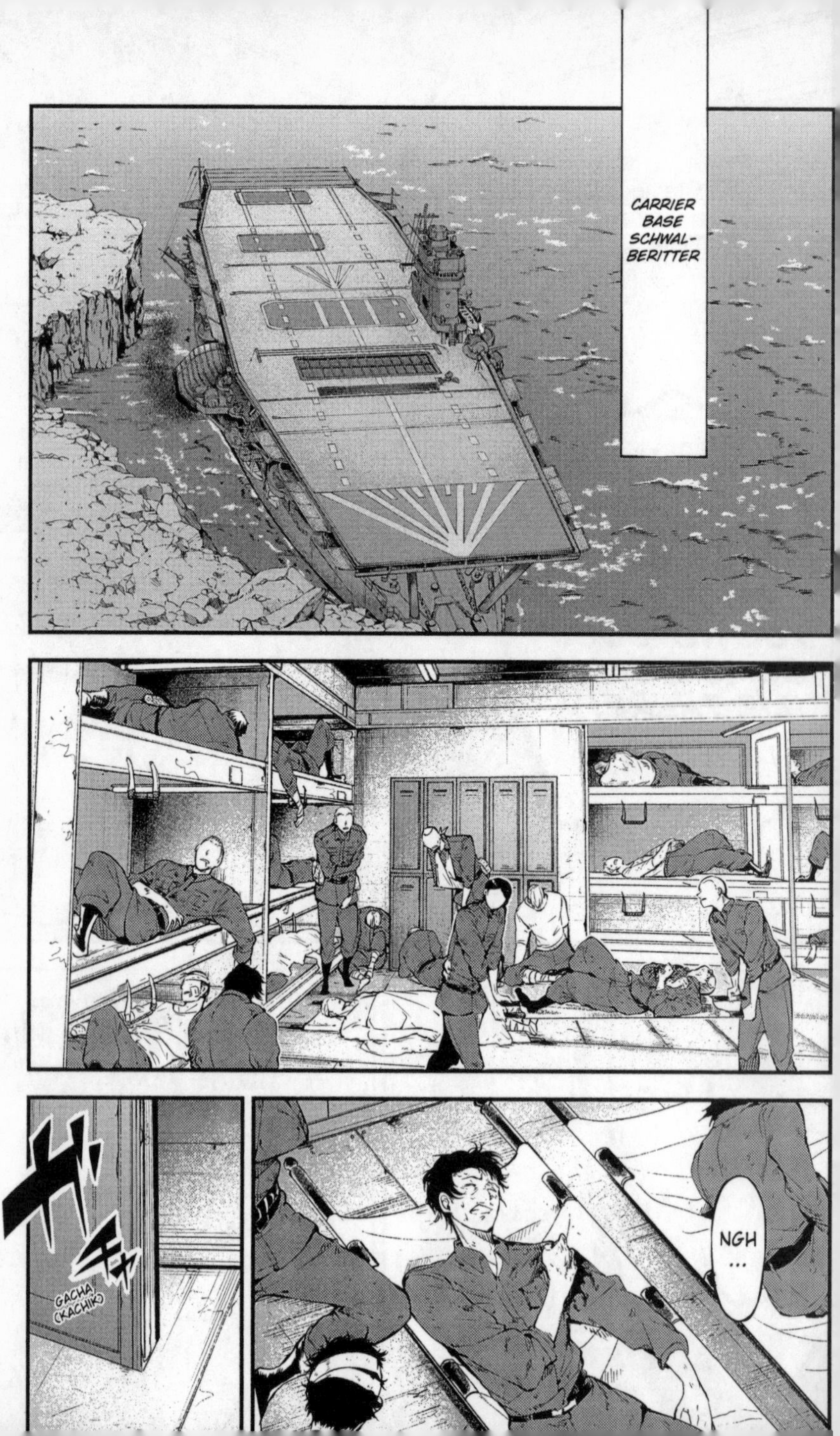
CARRIER BASE SCHWAL-BERITTER
NGH ...
GACHA (KACHIK)

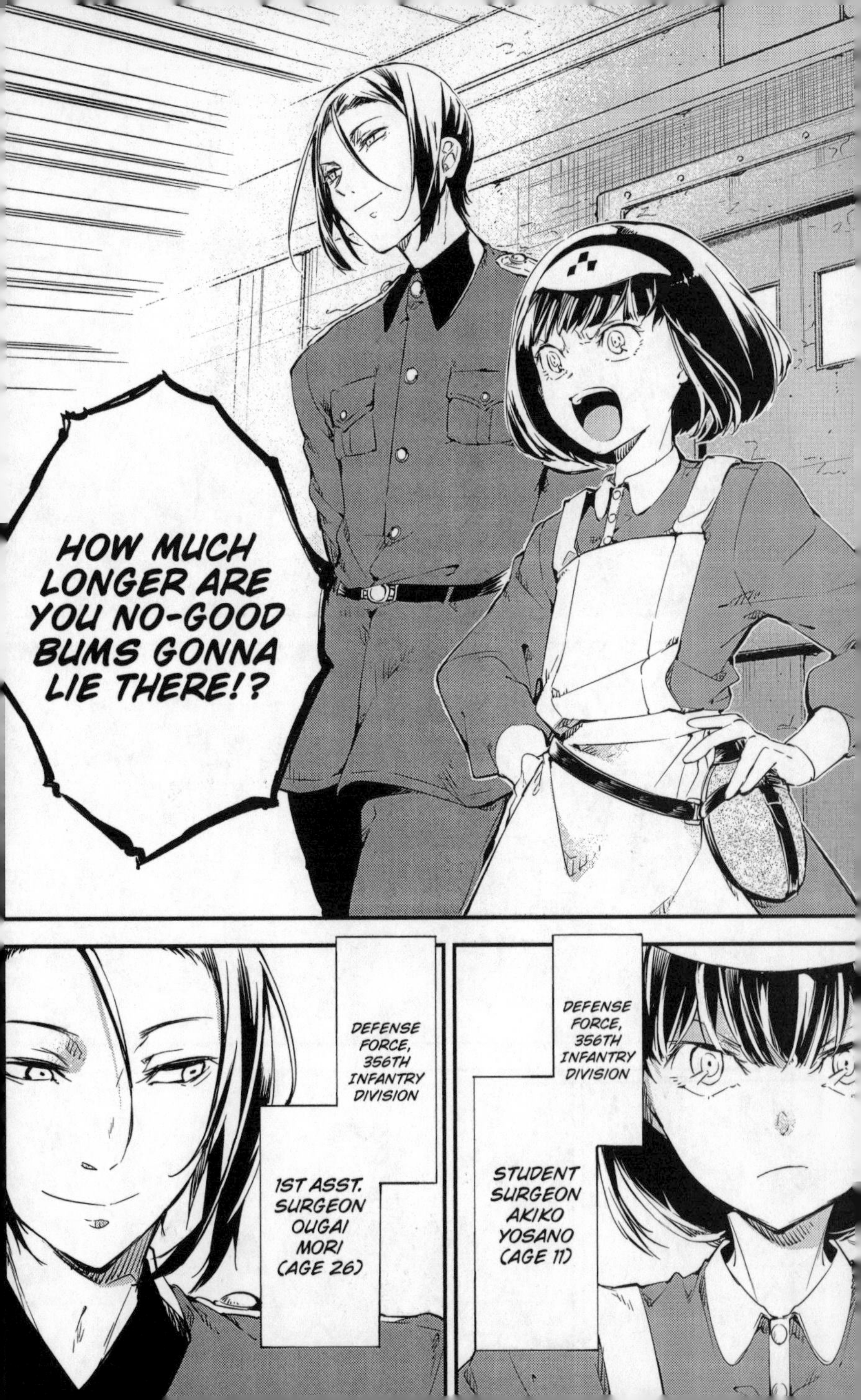
HOW MUCH LONGER ARE YOU NO-GOOD BUMS GONNA LIE THERE!?
DEFENSE FORCE, 356TH INFANTRY DIVISION
STUDENT SURGEON AKIKO YOSANO (AGE 11)
DEFENSE FORCE, 356TH INFANTRY DIVISION
1ST ASST. SURGEON OUGAI MORI (AGE 26)

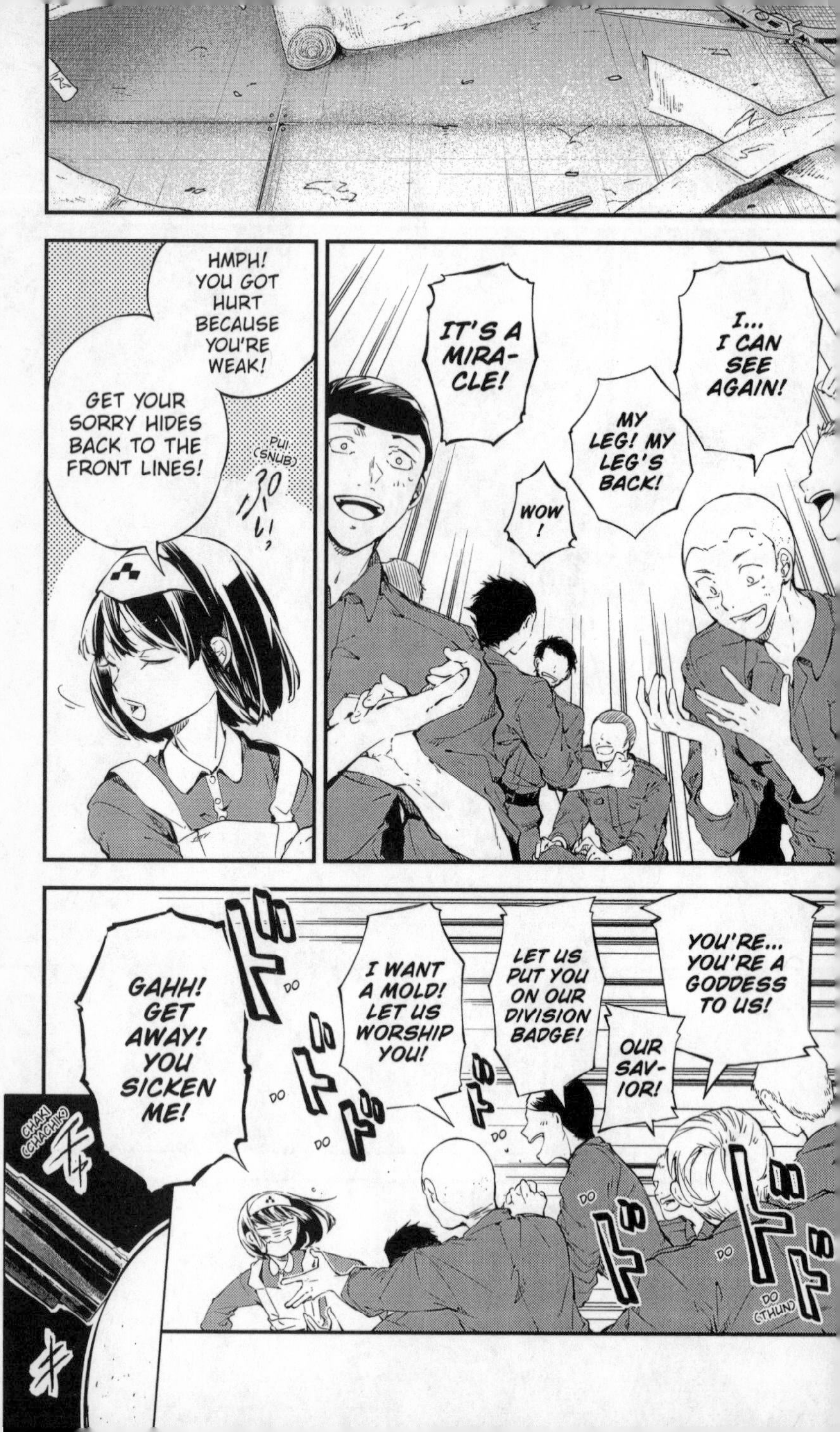
I... I CAN SEE AGAIN!
MY LEG! MY LEG'S BACK!
WOW!
IT'S A MIRACLE!
HMPH! YOU GOT HURT BECAUSE YOU'RE WEAK!
GET YOUR SORRY HIDES BACK TO THE FRONT LINES!
PUI (SNUB)
YOU'RE... YOU'RE A GODDESS TO US!
OUR SAVIOR!
LET US PUT YOU ON OUR DIVISION BADGE!
I WANT A MOLD! LET US WORSHIP YOU!
DO (THUN)
DO
DO
DO
DO
DO
GAHH! GET AWAY! YOU SICKEN ME!
CHAKI (CHACHIK)

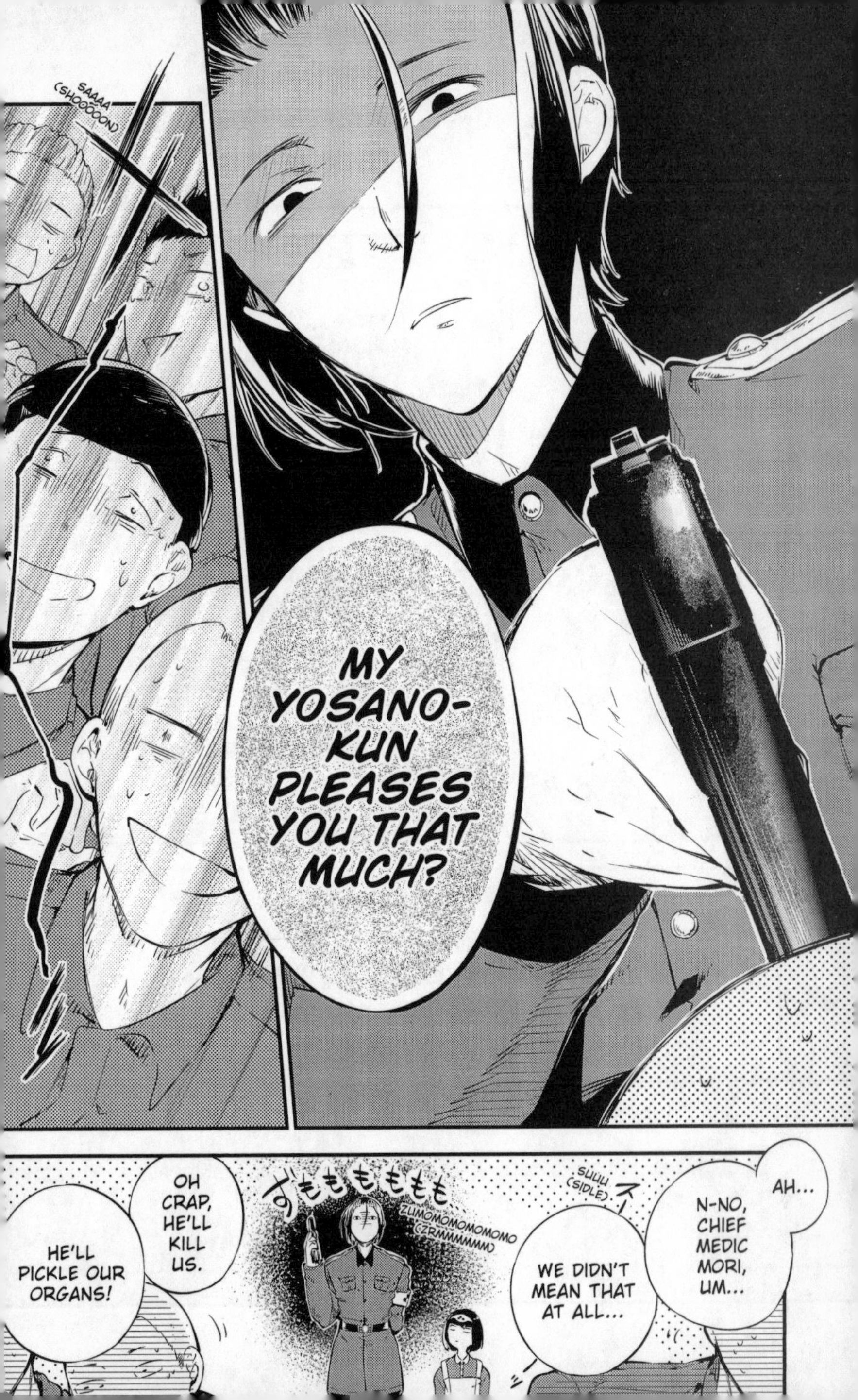
MY YOSANO-KUN PLEASES YOU THAT MUCH?
SAAAA (SHOOOOON)
AH...
N-NO, CHIEF MEDIC MORI, UM...
WE DIDN'T MEAN THAT AT ALL...
SUUU (SIDLE)
ZUMOMOMOMOMO (ZRMMMMMMM)
OH CRAP, HE'LL KILL US.
HE'LL PICKLE OUR ORGANS!

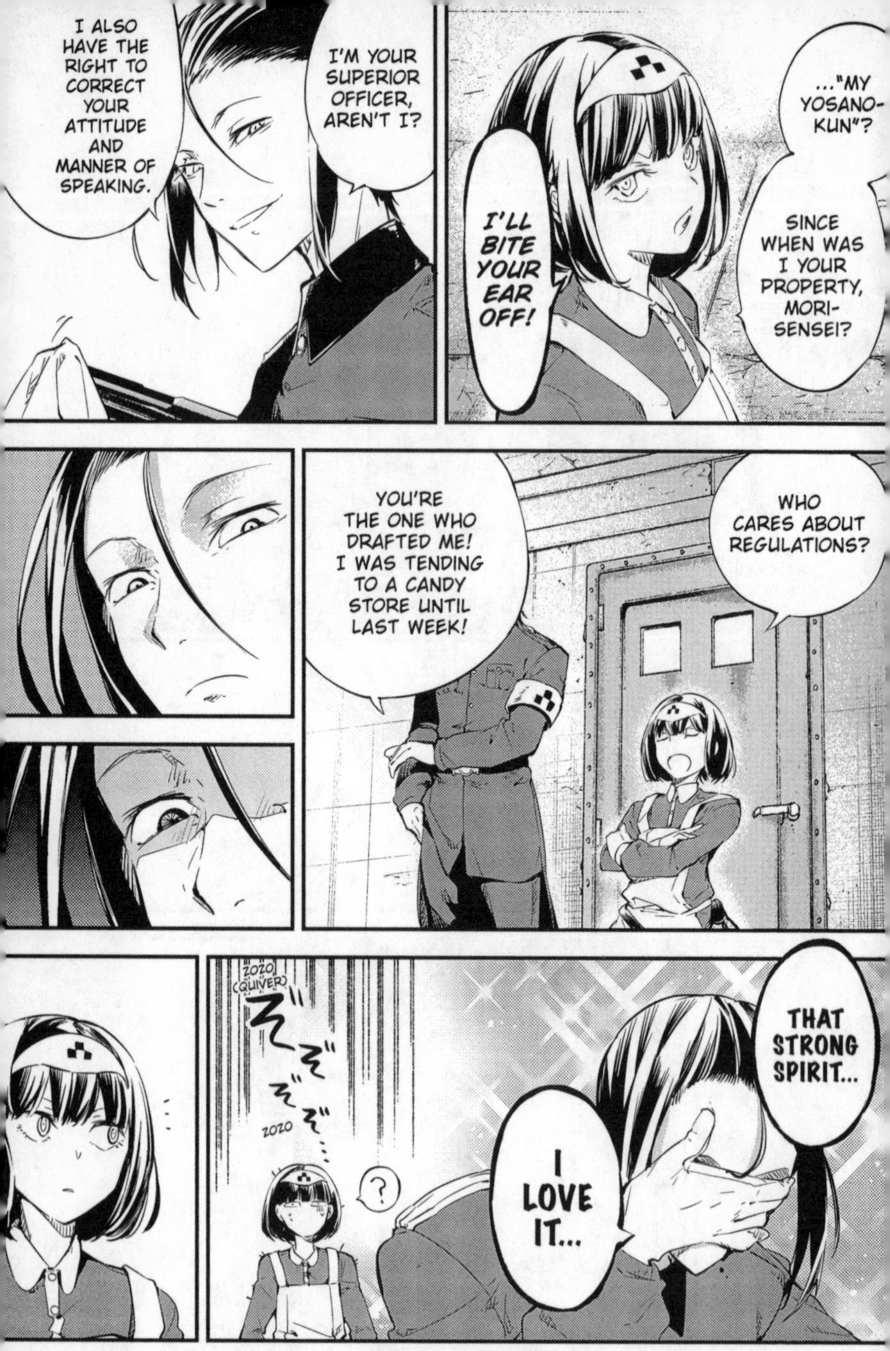
..."MY YOSANO-KUN"?
SINCE WHEN WAS I YOUR PROPERTY, MORI-SENSEI?
I'LL BITE YOUR EAR OFF!
I'M YOUR SUPERIOR OFFICER, AREN'T I?
I ALSO HAVE THE RIGHT TO CORRECT YOUR ATTITUDE AND MANNER OF SPEAKING.
WHO CARES ABOUT REGULATIONS?
YOU'RE THE ONE WHO DRAFTED ME! I WAS TENDING TO A CANDY STORE UNTIL LAST WEEK!
THAT STRONG SPIRIT...
I LOVE IT...
ZOZO (QUIVER)
ZOZO
?

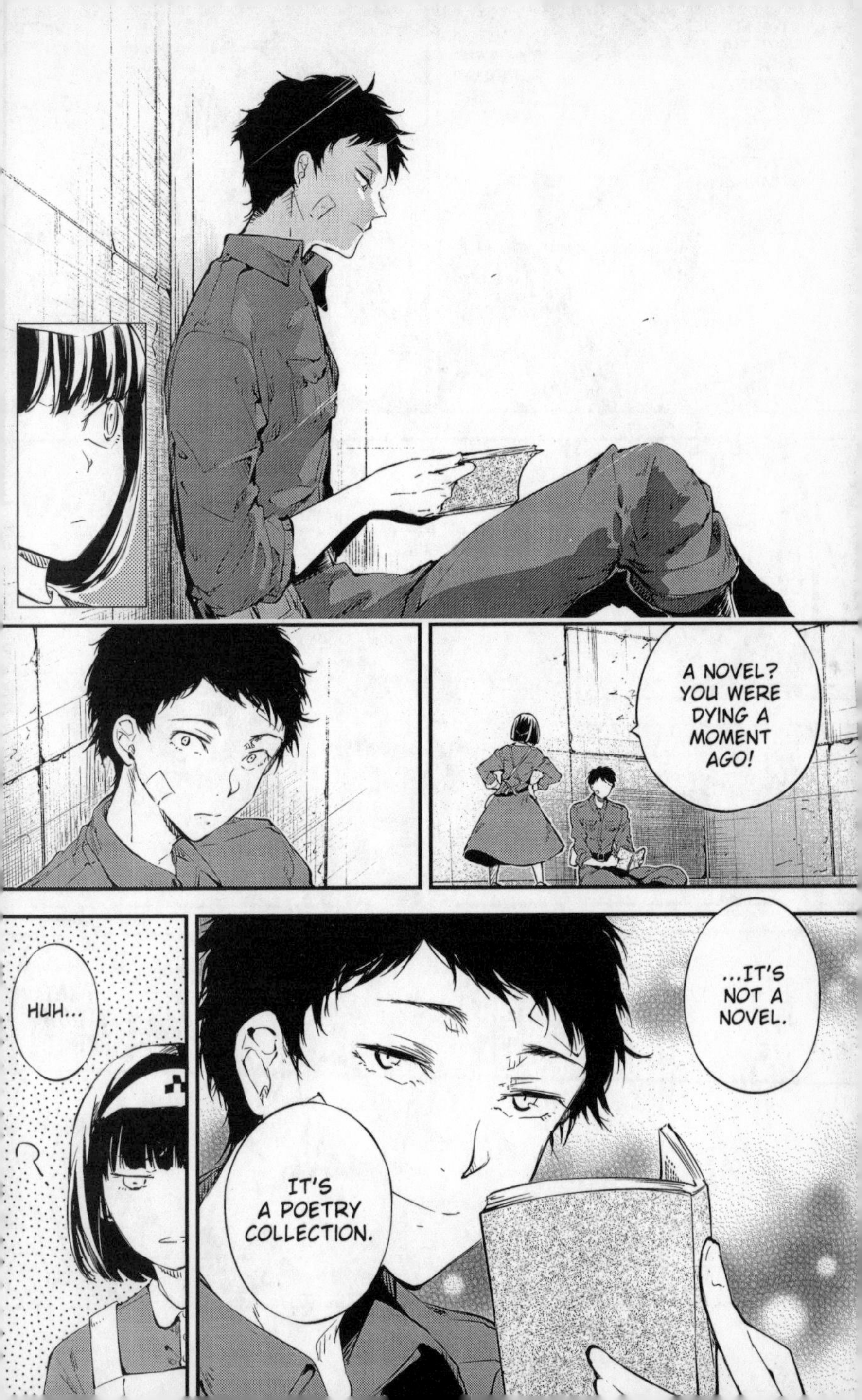
A NOVEL? YOU WERE DYING A MOMENT AGO!
...IT'S NOT A NOVEL.
IT'S A POETRY COLLECTION.
HUH...

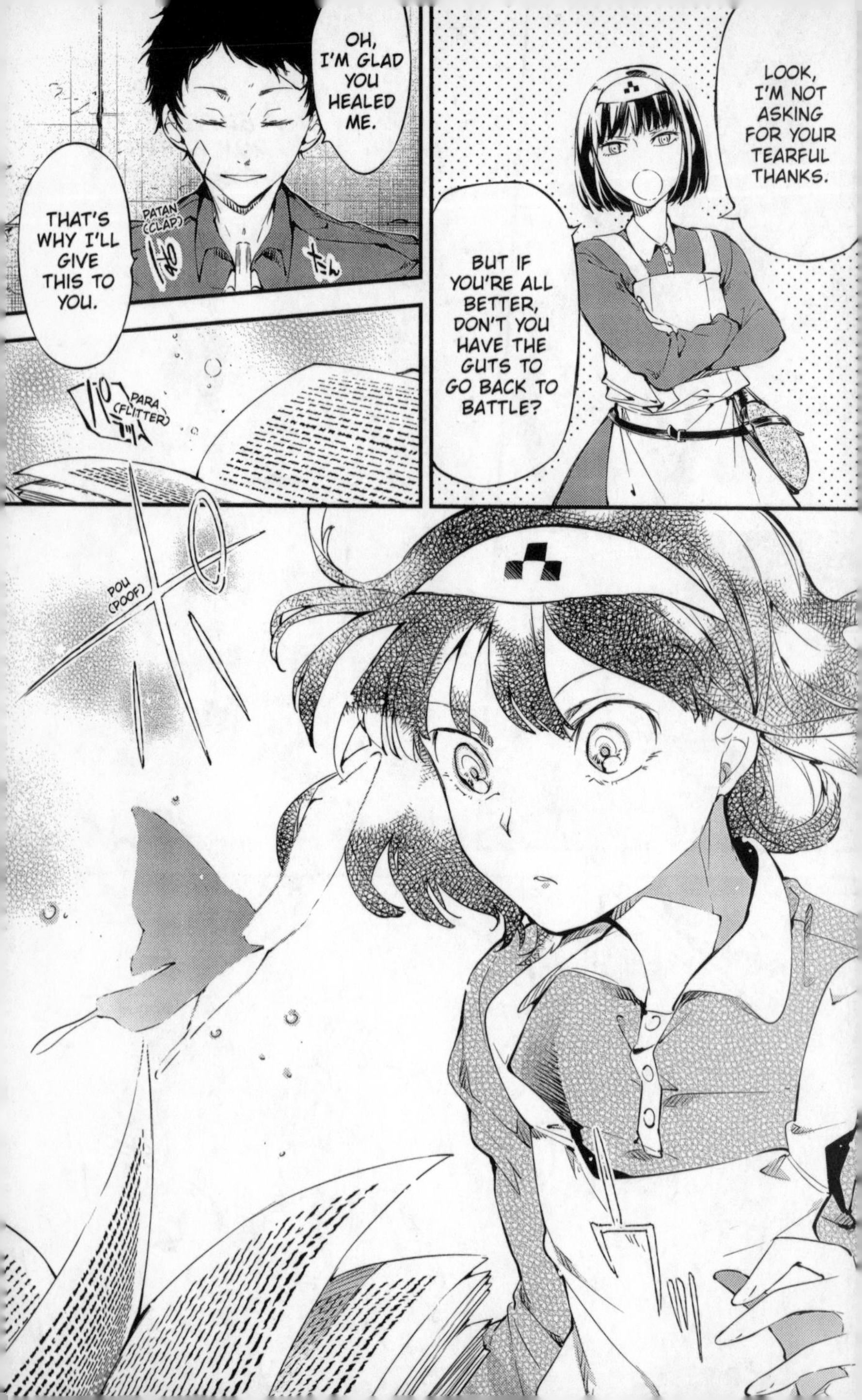
LOOK, I'M NOT ASKING FOR YOUR TEARFUL THANKS.
BUT IF YOU'RE ALL BETTER, DON'T YOU HAVE THE GUTS TO GO BACK TO BATTLE?
OH, I'M GLAD YOU HEALED ME.
PATAN (CLAP)
THAT'S WHY I'LL GIVE THIS TO YOU.
PARA (FLITTER)
POU (POOF)

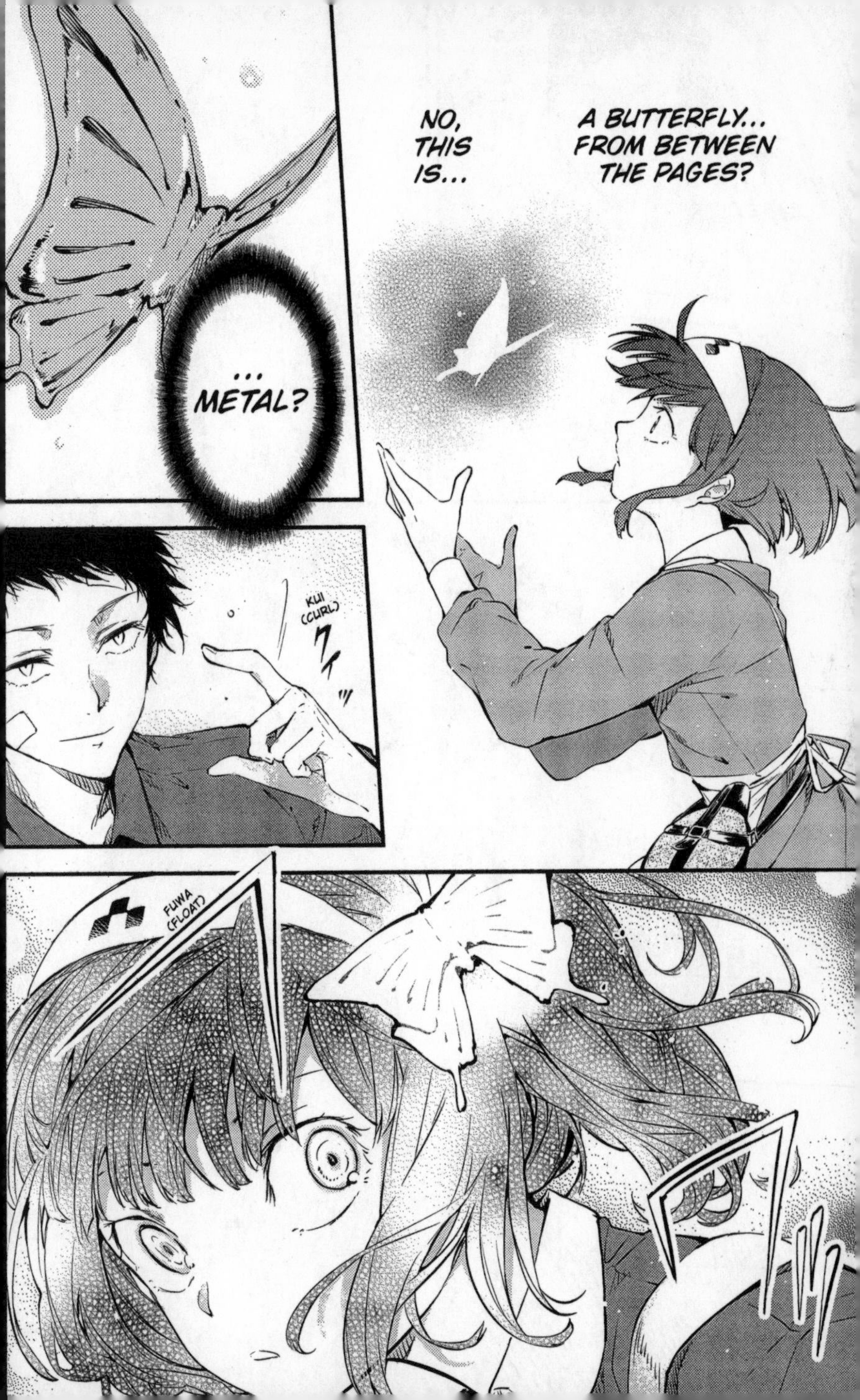
A BUTTERFLY... FROM BETWEEN THE PAGES?
NO, THIS IS...
... METAL?
KUI (CURL)
FUWA (FLOAT)

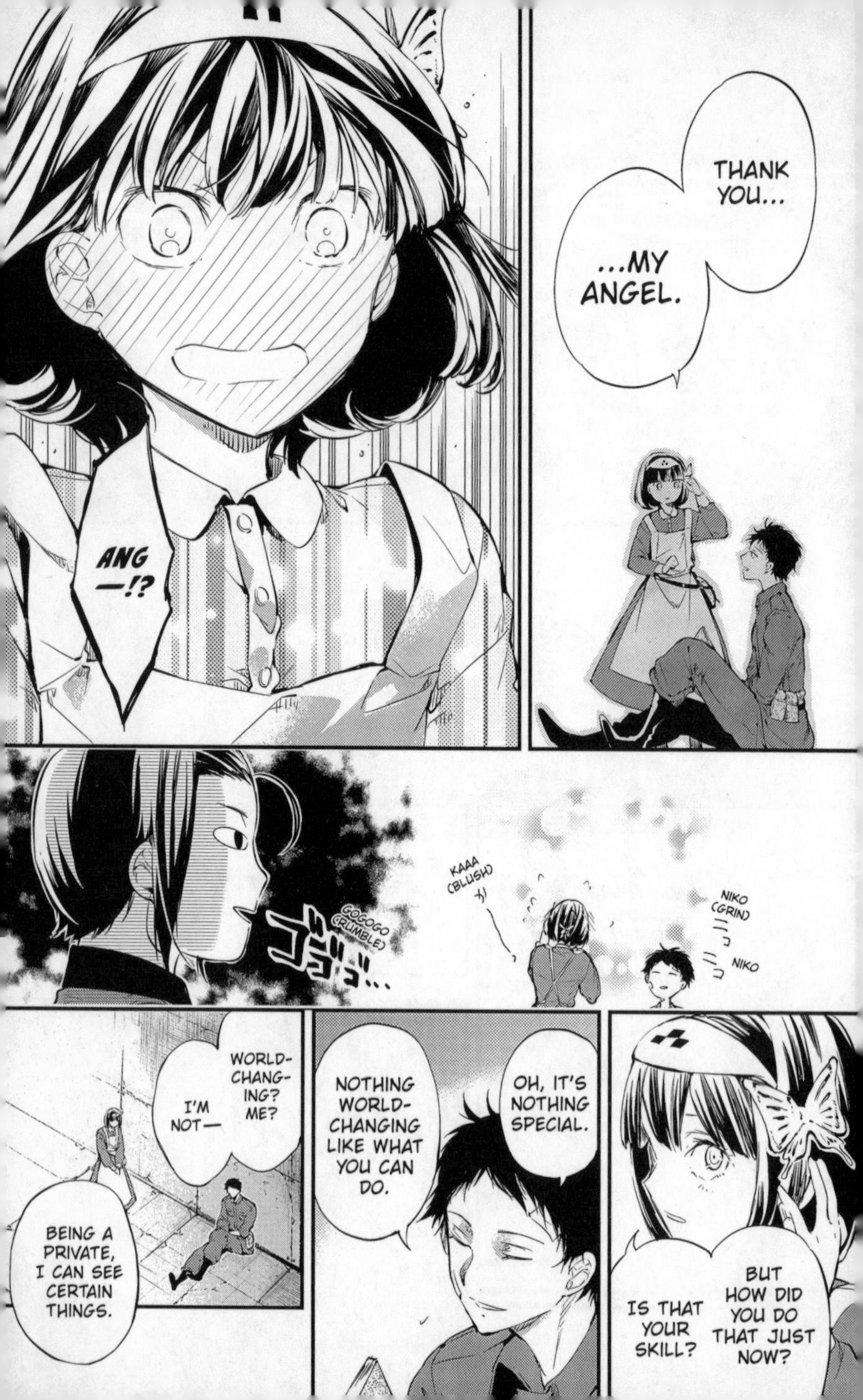
THANK YOU...
...MY ANGEL.
ANG—!?
KAAA (BLUSH)
NIKO (GRIN)
NIKO
GOGOGO (RUMBLE)
BUT HOW DID YOU DO THAT JUST NOW?
IS THAT YOUR SKILL?
OH, IT'S NOTHING SPECIAL.
NOTHING WORLD-CHANGING LIKE WHAT YOU CAN DO.
WORLD-CHANGING? ME?
I'M NOT—
BEING A PRIVATE, I CAN SEE CERTAIN THINGS.

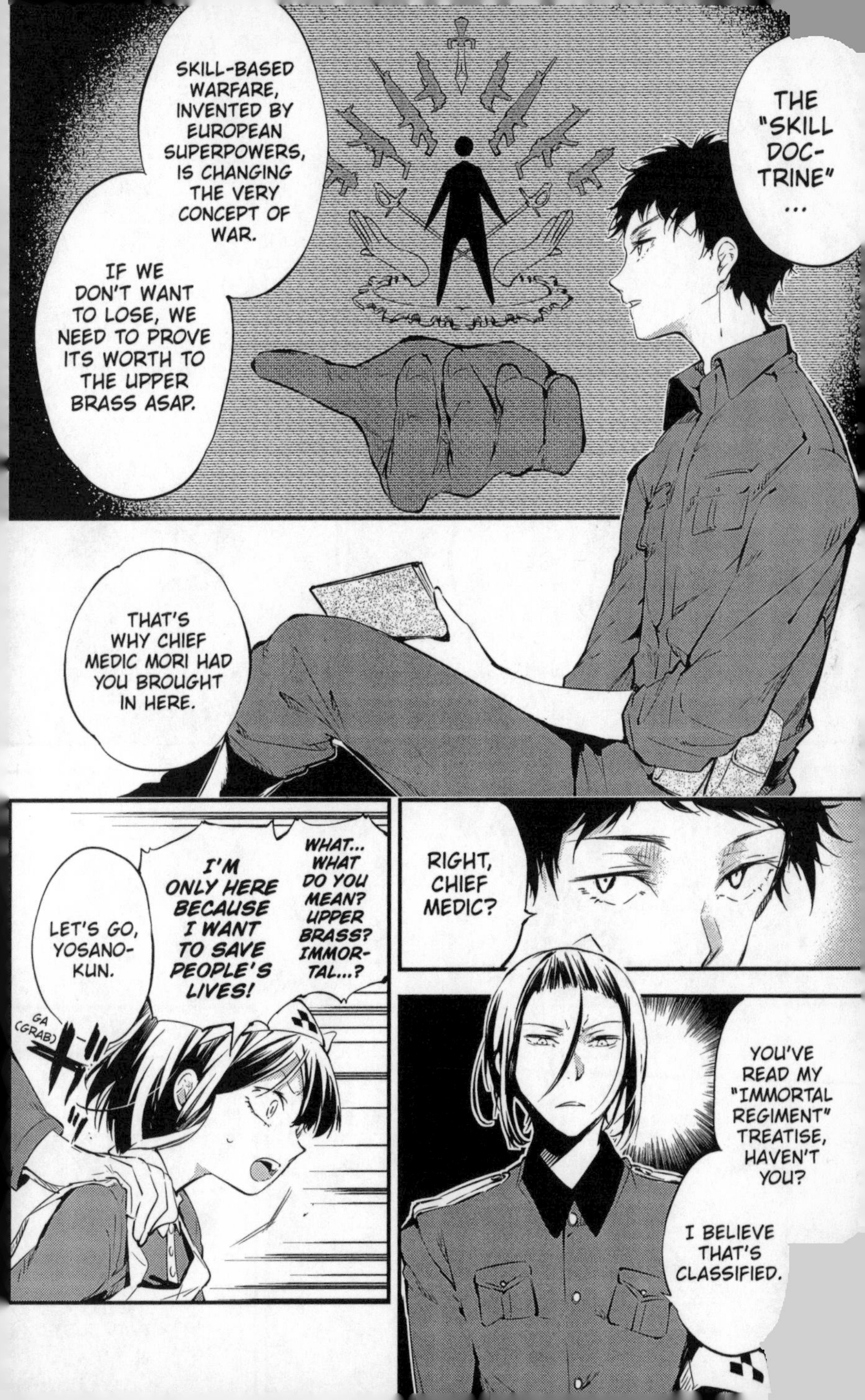
THE "SKILL DOCTRINE"...
SKILL-BASED WARFARE, INVENTED BY EUROPEAN SUPERPOWERS, IS CHANGING THE VERY CONCEPT OF WAR.
IF WE DON'T WANT TO LOSE, WE NEED TO PROVE ITS WORTH TO THE UPPER BRASS ASAP.
THAT'S WHY CHIEF MEDIC MORI HAD YOU BROUGHT IN HERE.
RIGHT, CHIEF MEDIC?
YOU'VE READ MY "IMMORTAL REGIMENT" TREATISE, HAVEN'T YOU?
I BELIEVE THAT'S CLASSIFIED.
WHAT... WHAT DO YOU MEAN? UPPER BRASS? IMMORTAL...?
I'M ONLY HERE BECAUSE I WANT TO SAVE PEOPLE'S LIVES!
LET'S GO, YOSANO-KUN.
GA (GRAB)

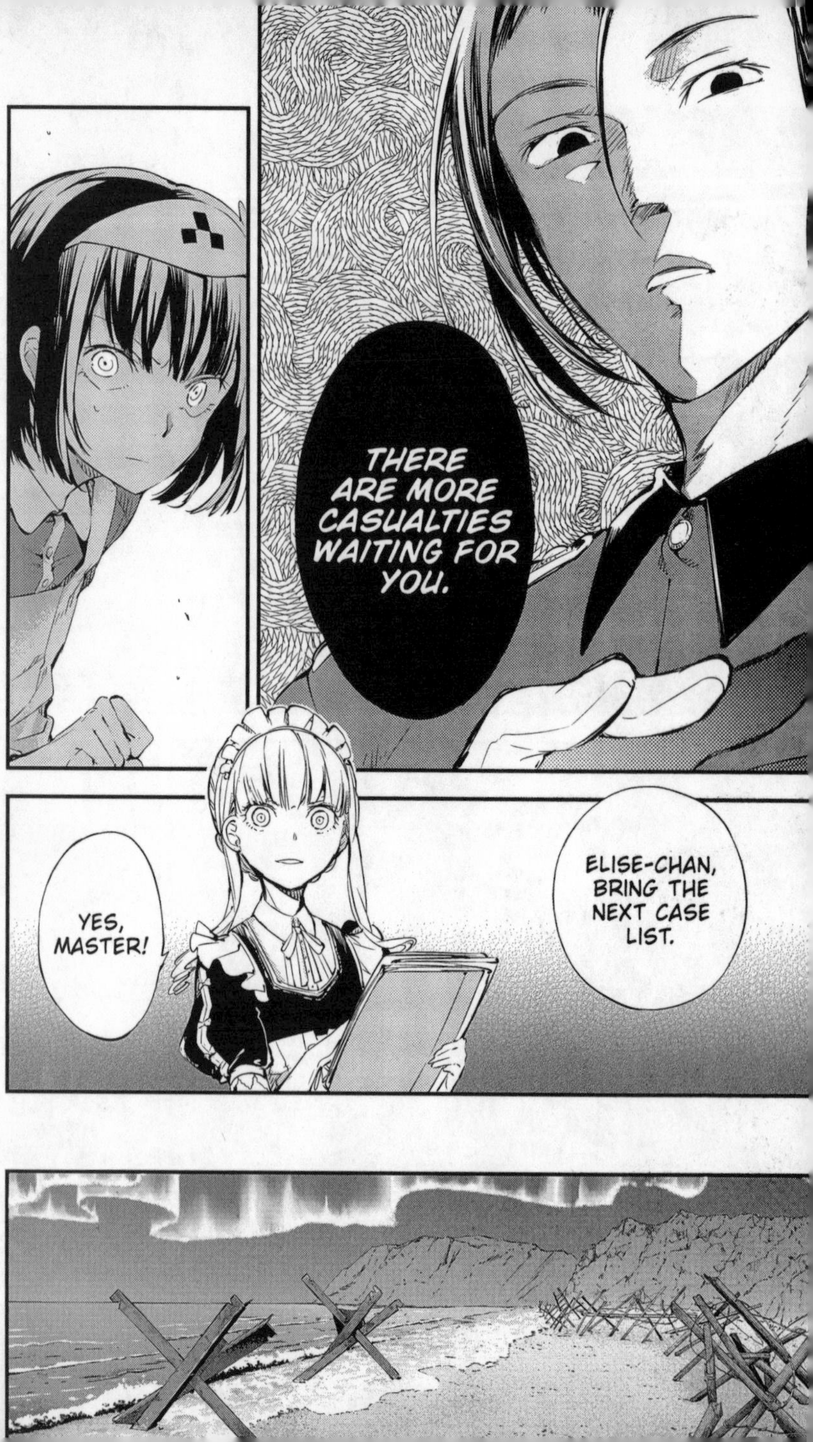
THERE ARE MORE CASUALTIES WAITING FOR YOU.
ELISE-CHAN, BRING THE NEXT CASE LIST.
YES, MASTER!

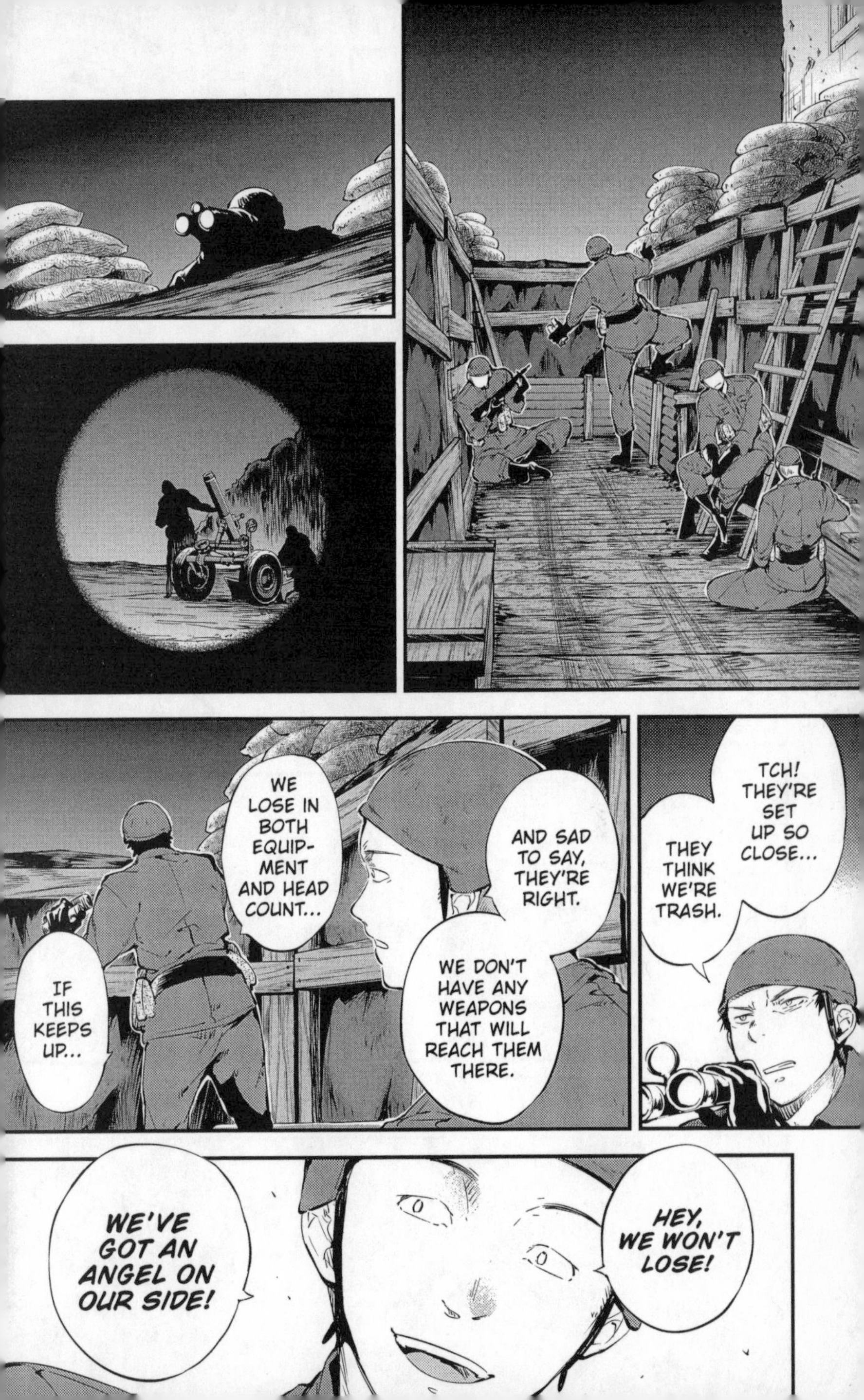
TCH! THEY'RE SET UP SO CLOSE...
THEY THINK WE'RE TRASH.
AND SAD TO SAY, THEY'RE RIGHT.
WE DON'T HAVE ANY WEAPONS THAT WILL REACH THEM THERE.
WE LOSE IN BOTH EQUIPMENT AND HEAD COUNT...
IF THIS KEEPS UP...
HEY, WE WON'T LOSE!
WE'VE GOT AN ANGEL ON OUR SIDE!

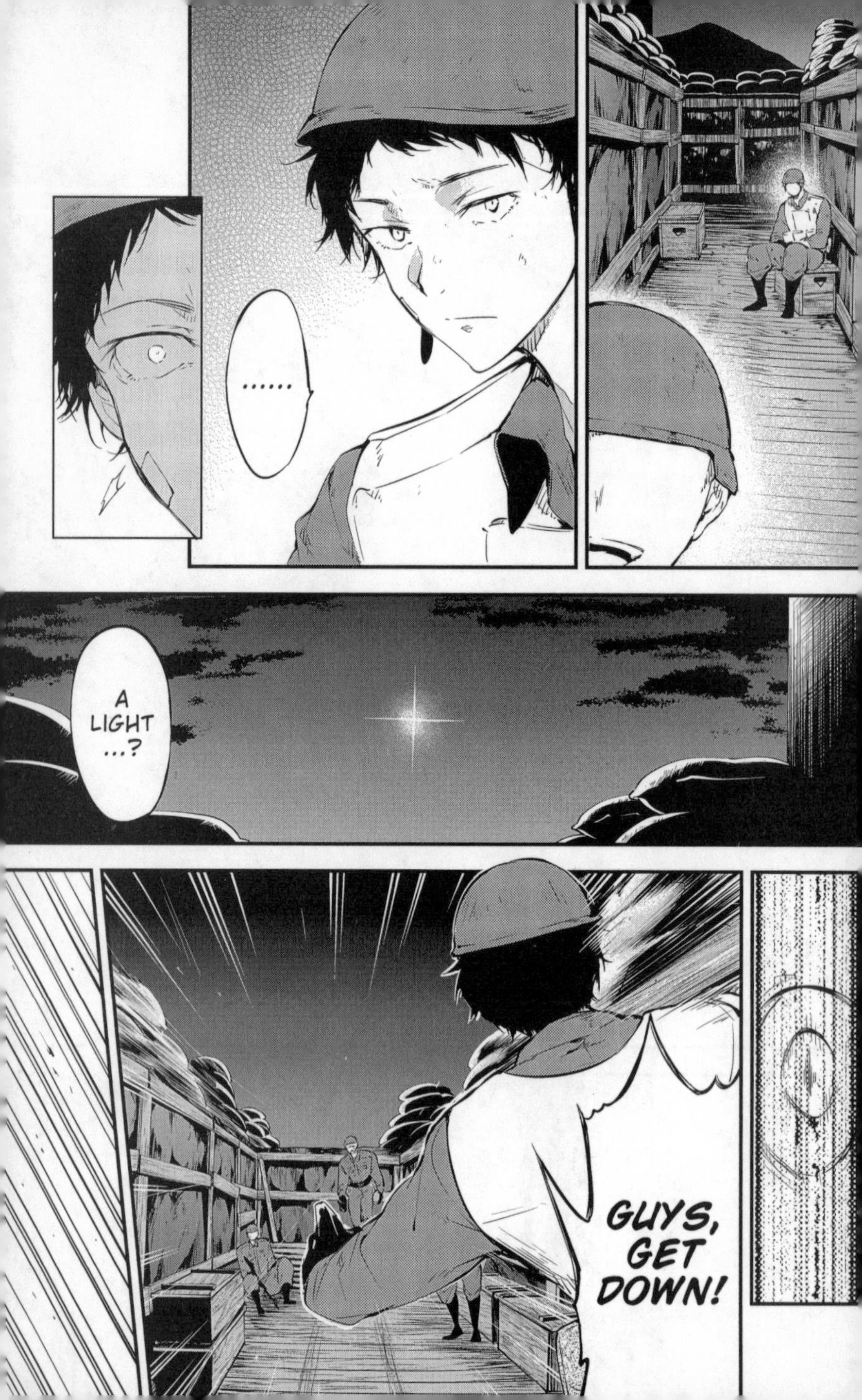
......
A LIGHT ...?
GUYS, GET DOWN!

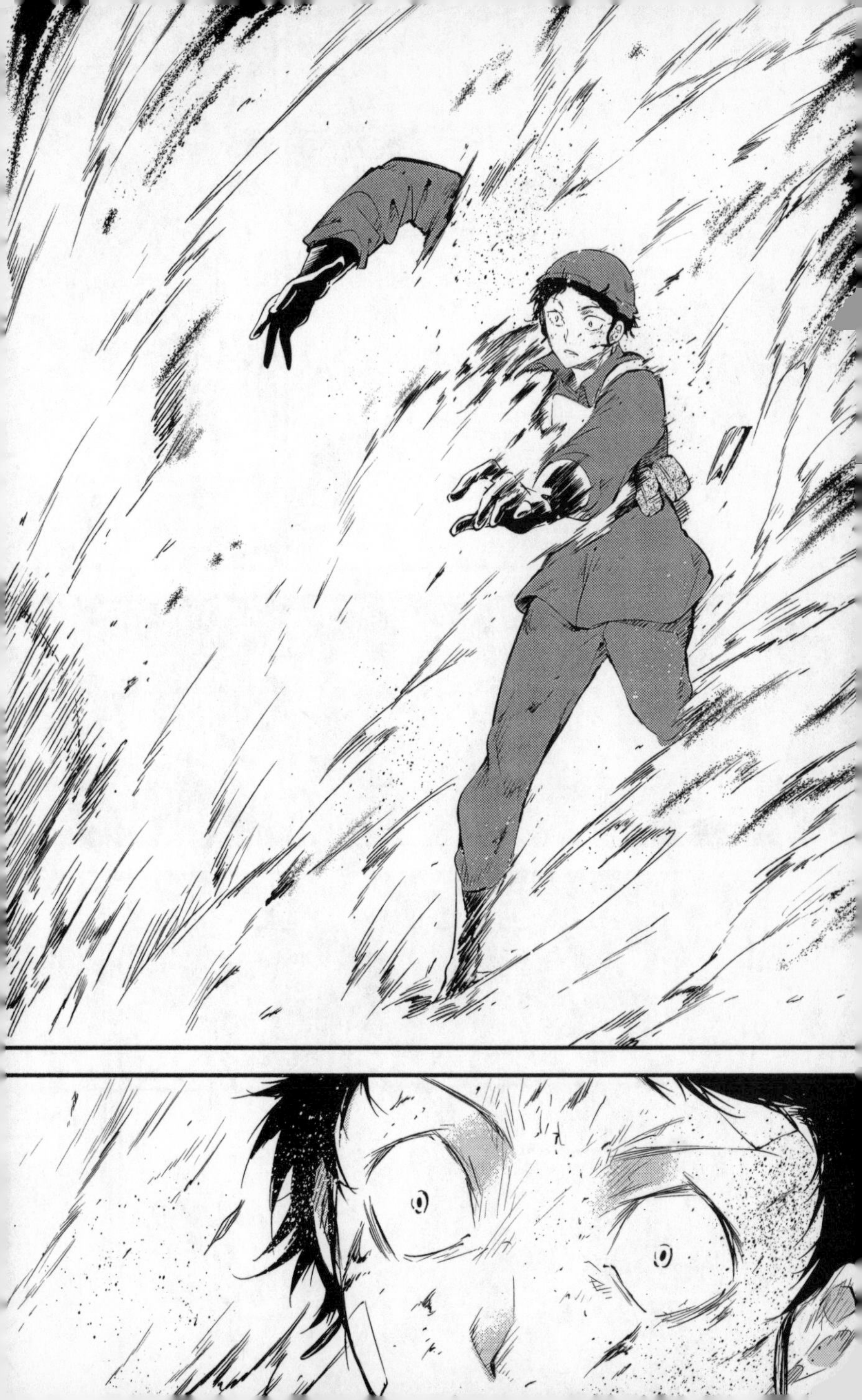

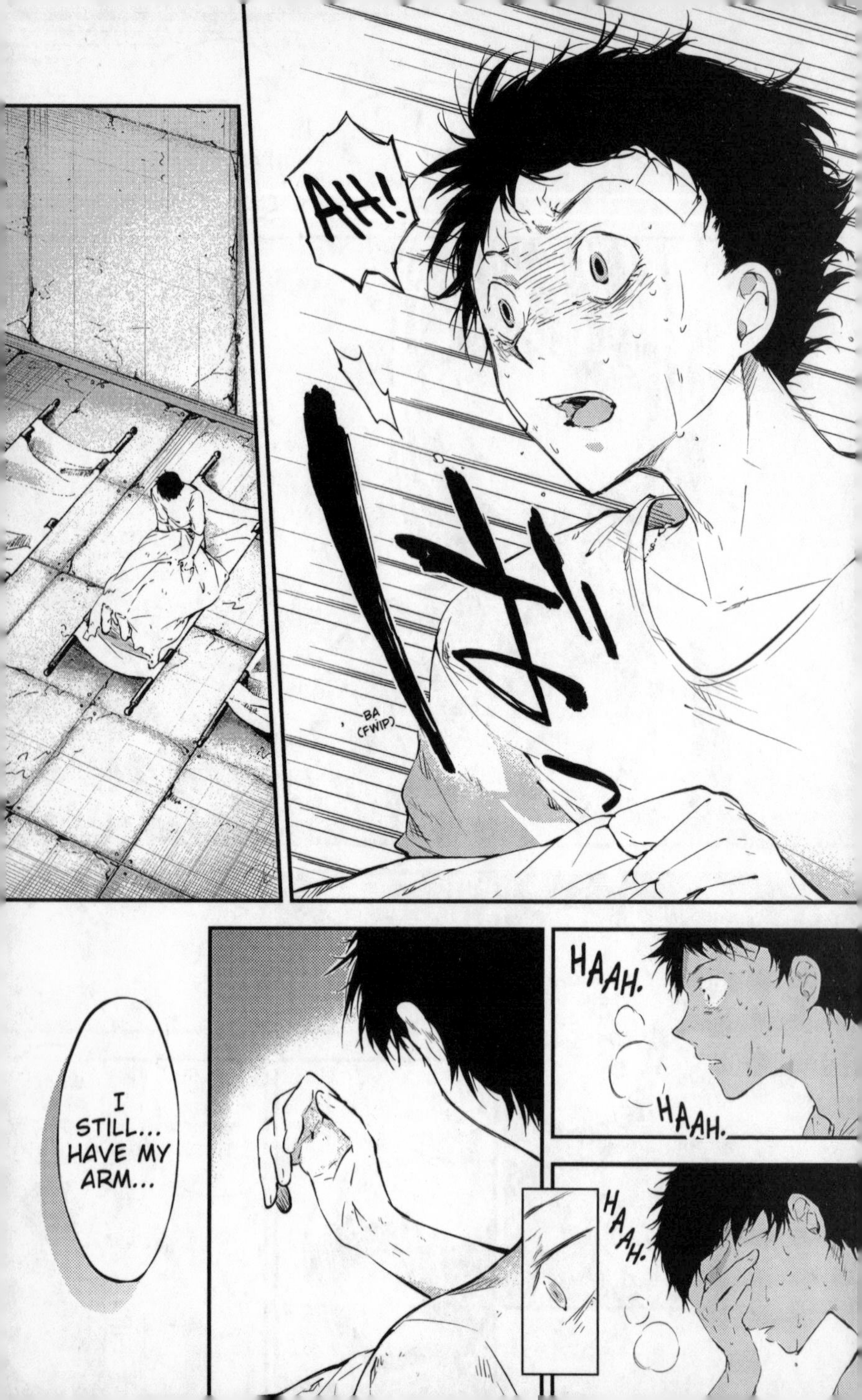
AH!
BA (FWIP)
HAAH.
HAAH.
HAAH.
I STILL... HAVE MY ARM...

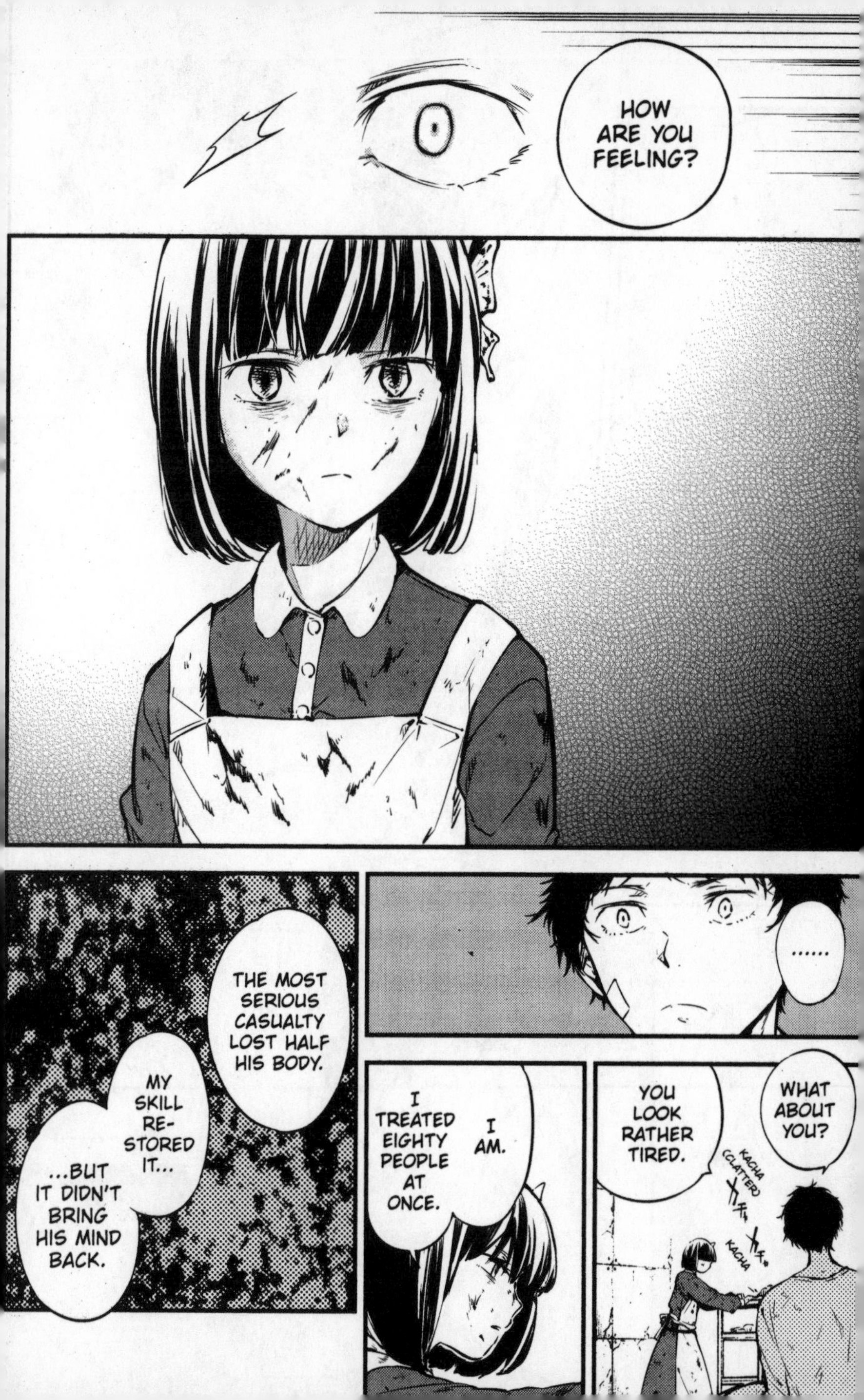
HOW ARE YOU FEELING?
......
WHAT ABOUT YOU?
YOU LOOK RATHER TIRED.
KACHA (CLATTER)
KACHA
I AM.
I TREATED EIGHTY PEOPLE AT ONCE.
THE MOST SERIOUS CASUALTY LOST HALF HIS BODY.
MY SKILL RE-STORED IT...
...BUT IT DIDN'T BRING HIS MIND BACK.

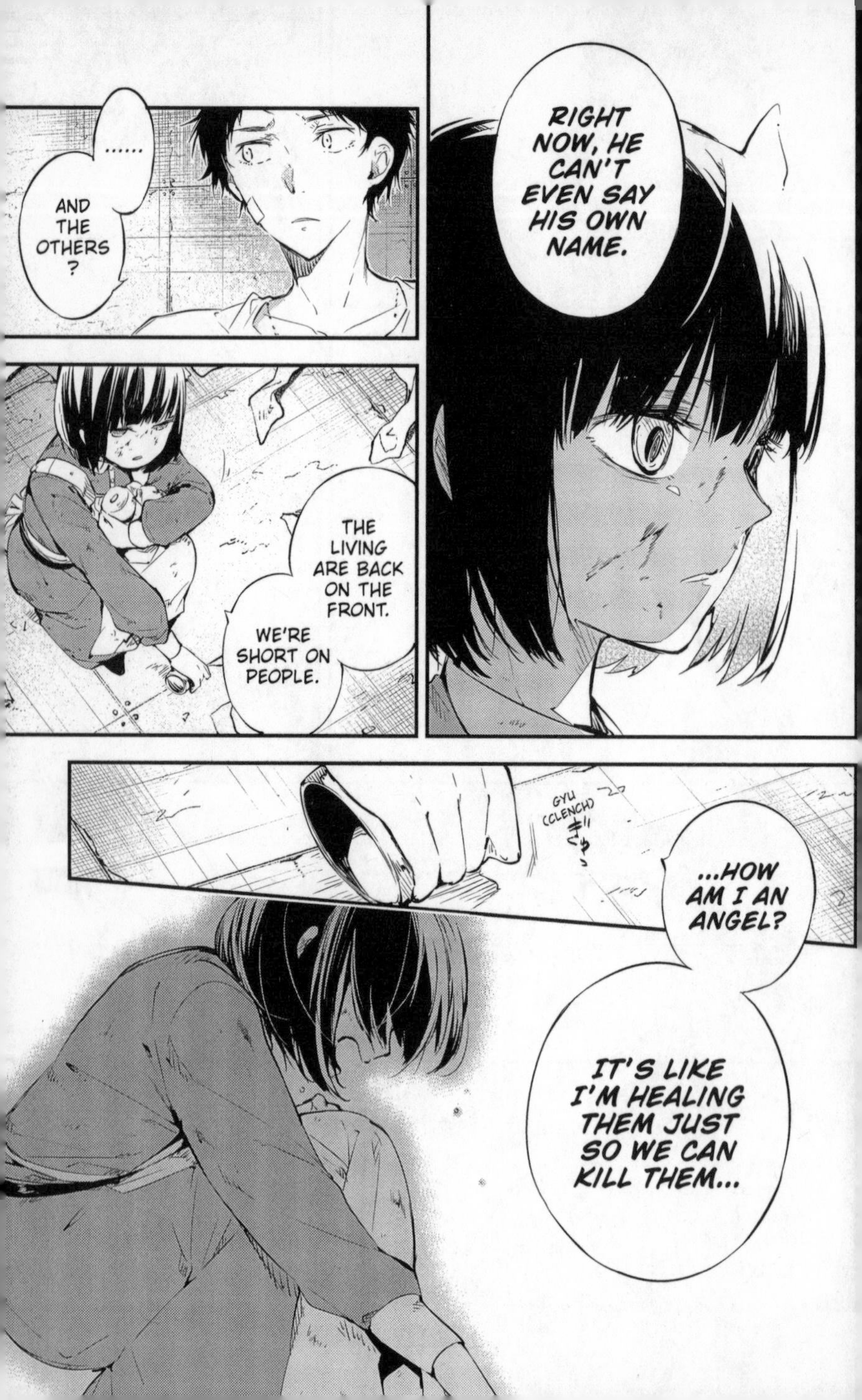
RIGHT NOW, HE CAN'T EVEN SAY HIS OWN NAME.
......
AND THE OTHERS?
THE LIVING ARE BACK ON THE FRONT.
WE'RE SHORT ON PEOPLE.
GYU (CLENCH)
...HOW AM I AN ANGEL?
IT'S LIKE I'M HEALING THEM JUST SO WE CAN KILL THEM...

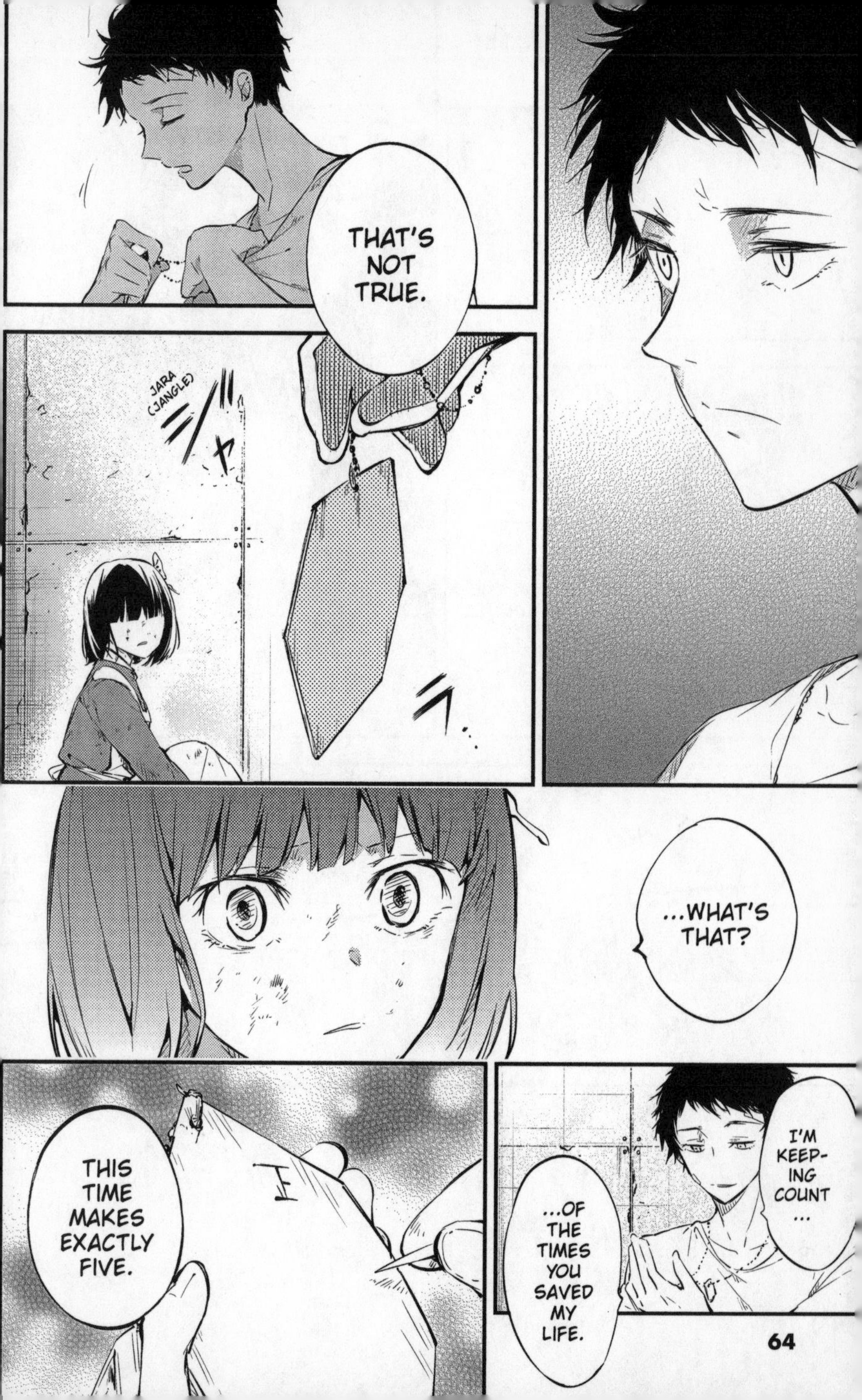
THAT'S NOT TRUE.
JARA (JANGLE)
...WHAT'S THAT?
I'M KEEP-ING COUNT...
...OF THE TIMES YOU SAVED MY LIFE.
THIS TIME MAKES EXACTLY FIVE.

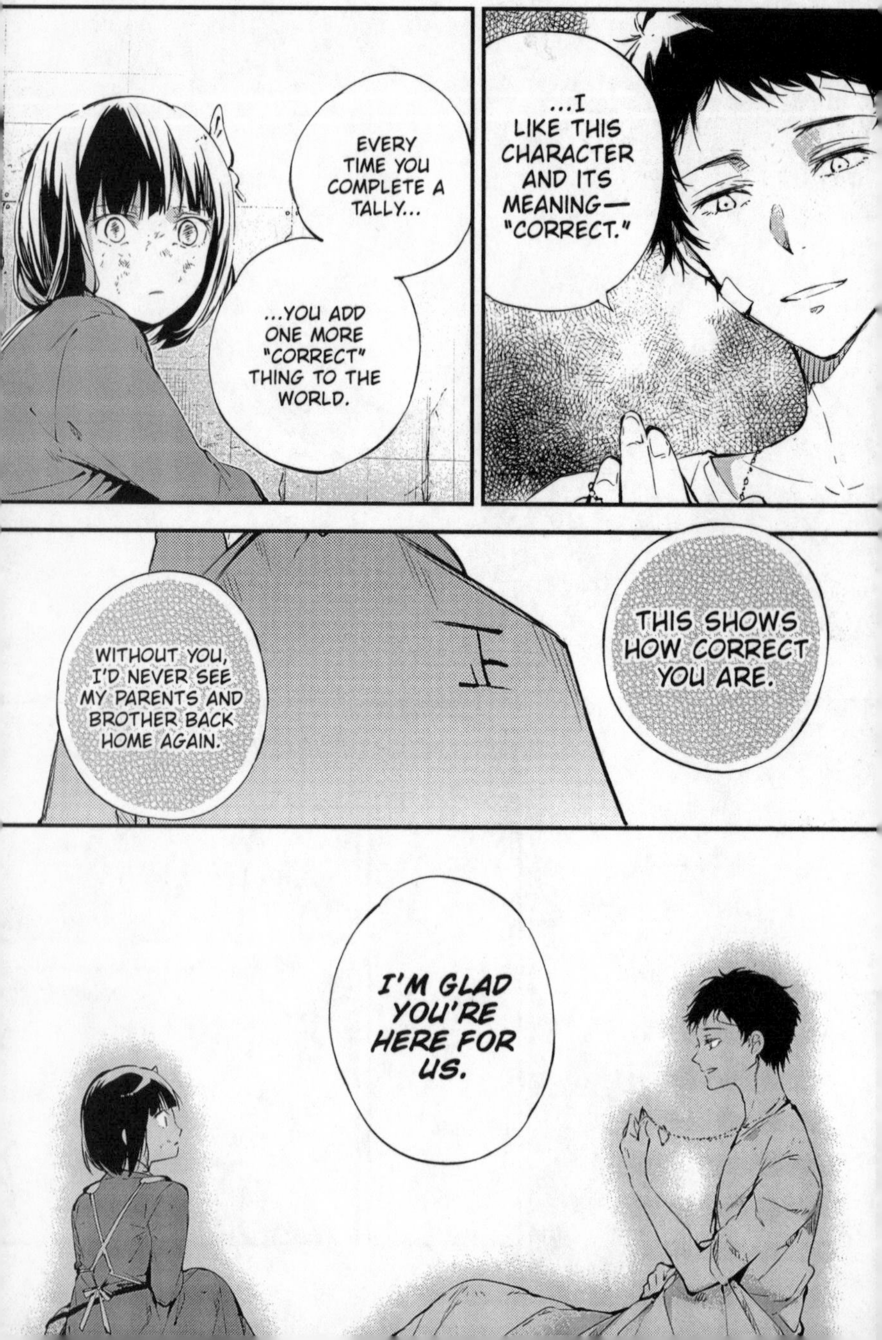
...I LIKE THIS CHARACTER AND ITS MEANING—"CORRECT."
EVERY TIME YOU COMPLETE A TALLY...
...YOU ADD ONE MORE "CORRECT" THING TO THE WORLD.
THIS SHOWS HOW CORRECT YOU ARE.
WITHOUT YOU, I'D NEVER SEE MY PARENTS AND BROTHER BACK HOME AGAIN.
I'M GLAD YOU'RE HERE FOR US.

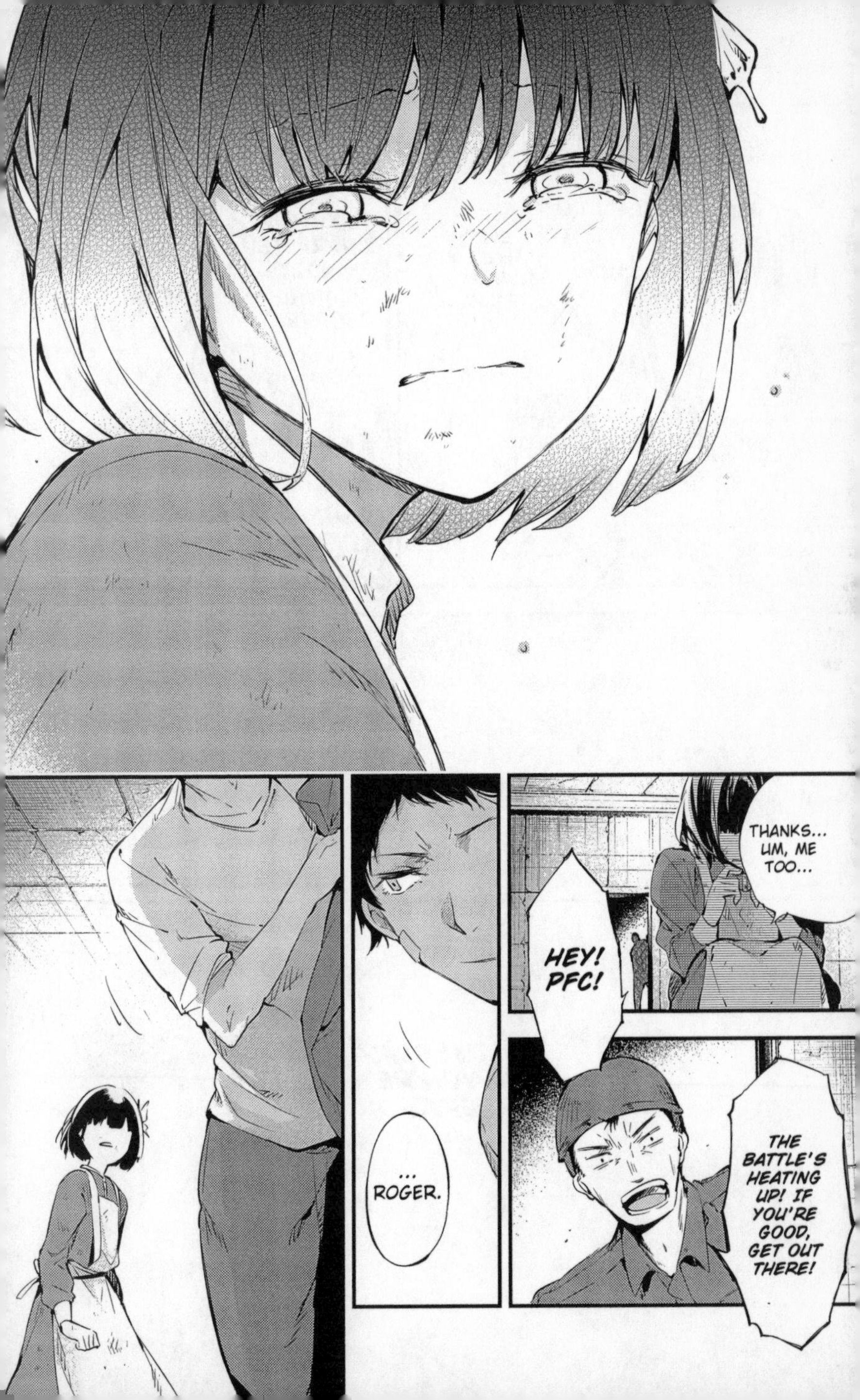
THANKS... UM, ME TOO...
HEY! PFC!
THE BATTLE'S HEATING UP! IF YOU'RE GOOD, GET OUT THERE!
... ROGER.

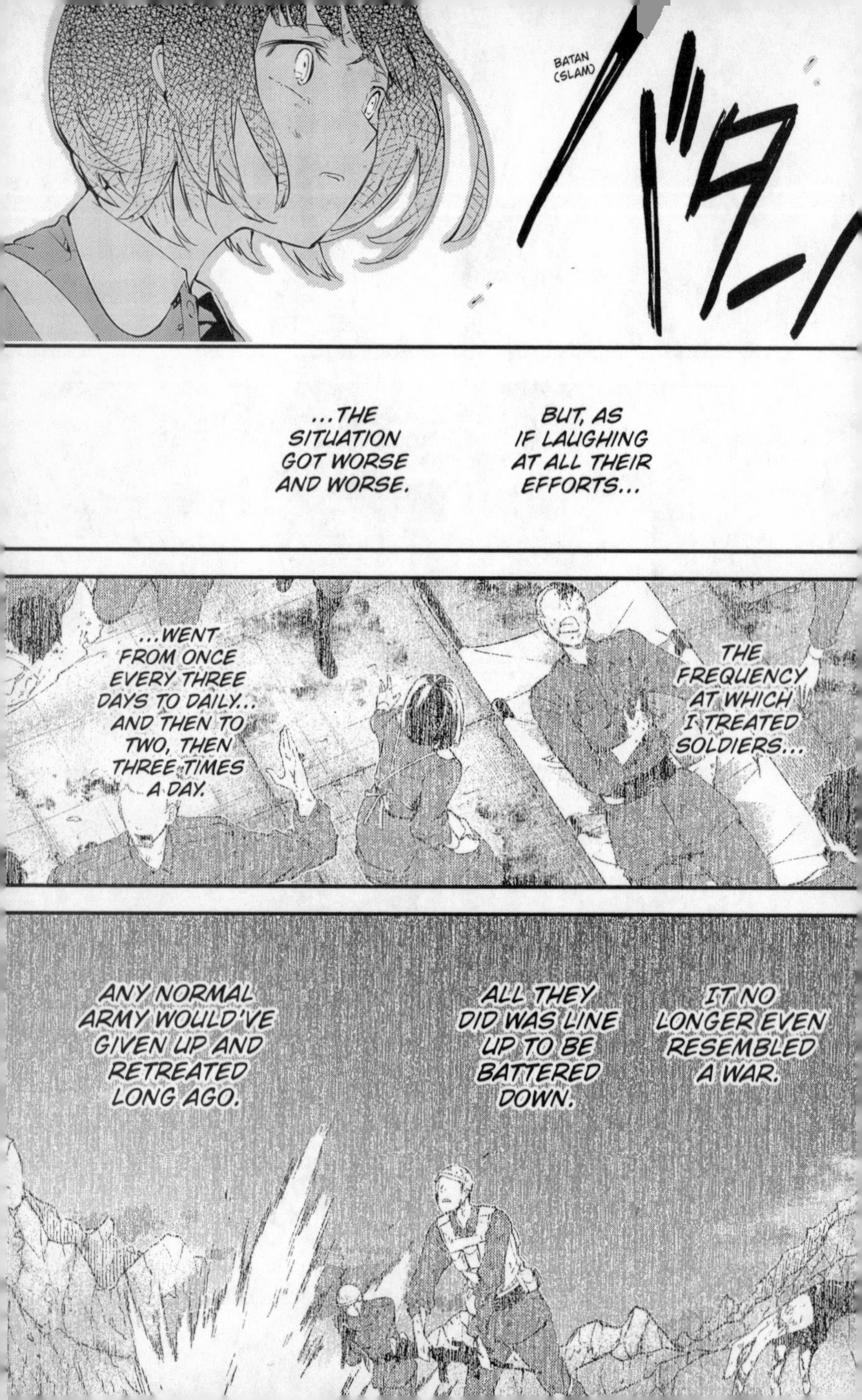
バタン
BATAN (SLAM)
BUT, AS IF LAUGHING AT ALL THEIR EFFORTS...
...THE SITUATION GOT WORSE AND WORSE.
THE FREQUENCY AT WHICH I TREATED SOLDIERS...
...WENT FROM ONCE EVERY THREE DAYS TO DAILY... AND THEN TO TWO, THEN THREE TIMES A DAY.
IT NO LONGER EVEN RESEMBLED A WAR.
ALL THEY DID WAS LINE UP TO BE BATTERED DOWN.
ANY NORMAL ARMY WOULD'VE GIVEN UP AND RETREATED LONG AGO.

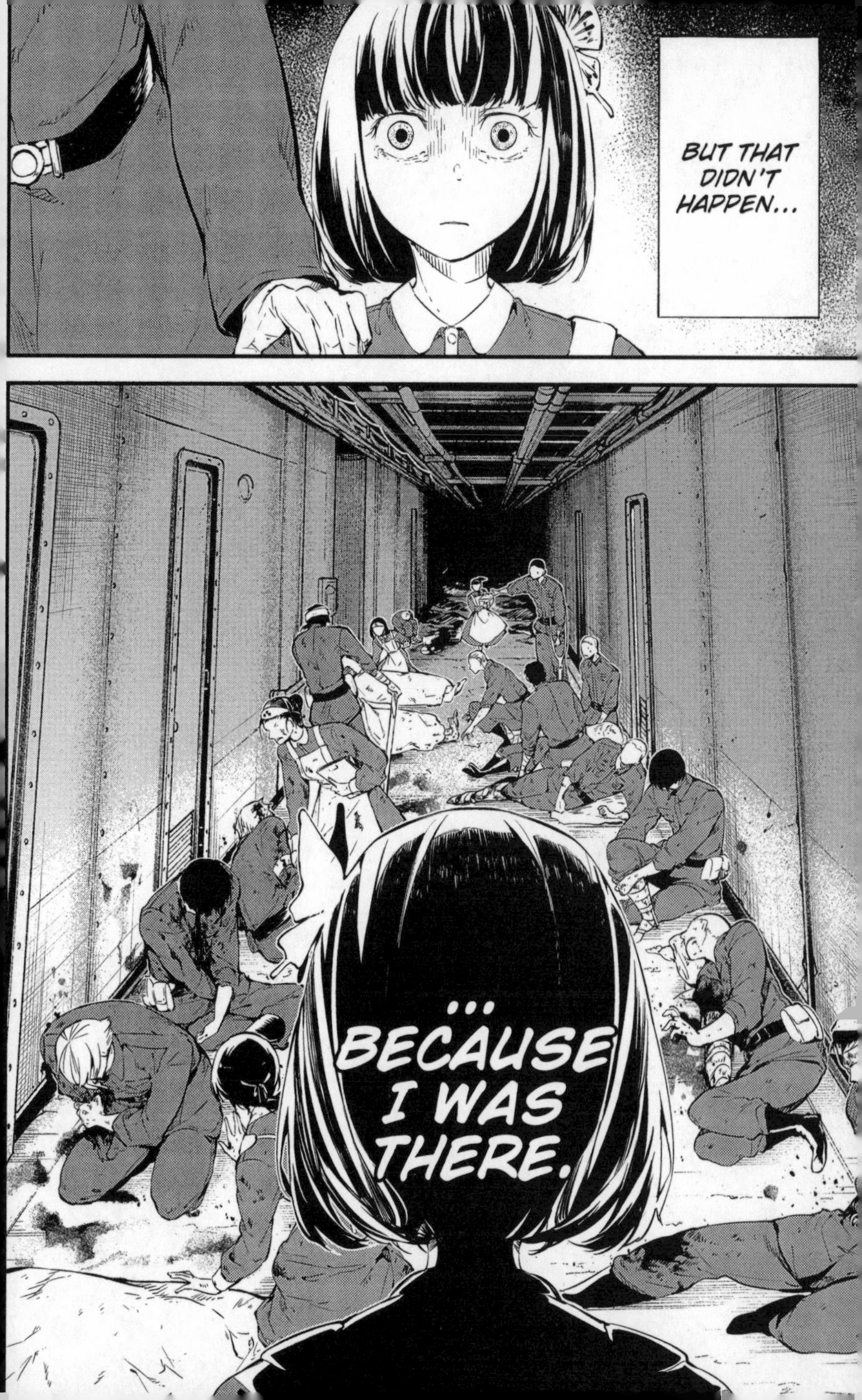
BUT THAT DIDN'T HAPPEN...
...BECAUSE I WAS THERE.

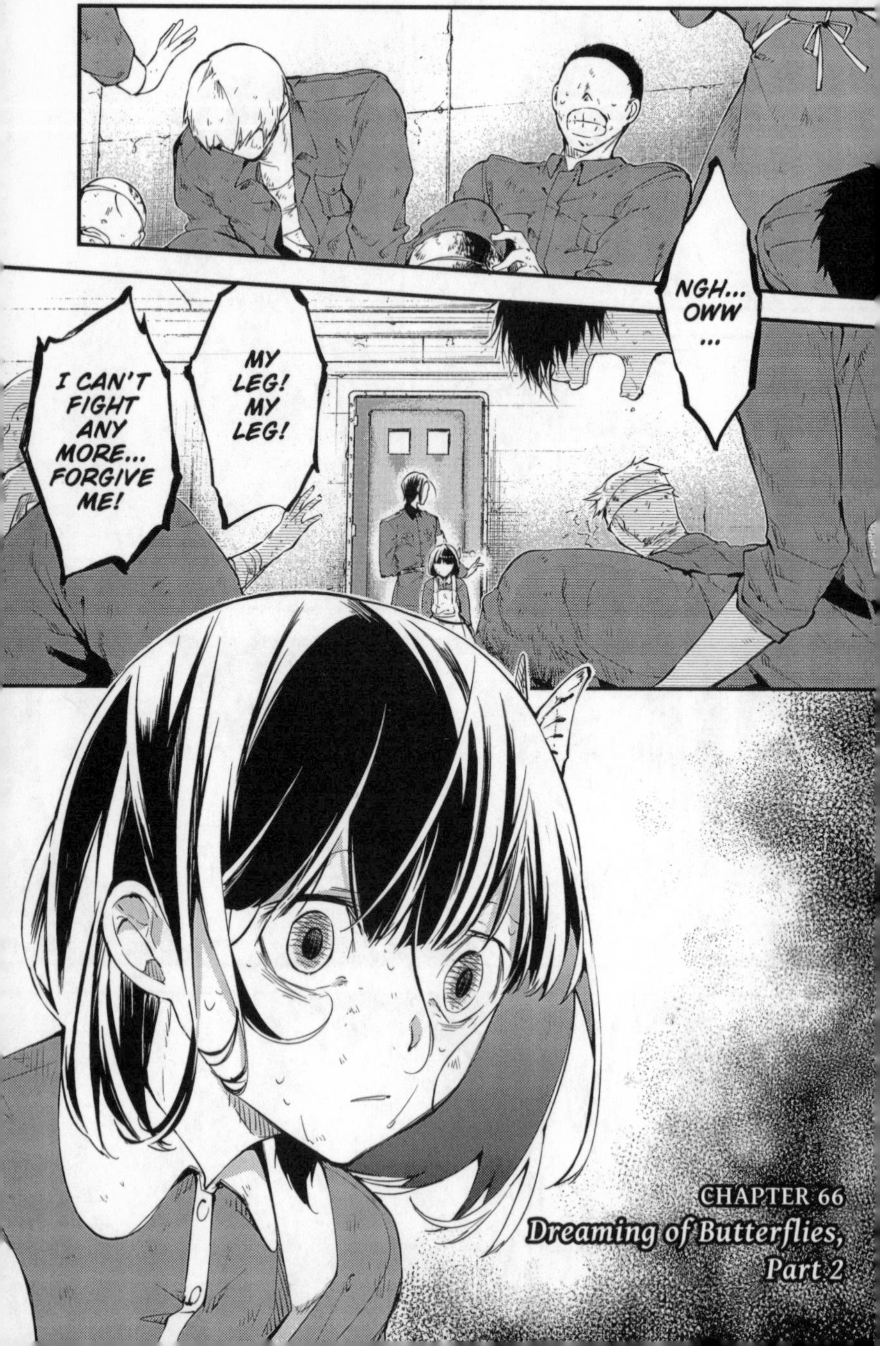
NGH... OWW ...
MY LEG! MY LEG!
I CAN'T FIGHT ANY MORE... FORGIVE ME!

CHAPTER 66
Dreaming of Butterflies, Part 2

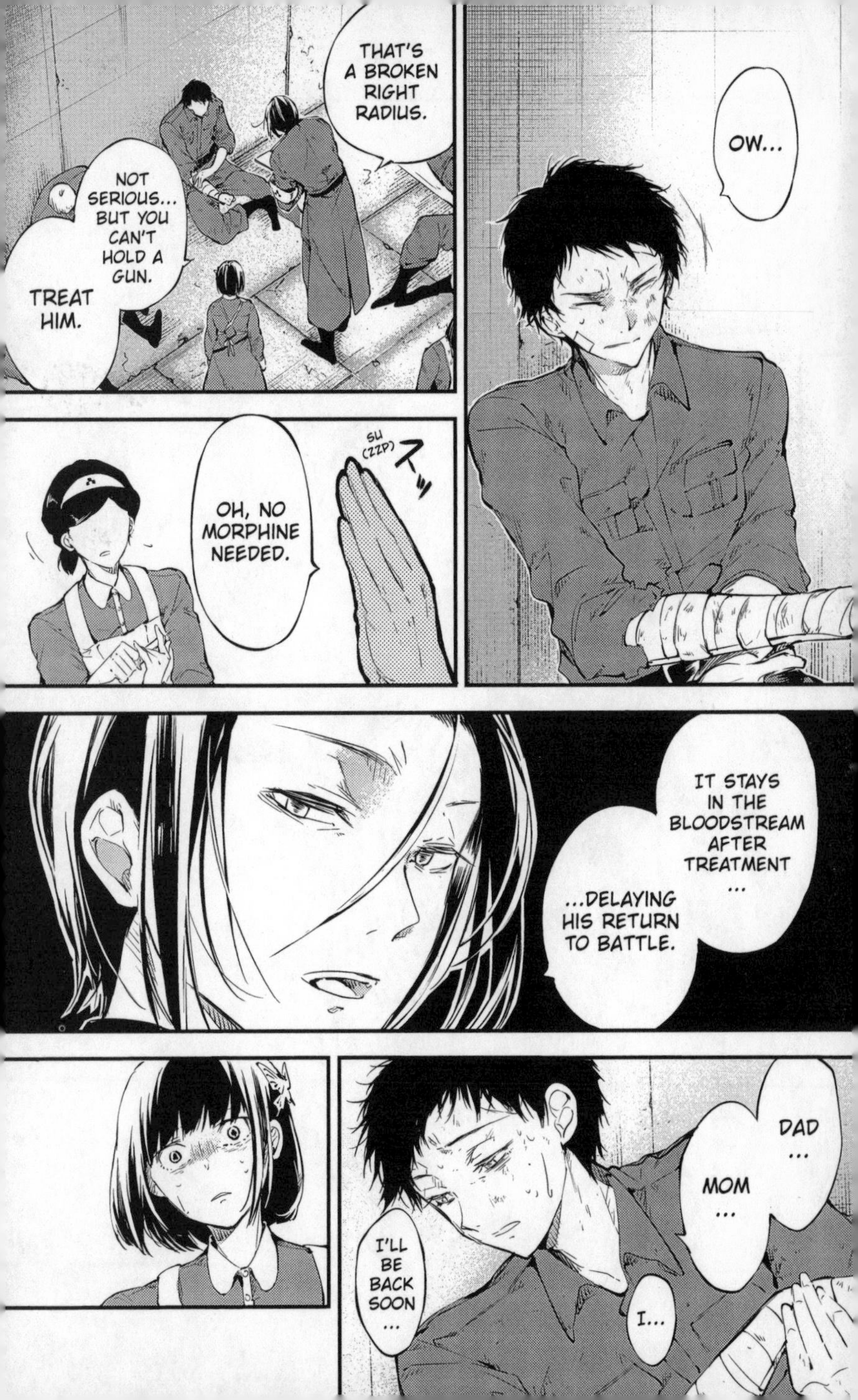
OW...
THAT'S A BROKEN RIGHT RADIUS.
NOT SERIOUS... BUT YOU CAN'T HOLD A GUN.
TREAT HIM.
スッ
SU (ZZZP)
OH, NO MORPHINE NEEDED.
IT STAYS IN THE BLOODSTREAM AFTER TREATMENT...
...DELAYING HIS RETURN TO BATTLE.
DAD...
MOM...
I...
I'LL BE BACK SOON...

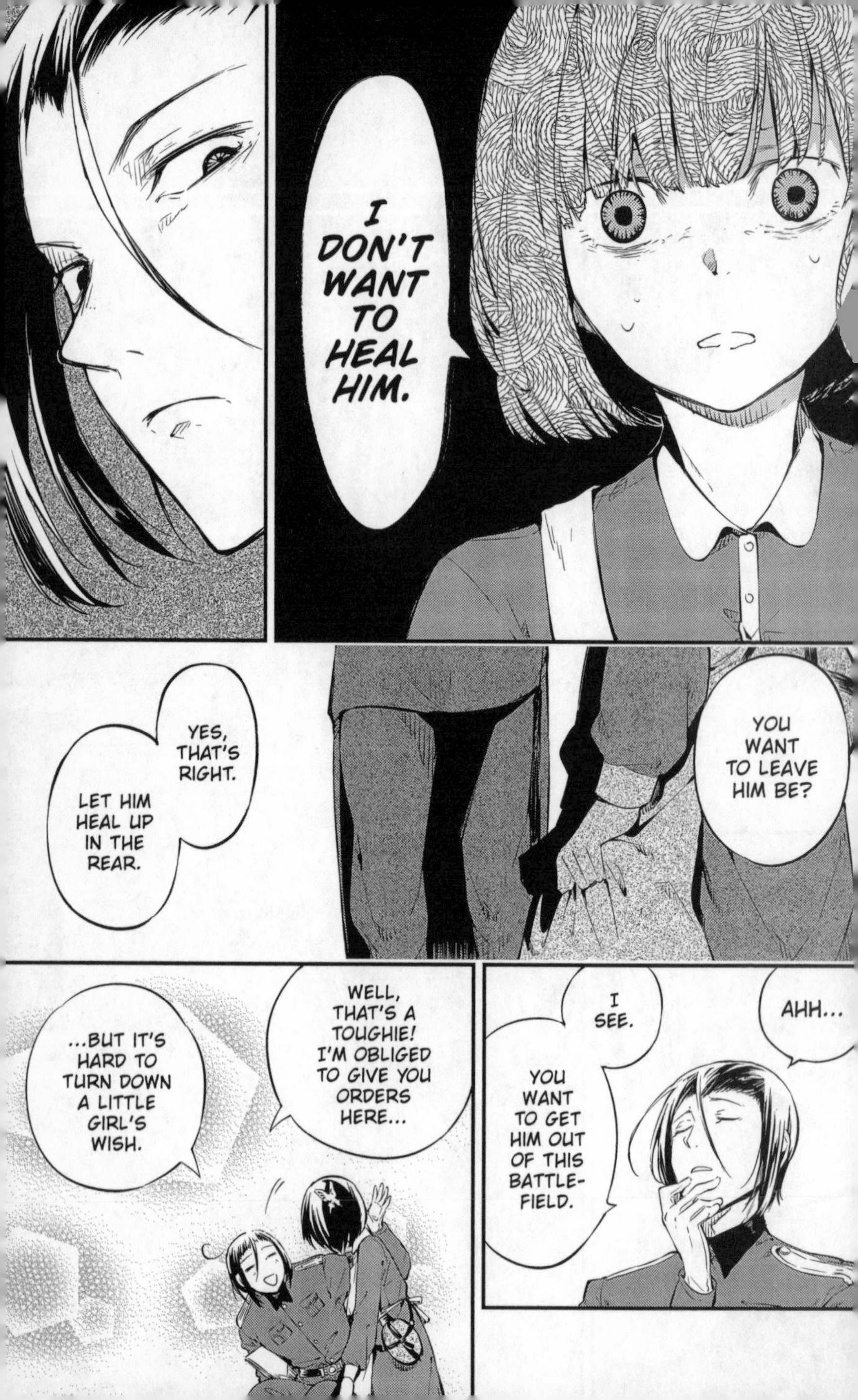
I DON'T WANT TO HEAL HIM.
YOU WANT TO LEAVE HIM BE?
YES, THAT'S RIGHT.
LET HIM HEAL UP IN THE REAR.
AHH...
I SEE.
YOU WANT TO GET HIM OUT OF THIS BATTLE-FIELD.
WELL, THAT'S A TOUGHIE! I'M OBLIGED TO GIVE YOU ORDERS HERE...
...BUT IT'S HARD TO TURN DOWN A LITTLE GIRL'S WISH.

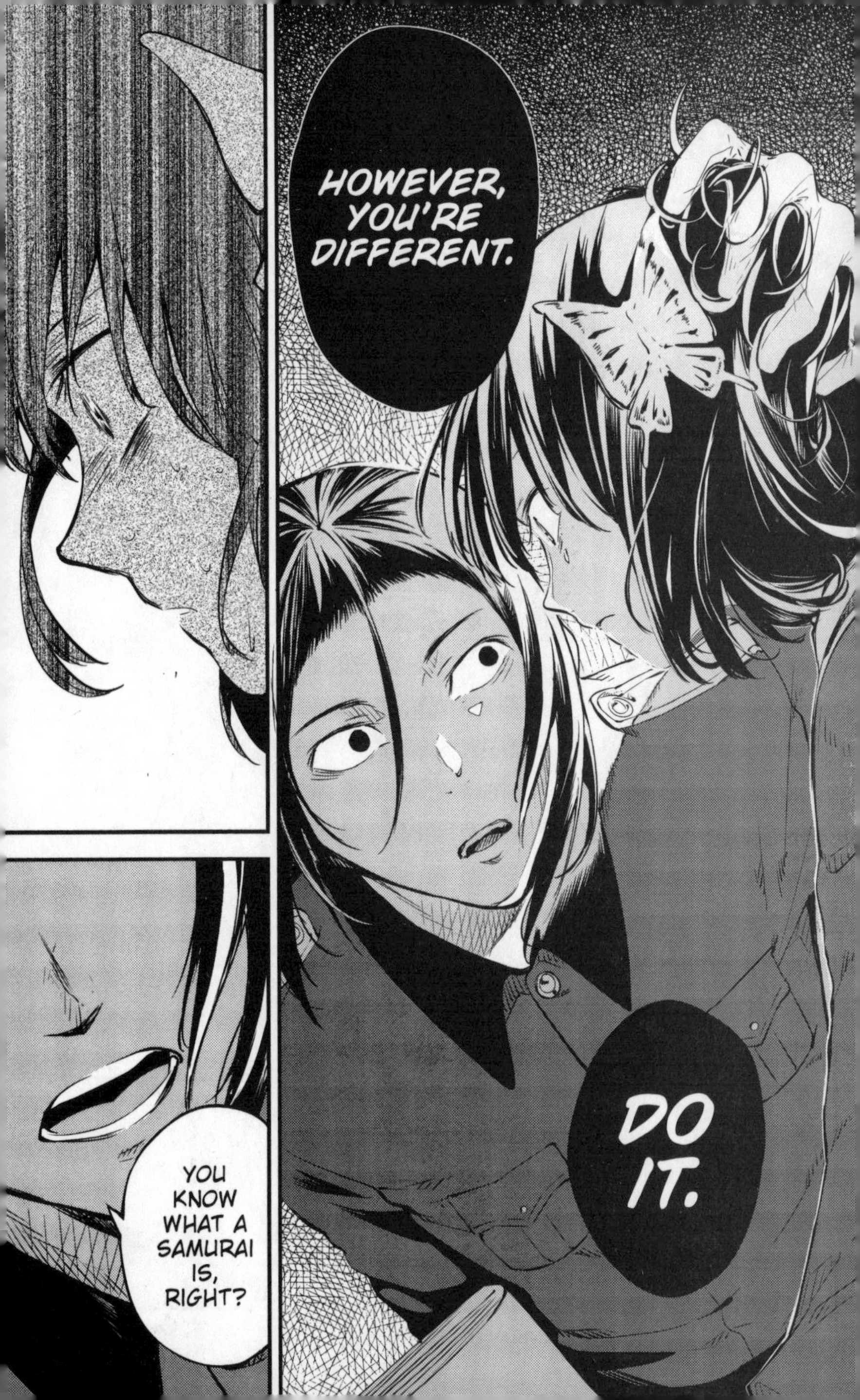
HOWEVER, YOU'RE DIFFERENT.
DO IT.
YOU KNOW WHAT A SAMURAI IS, RIGHT?

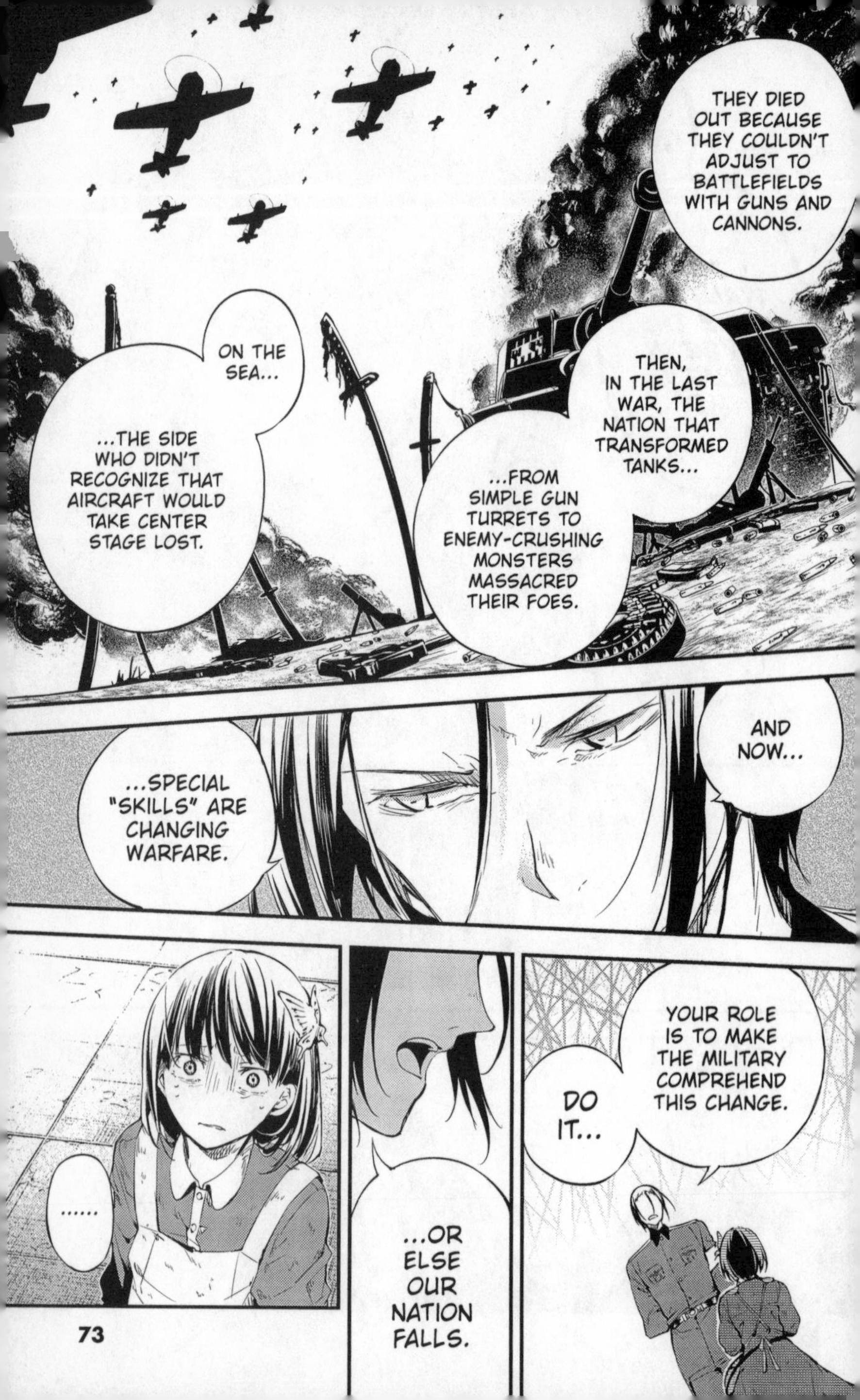
THEY DIED OUT BECAUSE THEY COULDN'T ADJUST TO BATTLEFIELDS WITH GUNS AND CANNONS.
THEN, IN THE LAST WAR, THE NATION THAT TRANSFORMED TANKS...
...FROM SIMPLE GUN TURRETS TO ENEMY-CRUSHING MONSTERS MASSACRED THEIR FOES.
ON THE SEA...
...THE SIDE WHO DIDN'T RECOGNIZE THAT AIRCRAFT WOULD TAKE CENTER STAGE LOST.
AND NOW...
...SPECIAL "SKILLS" ARE CHANGING WARFARE.
YOUR ROLE IS TO MAKE THE MILITARY COMPREHEND THIS CHANGE.
DO IT...
...OR ELSE OUR NATION FALLS.
......

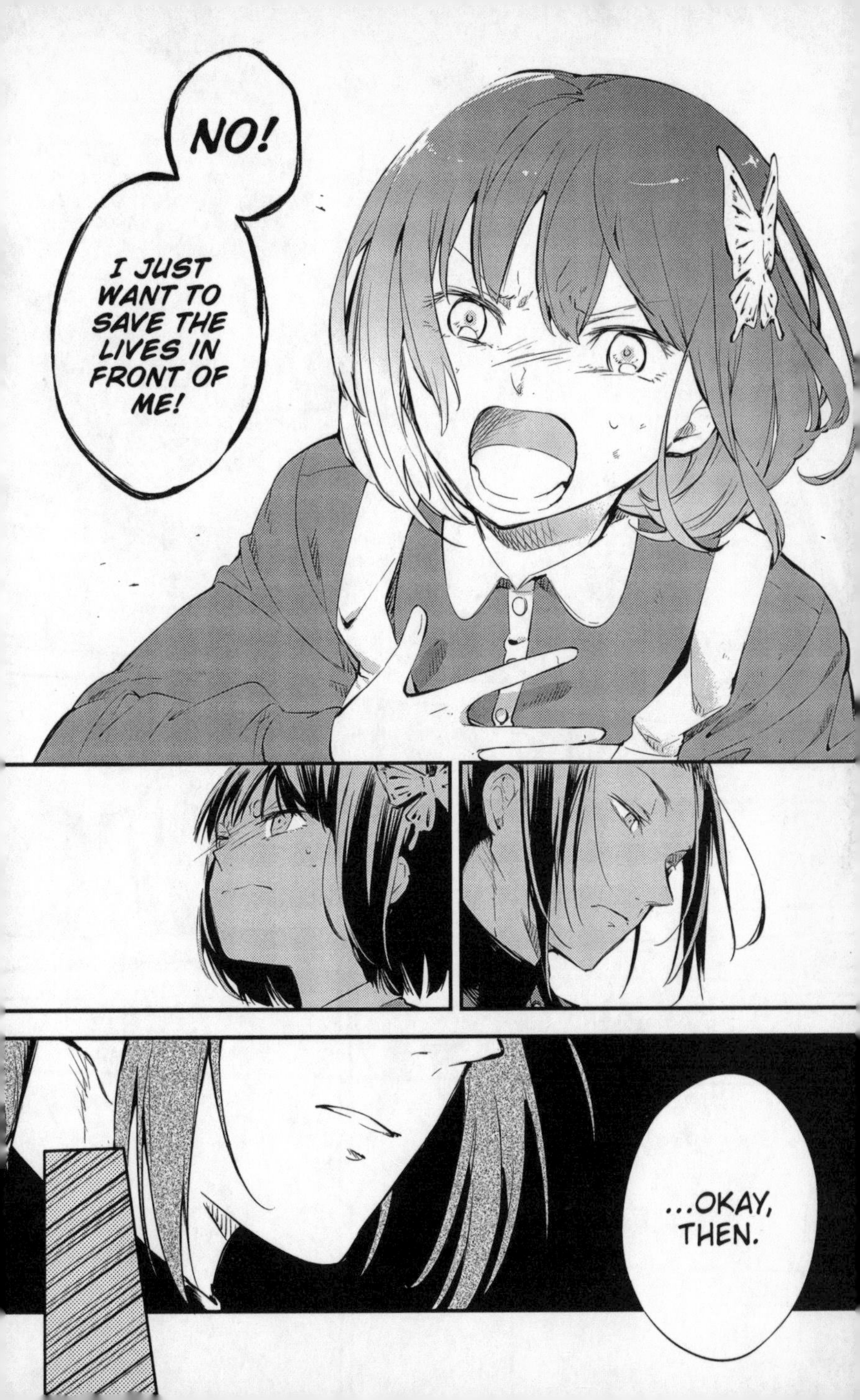
NO!
I JUST WANT TO SAVE THE LIVES IN FRONT OF ME!
...OKAY, THEN.

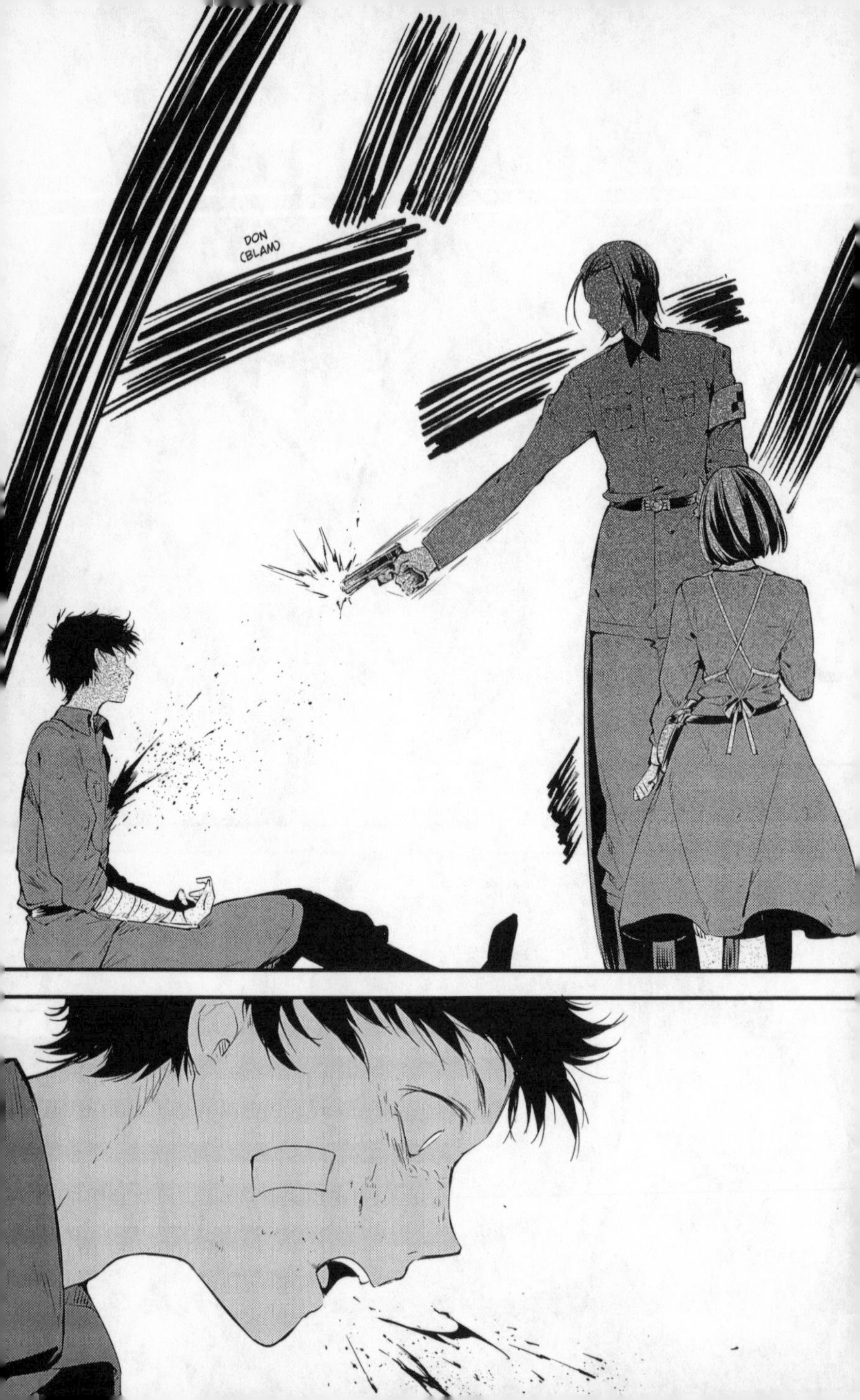
DON
(BLAM)

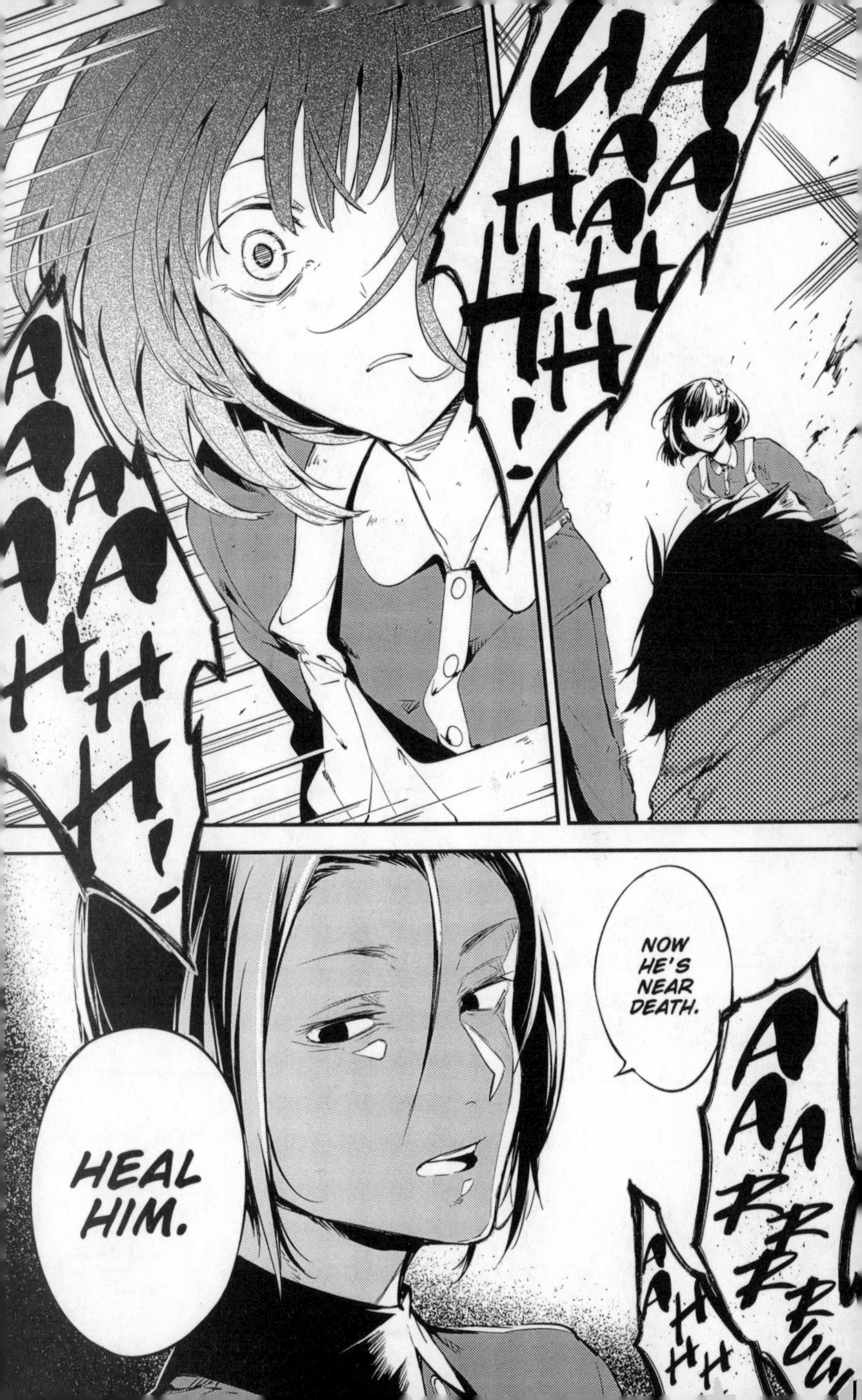
UAAAHAAAHHHHH!!
AAAAAAHHHH!!
NOW HE'S NEAR DEATH.
HEAL HIM.
AAARRRR
AAAHHHH

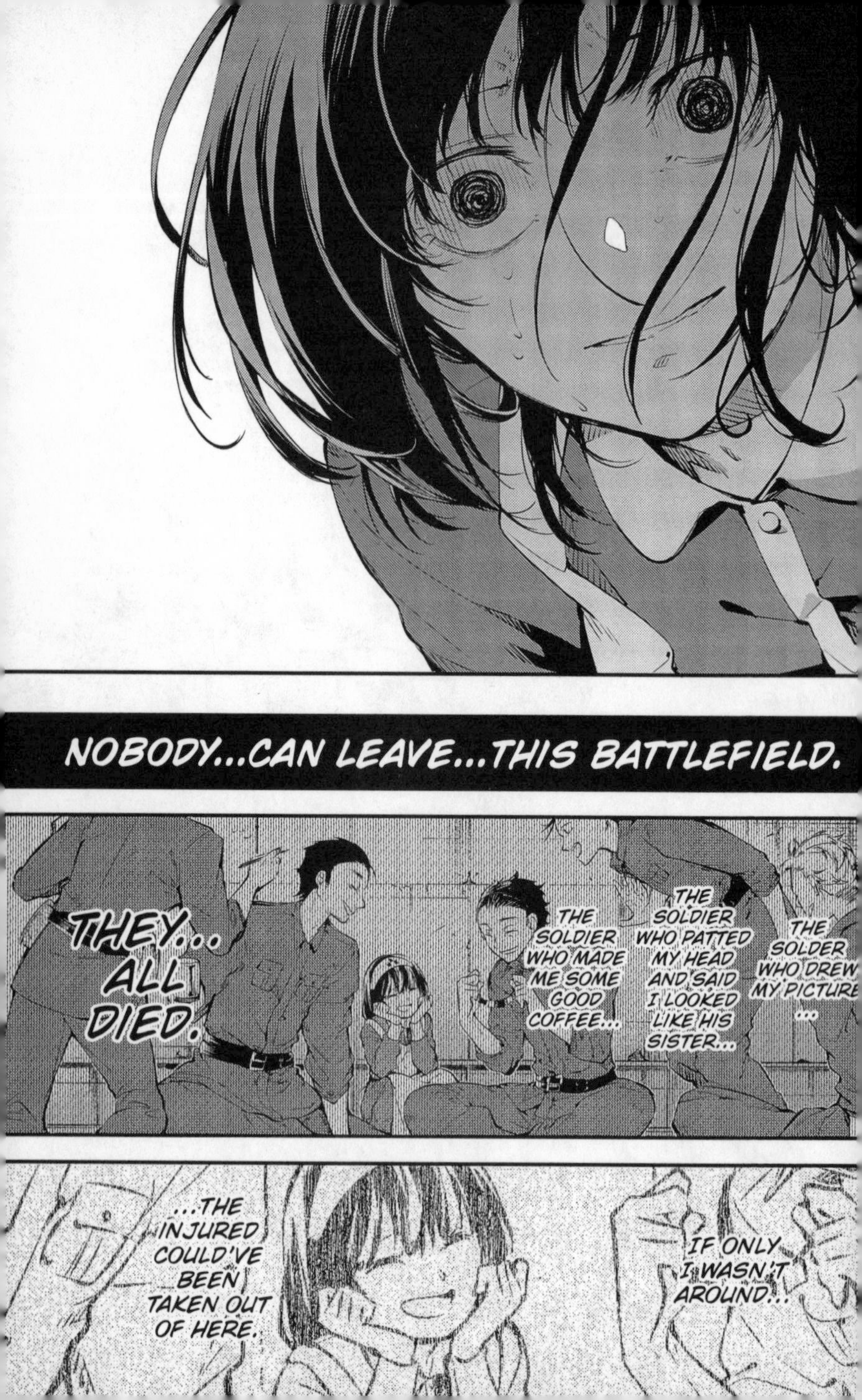
NOBODY...CAN LEAVE...THIS BATTLEFIELD.
THE SOLDER WHO DREW MY PICTURE...
THE SOLDIER WHO PATTED MY HEAD AND SAID I LOOKED LIKE HIS SISTER...
THE SOLDIER WHO MADE ME SOME GOOD COFFEE...
THEY... ALL DIED.
IF ONLY I WASN'T AROUND...
...THE INJURED COULD'VE BEEN TAKEN OUT OF HERE.

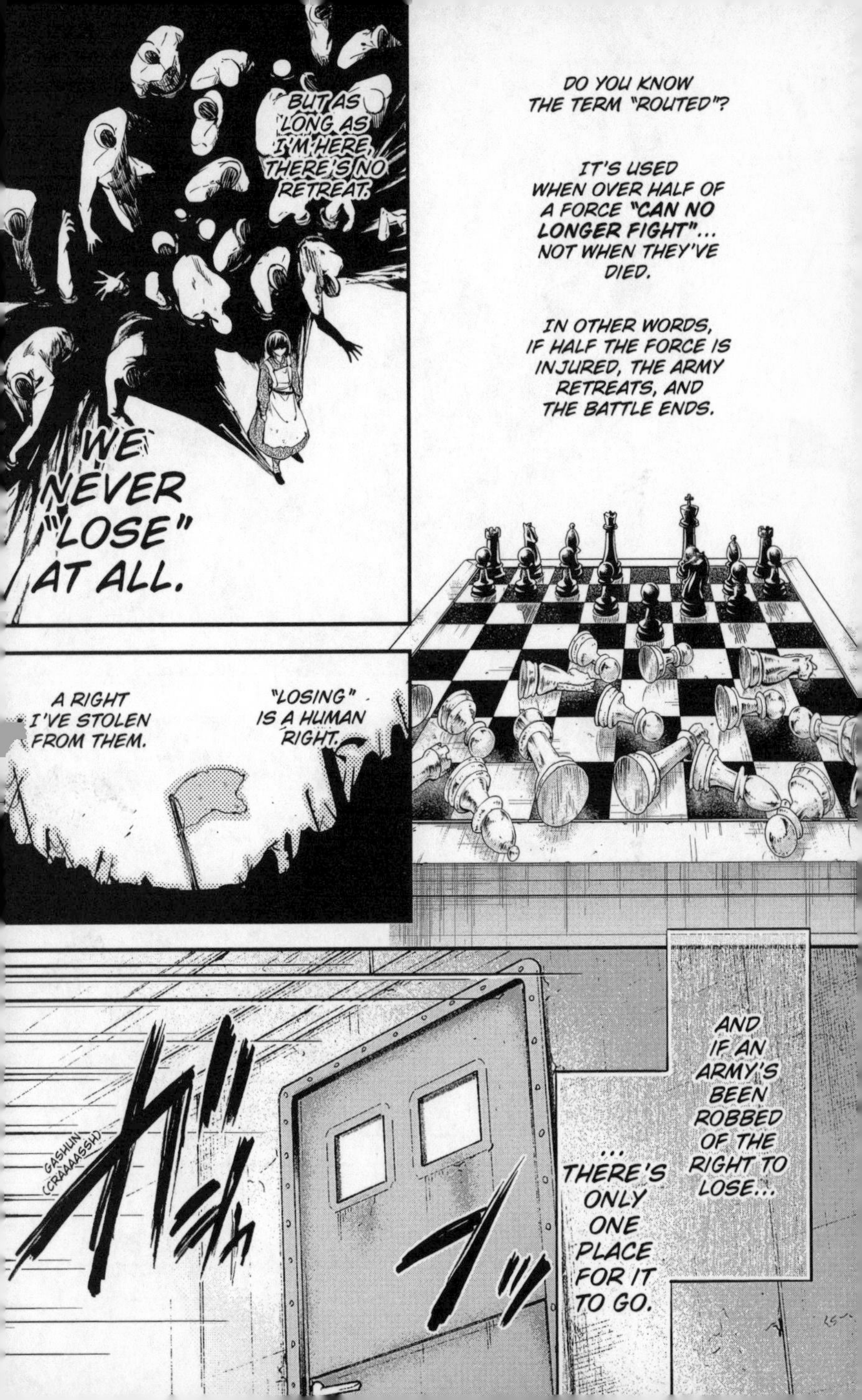
DO YOU KNOW THE TERM "ROUTED"?
IT'S USED WHEN OVER HALF OF A FORCE "CAN NO LONGER FIGHT"... NOT WHEN THEY'VE DIED.
IN OTHER WORDS, IF HALF THE FORCE IS INJURED, THE ARMY RETREATS, AND THE BATTLE ENDS.
BUT AS LONG AS I'M HERE, THERE'S NO RETREAT.
WE NEVER "LOSE" AT ALL.
"LOSING" IS A HUMAN RIGHT.
A RIGHT I'VE STOLEN FROM THEM.
AND IF AN ARMY'S BEEN ROBBED OF THE RIGHT TO LOSE...
...THERE'S ONLY ONE PLACE FOR IT TO GO.
GASHUN (CRAAASSH)

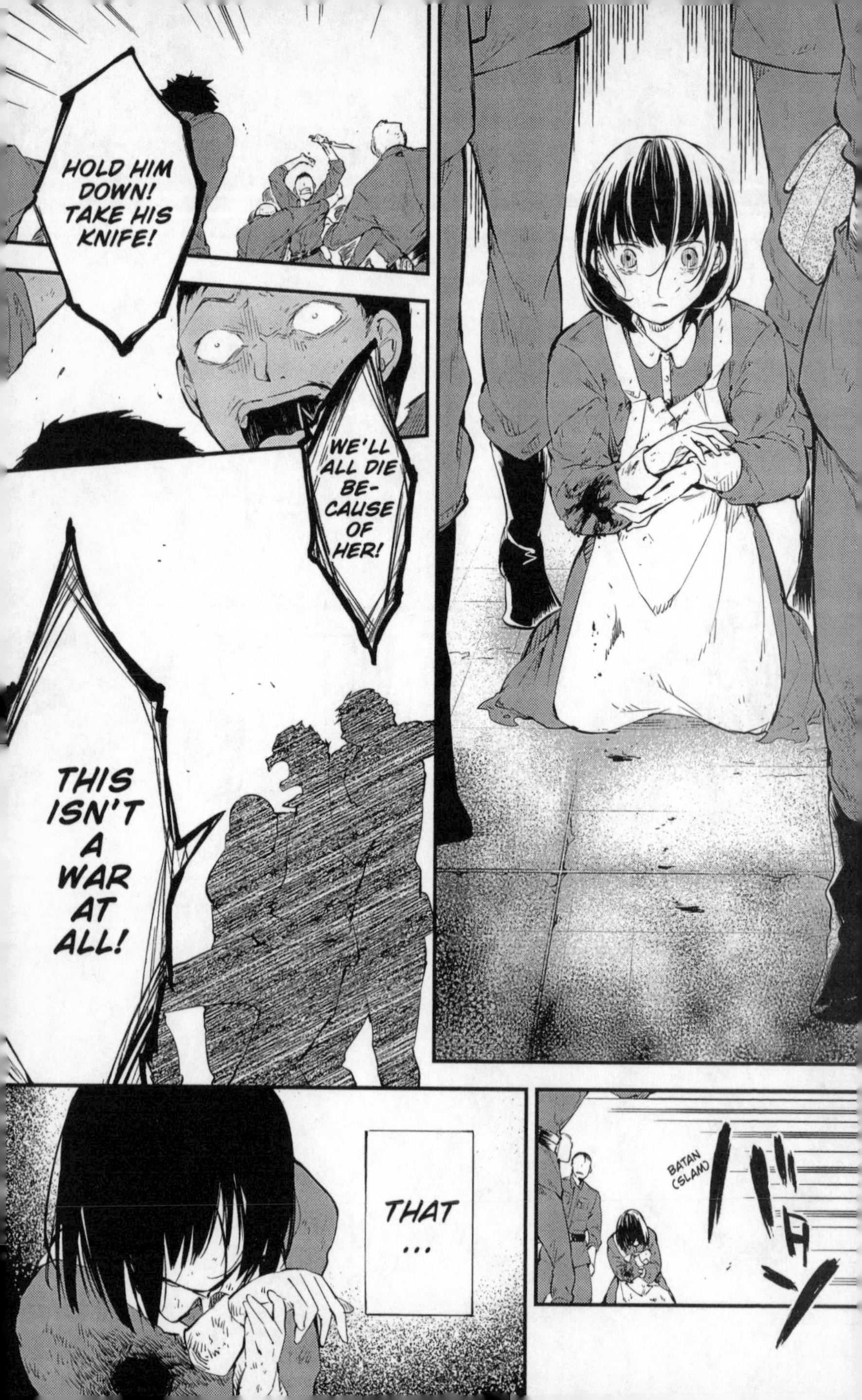
HOLD HIM DOWN! TAKE HIS KNIFE!
WE'LL ALL DIE BE-CAUSE OF HER!
THIS ISN'T A WAR AT ALL!
BATAN (SLAM)
THAT ...

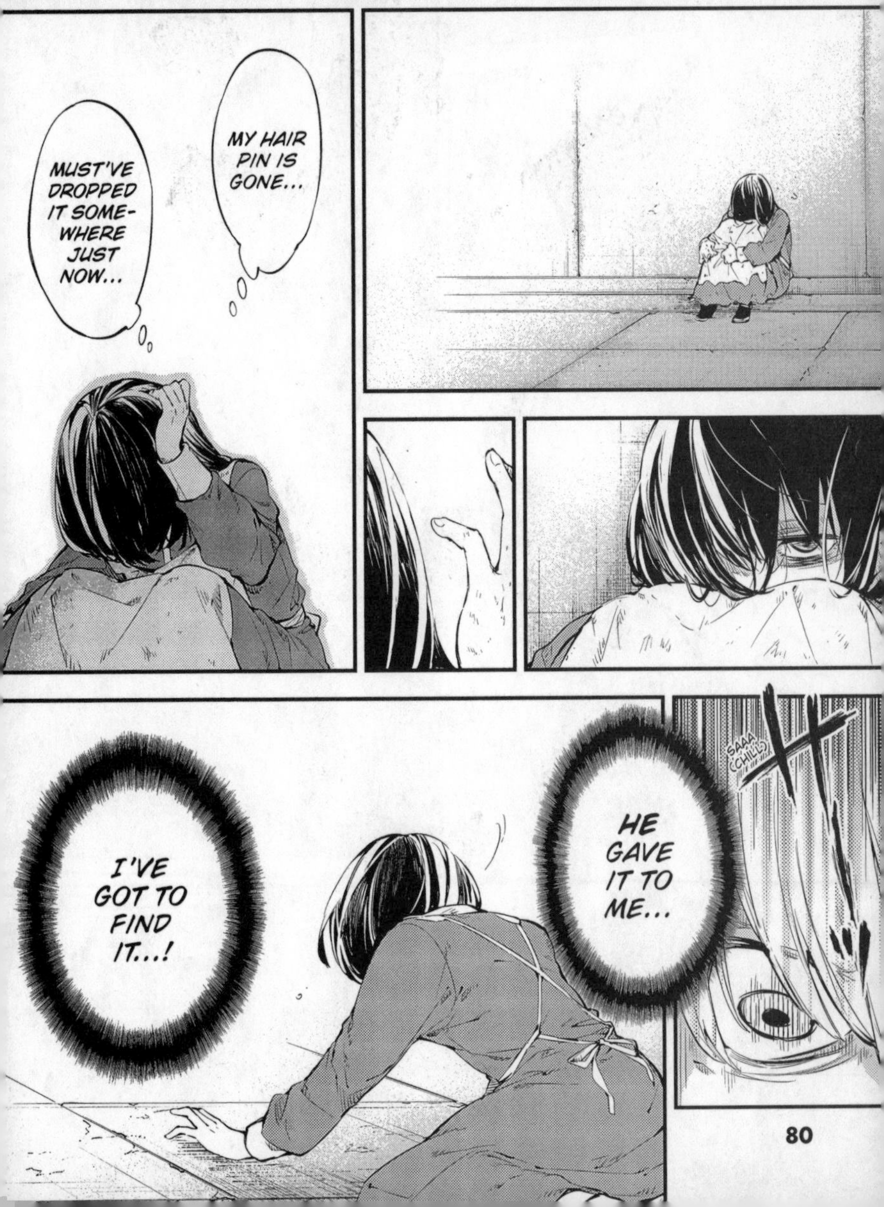
MY HAIR PIN IS GONE...
MUST'VE DROPPED IT SOME-WHERE JUST NOW...
SAAA (CHILL)
HE GAVE IT TO ME...
I'VE GOT TO FIND IT...!

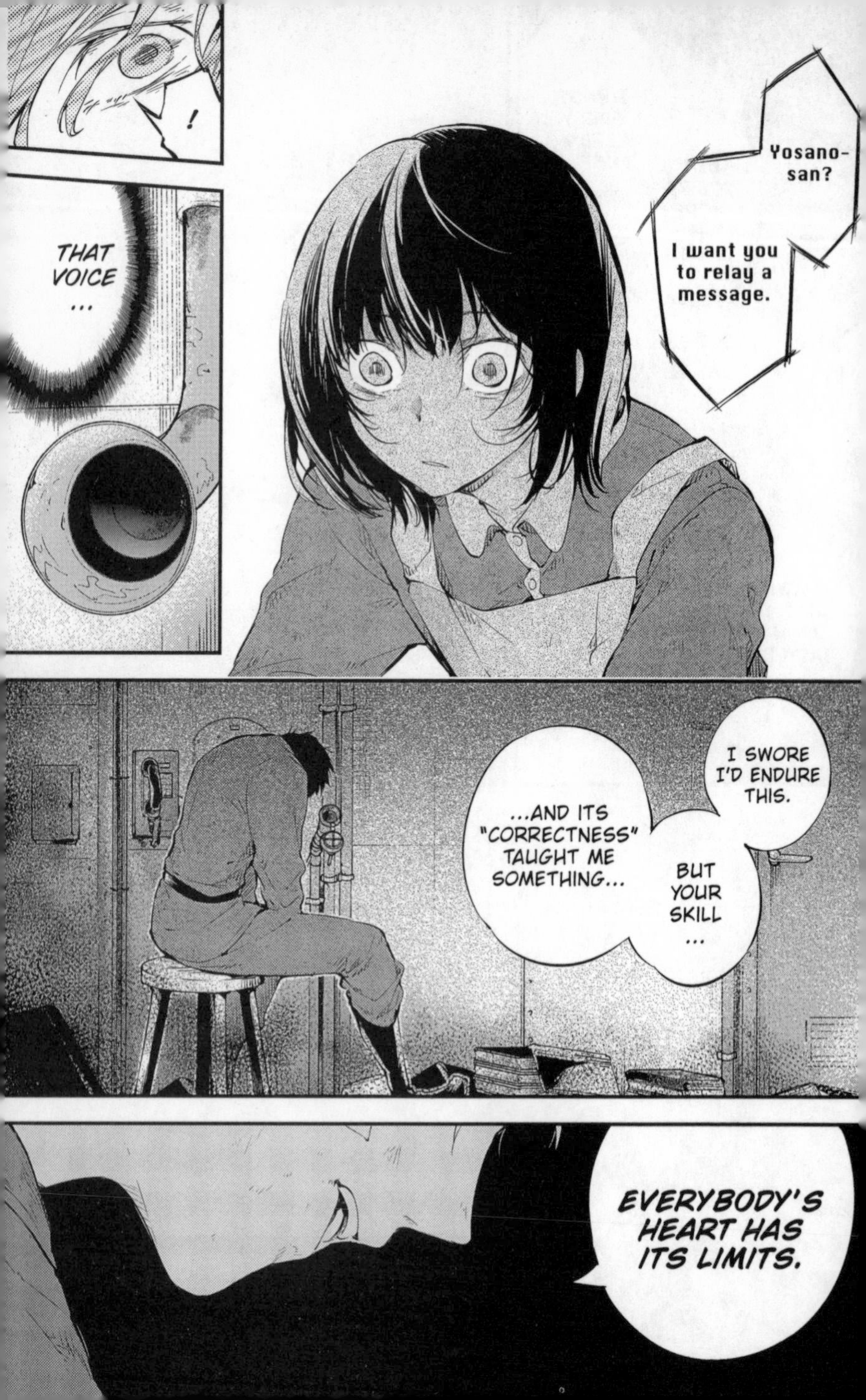
Yosano-san?
I want you to relay a message.
!
THAT VOICE ...
I SWORE I'D ENDURE THIS.
BUT YOUR SKILL ...
...AND ITS "CORRECTNESS" TAUGHT ME SOMETHING...
EVERYBODY'S HEART HAS ITS LIMITS.

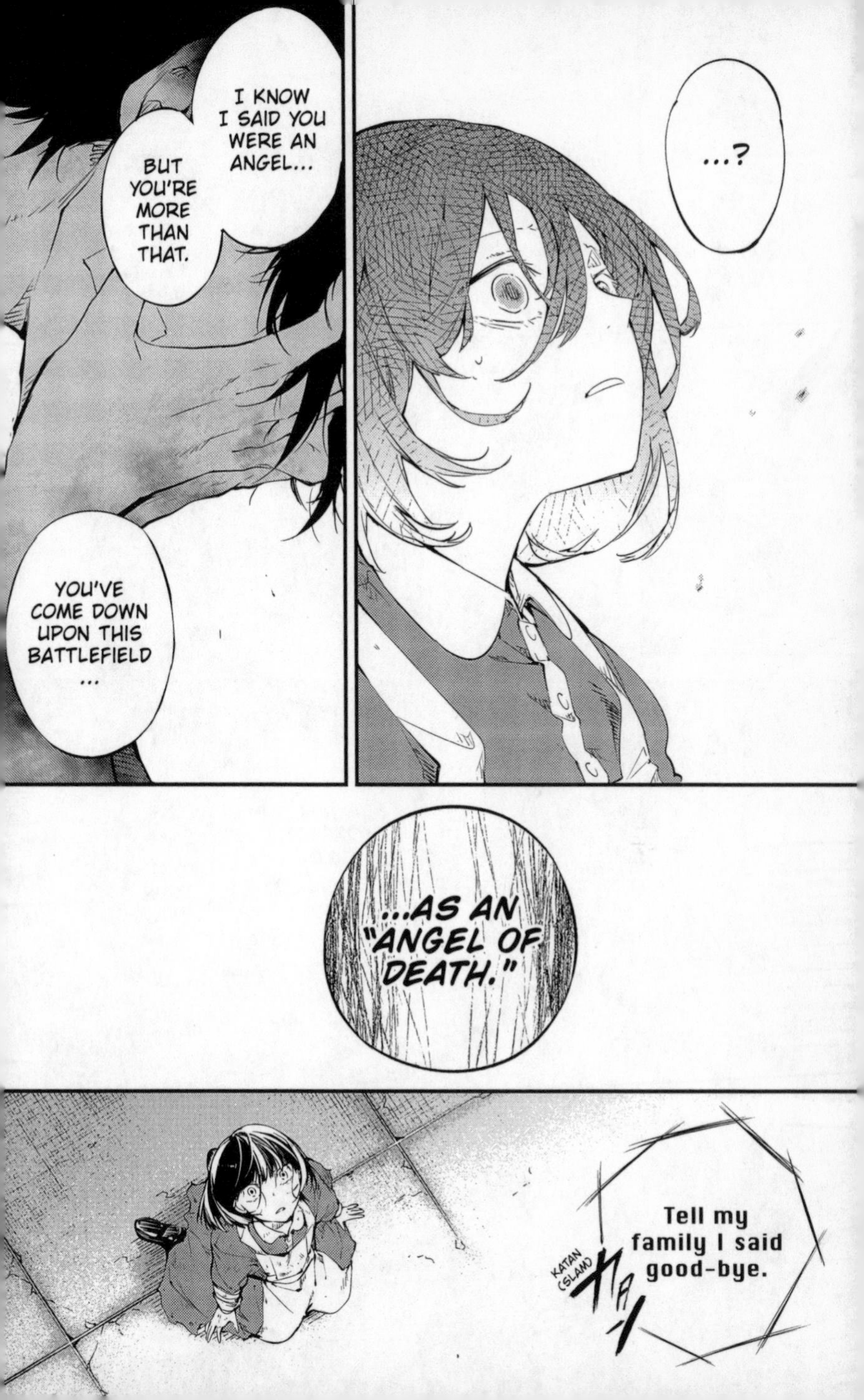
...?
I KNOW I SAID YOU WERE AN ANGEL...
BUT YOU'RE MORE THAN THAT.
YOU'VE COME DOWN UPON THIS BATTLEFIELD ...
..AS AN "ANGEL OF DEATH."
Tell my family I said good-bye.
KATAN (SLAM)

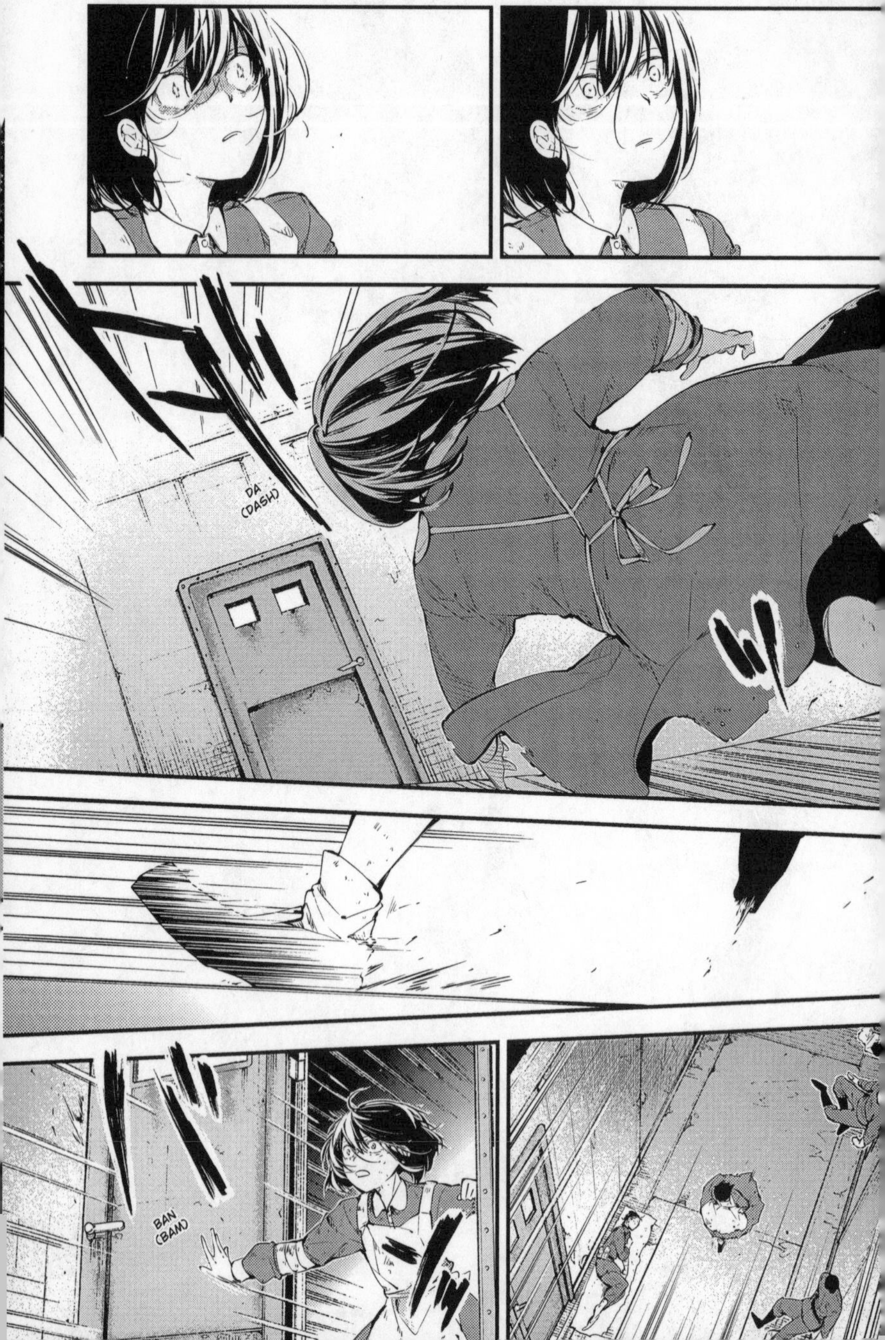
DA
(DASH)
BAN
(BAM)

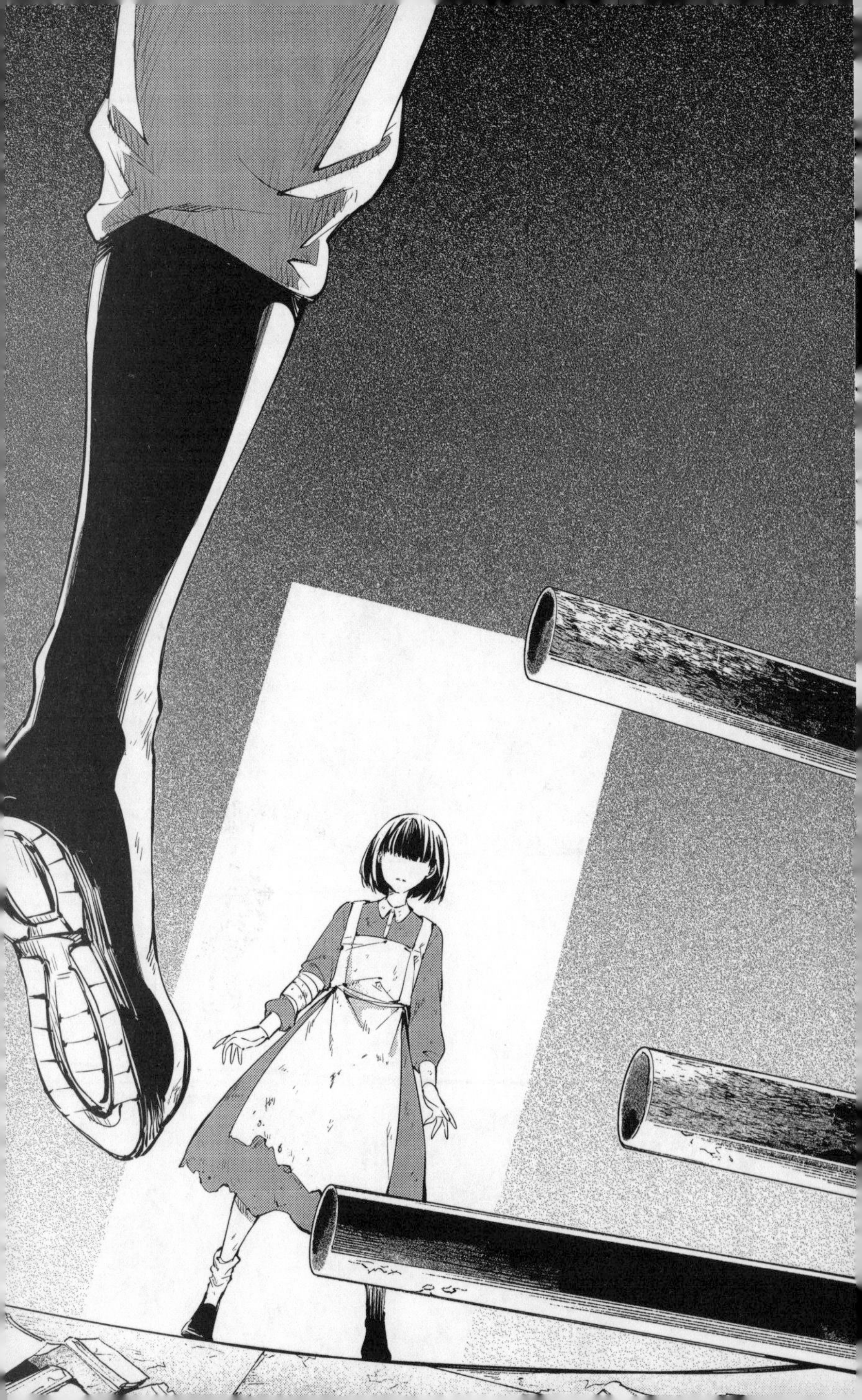

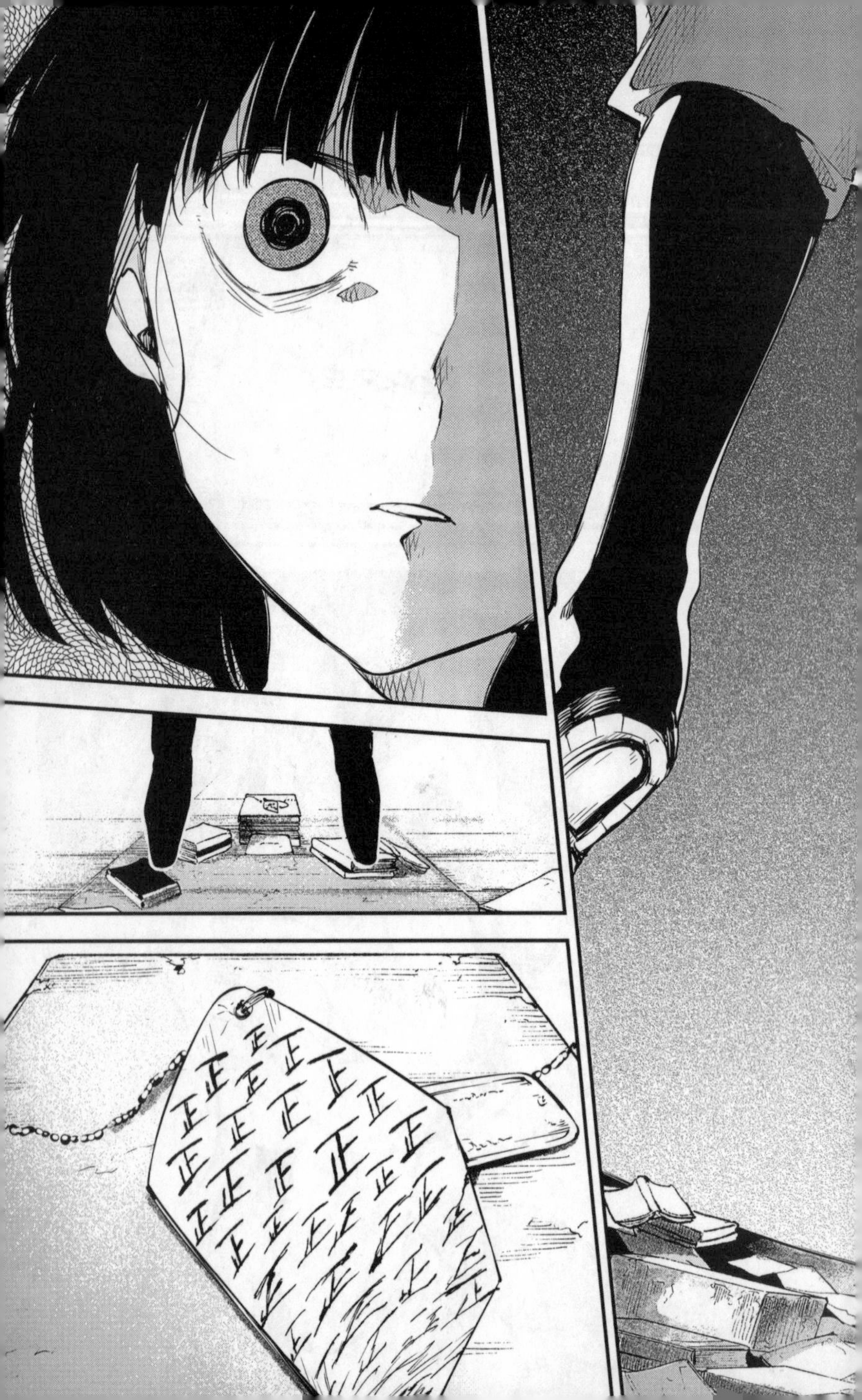

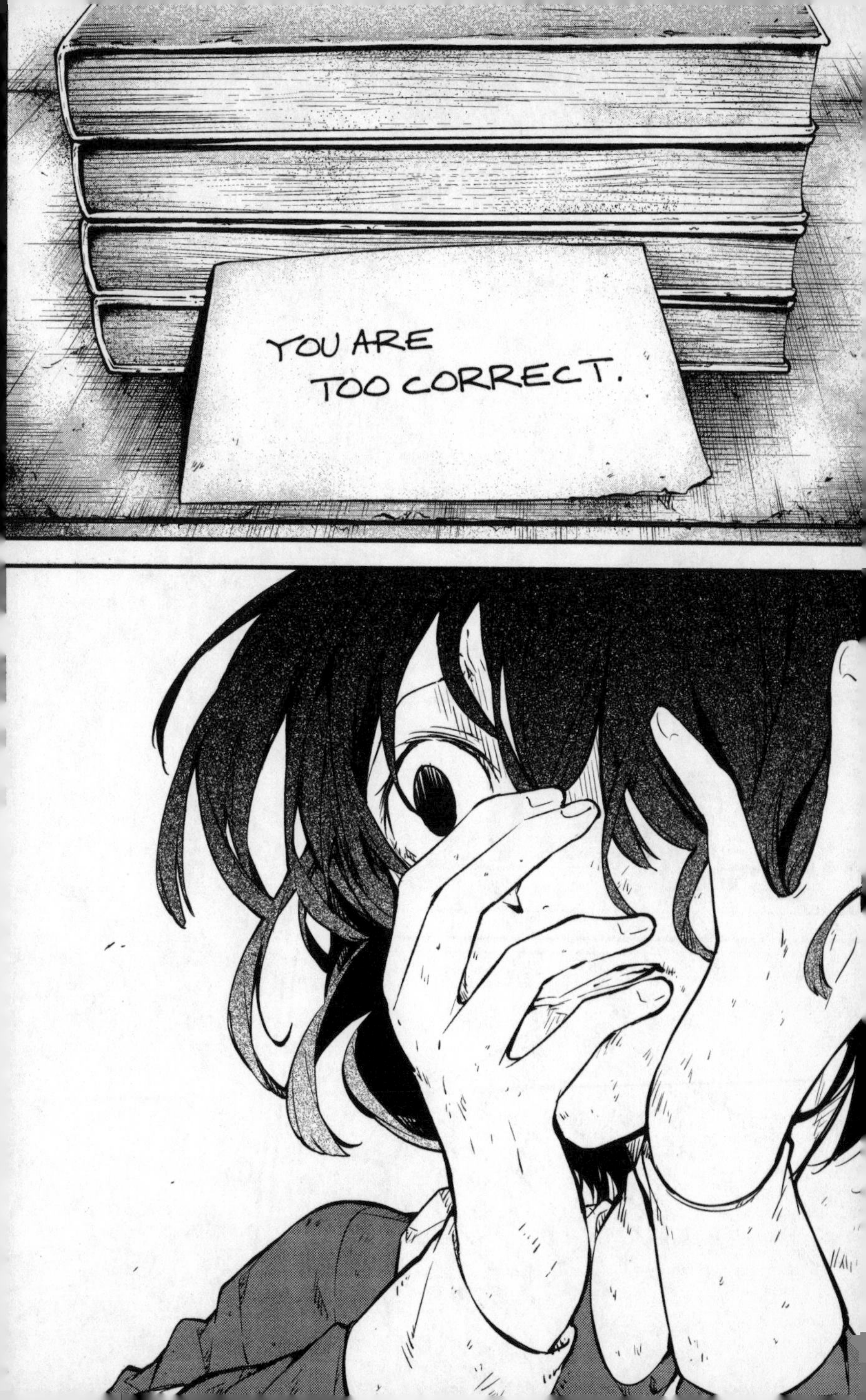
YOU ARE TOO CORRECT.

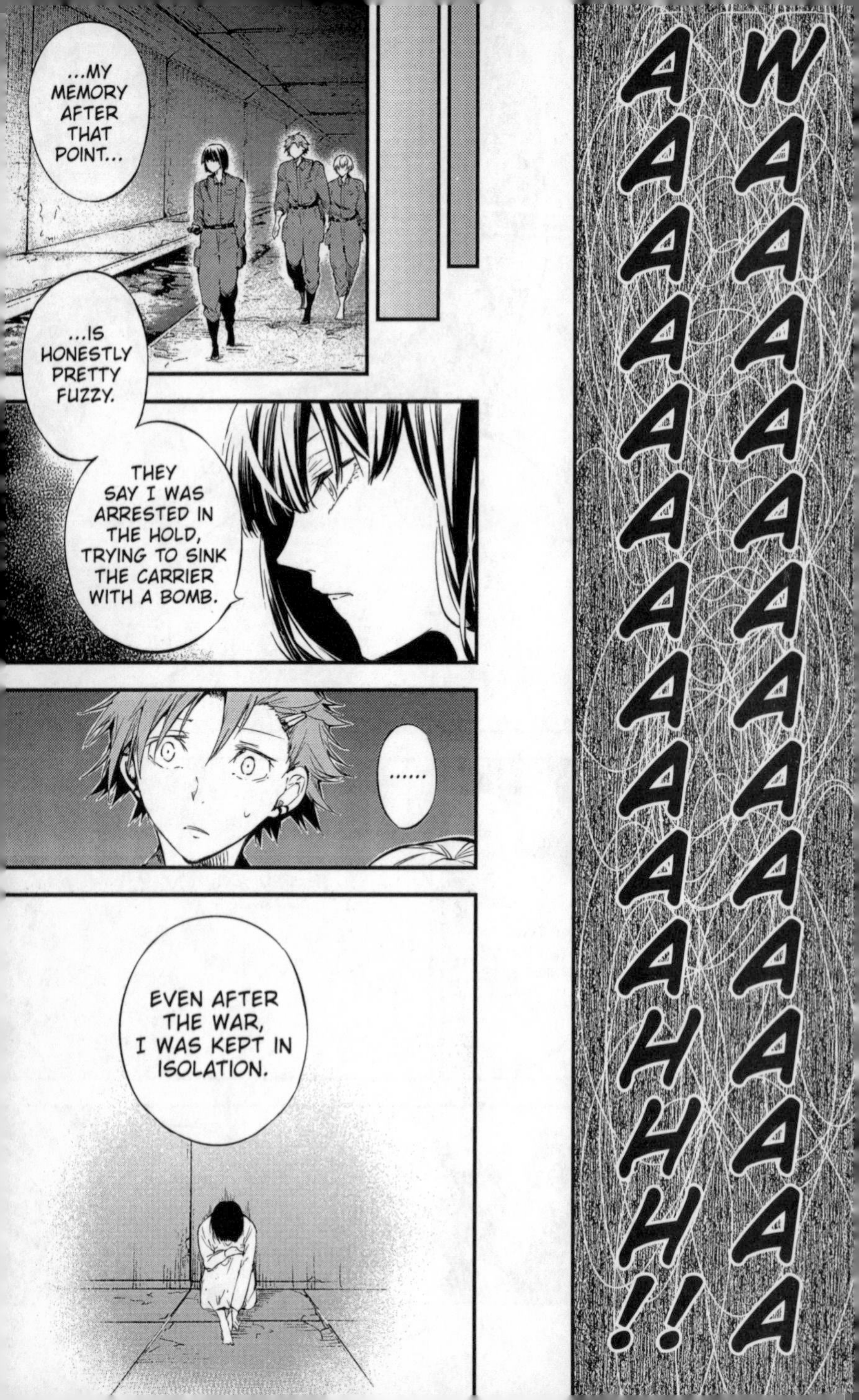
WAAAAAAAAAAAAAAAAAAAAAAAAAAAAAHHHH!!
...MY MEMORY AFTER THAT POINT...
...IS HONESTLY PRETTY FUZZY.
THEY SAY I WAS ARRESTED IN THE HOLD, TRYING TO SINK THE CARRIER WITH A BOMB.
......
EVEN AFTER THE WAR, I WAS KEPT IN ISOLATION.

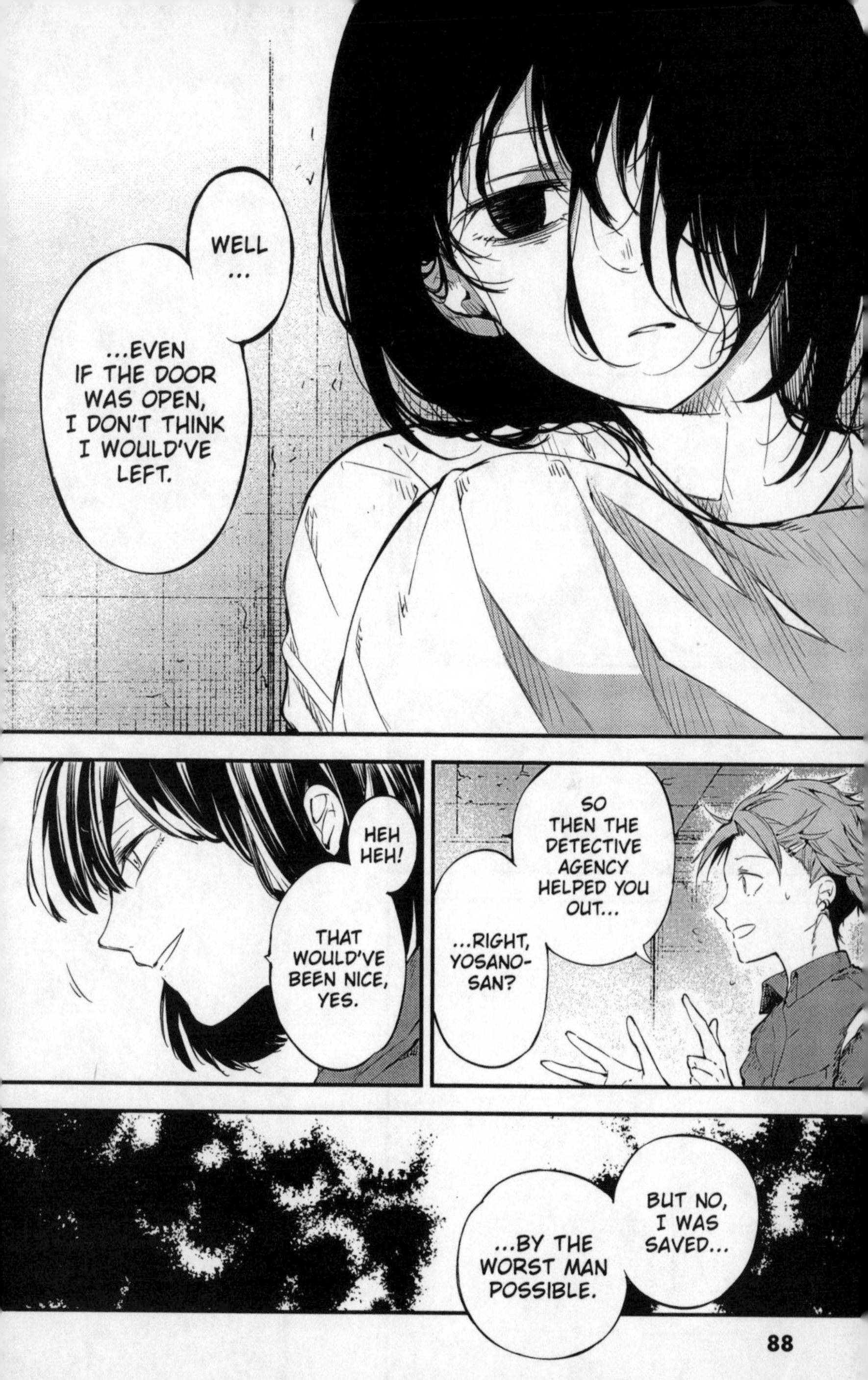
WELL ...
...EVEN IF THE DOOR WAS OPEN, I DON'T THINK I WOULD'VE LEFT.
SO THEN THE DETECTIVE AGENCY HELPED YOU OUT...
...RIGHT, YOSANO-SAN?
HEH HEH!
THAT WOULD'VE BEEN NICE, YES.
BUT NO, I WAS SAVED...
...BY THE WORST MAN POSSIBLE.

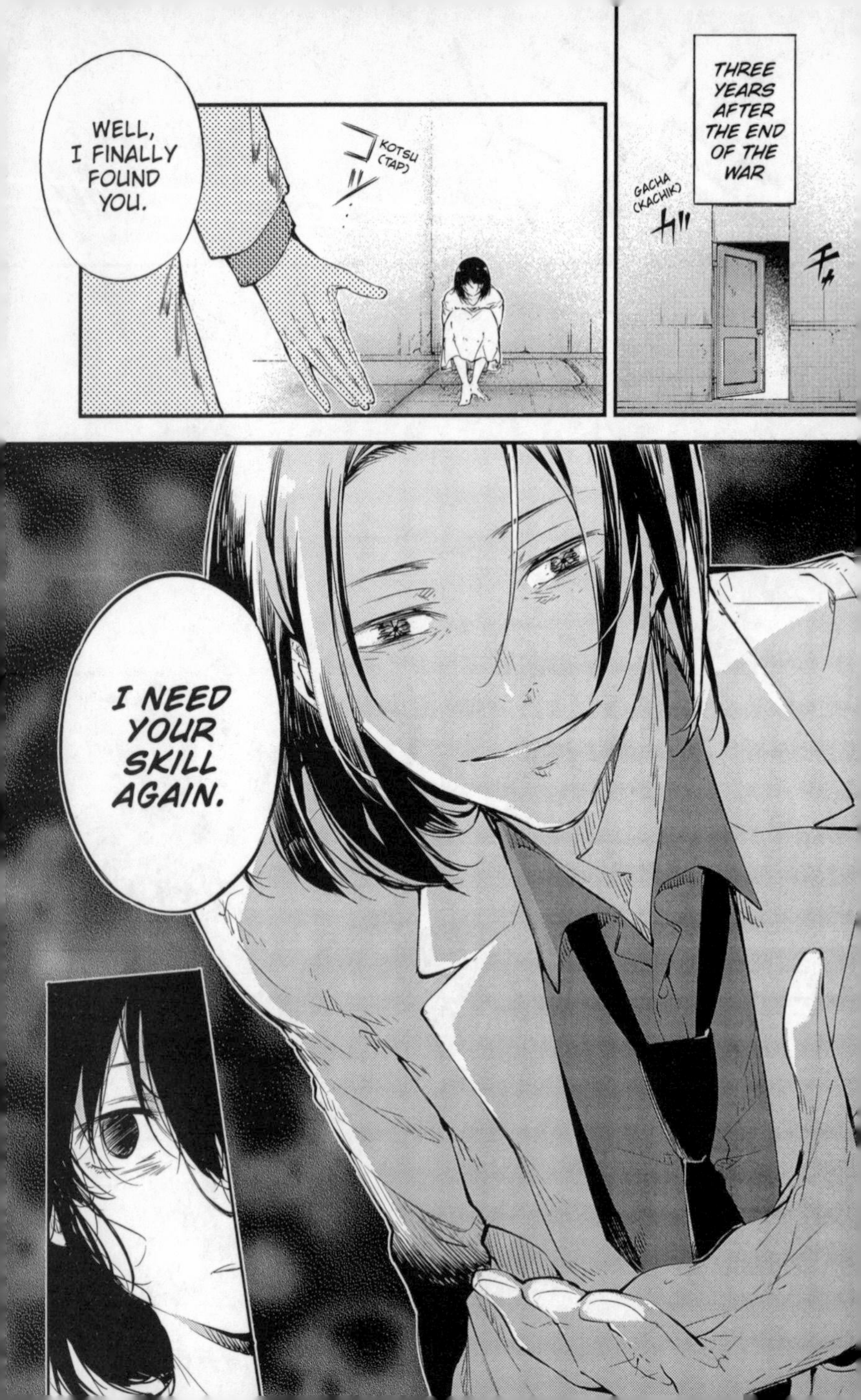
THREE YEARS AFTER THE END OF THE WAR
GACHA (KACHIK)
KOTSU (TAP)
WELL, I FINALLY FOUND YOU.
I NEED YOUR SKILL AGAIN.

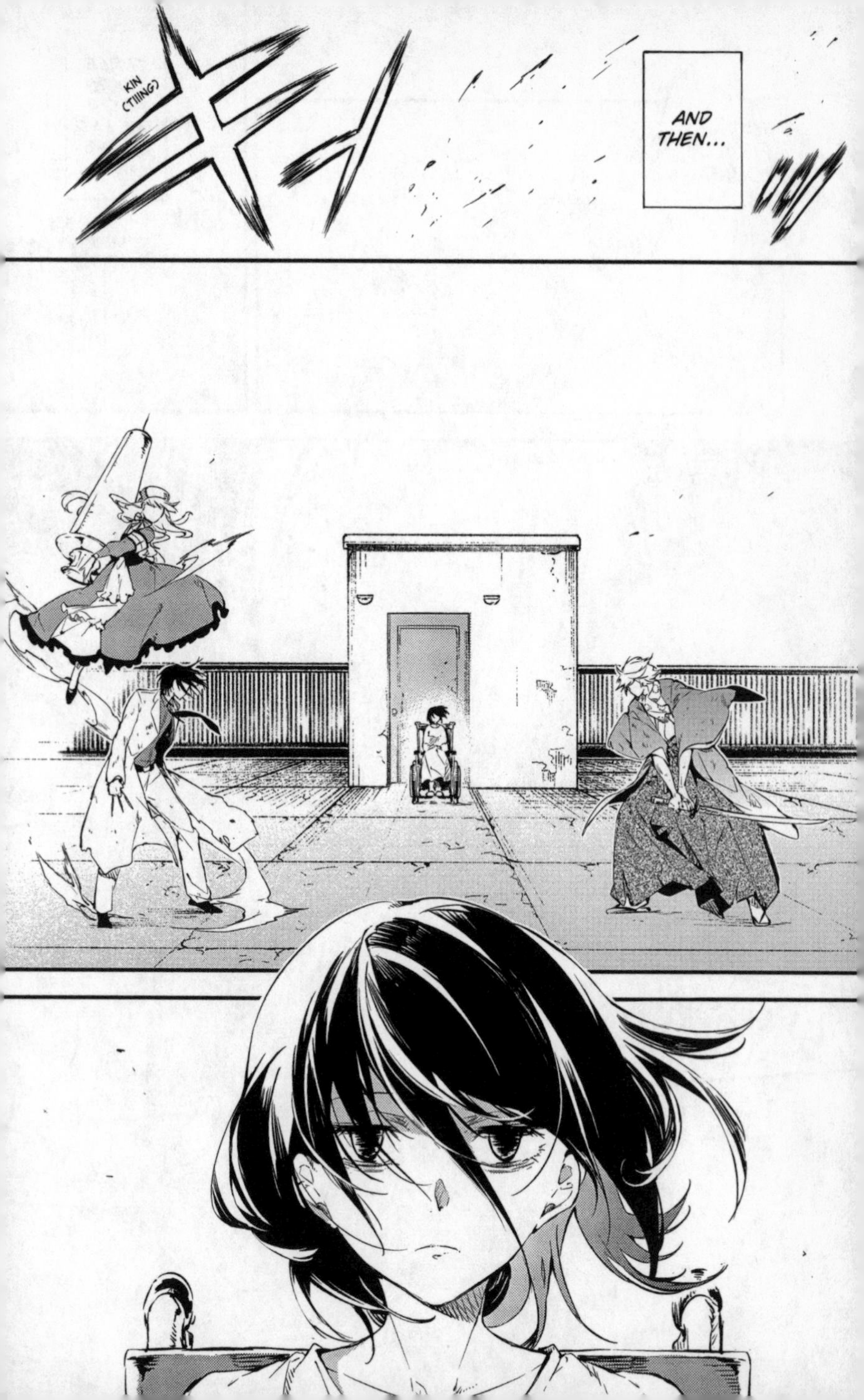
AND THEN...
KIN (TIIING)

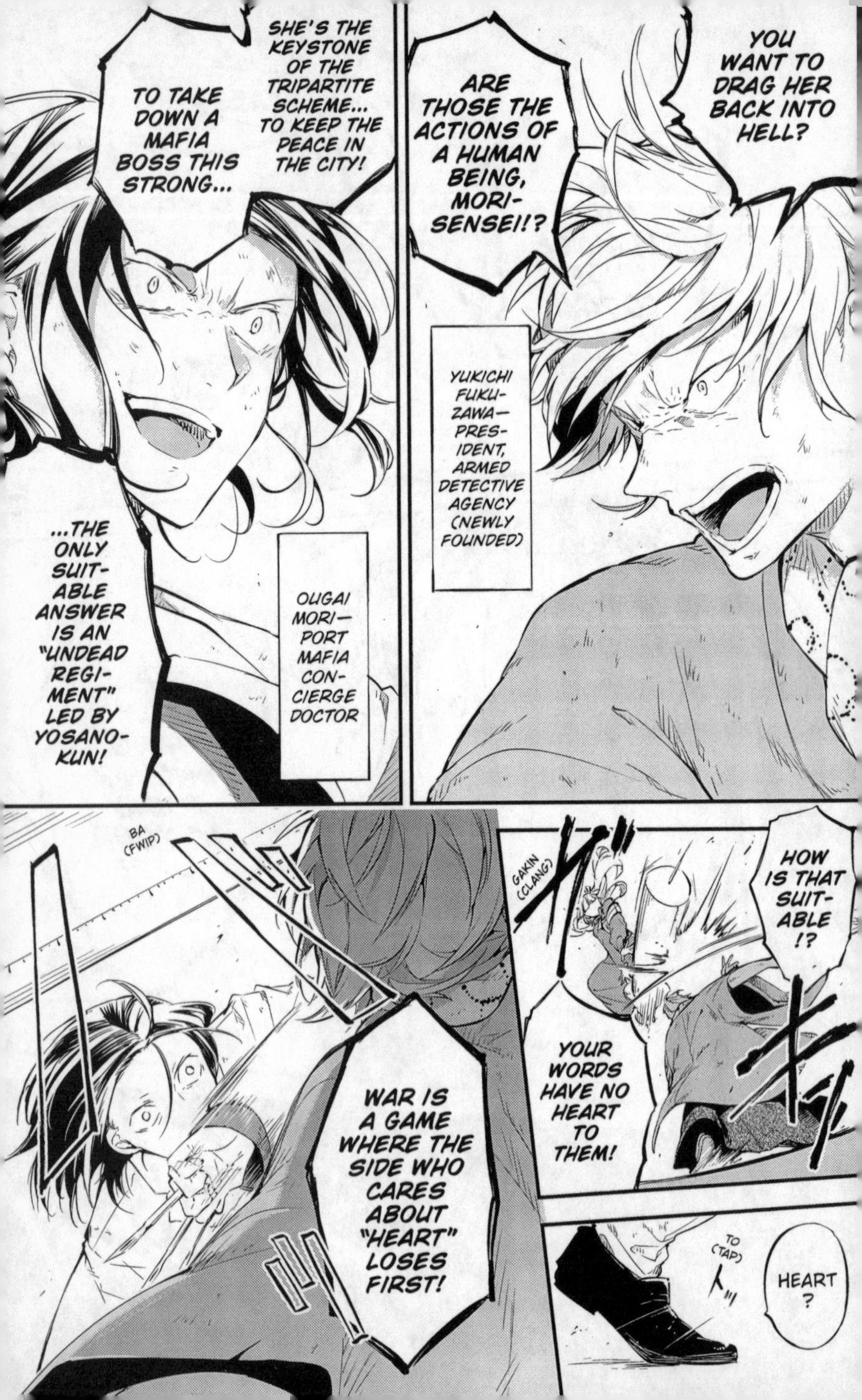
YOU WANT TO DRAG HER BACK INTO HELL?
ARE THOSE THE ACTIONS OF A HUMAN BEING, MORI-SENSEI!?
YUKICHI FUKUZAWA—PRESIDENT, ARMED DETECTIVE AGENCY (NEWLY FOUNDED)
SHE'S THE KEYSTONE OF THE TRIPARTITE SCHEME... TO KEEP THE PEACE IN THE CITY!
TO TAKE DOWN A MAFIA BOSS THIS STRONG...
...THE ONLY SUITABLE ANSWER IS AN "UNDEAD REGIMENT" LED BY YOSANO-KUN!
OUGAI MORI—PORT MAFIA CONCIERGE DOCTOR
GAKIN (CLANG)
HOW IS THAT SUITABLE!?
YOUR WORDS HAVE NO HEART TO THEM!
TO (TAP)
HEART?
BA (FWIP)
WAR IS A GAME WHERE THE SIDE WHO CARES ABOUT "HEART" LOSES FIRST!

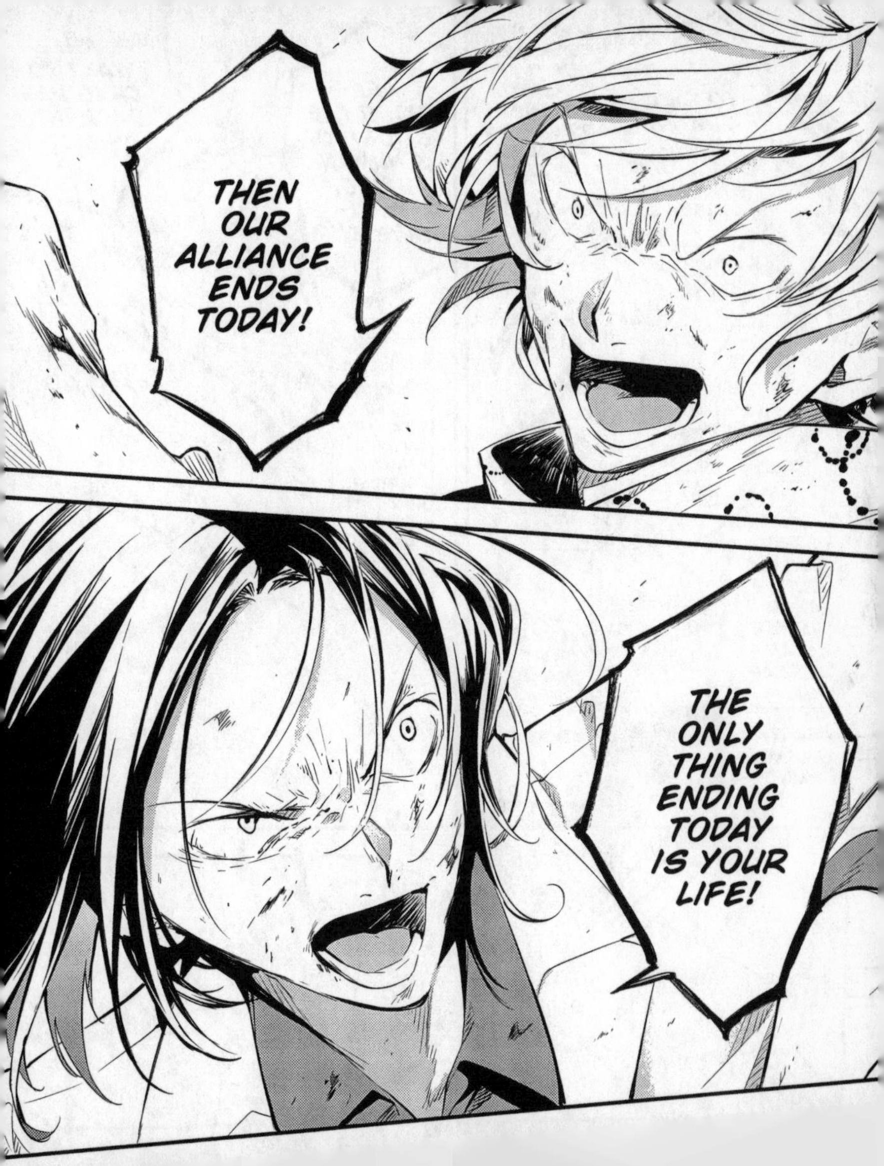
THEN OUR ALLIANCE ENDS TODAY!
THE ONLY THING ENDING TODAY IS YOUR LIFE!

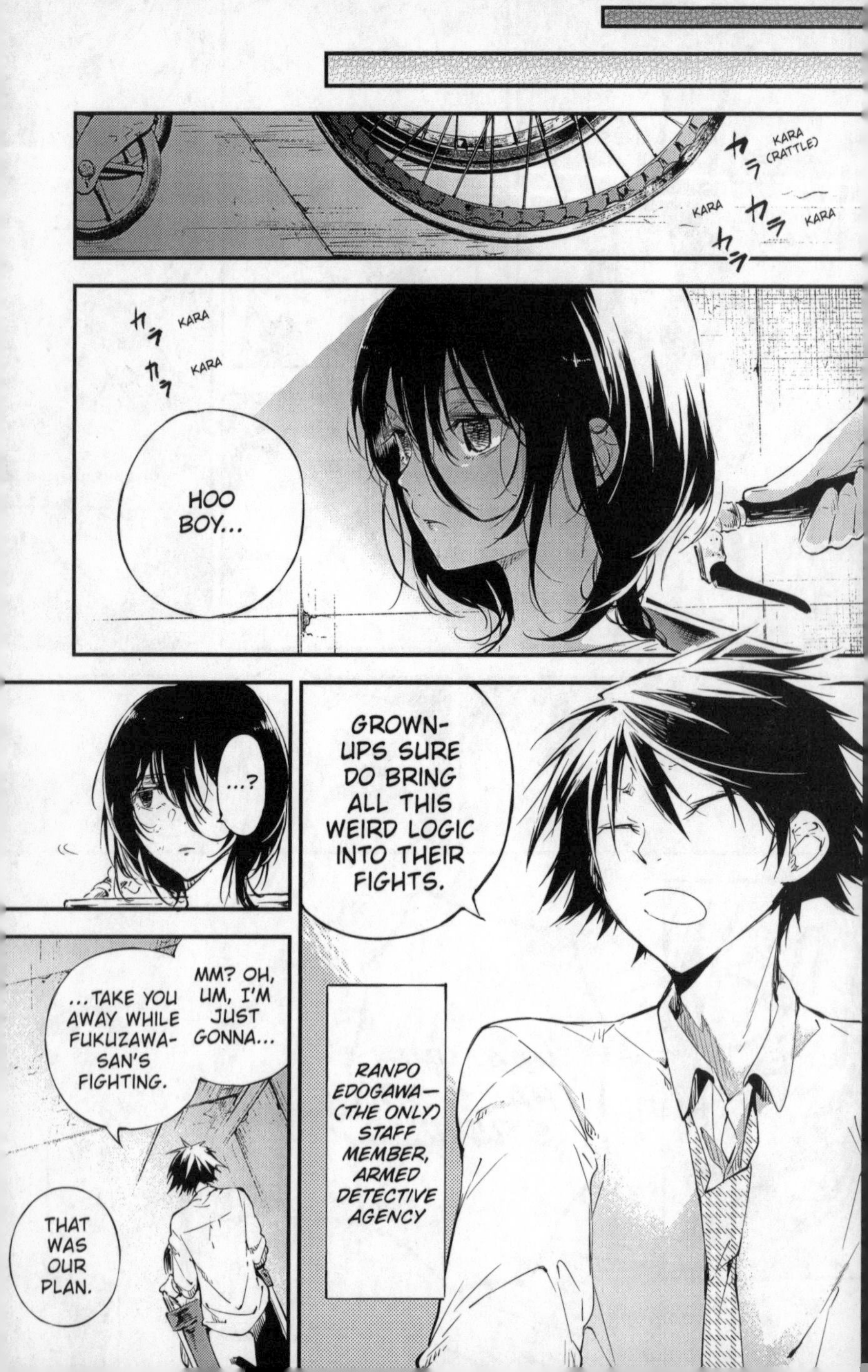

カラ KARA (RATTLE)
KARA カラ KARA
カラ
カラ KARA
カラ KARA
HOO BOY...
GROWN-UPS SURE DO BRING ALL THIS WEIRD LOGIC INTO THEIR FIGHTS.
RANPO EDOGAWA—(THE ONLY) STAFF MEMBER, ARMED DETECTIVE AGENCY
...?
MM? OH, UM, I'M JUST GONNA...
...TAKE YOU AWAY WHILE FUKUZAWA-SAN'S FIGHTING.
THAT WAS OUR PLAN.

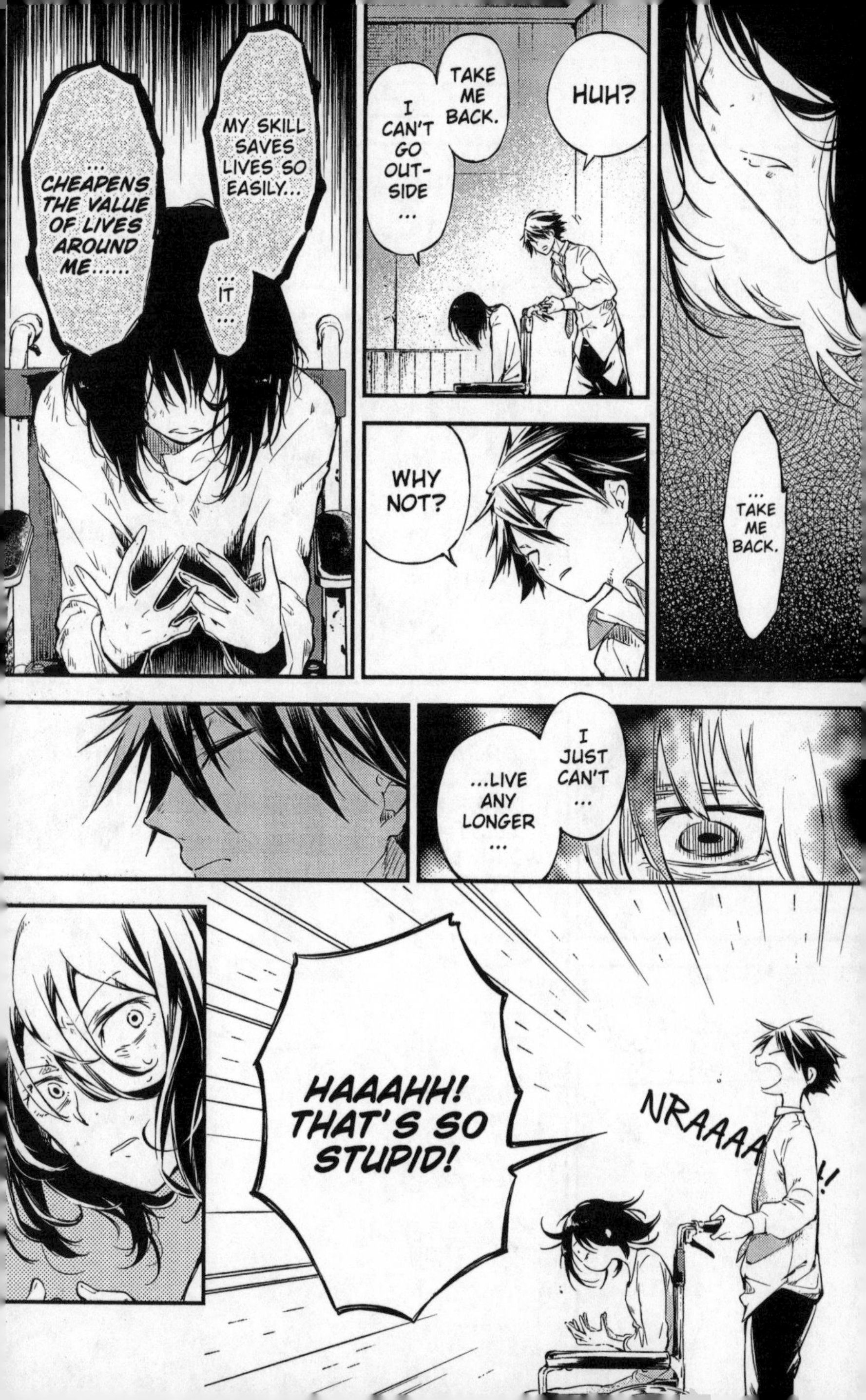
... TAKE ME BACK.
HUH?
TAKE ME BACK.
I CAN'T GO OUT-SIDE ...
WHY NOT?
MY SKILL SAVES LIVES SO EASILY...
... IT ...
... CHEAPENS THE VALUE OF LIVES AROUND ME......
I JUST CAN'T ...
...LIVE ANY LONGER ...
NRAAAA!!
HAAAHH! THAT'S SO STUPID!

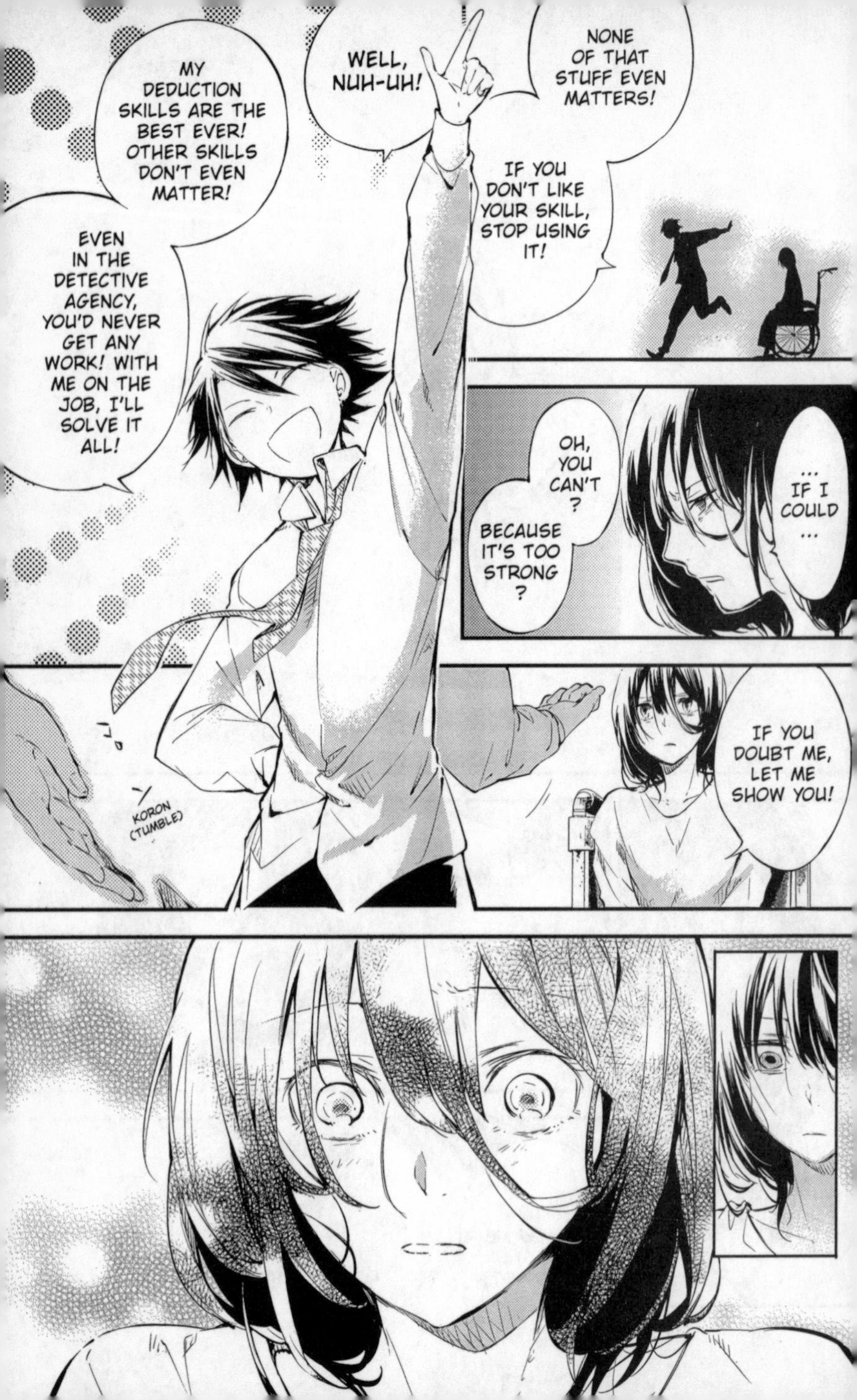
IF YOU DON'T LIKE YOUR SKILL, STOP USING IT!
... IF I COULD ...
OH, YOU CAN'T?
BECAUSE IT'S TOO STRONG?
WELL, NUH-UH!
NONE OF THAT STUFF EVEN MATTERS!
MY DEDUCTION SKILLS ARE THE BEST EVER! OTHER SKILLS DON'T EVEN MATTER!
EVEN IN THE DETECTIVE AGENCY, YOU'D NEVER GET ANY WORK! WITH ME ON THE JOB, I'LL SOLVE IT ALL!
KORON (TUMBLE)
IF YOU DOUBT ME, LET ME SHOW YOU!

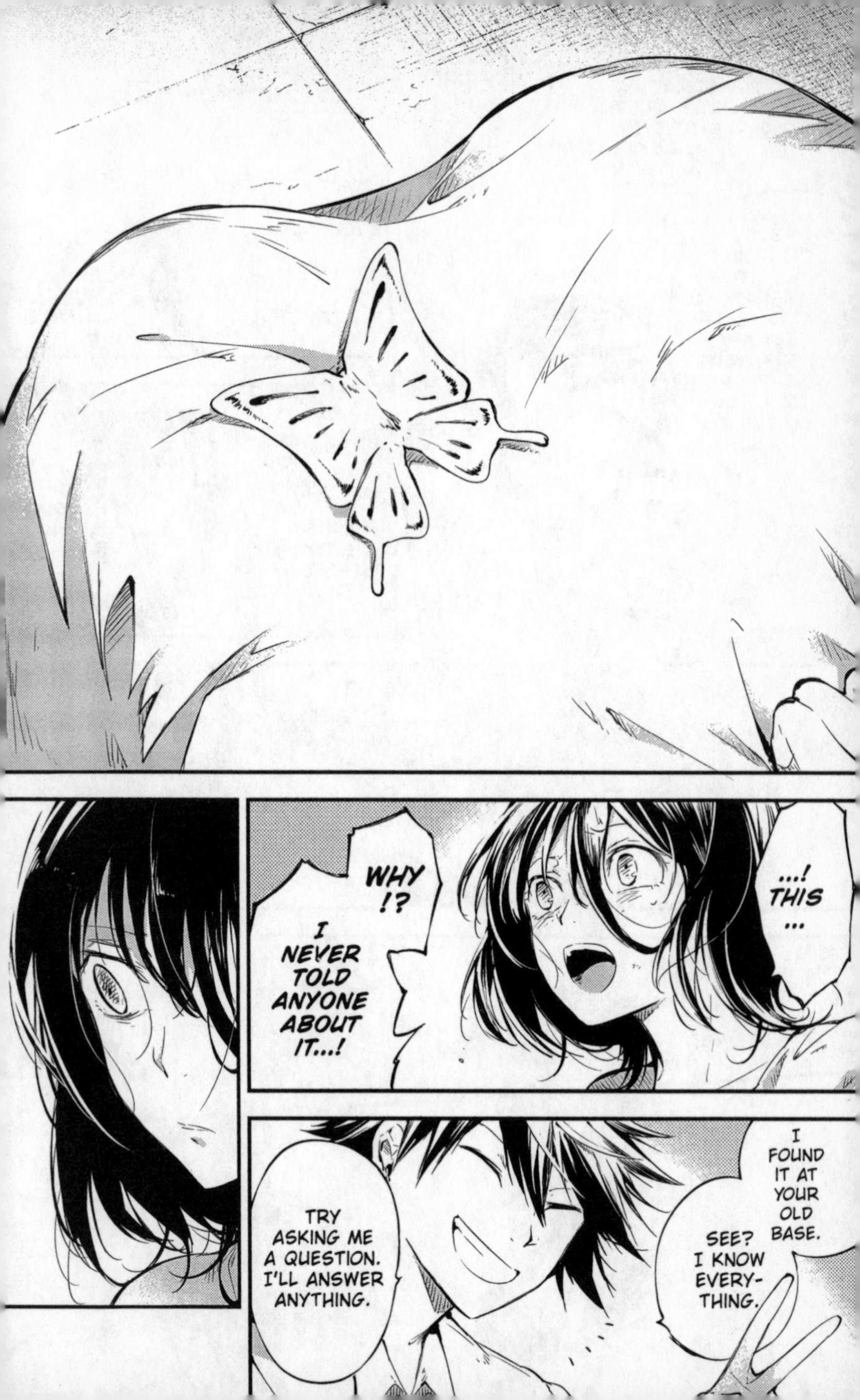
...! THIS ...
WHY !?
I NEVER TOLD ANYONE ABOUT IT...!
I FOUND IT AT YOUR OLD BASE.
SEE? I KNOW EVERY-THING.
TRY ASKING ME A QUESTION. I'LL ANSWER ANYTHING.

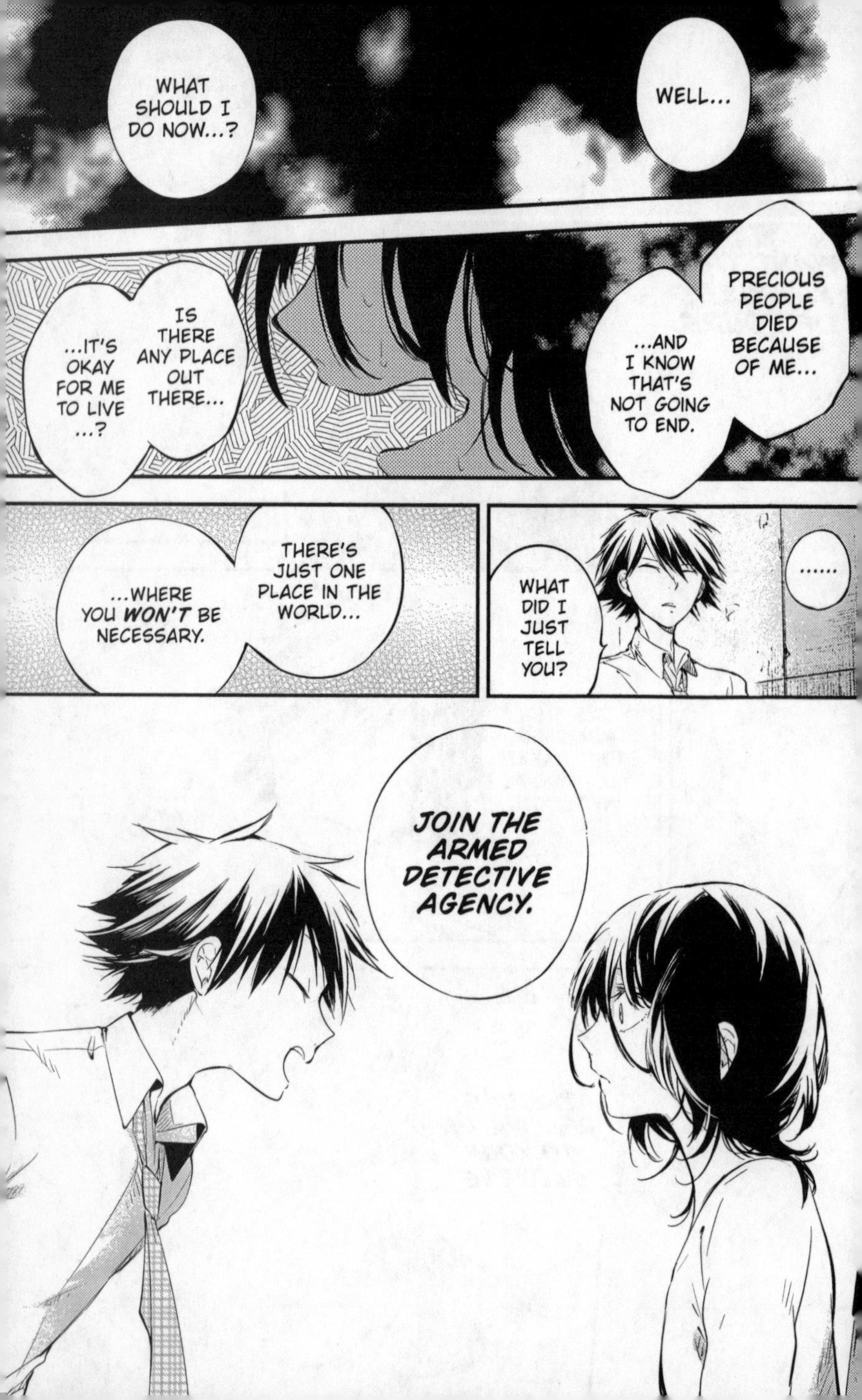
WELL...
WHAT SHOULD I DO NOW...?
PRECIOUS PEOPLE DIED BECAUSE OF ME...
...AND I KNOW THAT'S NOT GOING TO END.
IS THERE ANY PLACE OUT THERE...
...IT'S OKAY FOR ME TO LIVE ...?
......
WHAT DID I JUST TELL YOU?
THERE'S JUST ONE PLACE IN THE WORLD...
...WHERE YOU **WON'T** BE NECESSARY.
JOIN THE ARMED DETECTIVE AGENCY.

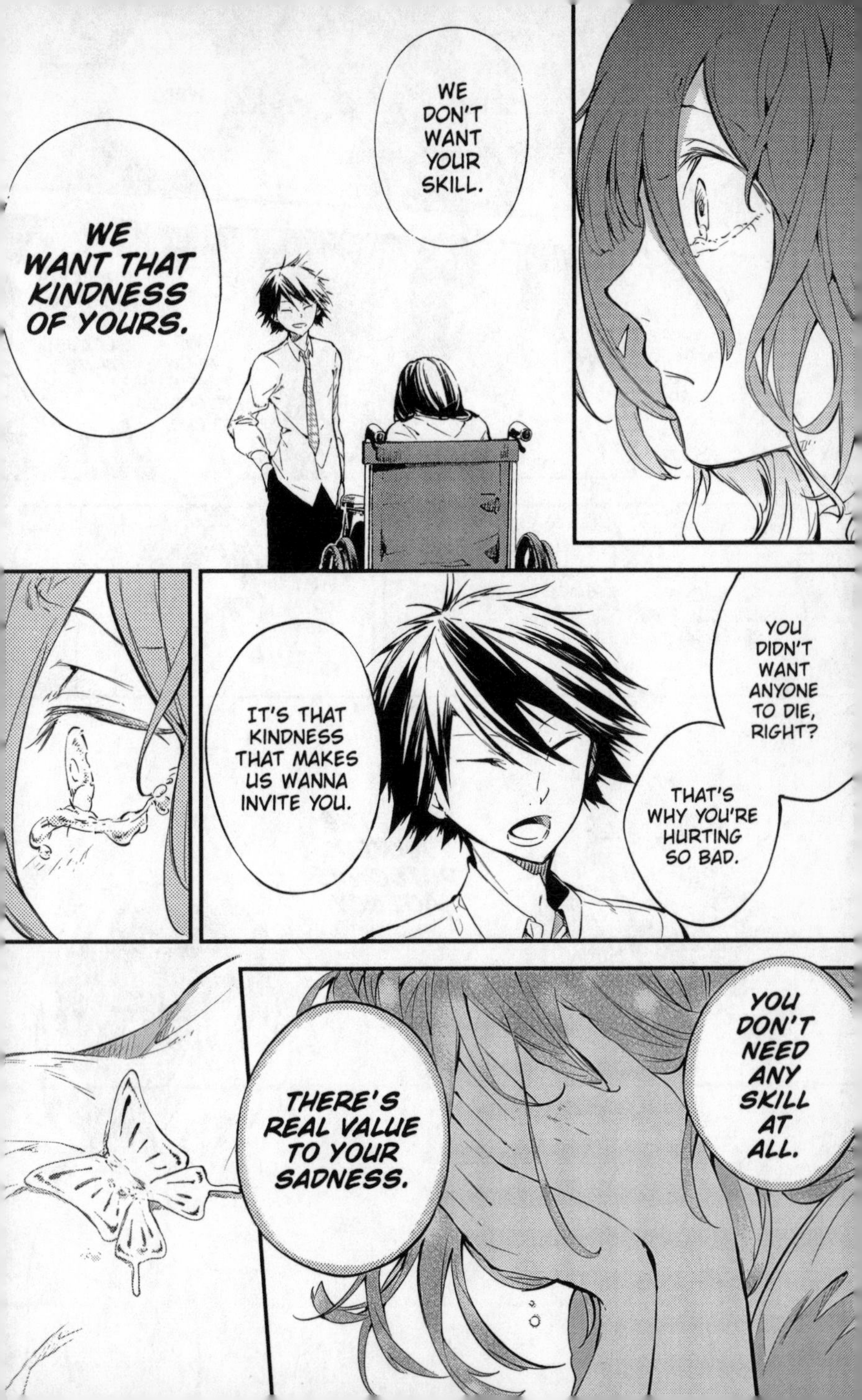
WE DON'T WANT YOUR SKILL.
WE WANT THAT KINDNESS OF YOURS.
YOU DIDN'T WANT ANYONE TO DIE, RIGHT?
THAT'S WHY YOU'RE HURTING SO BAD.
IT'S THAT KINDNESS THAT MAKES US WANNA INVITE YOU.
YOU DON'T NEED ANY SKILL AT ALL.
THERE'S REAL VALUE TO YOUR SADNESS.

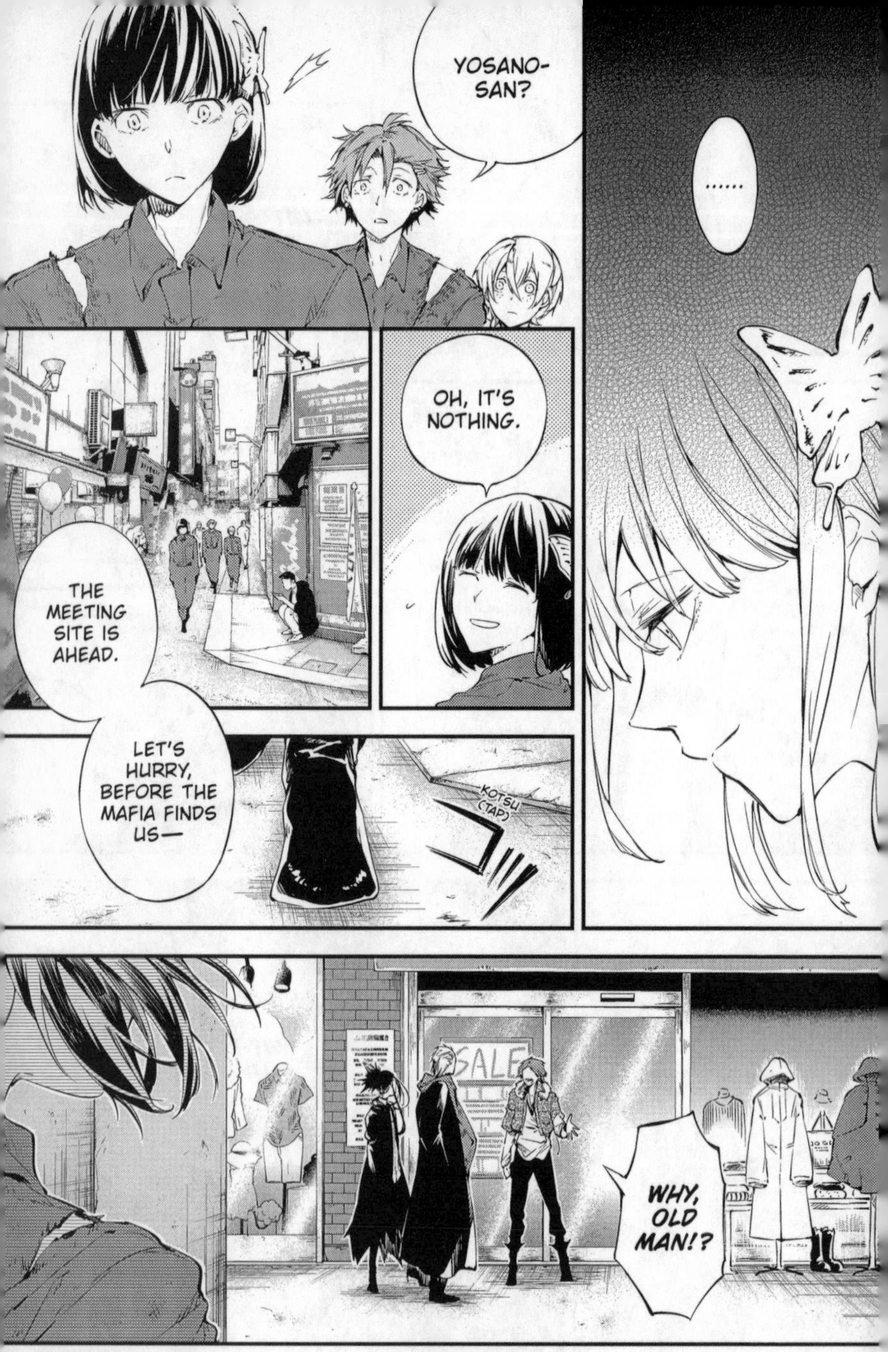
......
YOSANO-SAN?
OH, IT'S NOTHING.
THE MEETING SITE IS AHEAD.
LET'S HURRY, BEFORE THE MAFIA FINDS US—
KOTSU (TAP)
WHY, OLD MAN!?

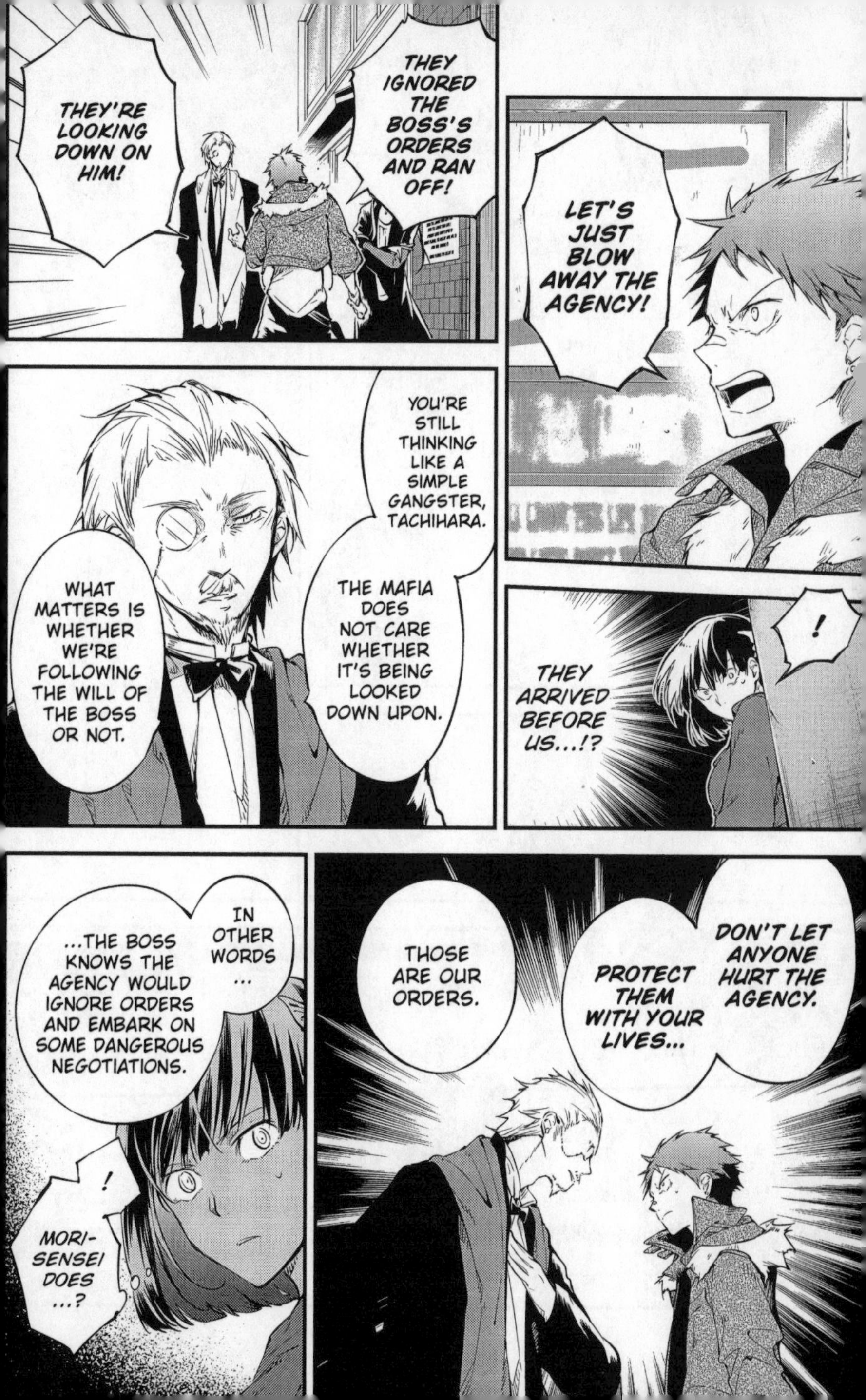
THEY IGNORED THE BOSS'S ORDERS AND RAN OFF!
THEY'RE LOOKING DOWN ON HIM!
LET'S JUST BLOW AWAY THE AGENCY!
YOU'RE STILL THINKING LIKE A SIMPLE GANGSTER, TACHIHARA.
THE MAFIA DOES NOT CARE WHETHER IT'S BEING LOOKED DOWN UPON.
WHAT MATTERS IS WHETHER WE'RE FOLLOWING THE WILL OF THE BOSS OR NOT.
!
THEY ARRIVED BEFORE US...!?
DON'T LET ANYONE HURT THE AGENCY.
PROTECT THEM WITH YOUR LIVES...
THOSE ARE OUR ORDERS.
IN OTHER WORDS...
...THE BOSS KNOWS THE AGENCY WOULD IGNORE ORDERS AND EMBARK ON SOME DANGEROUS NEGOTIATIONS.
!
MORI-SENSEI DOES...?

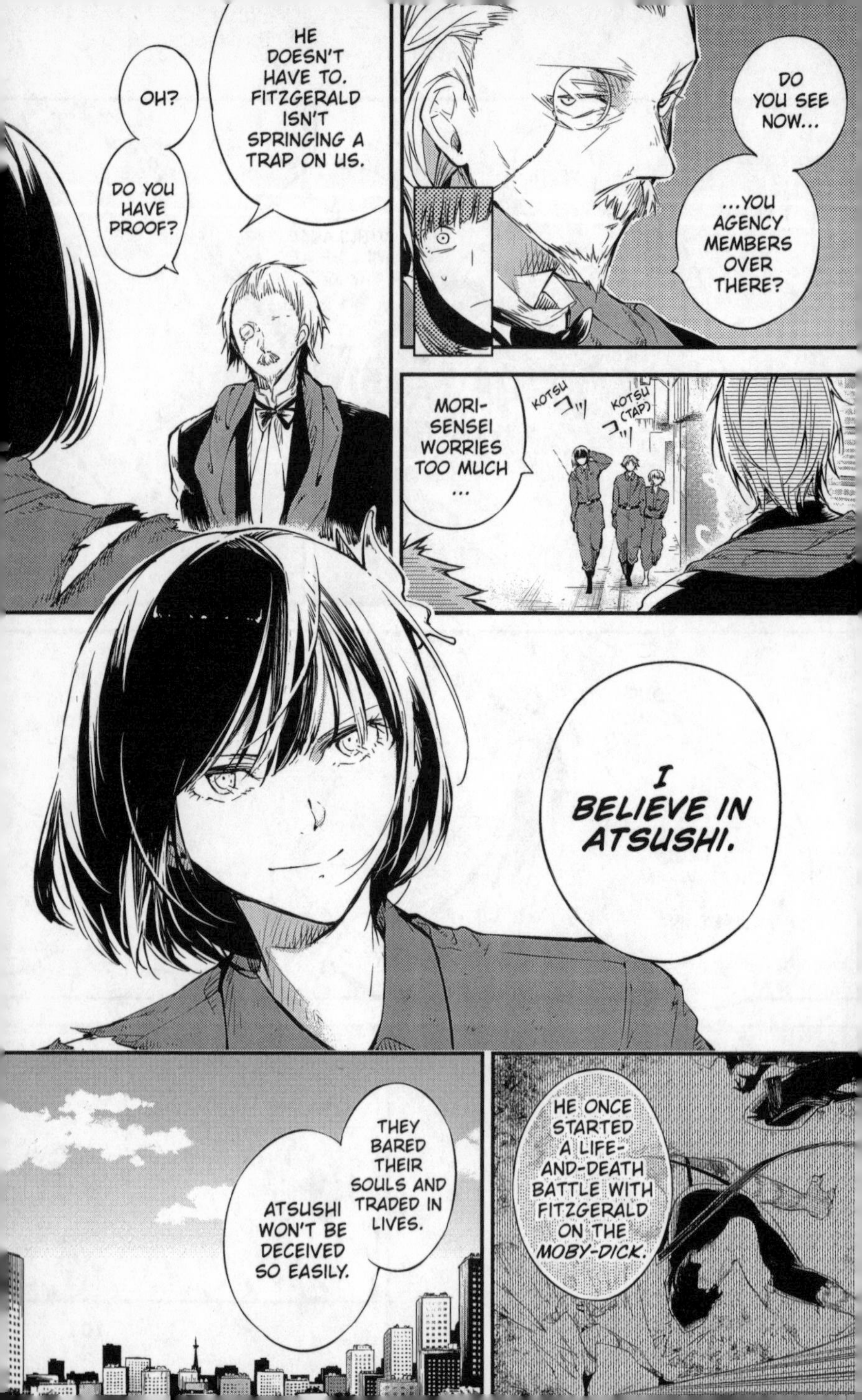
DO YOU SEE NOW...
...YOU AGENCY MEMBERS OVER THERE?
KOTSU
KOTSU (TAP)
MORI-SENSEI WORRIES TOO MUCH...
HE DOESN'T HAVE TO. FITZGERALD ISN'T SPRINGING A TRAP ON US.
OH?
DO YOU HAVE PROOF?
I BELIEVE IN ATSUSHI.
HE ONCE STARTED A LIFE-AND-DEATH BATTLE WITH FITZGERALD ON THE *MOBY-DICK*.
THEY BARED THEIR SOULS AND TRADED IN LIVES.
ATSUSHI WON'T BE DECEIVED SO EASILY.

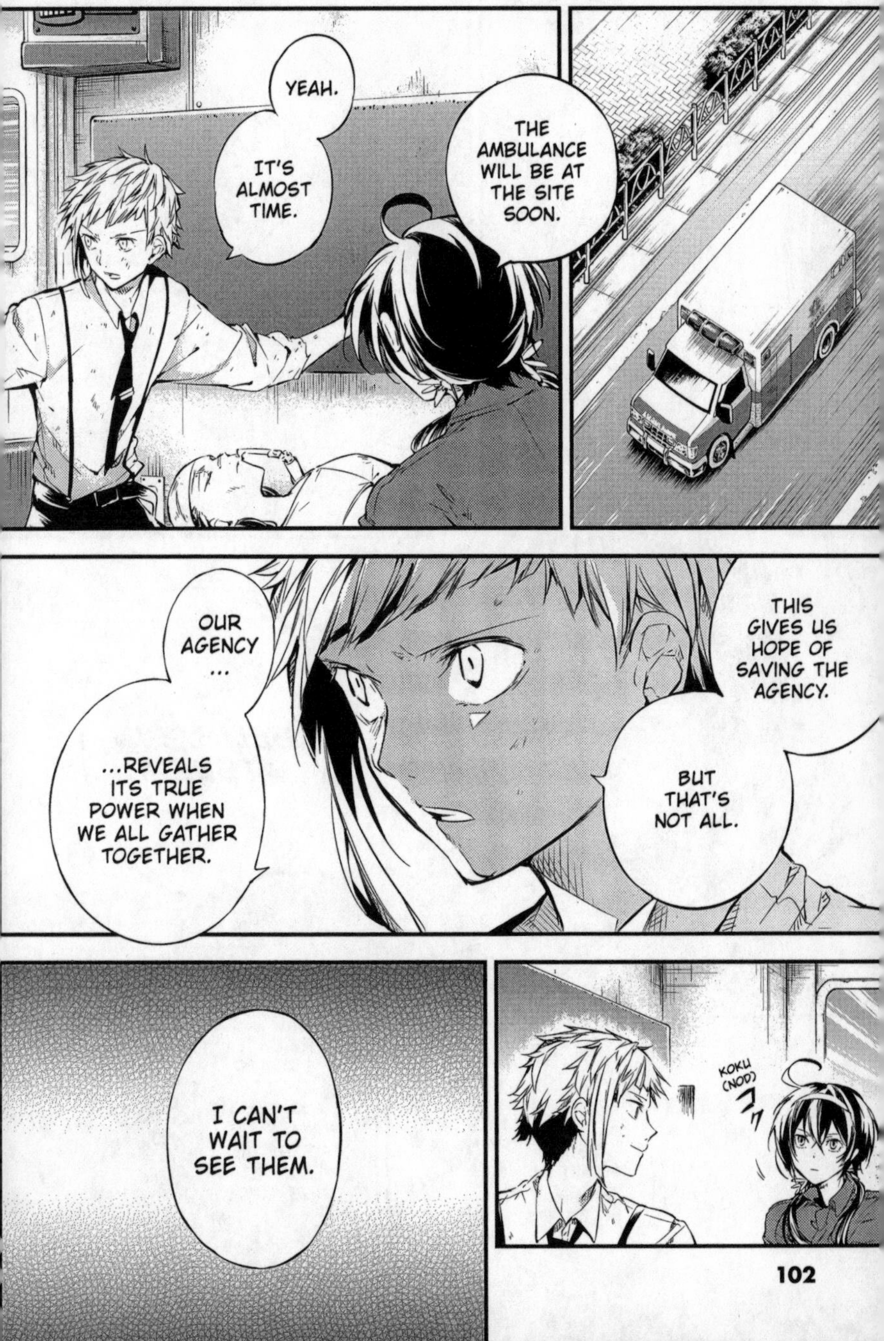
THE AMBULANCE WILL BE AT THE SITE SOON.
YEAH.
IT'S ALMOST TIME.
THIS GIVES US HOPE OF SAVING THE AGENCY.
BUT THAT'S NOT ALL.
OUR AGENCY...
...REVEALS ITS TRUE POWER WHEN WE ALL GATHER TOGETHER.
KOKU (NOD)
I CAN'T WAIT TO SEE THEM.

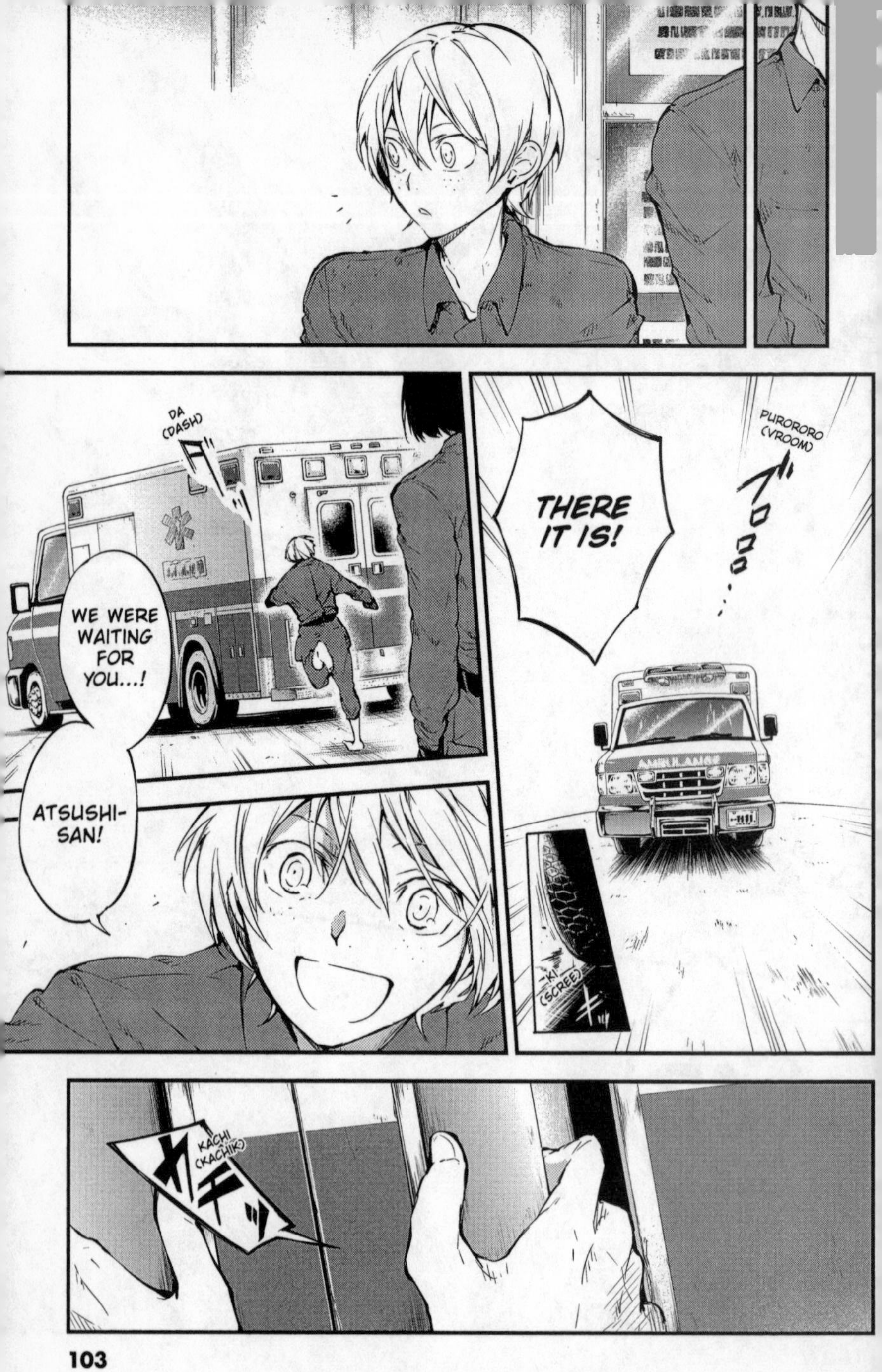
PURORORO (VROOM)
THERE IT IS!
KI (SCREE)
DA (DASH)
WE WERE WAITING FOR YOU...!
ATSUSHI-SAN!
KACHI (KACHIK)

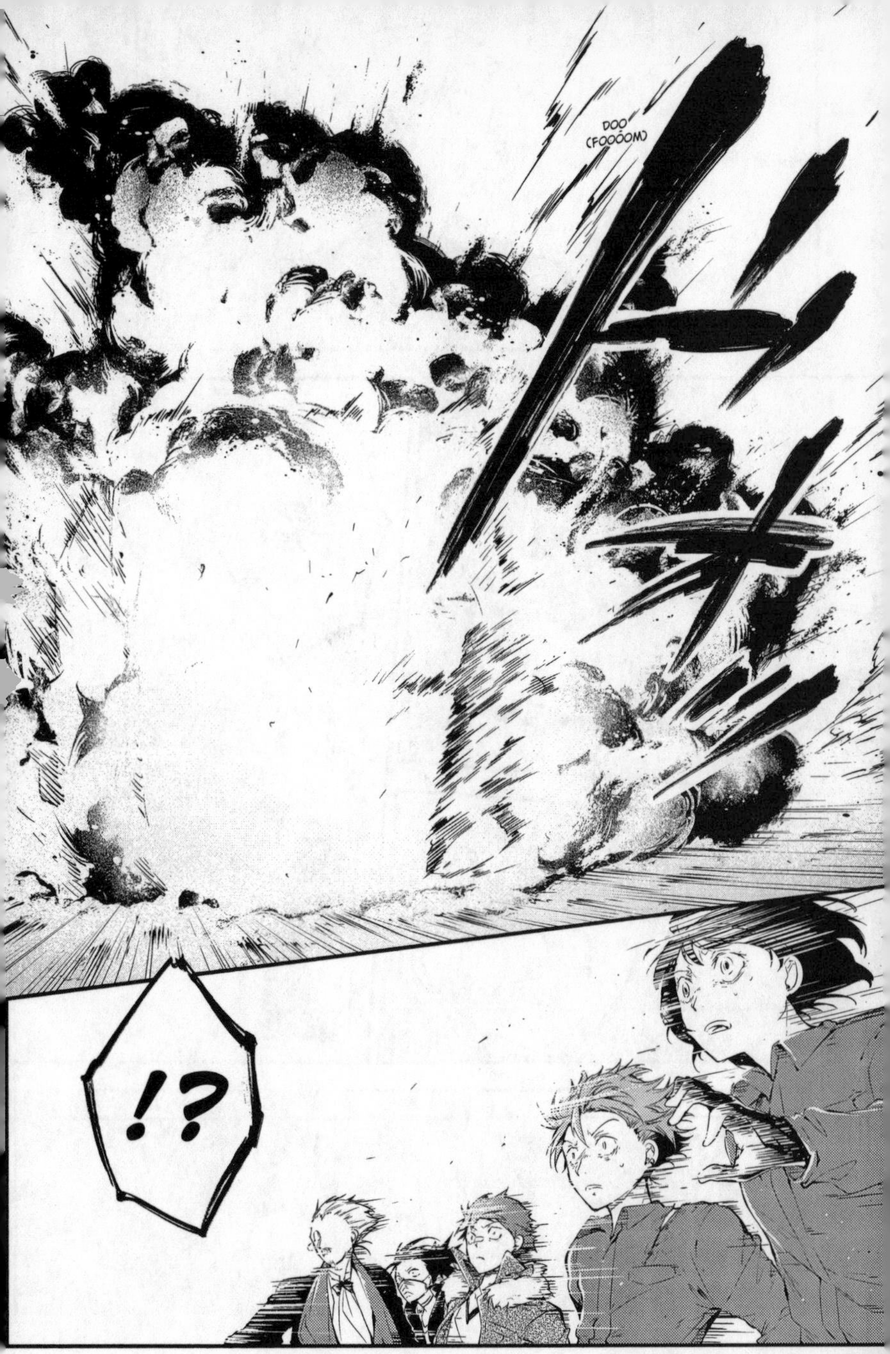
DOO
(FOOOOM)
!?

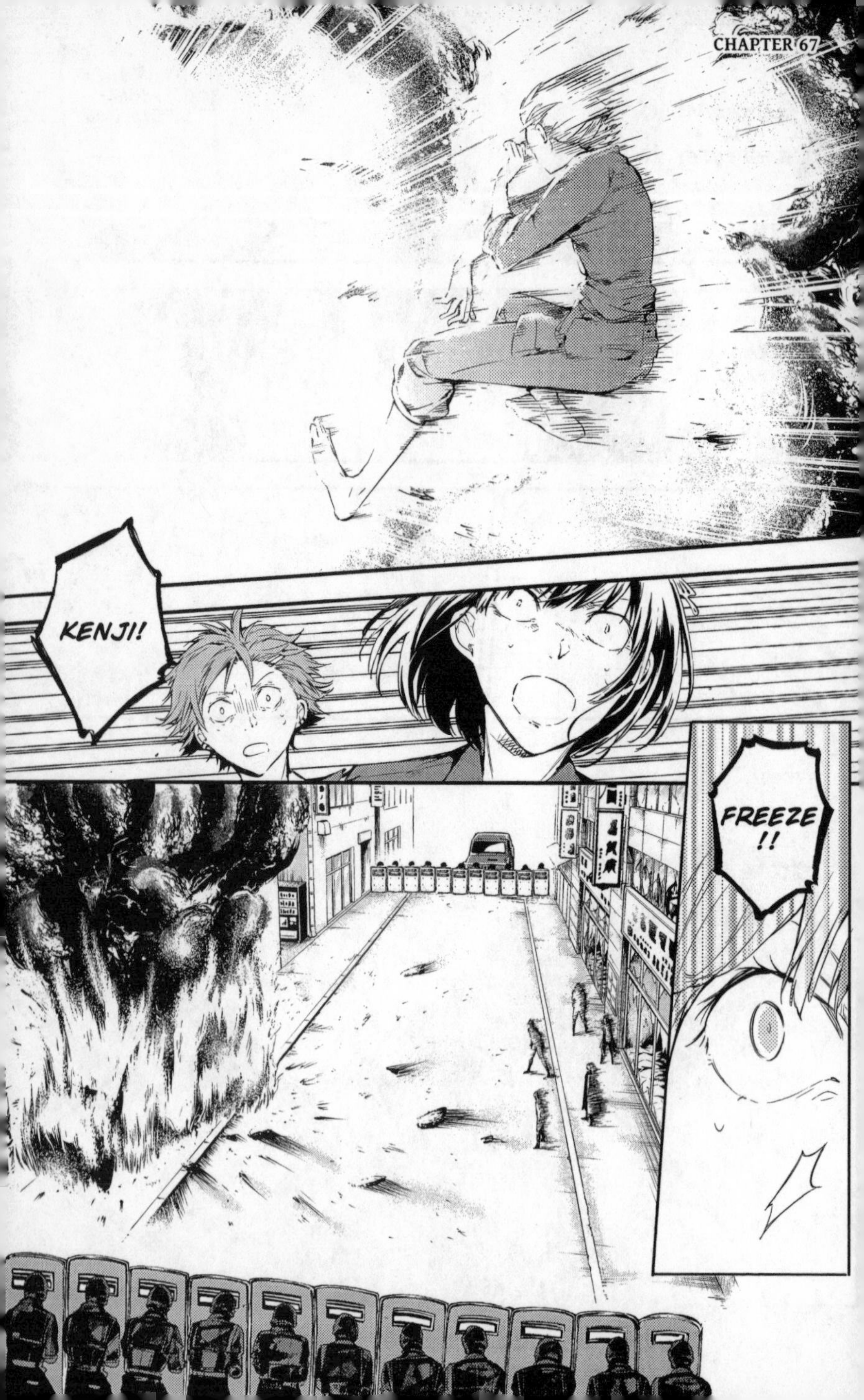
CHAPTER 67
KENJI!
FREEZE !!

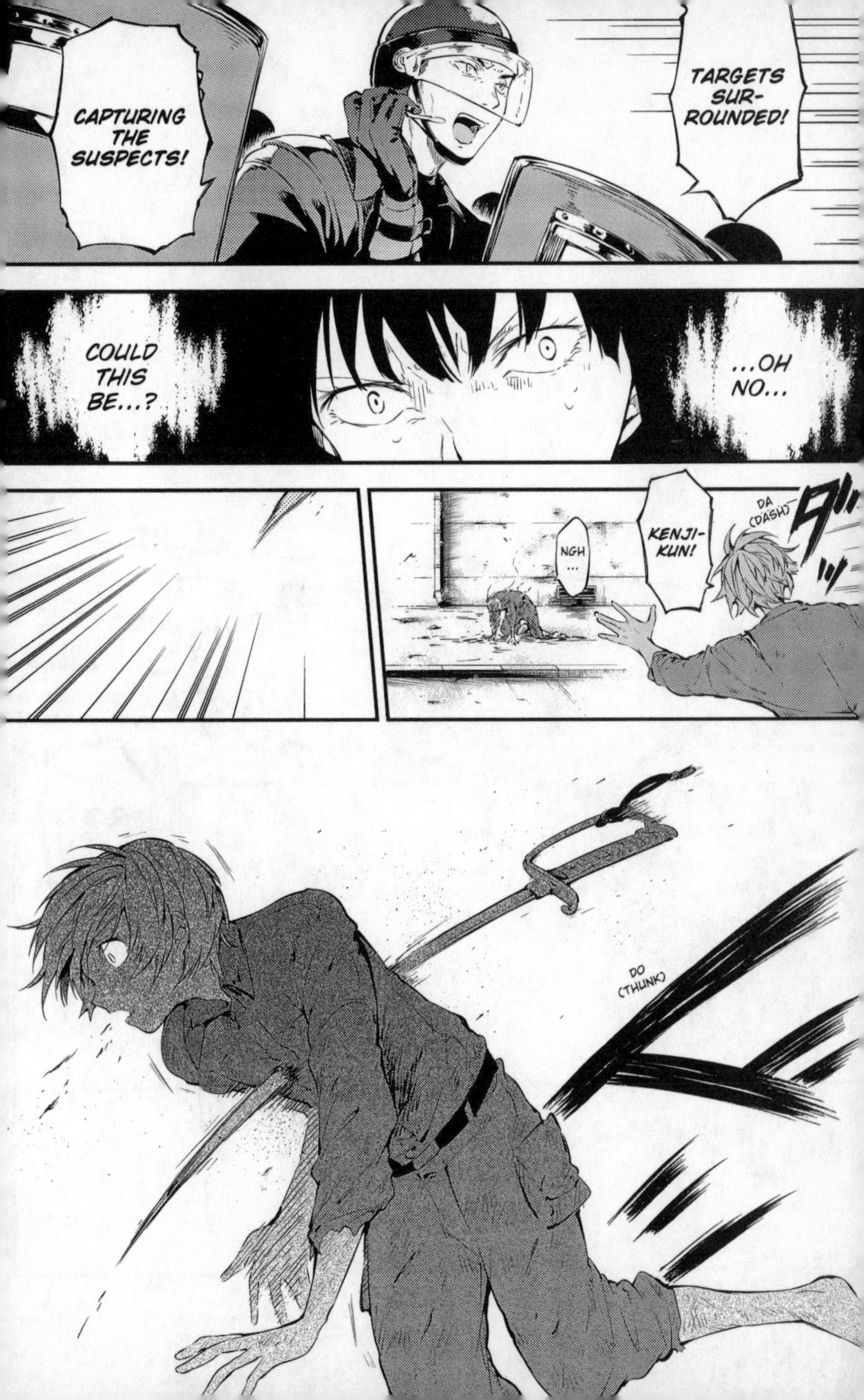
TARGETS SUR-ROUNDED!
CAPTURING THE SUSPECTS!
...OH NO...
COULD THIS BE...?
DA (DASH)
KENJI-KUN!
NGH...
DO (THUNK)

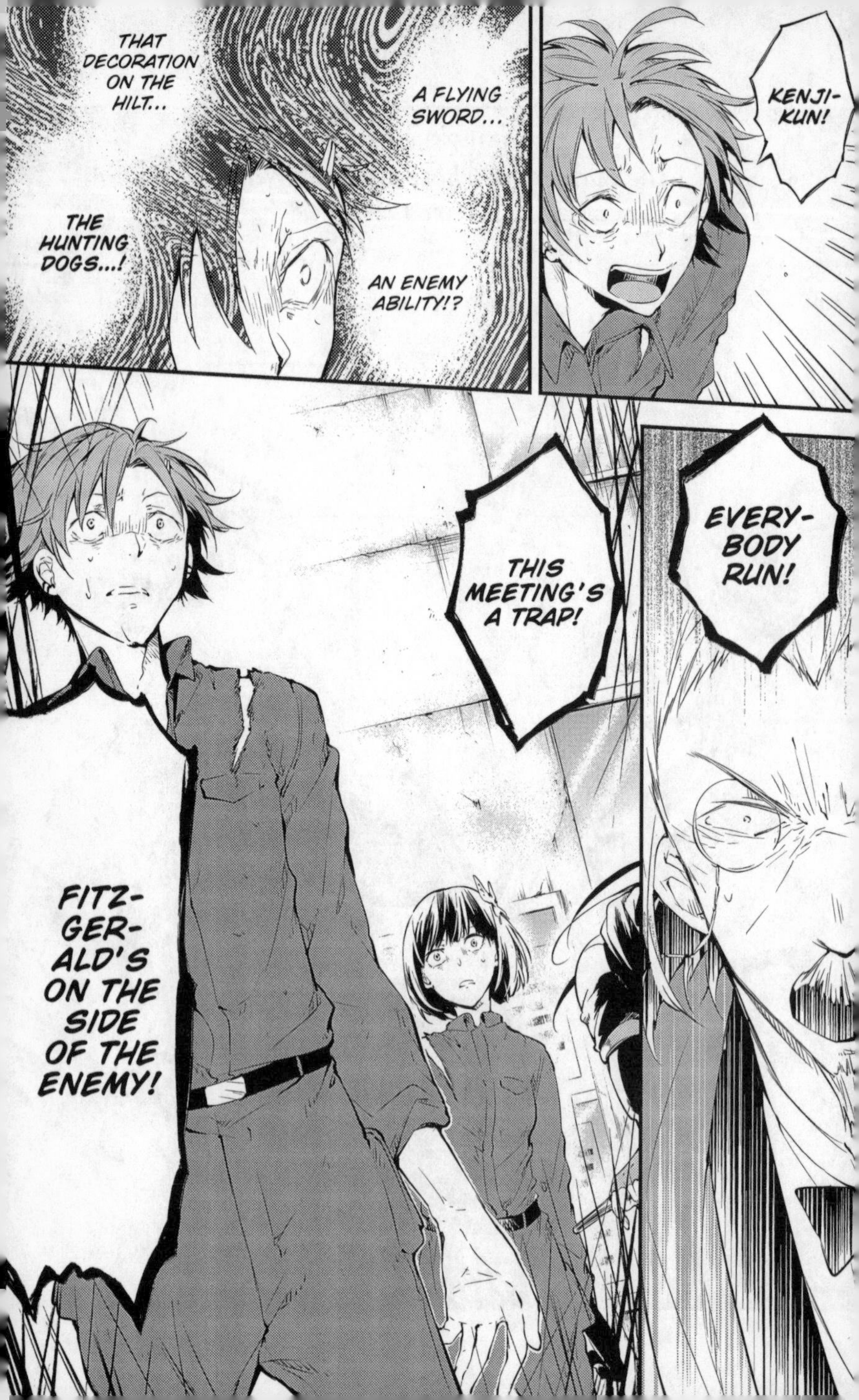
KENJI-KUN!
A FLYING SWORD...
AN ENEMY ABILITY!?
THAT DECORATION ON THE HILT...
THE HUNTING DOGS...!
EVERY-BODY RUN!
THIS MEETING'S A TRAP!
FITZ-GER-ALD'S ON THE SIDE OF THE ENEMY!

CHAPTER 67

The Sadness of Those Without Wings, Part 1

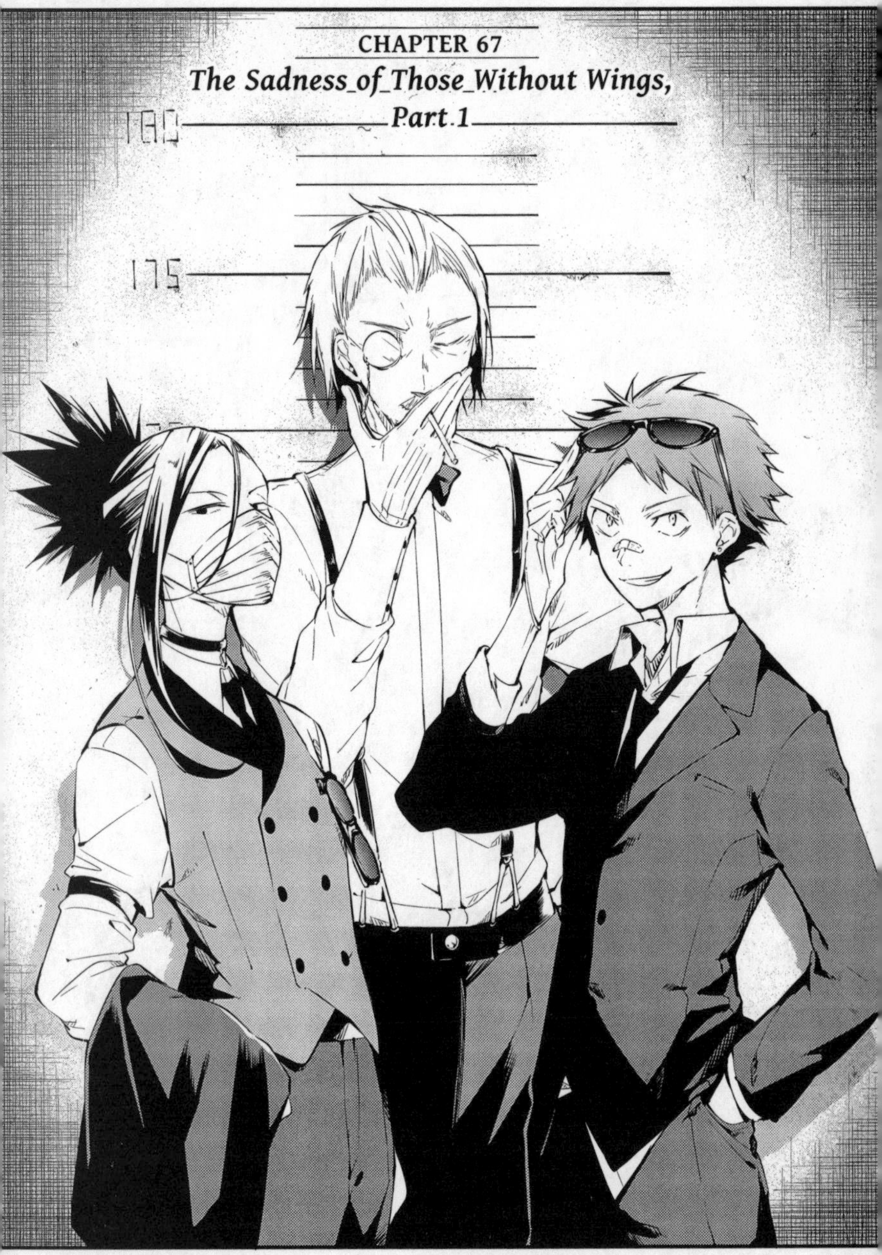
180
175

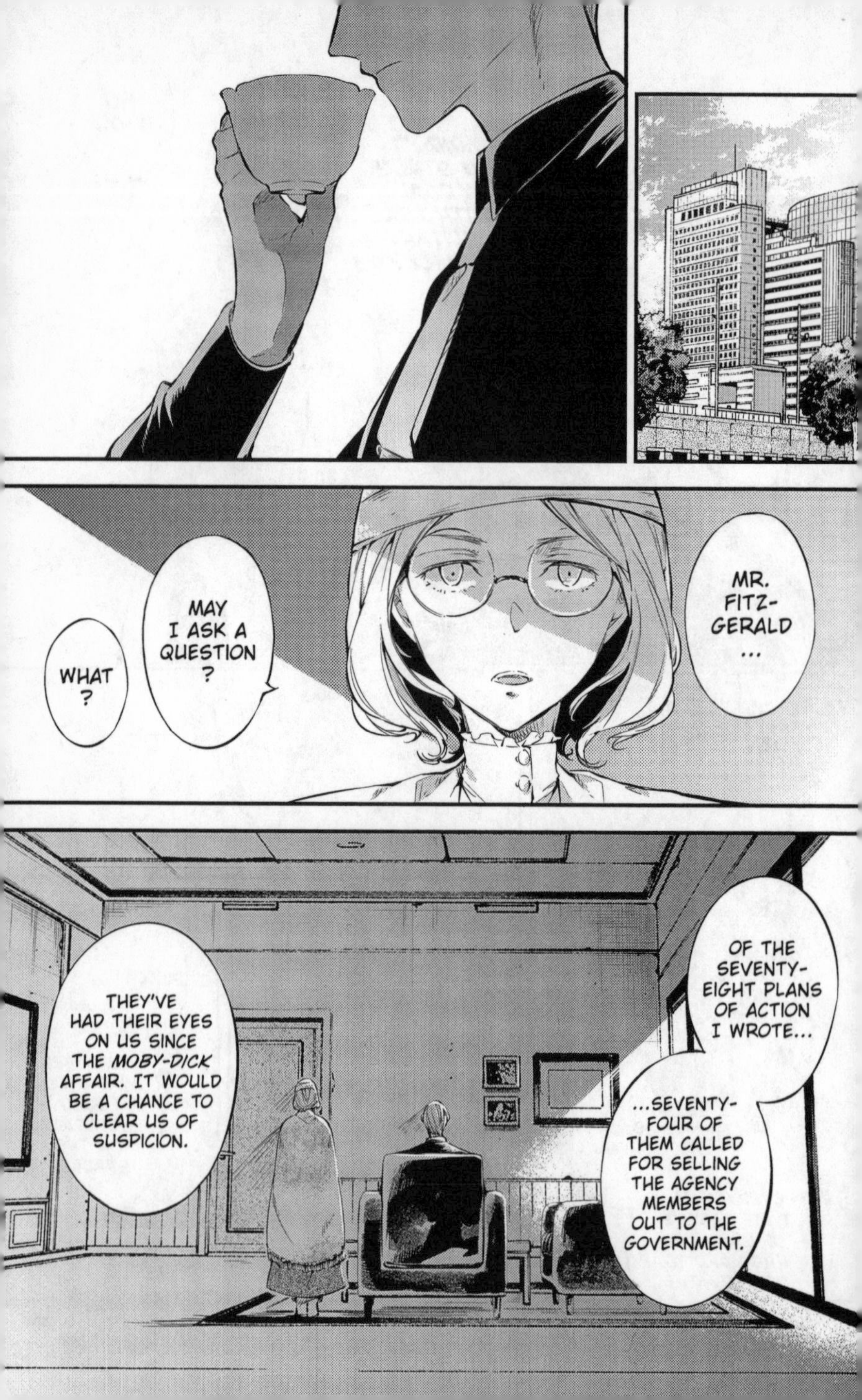
MR. FITZ-GERALD...
MAY I ASK A QUESTION?
WHAT?
OF THE SEVENTY-EIGHT PLANS OF ACTION I WROTE...
...SEVENTY-FOUR OF THEM CALLED FOR SELLING THE AGENCY MEMBERS OUT TO THE GOVERNMENT.
THEY'VE HAD THEIR EYES ON US SINCE THE *MOBY-DICK* AFFAIR. IT WOULD BE A CHANCE TO CLEAR US OF SUSPICION.

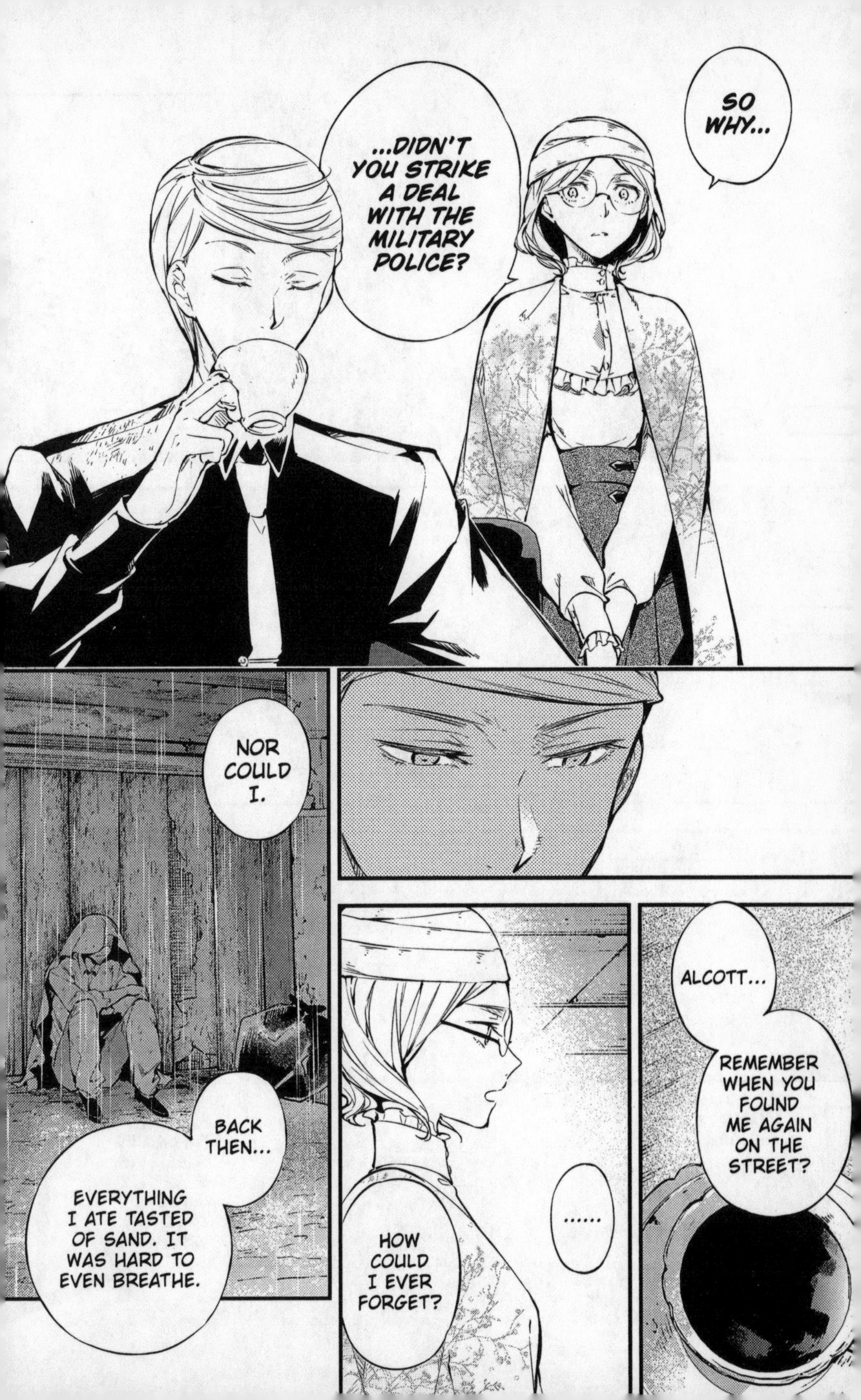
SO WHY...
...DIDN'T YOU STRIKE A DEAL WITH THE MILITARY POLICE?
ALCOTT...
REMEMBER WHEN YOU FOUND ME AGAIN ON THE STREET?
......
HOW COULD I EVER FORGET?
NOR COULD I.
BACK THEN...
EVERYTHING I ATE TASTED OF SAND. IT WAS HARD TO EVEN BREATHE.

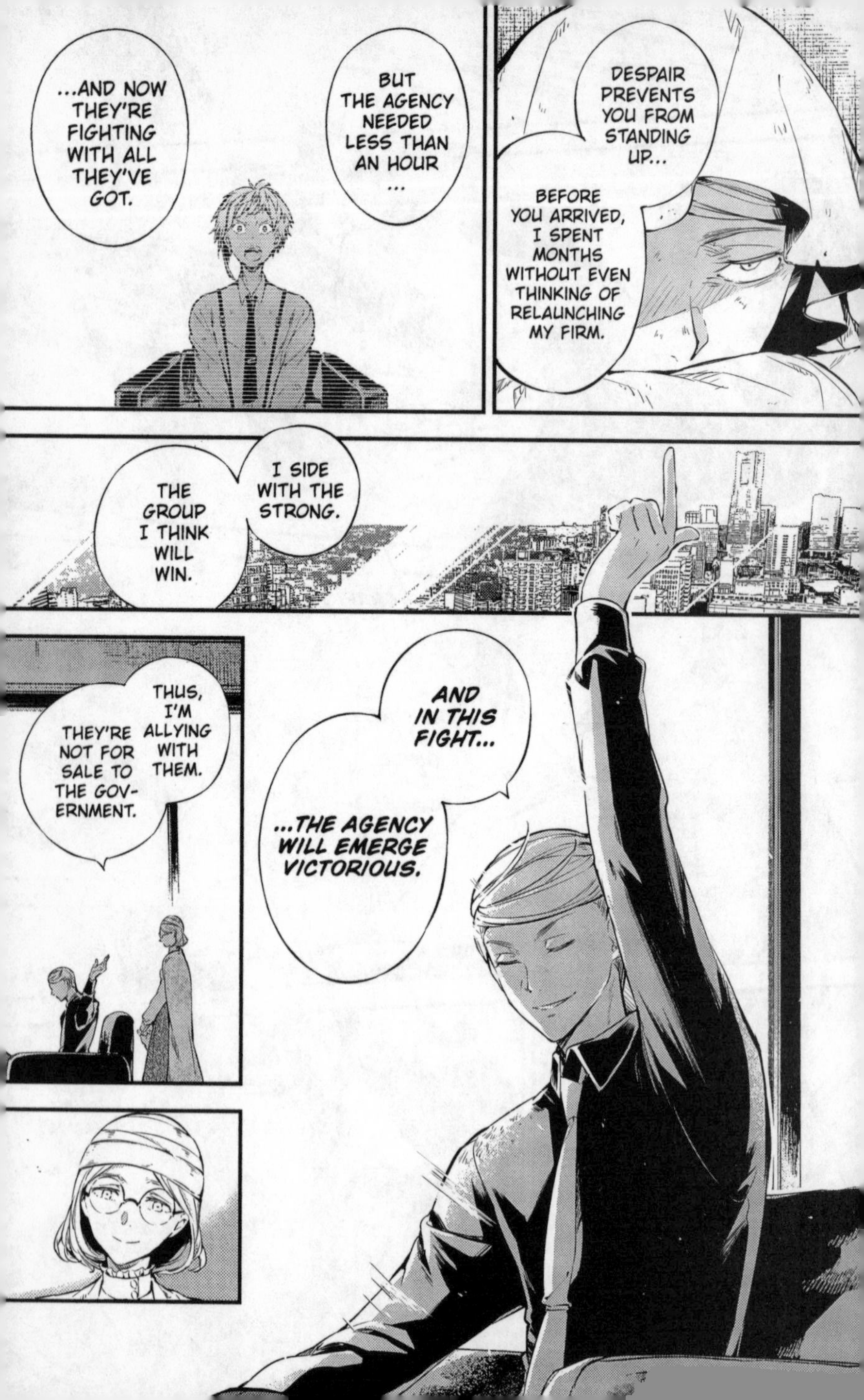
DESPAIR PREVENTS YOU FROM STANDING UP...
BEFORE YOU ARRIVED, I SPENT MONTHS WITHOUT EVEN THINKING OF RELAUNCHING MY FIRM.
BUT THE AGENCY NEEDED LESS THAN AN HOUR ...
...AND NOW THEY'RE FIGHTING WITH ALL THEY'VE GOT.
I SIDE WITH THE STRONG.
THE GROUP I THINK WILL WIN.
AND IN THIS FIGHT...
...THE AGENCY WILL EMERGE VICTORIOUS.
THUS, I'M ALLYING WITH THEM.
THEY'RE NOT FOR SALE TO THE GOV-ERNMENT.

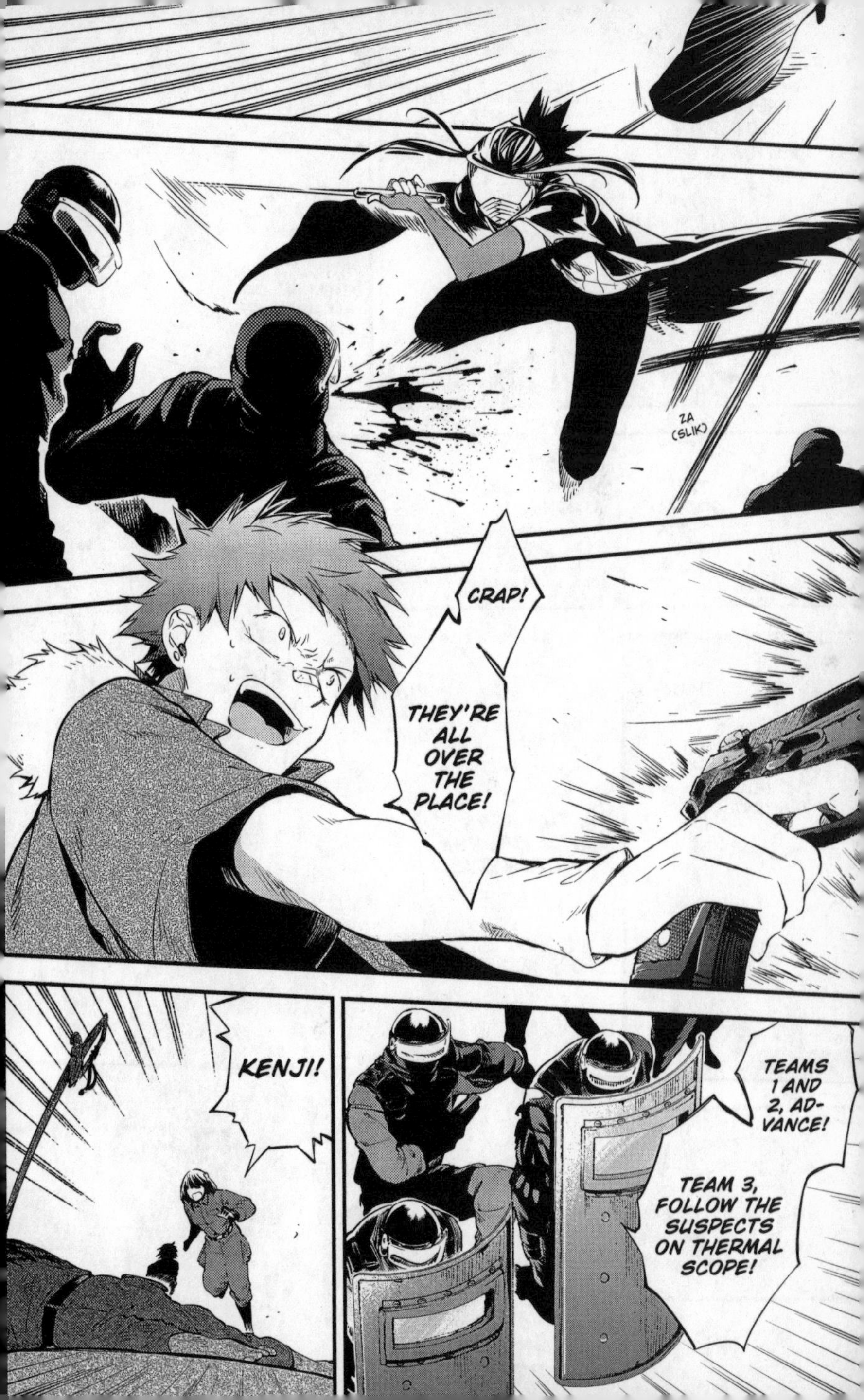
ZA
(SLIK)
CRAP!
THEY'RE ALL OVER THE PLACE!
TEAMS 1 AND 2, AD-VANCE!
TEAM 3, FOLLOW THE SUSPECTS ON THERMAL SCOPE!
KENJI!

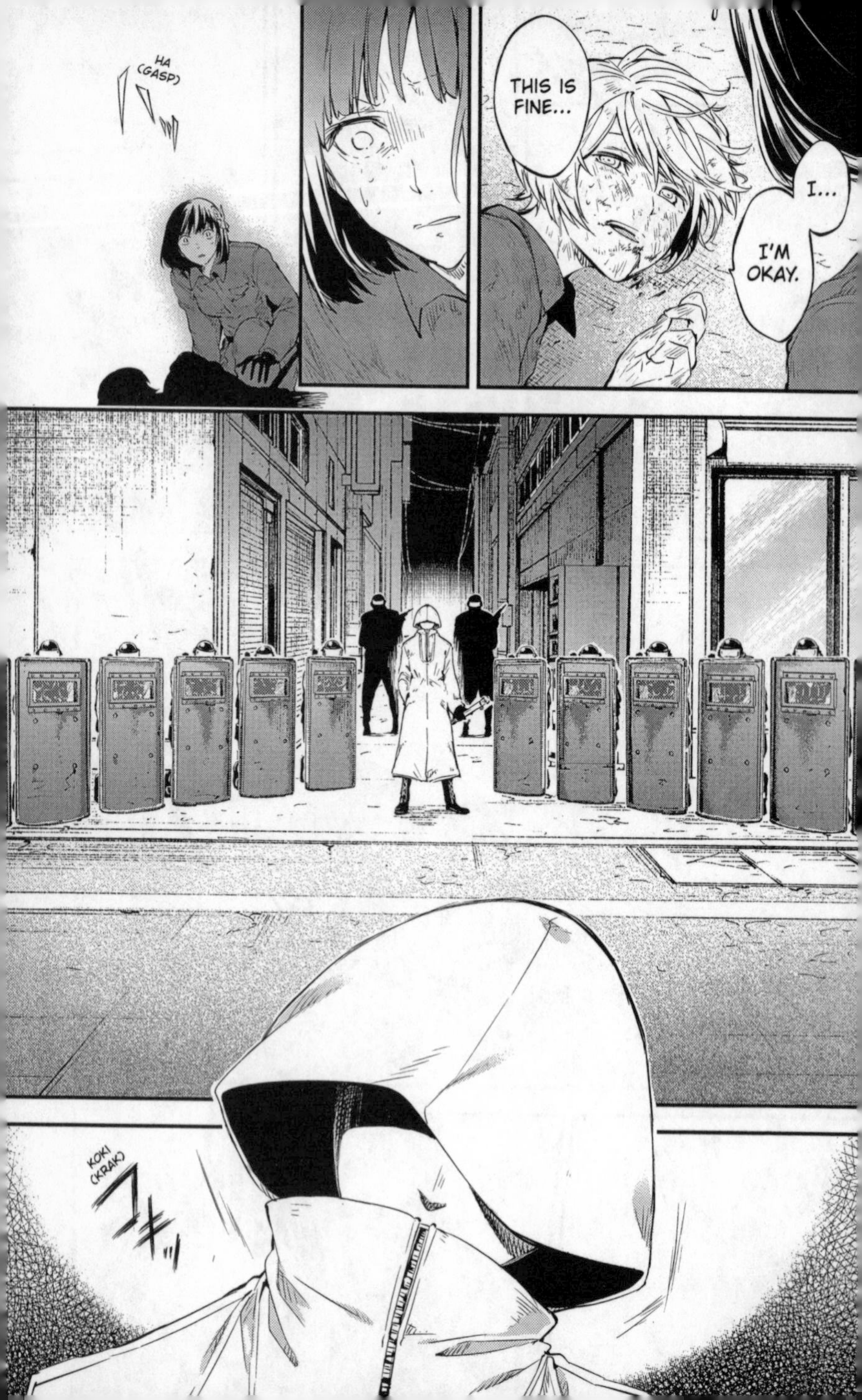
THIS IS FINE...
I...
I'M OKAY.
HA (GASP)
KOKI (KRAK)

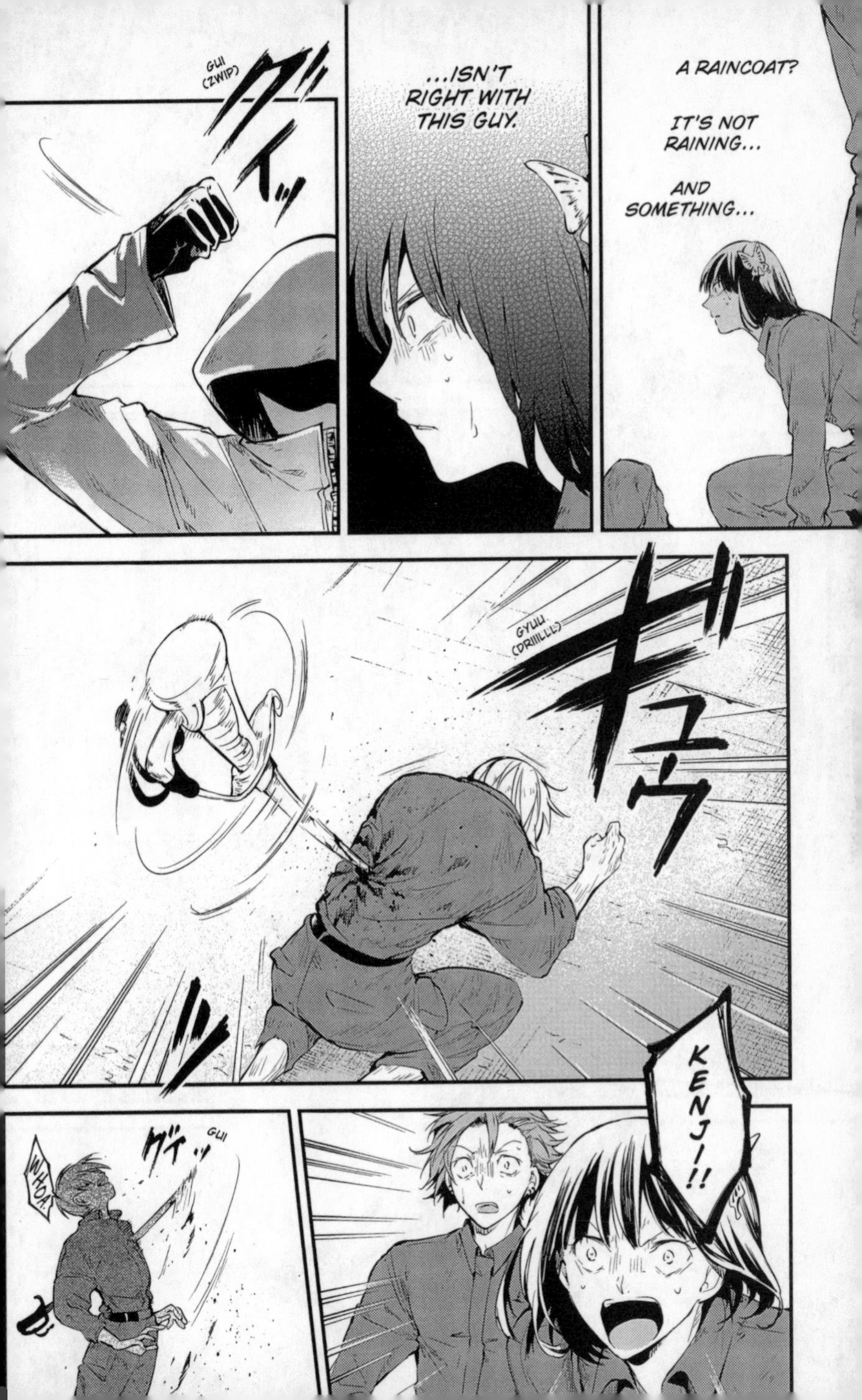
A RAINCOAT?
IT'S NOT RAINING...
AND SOMETHING...
...ISN'T RIGHT WITH THIS GUY.
GUI (ZWIP)
GYUU (DRIIIILLL)
KENJI!!
GUI
WHOA!

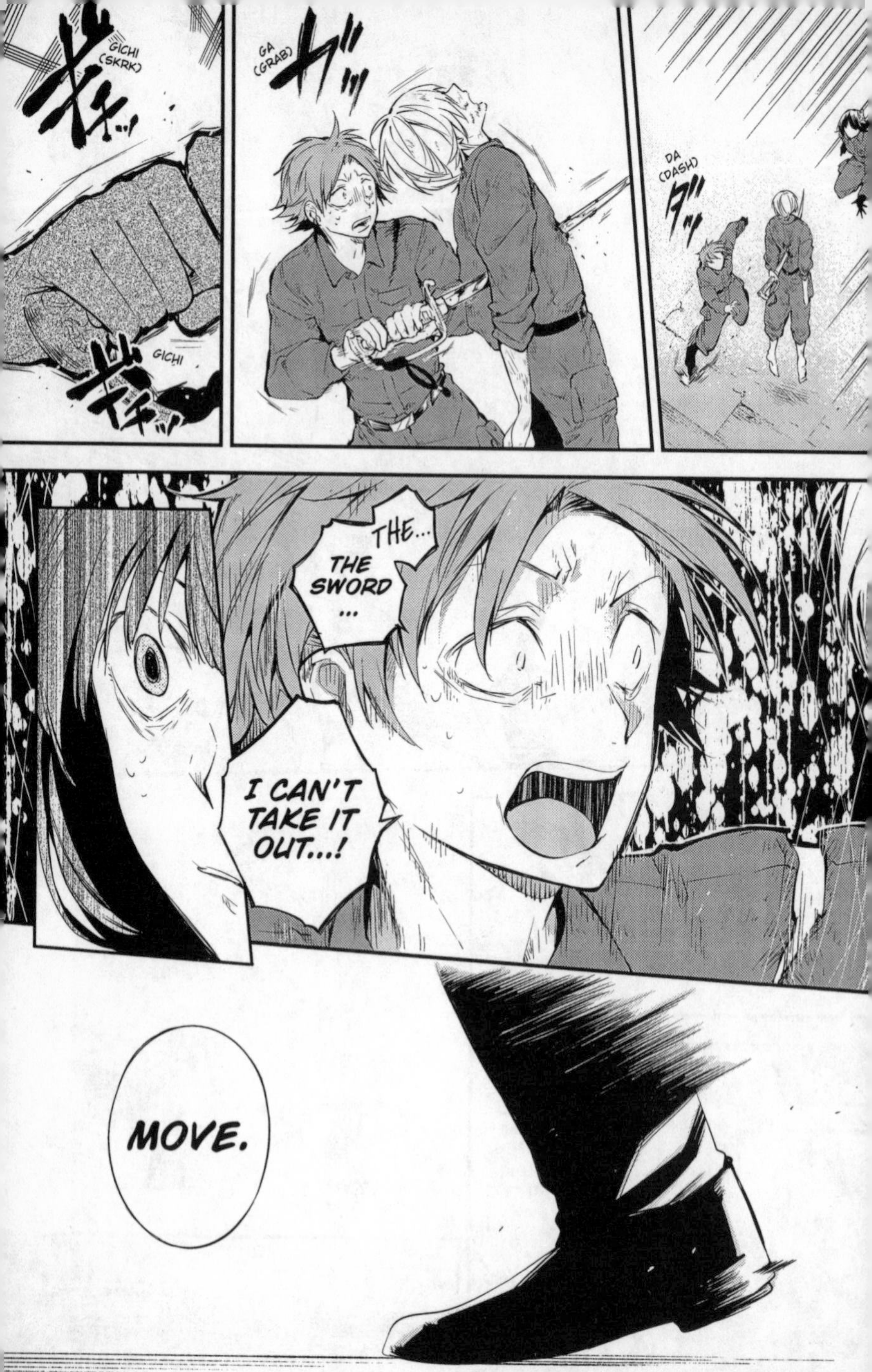
DA (DASH)
GA (GRAB)
GICHI (SKRK)
GICHI
THE... THE SWORD...
I CAN'T TAKE IT OUT...!
MOVE.

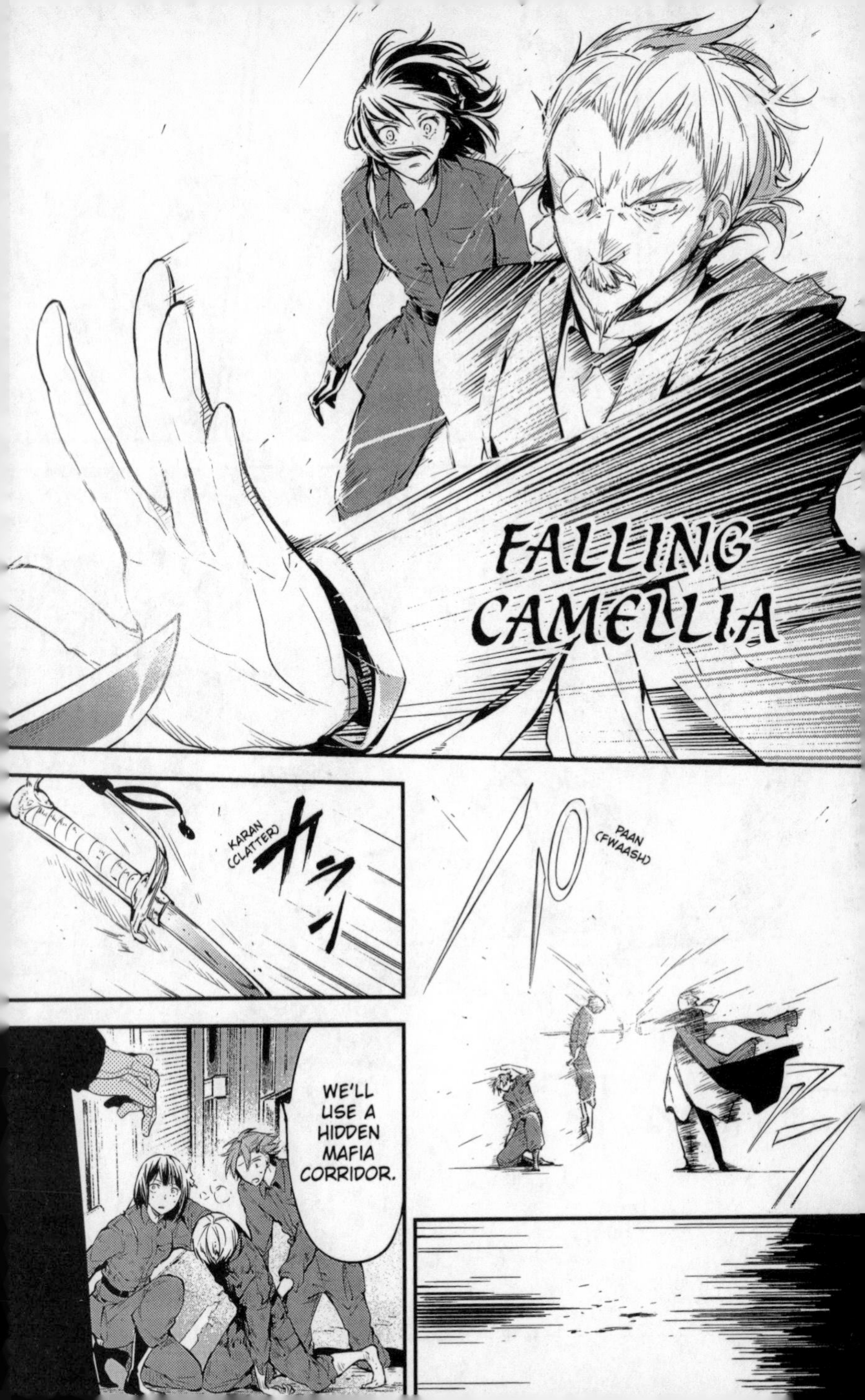
FALLING CAMELLIA
PAAN (FWAASH)
KARAN (CLATTER)
WE'LL USE A HIDDEN MAFIA CORRIDOR.

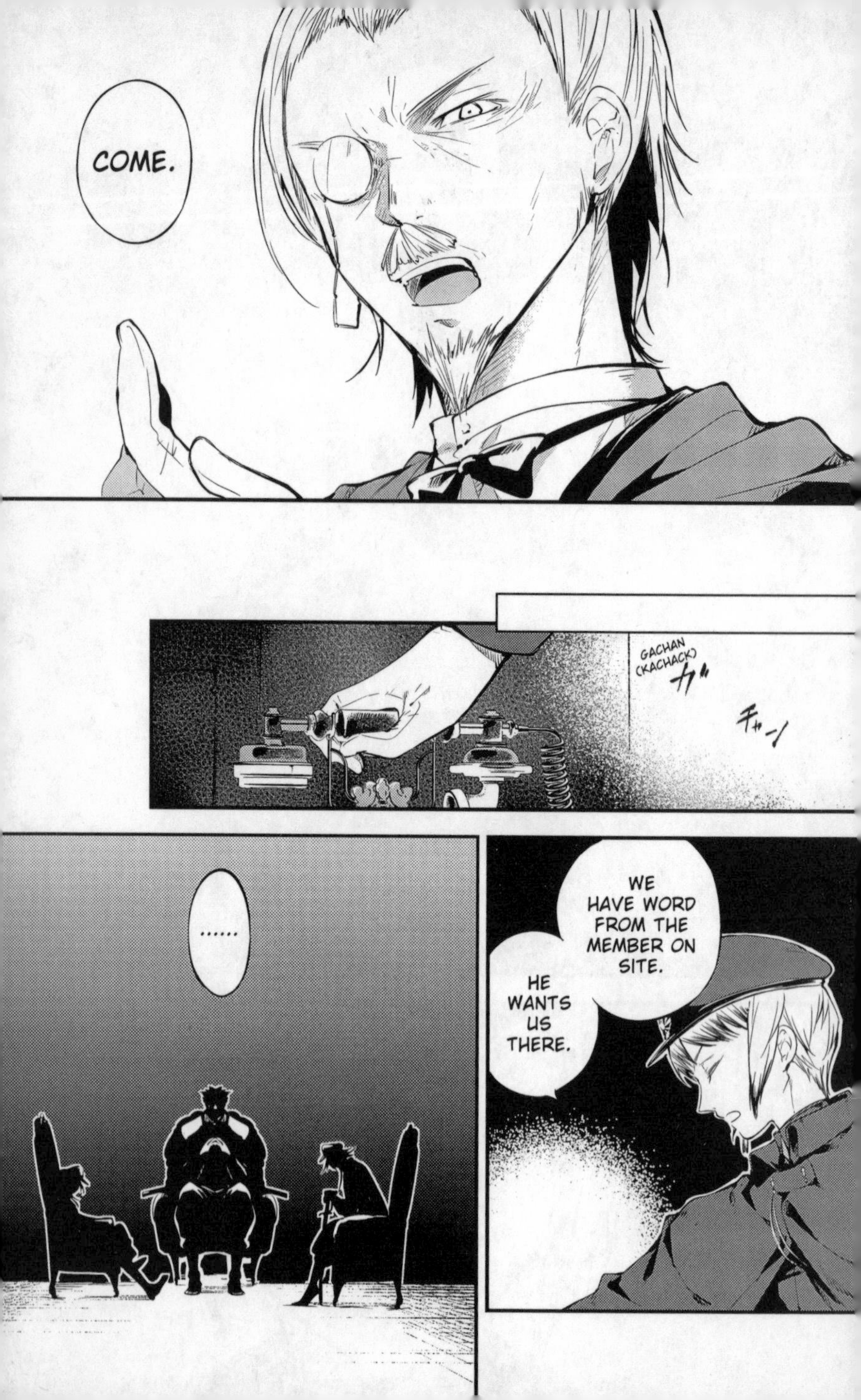
COME.
GACHAN (KACHACK)
ガチャン
WE HAVE WORD FROM THE MEMBER ON SITE.
HE WANTS US THERE.
......

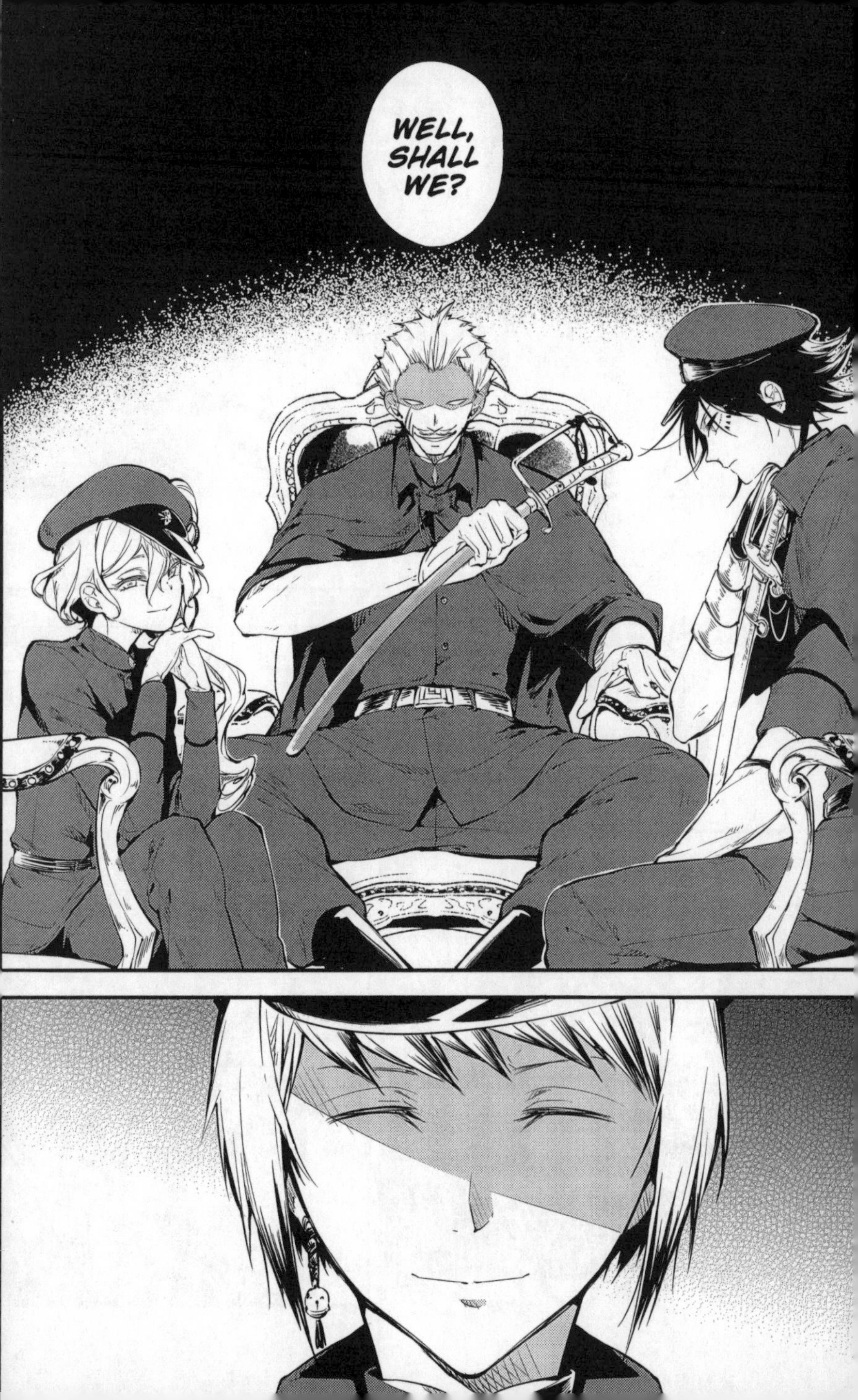
WELL, SHALL WE?

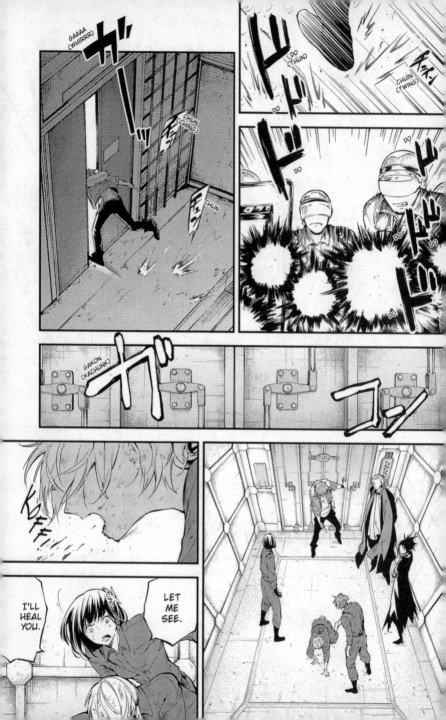

GAAAA
(WHIRRR)

ガ

CHUN
(CHING)

チュン

チュン

ビ
DO

DO
(THUN)

ビ

チュン
CHUN
(TWING)

ド
DO

DO

DO

ビ
DO

ビ
DO

ビ

ビ

DO

GAKON
(KACHUNK)

ガ

コン

KOFF!

LET
ME
SEE.

I'LL
HEAL
YOU.

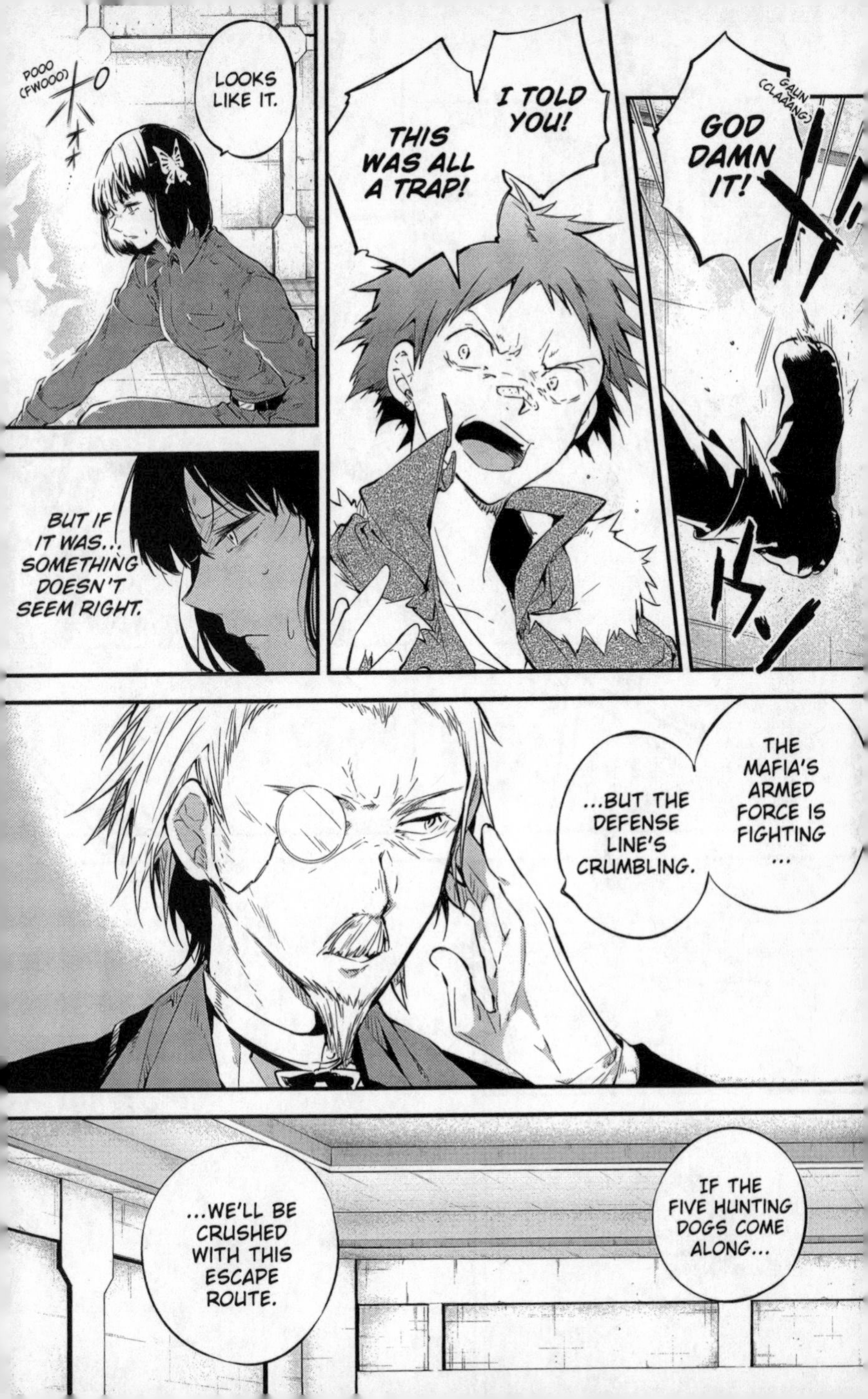
GAUN (CLAAANG)
GOD DAMN IT!
I TOLD YOU!
THIS WAS ALL A TRAP!
POOO (FWOOO)
LOOKS LIKE IT.
BUT IF IT WAS... SOMETHING DOESN'T SEEM RIGHT.
THE MAFIA'S ARMED FORCE IS FIGHTING...
...BUT THE DEFENSE LINE'S CRUMBLING.
IF THE FIVE HUNTING DOGS COME ALONG...
...WE'LL BE CRUSHED WITH THIS ESCAPE ROUTE.

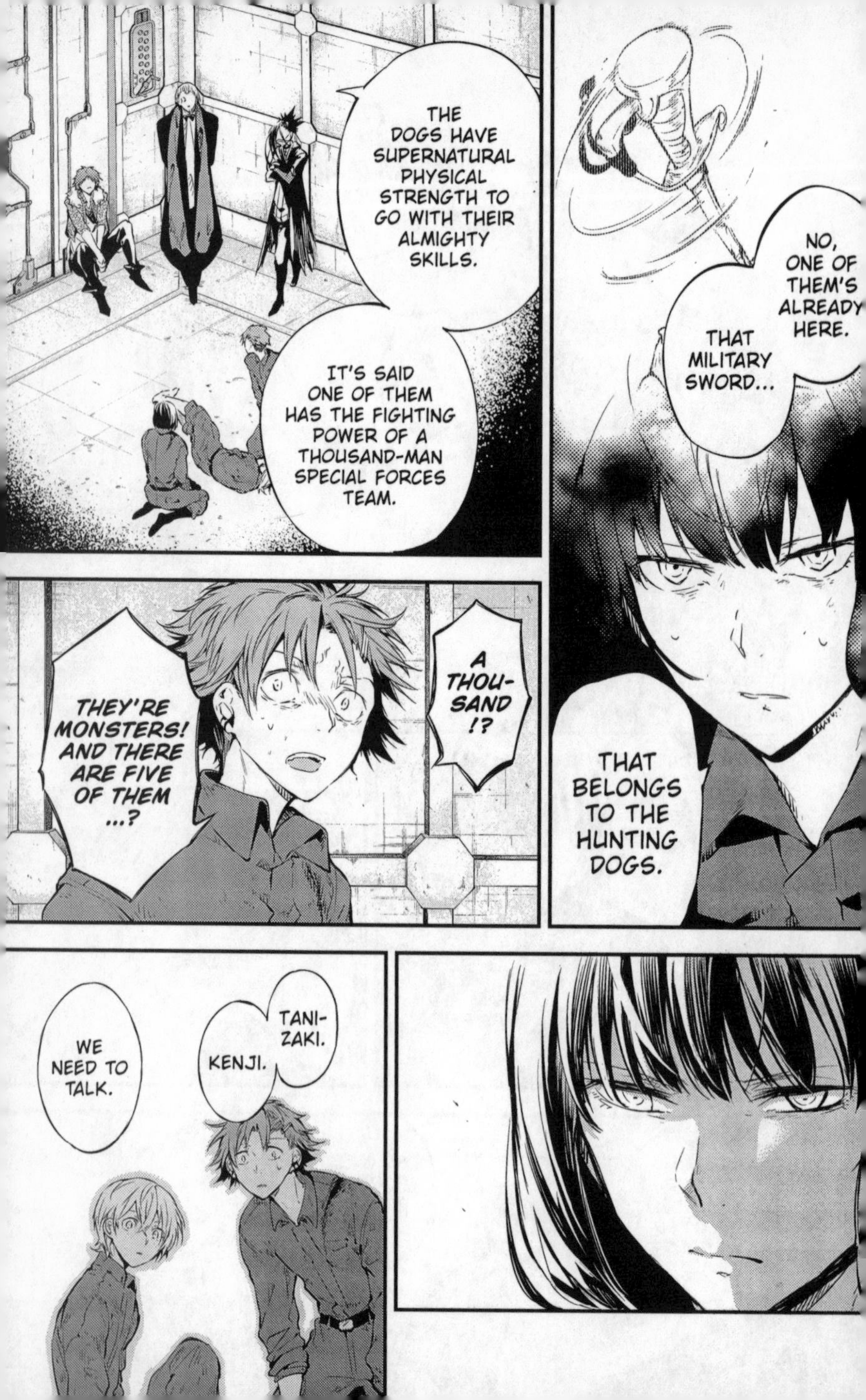
NO, ONE OF THEM'S ALREADY HERE.
THAT MILITARY SWORD...
THAT BELONGS TO THE HUNTING DOGS.
THE DOGS HAVE SUPERNATURAL PHYSICAL STRENGTH TO GO WITH THEIR ALMIGHTY SKILLS.
IT'S SAID ONE OF THEM HAS THE FIGHTING POWER OF A THOUSAND-MAN SPECIAL FORCES TEAM.
A THOU-SAND!?
THEY'RE MONSTERS! AND THERE ARE FIVE OF THEM ...?
TANI-ZAKI.
KENJI.
WE NEED TO TALK.

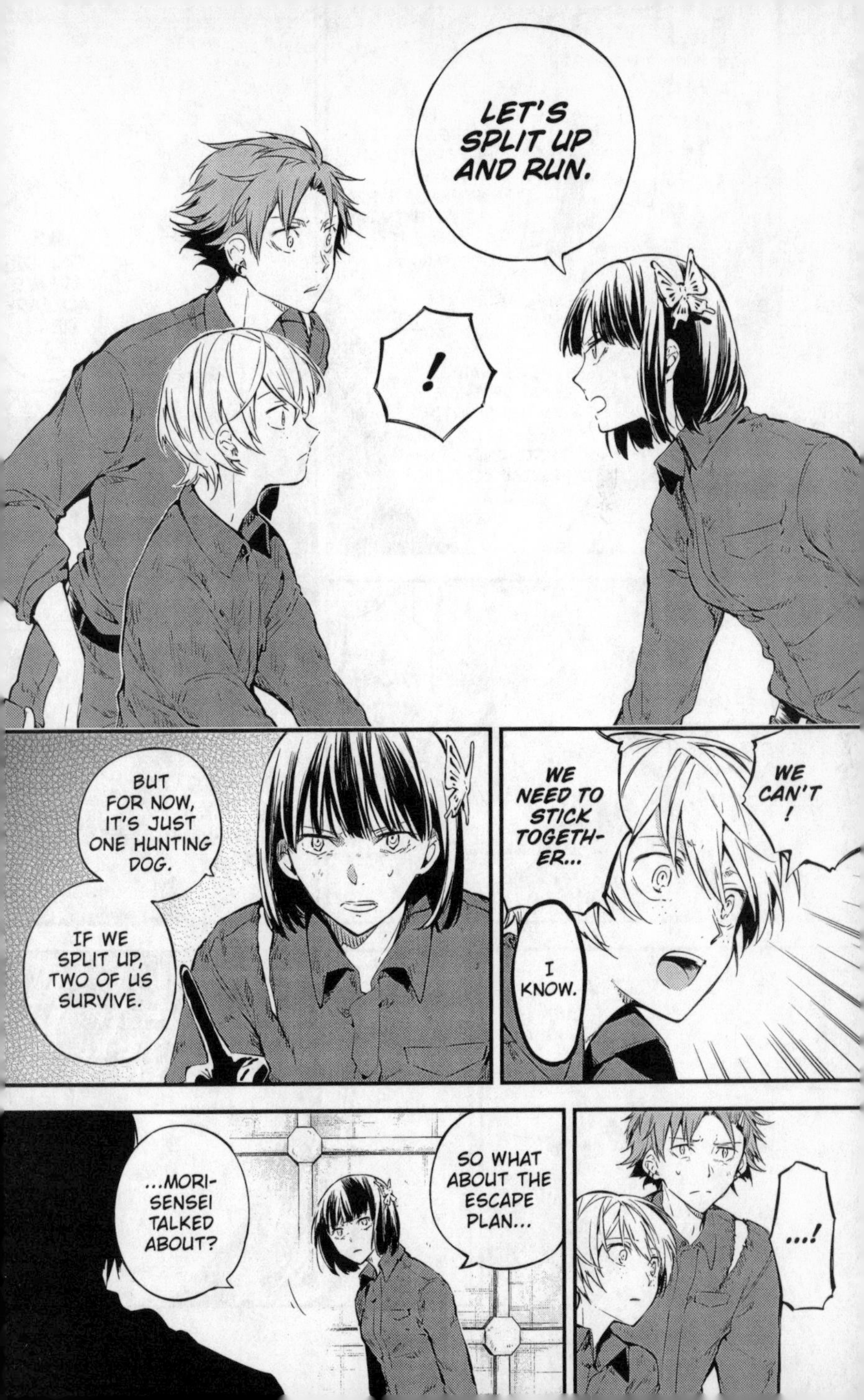
LET'S SPLIT UP AND RUN.
!
WE CAN'T!
WE NEED TO STICK TOGETHER...
I KNOW.
BUT FOR NOW, IT'S JUST ONE HUNTING DOG.
IF WE SPLIT UP, TWO OF US SURVIVE.
...!
SO WHAT ABOUT THE ESCAPE PLAN...
...MORI-SENSEI TALKED ABOUT?

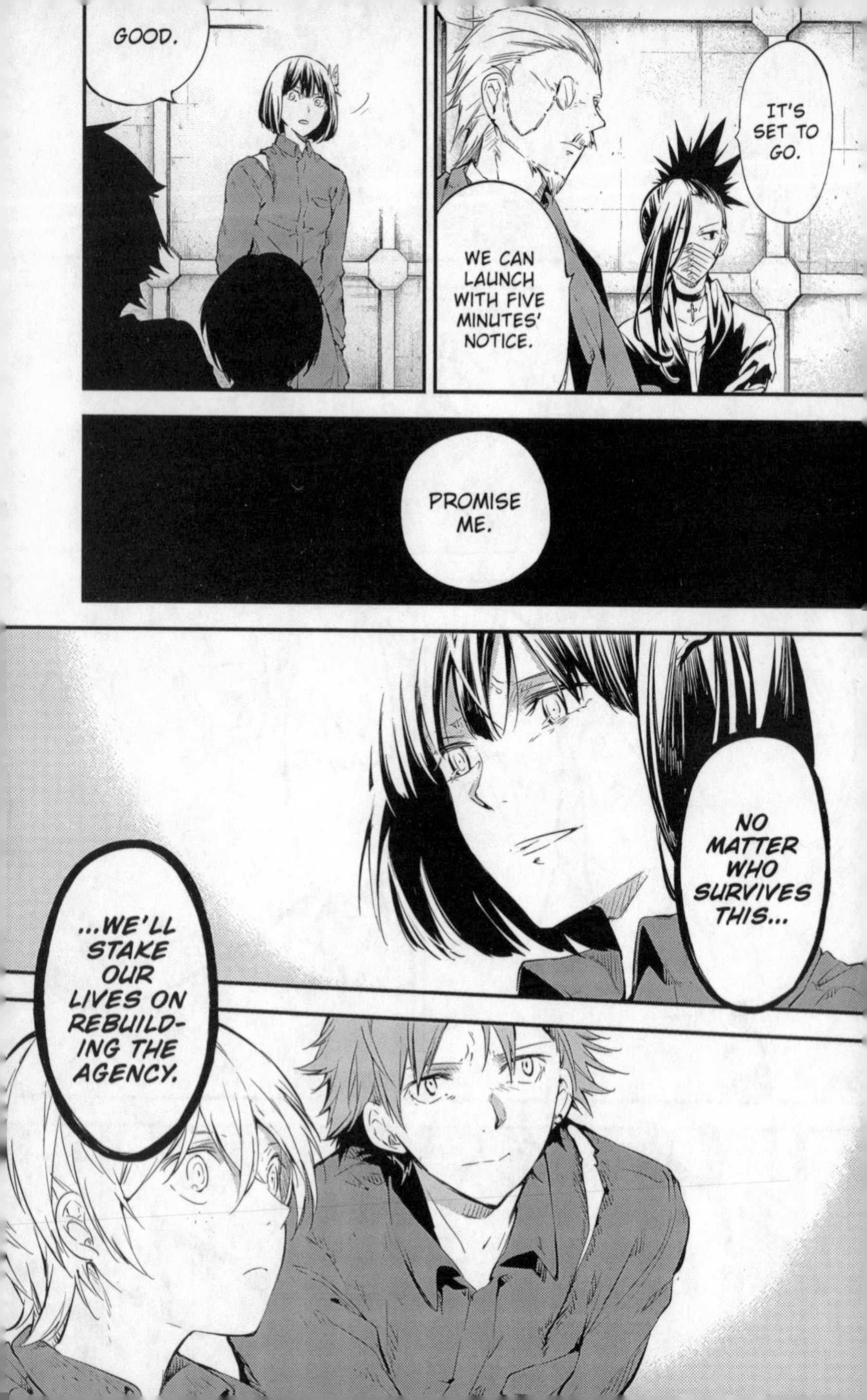
IT'S SET TO GO.
WE CAN LAUNCH WITH FIVE MINUTES' NOTICE.
GOOD.
PROMISE ME.
NO MATTER WHO SURVIVES THIS...
...WE'LL STAKE OUR LIVES ON REBUILD-ING THE AGENCY.

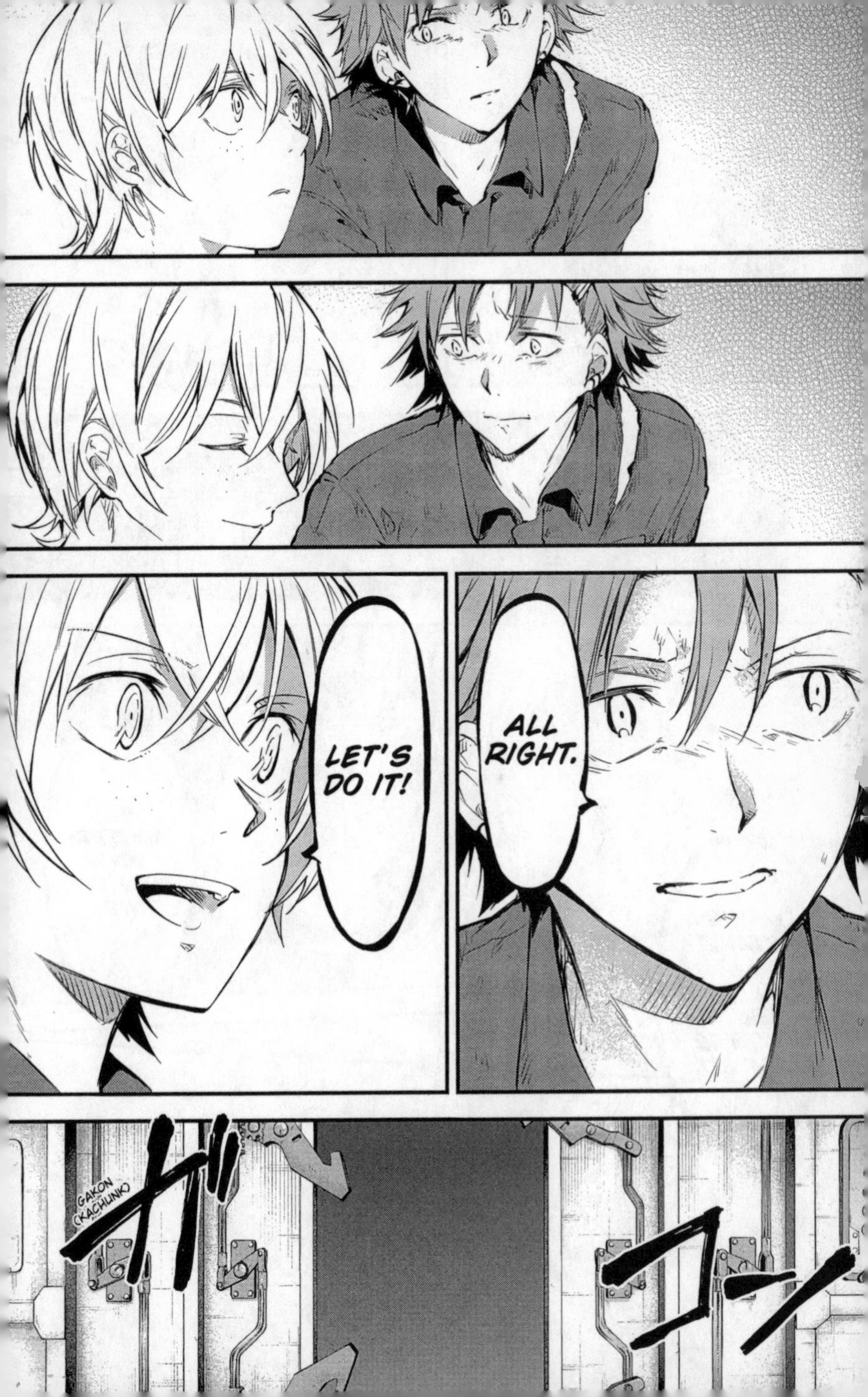
ALL RIGHT.
LET'S DO IT!
GAKON (KACHUNK)

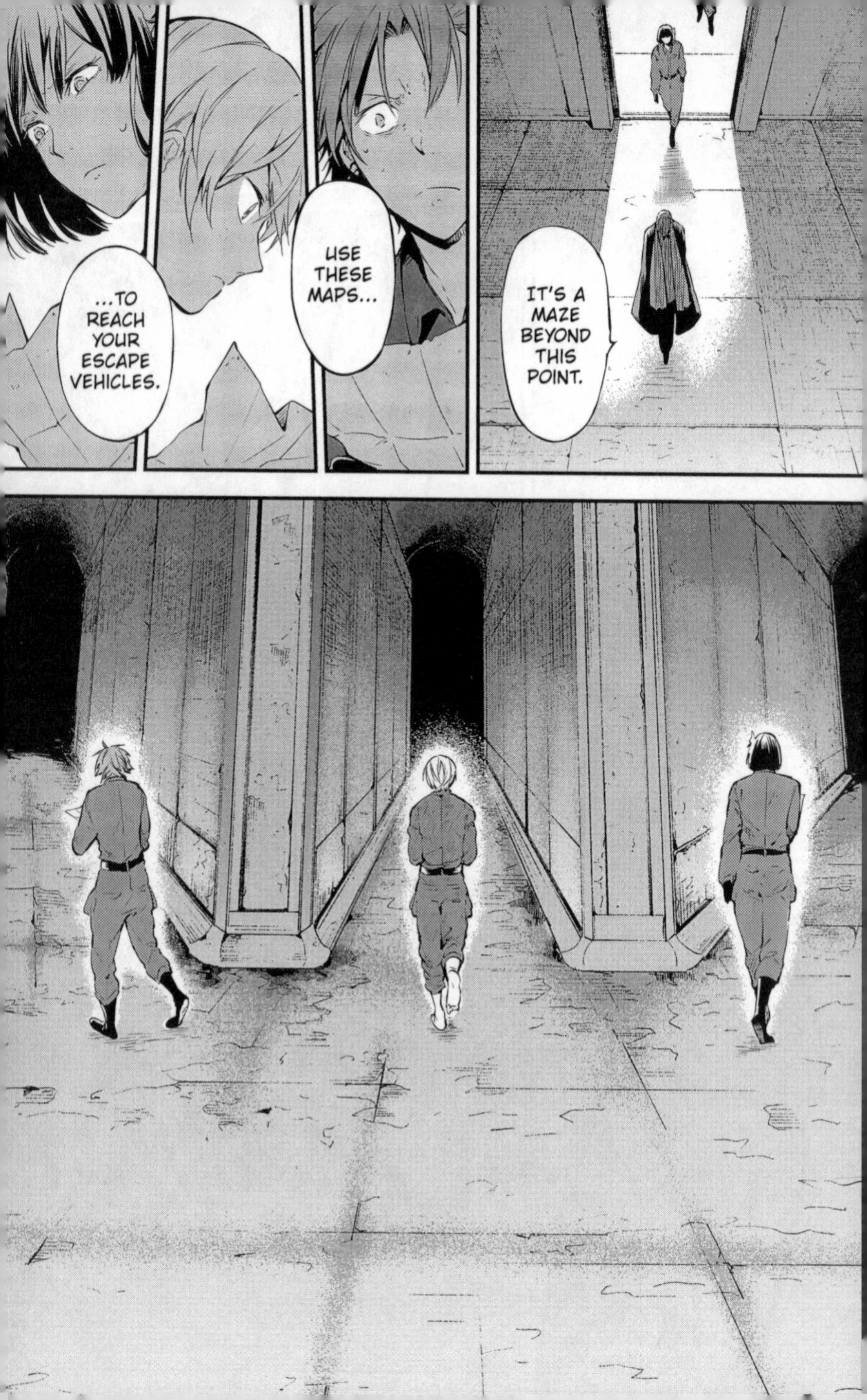
IT'S A MAZE BEYOND THIS POINT.
USE THESE MAPS...
...TO REACH YOUR ESCAPE VEHICLES.

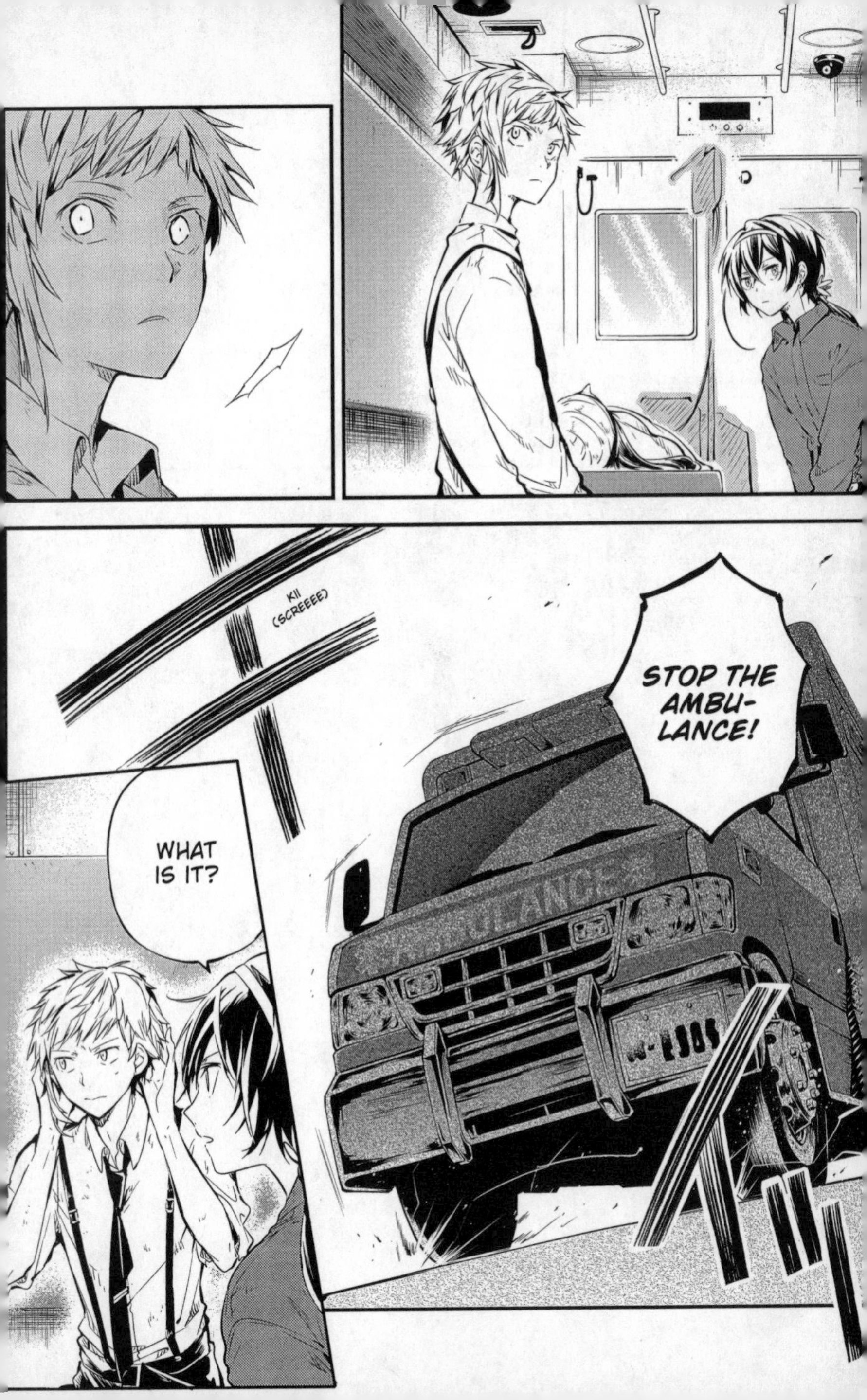
STOP THE AMBU-LANCE!
KII (SCREEEE)
WHAT IS IT?

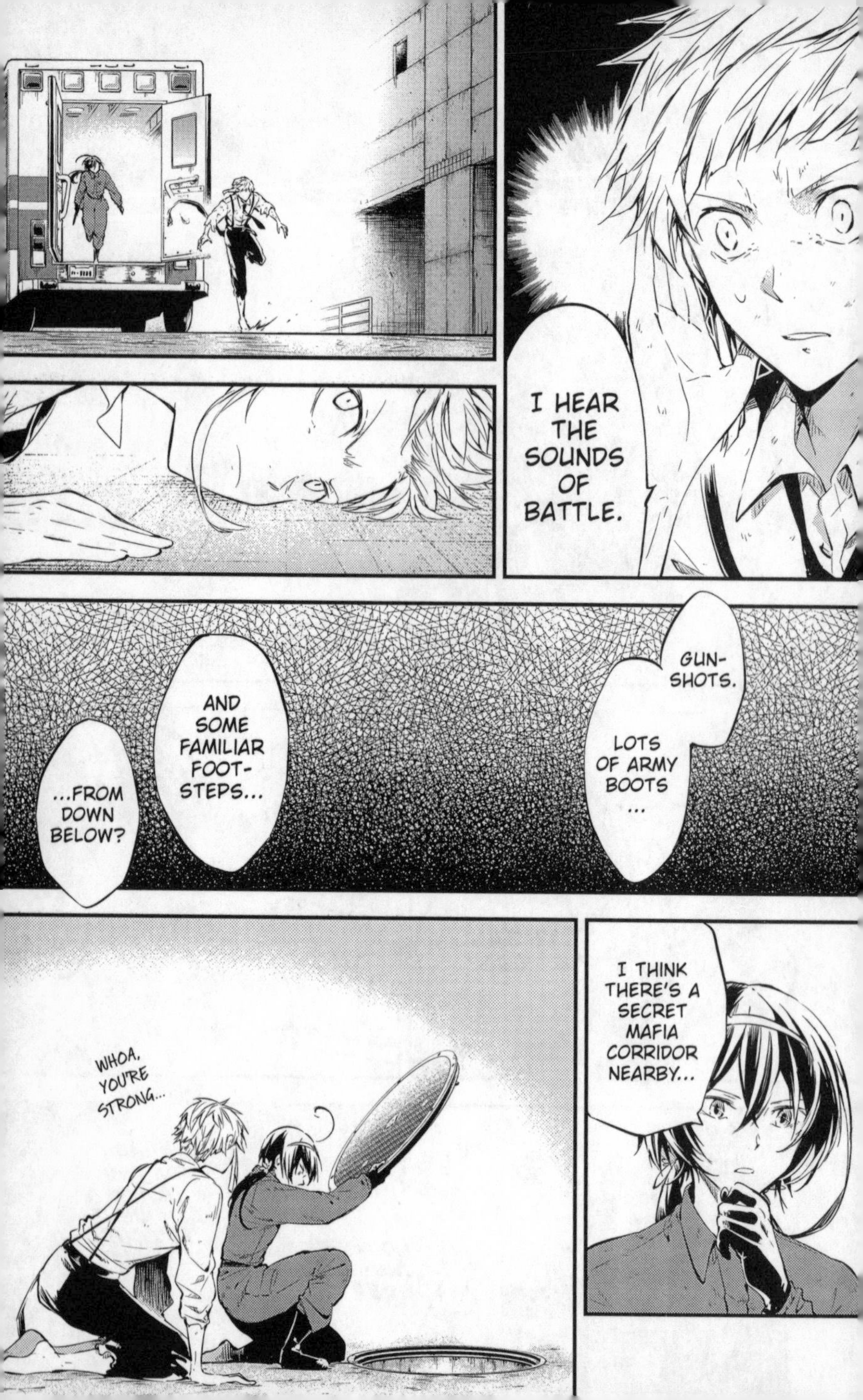
I HEAR THE SOUNDS OF BATTLE.
GUN-SHOTS.
LOTS OF ARMY BOOTS ...
AND SOME FAMILIAR FOOT-STEPS...
...FROM DOWN BELOW?
I THINK THERE'S A SECRET MAFIA CORRIDOR NEARBY...
WHOA, YOU'RE STRONG...

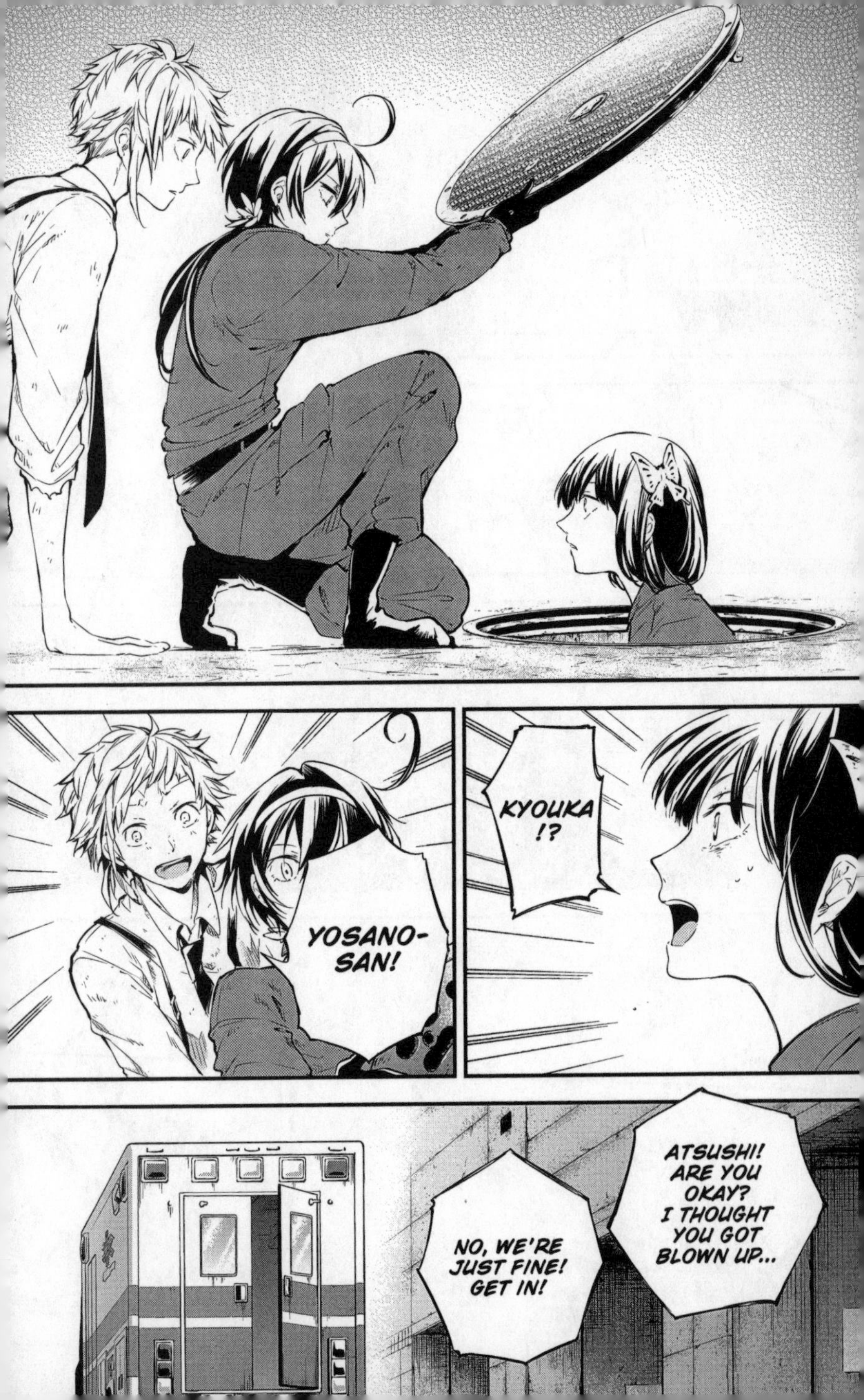
KYOUKA!?
YOSANO-SAN!
ATSUSHI! ARE YOU OKAY? I THOUGHT YOU GOT BLOWN UP...
NO, WE'RE JUST FINE! GET IN!

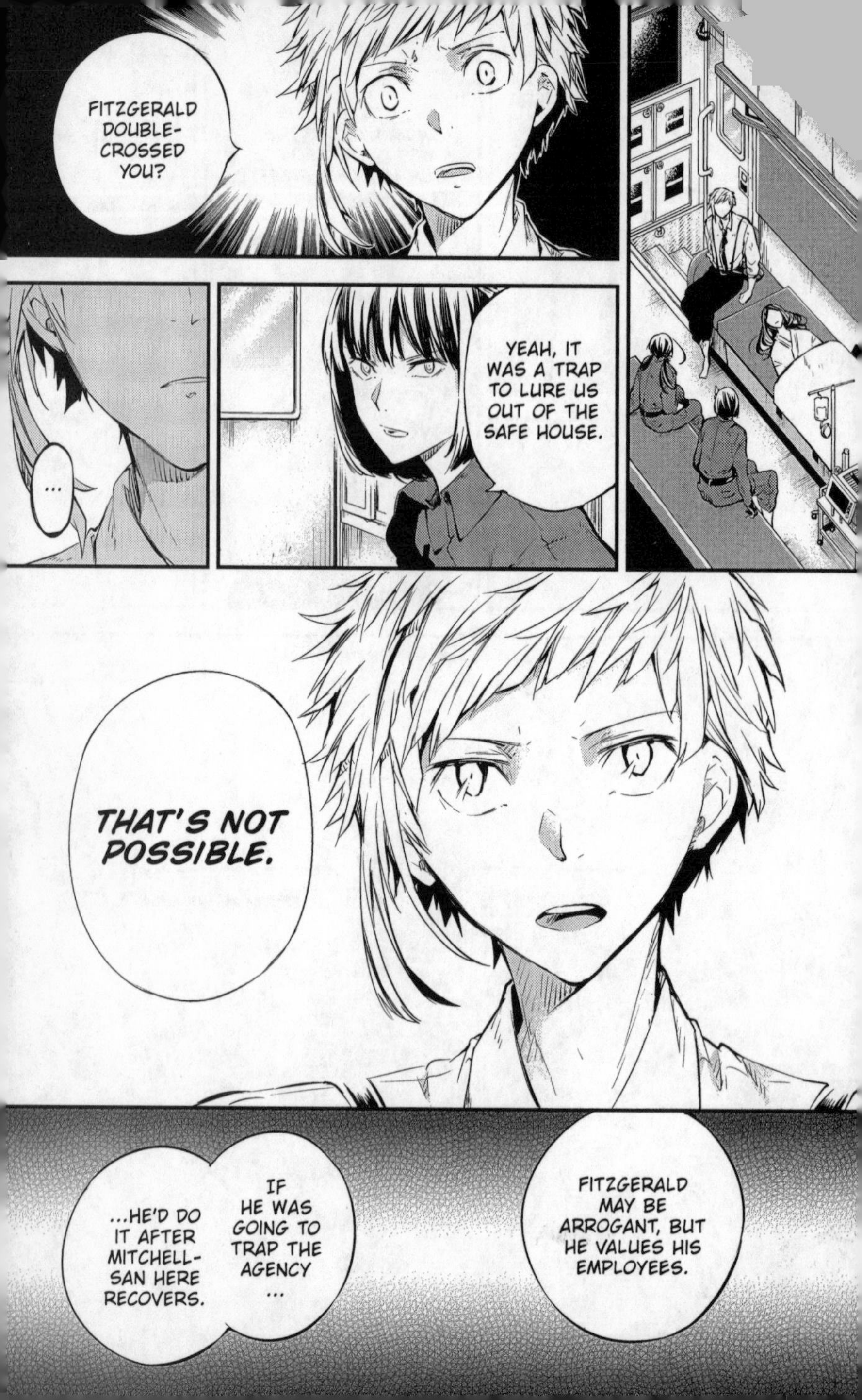
FITZGERALD DOUBLE-CROSSED YOU?
YEAH, IT WAS A TRAP TO LURE US OUT OF THE SAFE HOUSE.
...
THAT'S NOT POSSIBLE.
FITZGERALD MAY BE ARROGANT, BUT HE VALUES HIS EMPLOYEES.
IF HE WAS GOING TO TRAP THE AGENCY...
...HE'D DO IT AFTER MITCHELL-SAN HERE RECOVERS.

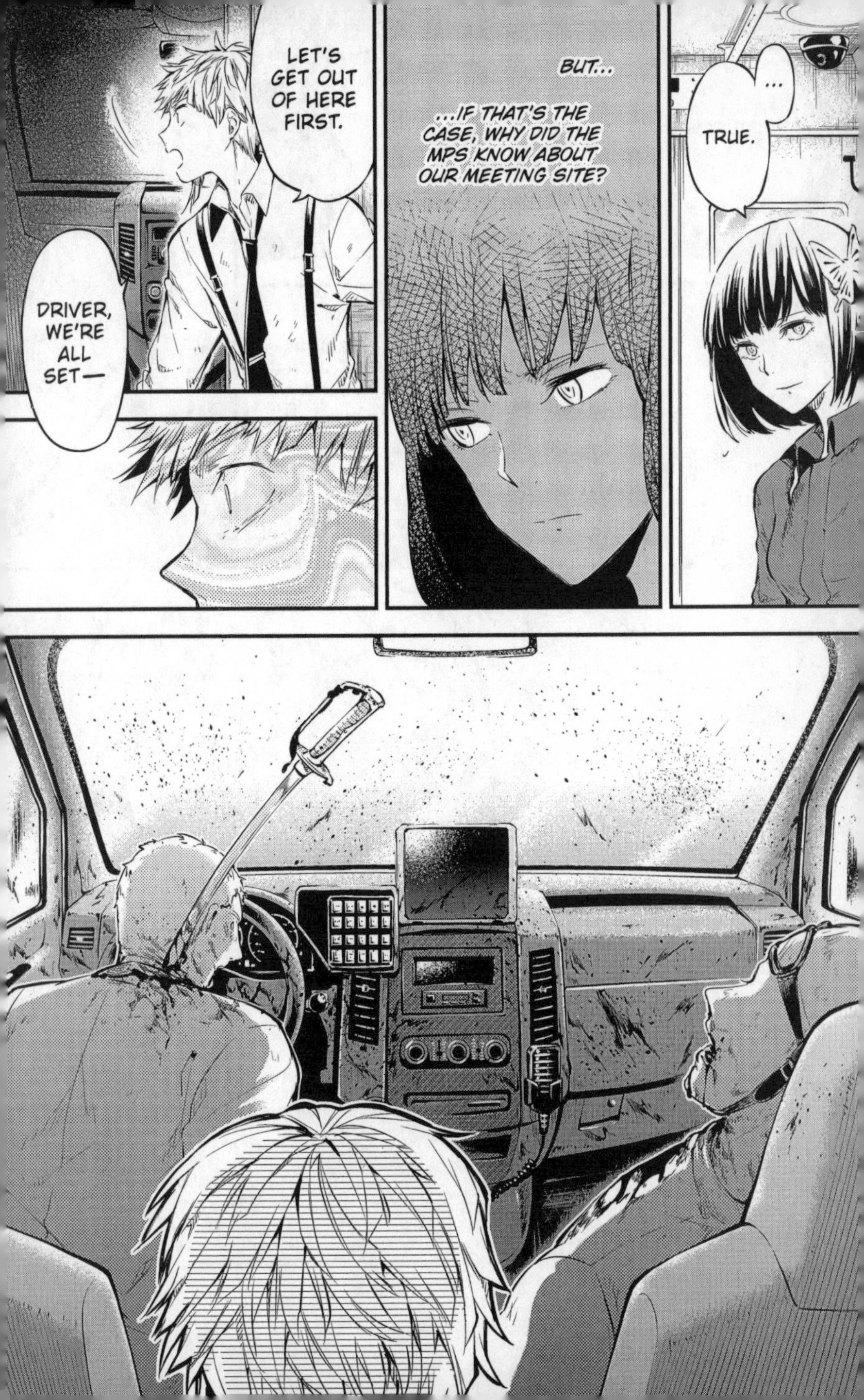
...
TRUE.
BUT...
...IF THAT'S THE CASE, WHY DID THE MPS KNOW ABOUT OUR MEETING SITE?
LET'S GET OUT OF HERE FIRST.
DRIVER, WE'RE ALL SET—

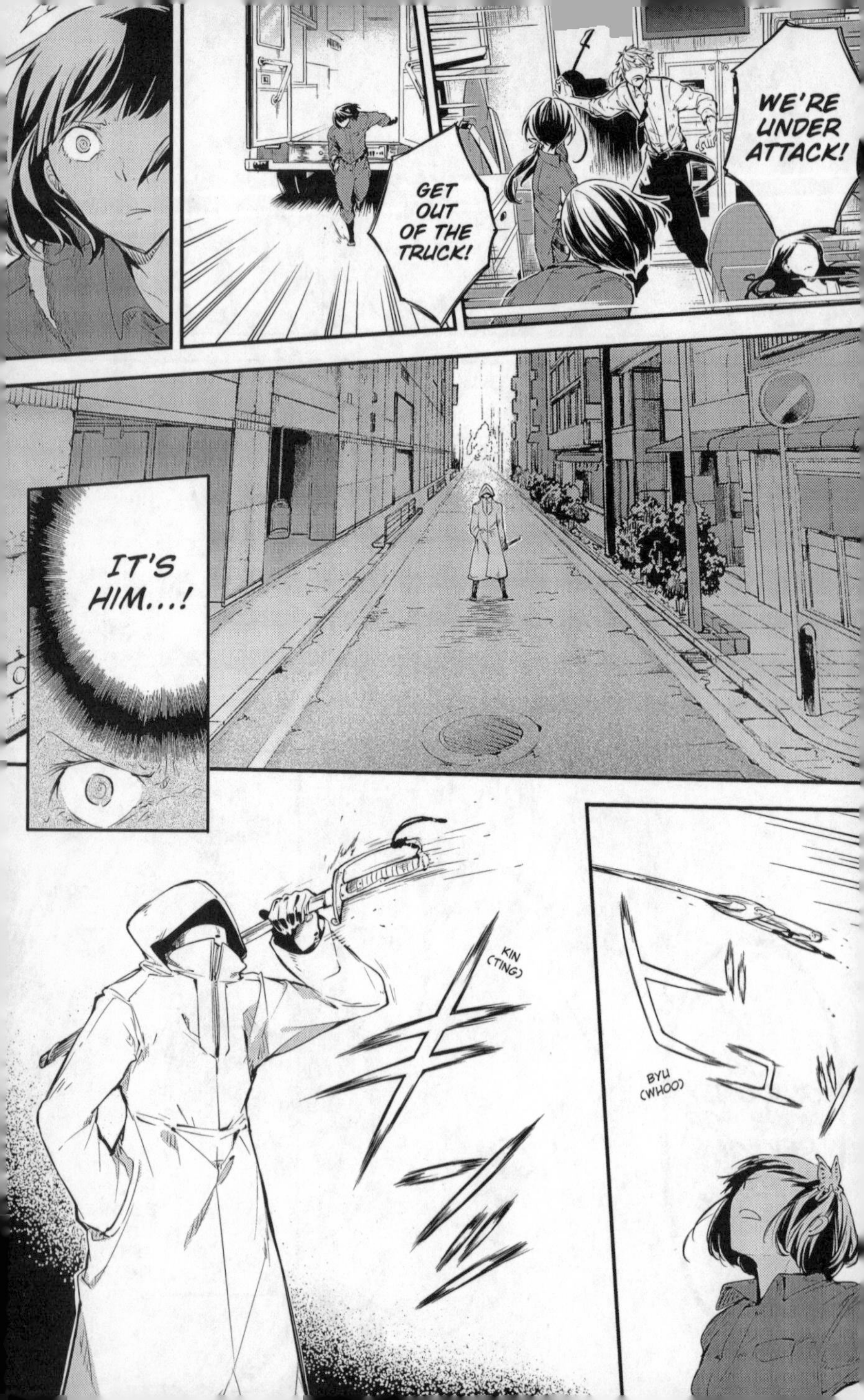
WE'RE UNDER ATTACK!
GET OUT OF THE TRUCK!
IT'S HIM...!
BYU (WHOO)
KIN (TING)

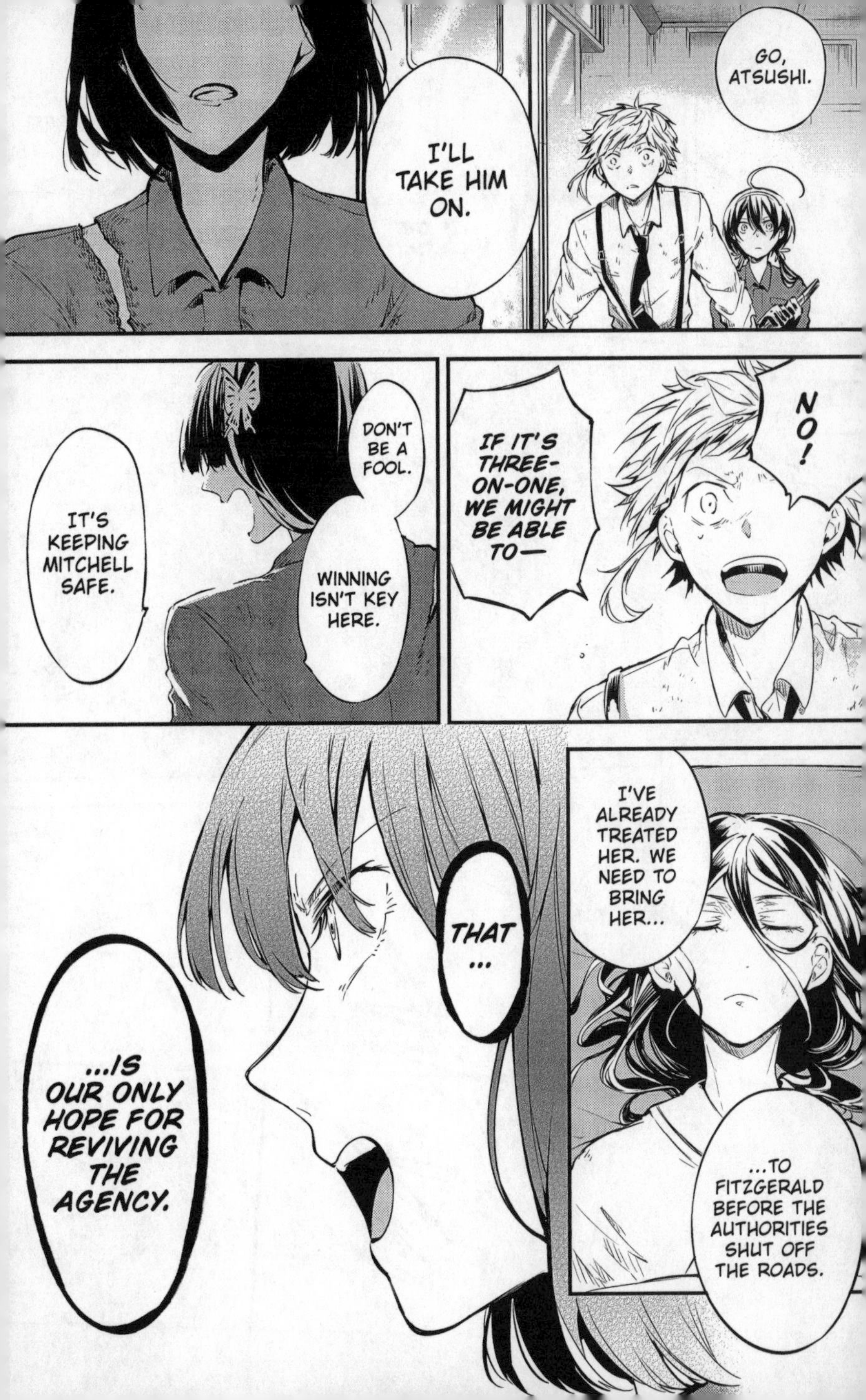
GO, ATSUSHI.
I'LL TAKE HIM ON.
NO!
IF IT'S THREE-ON-ONE, WE MIGHT BE ABLE TO—
DON'T BE A FOOL.
WINNING ISN'T KEY HERE.
IT'S KEEPING MITCHELL SAFE.
I'VE ALREADY TREATED HER. WE NEED TO BRING HER...
...TO FITZGERALD BEFORE THE AUTHORITIES SHUT OFF THE ROADS.
THAT...
...IS OUR ONLY HOPE FOR REVIVING THE AGENCY.

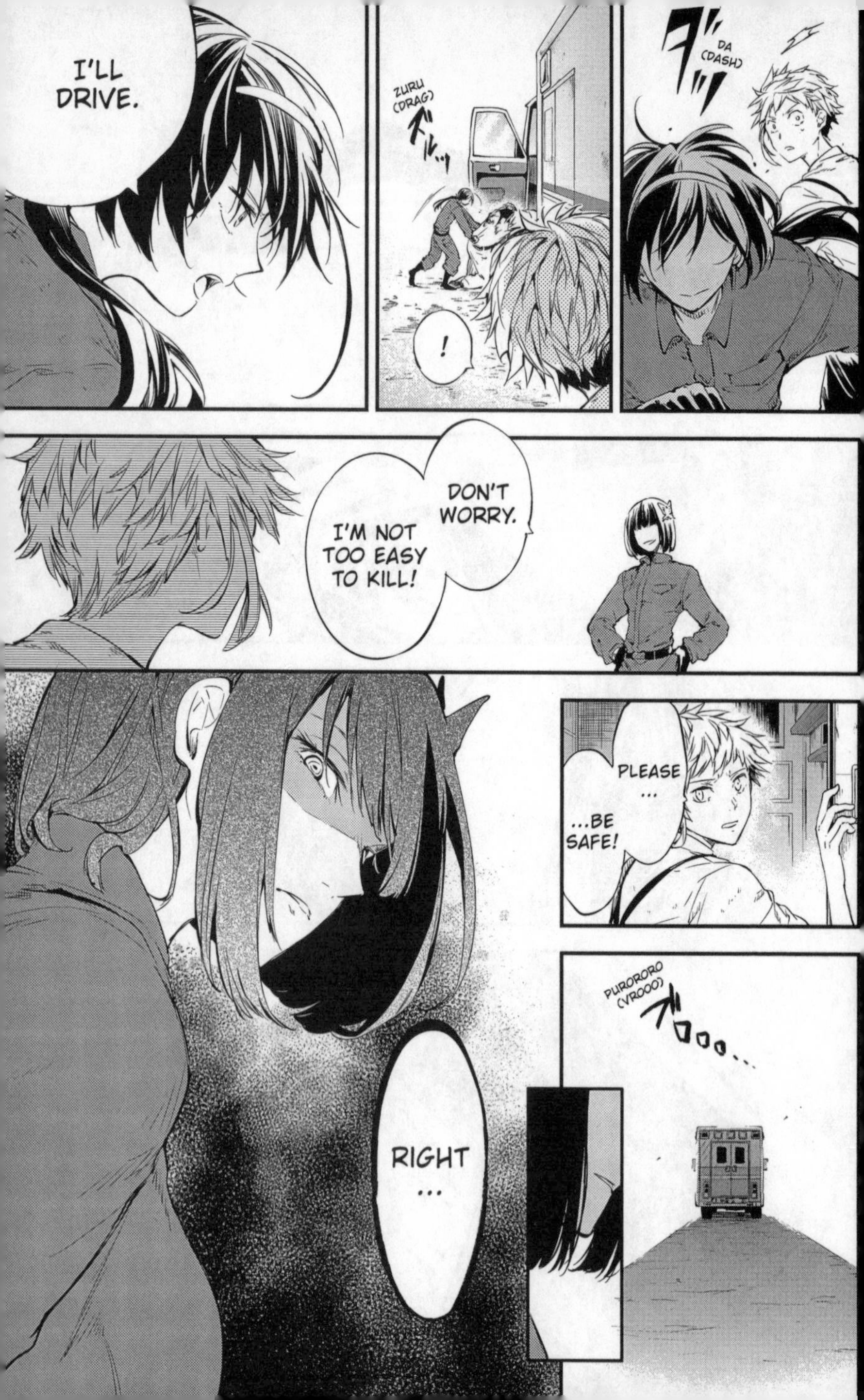
DA (DASH)
ZURU (DRAG)
!
I'LL DRIVE.
DON'T WORRY.
I'M NOT TOO EASY TO KILL!
PLEASE ...
...BE SAFE!
PURORORO (VROOO)
RIGHT ...

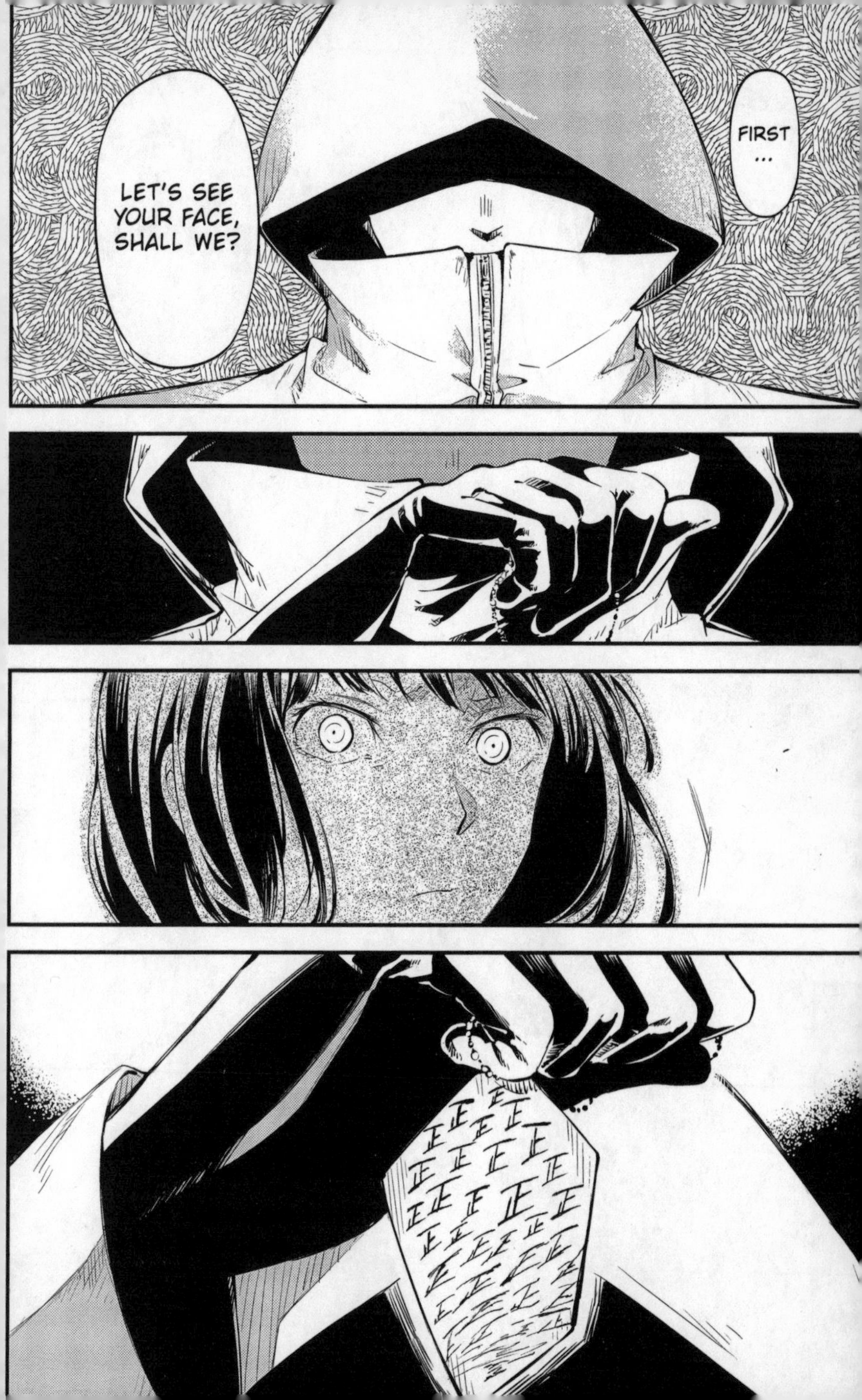
FIRST ...
LET'S SEE YOUR FACE, SHALL WE?

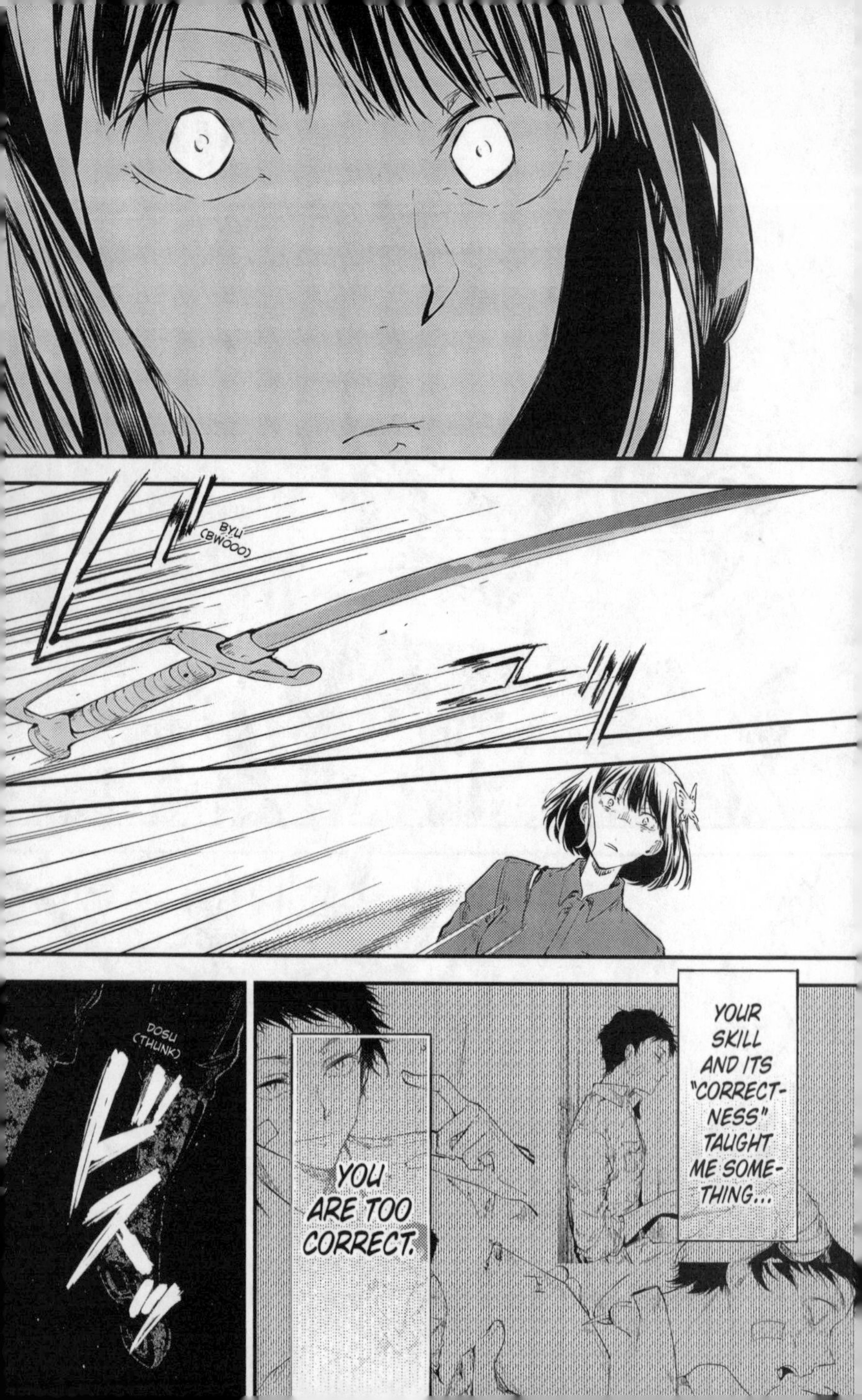
BYU (BWOOO)
YOUR SKILL AND ITS "CORRECTNESS" TAUGHT ME SOMETHING...
YOU ARE TOO CORRECT.
DOSU (THUNK)

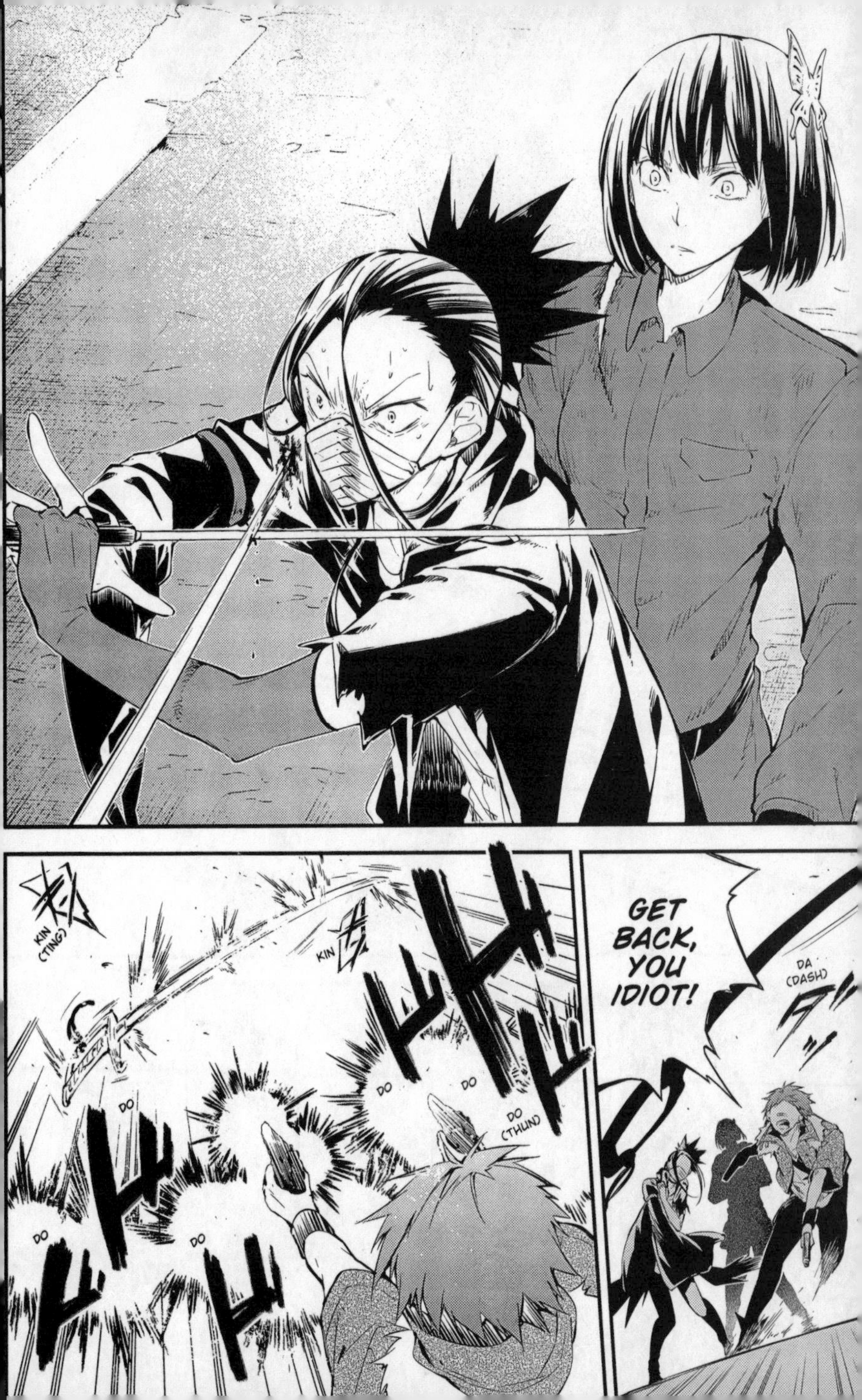
GET BACK, YOU IDIOT!
DA (DASH)
KIN
KIN (TING)
DO (THUD)
DO
DO
DO
DO
DO

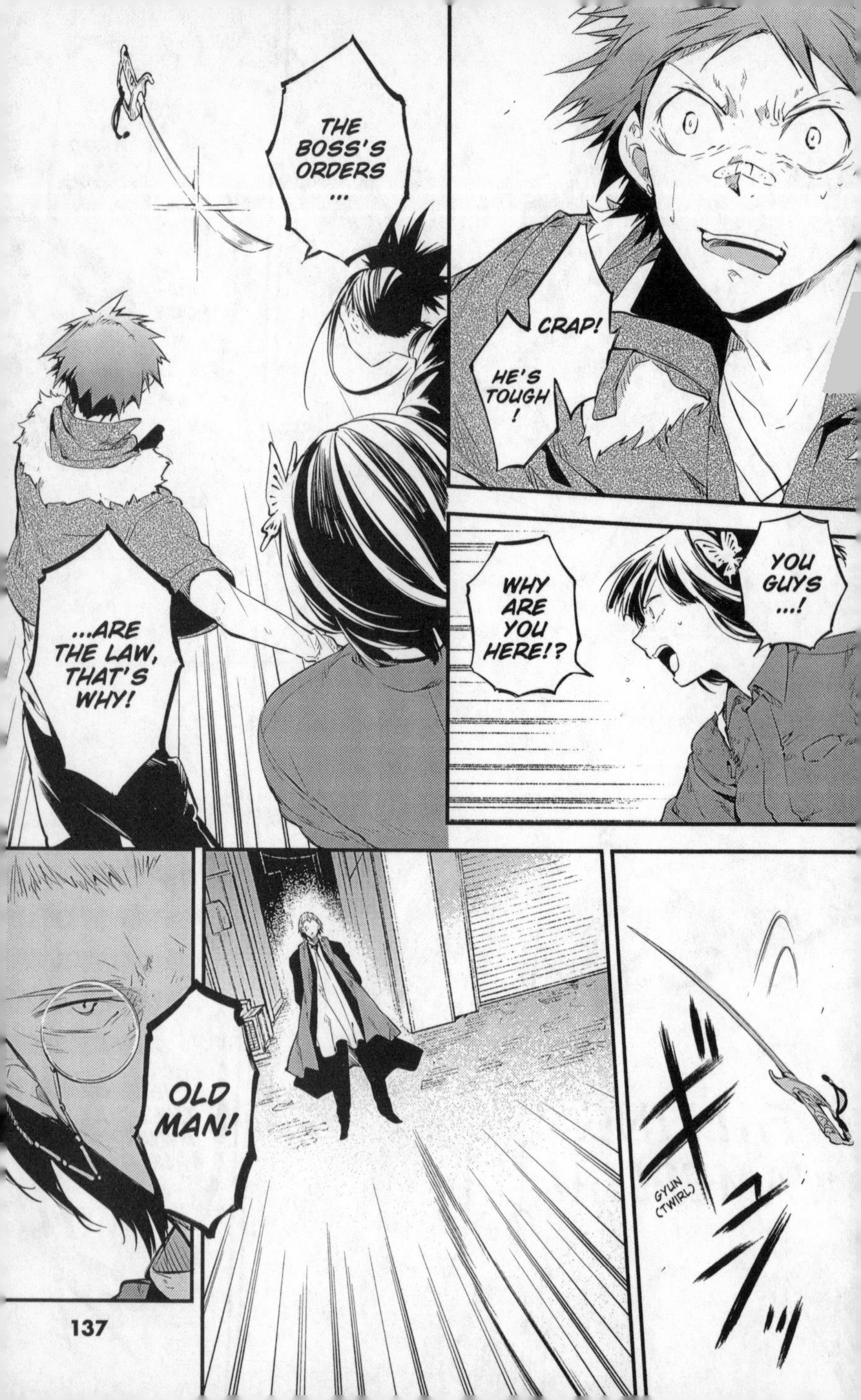
CRAP!
HE'S TOUGH!
YOU GUYS ...!
WHY ARE YOU HERE!?
THE BOSS'S ORDERS ...
...ARE THE LAW, THAT'S WHY!
GYUN (TWIRL)
OLD MAN!

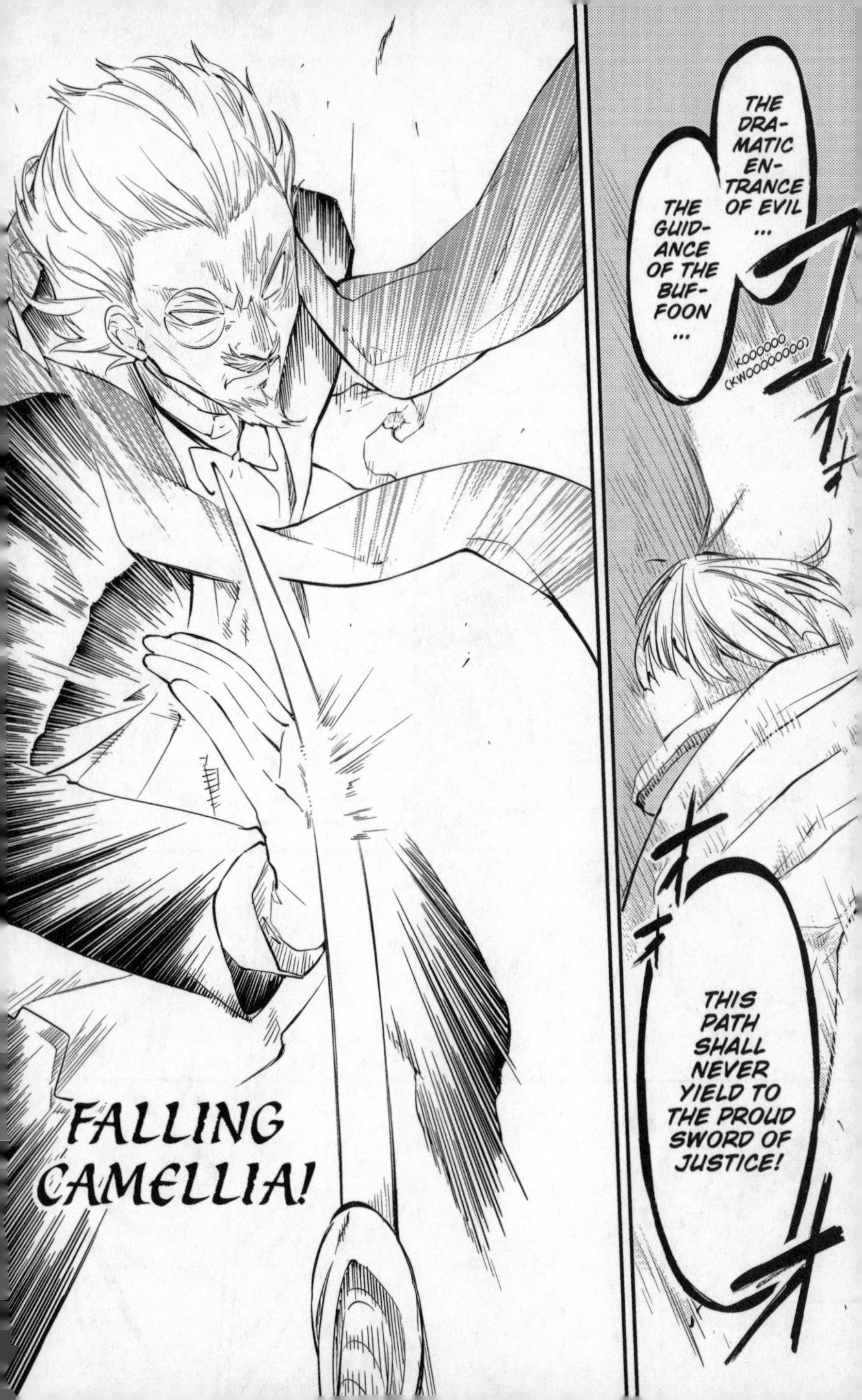
THE DRA-MATIC EN-TRANCE OF EVIL...
THE GUID-ANCE OF THE BUF-FOON...
KOOOOOO (KWOOOOOOOOO)
THIS PATH SHALL NEVER YIELD TO THE PROUD SWORD OF JUSTICE!
FALLING CAMELLIA!

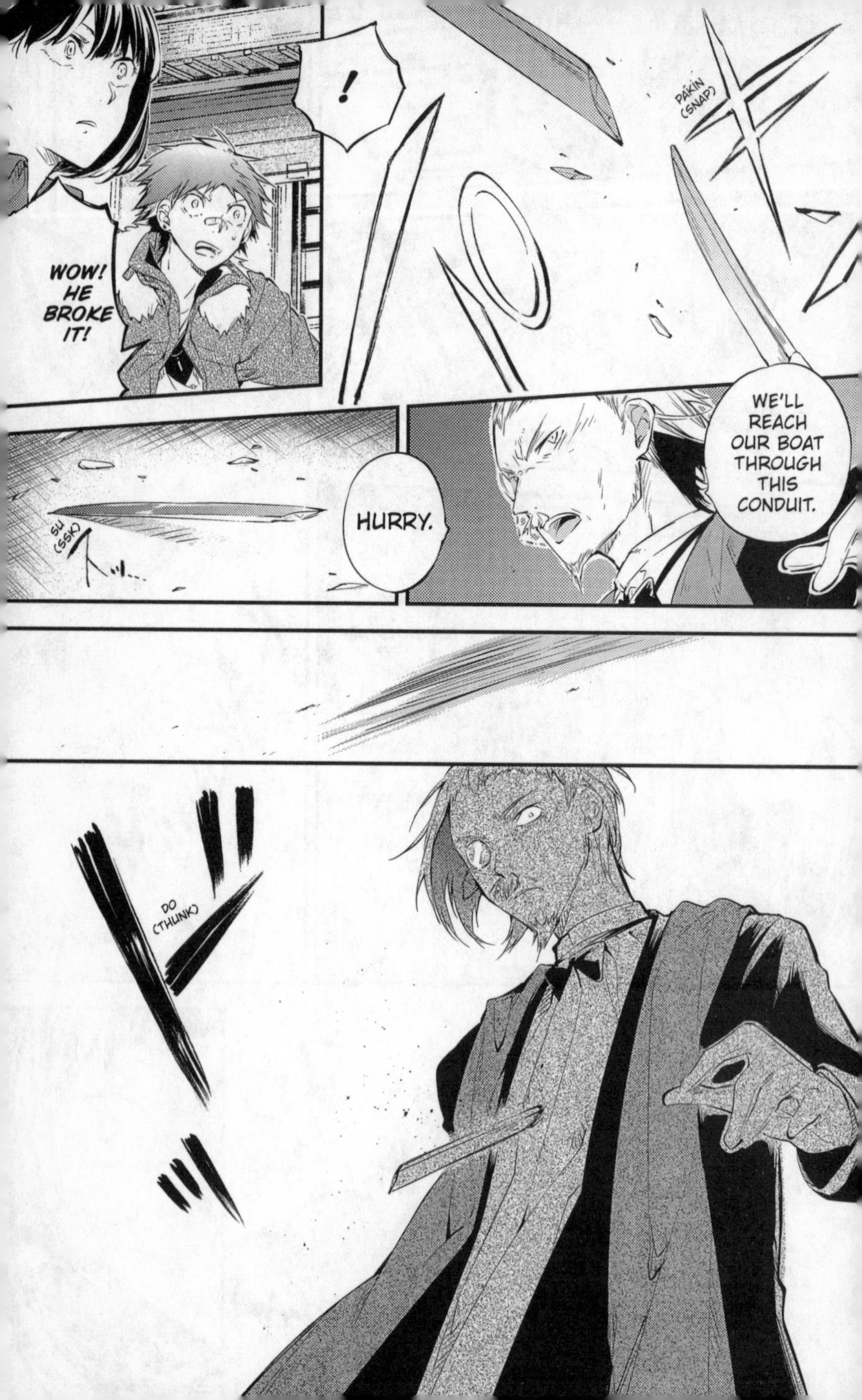
PAKIN (SNAP)
!
WOW! HE BROKE IT!
WE'LL REACH OUR BOAT THROUGH THIS CONDUIT.
HURRY.
SU (SSK)
DO (THUNK)

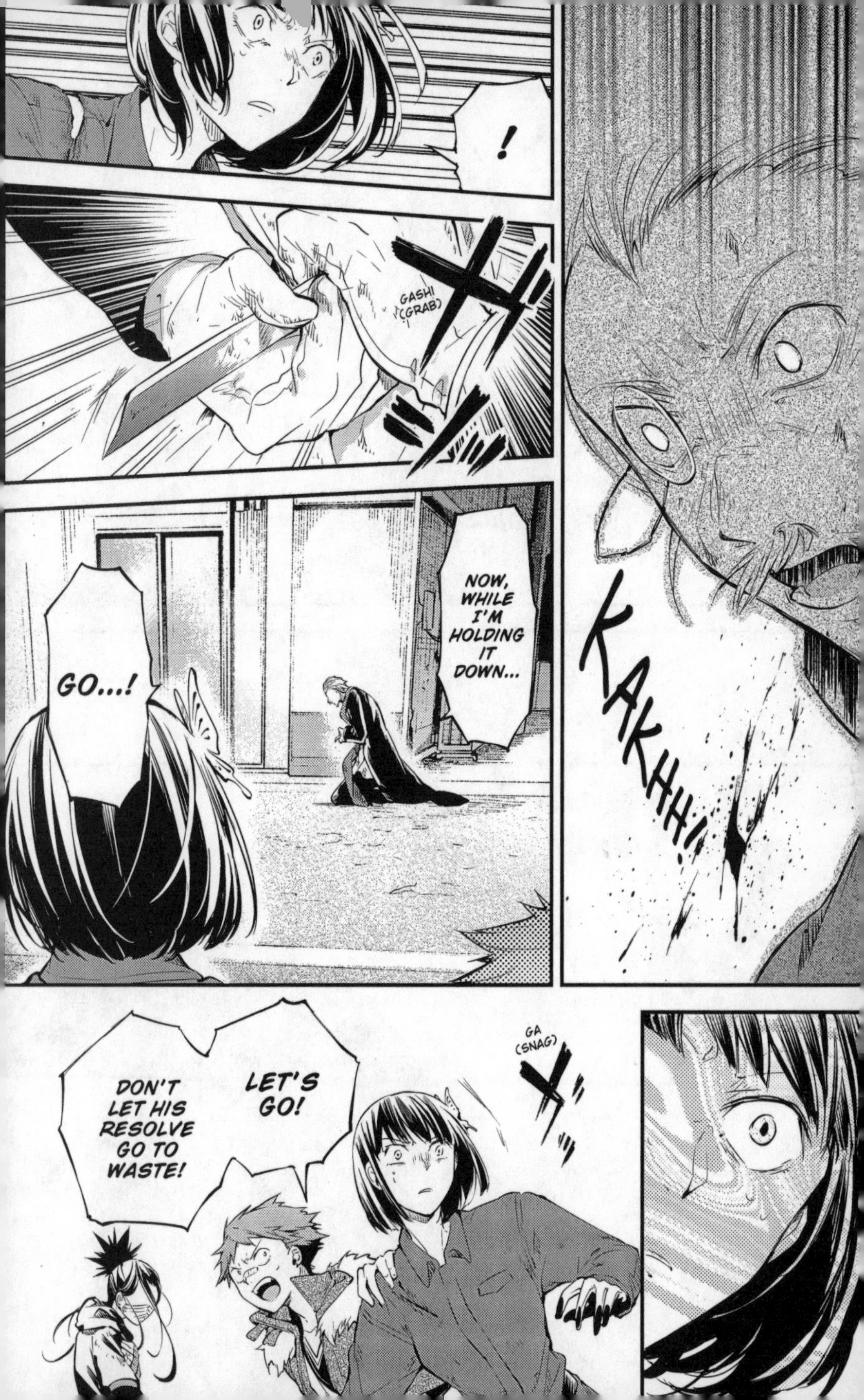
KAKHH!!
!
GASHI (GRAB)
NOW, WHILE I'M HOLDING IT DOWN...
GO...!
GA (SNAG)
LET'S GO!
DON'T LET HIS RESOLVE GO TO WASTE!

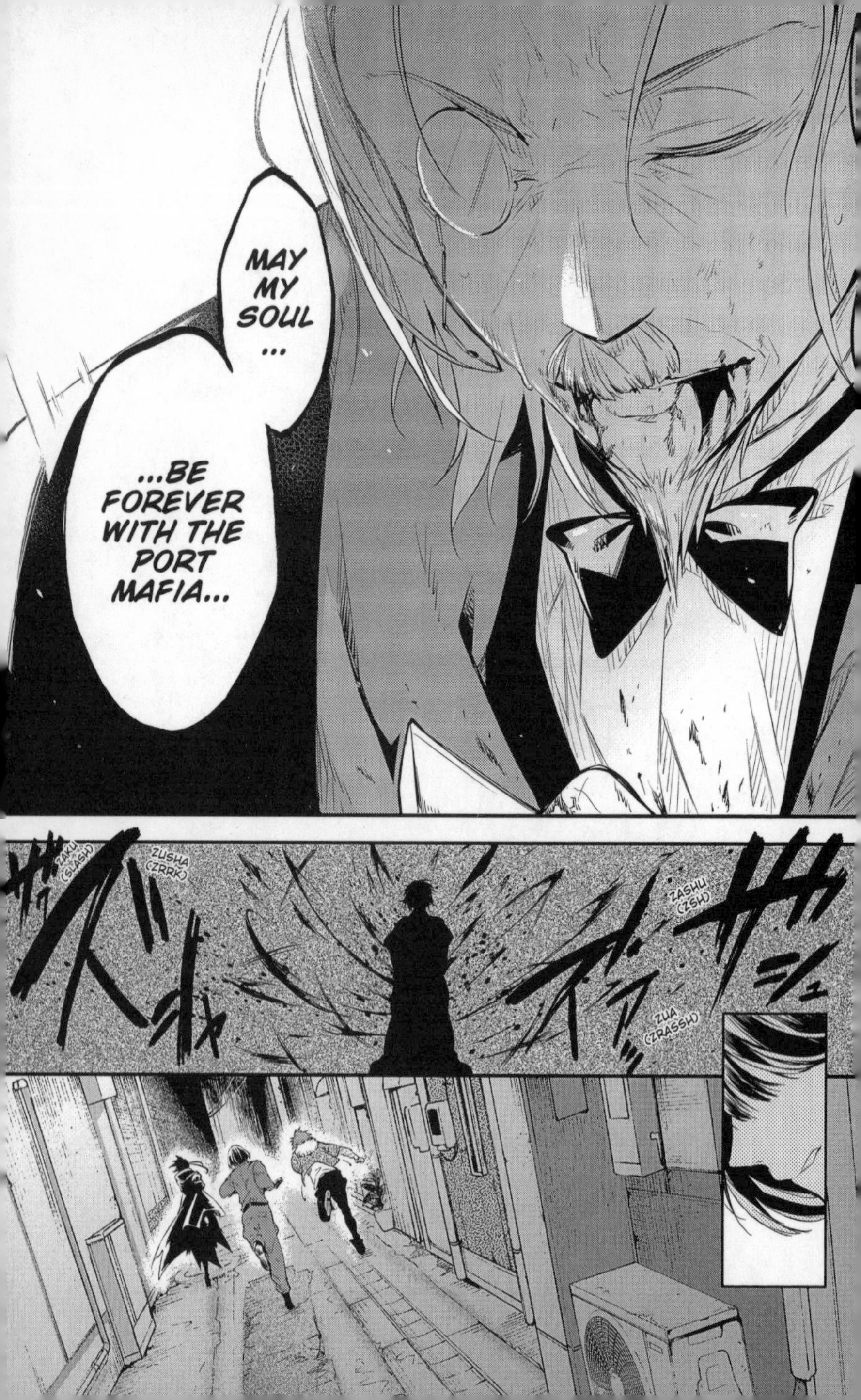
MAY MY SOUL ...
...BE FOREVER WITH THE PORT MAFIA...
ZASHU (ZSH)
ZUA (ZRASSH)
ZUSHA (ZRRK)
ZAKU (SLASH)

BUNGO
STRAY DOGS

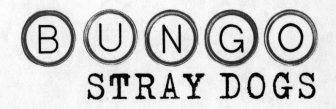

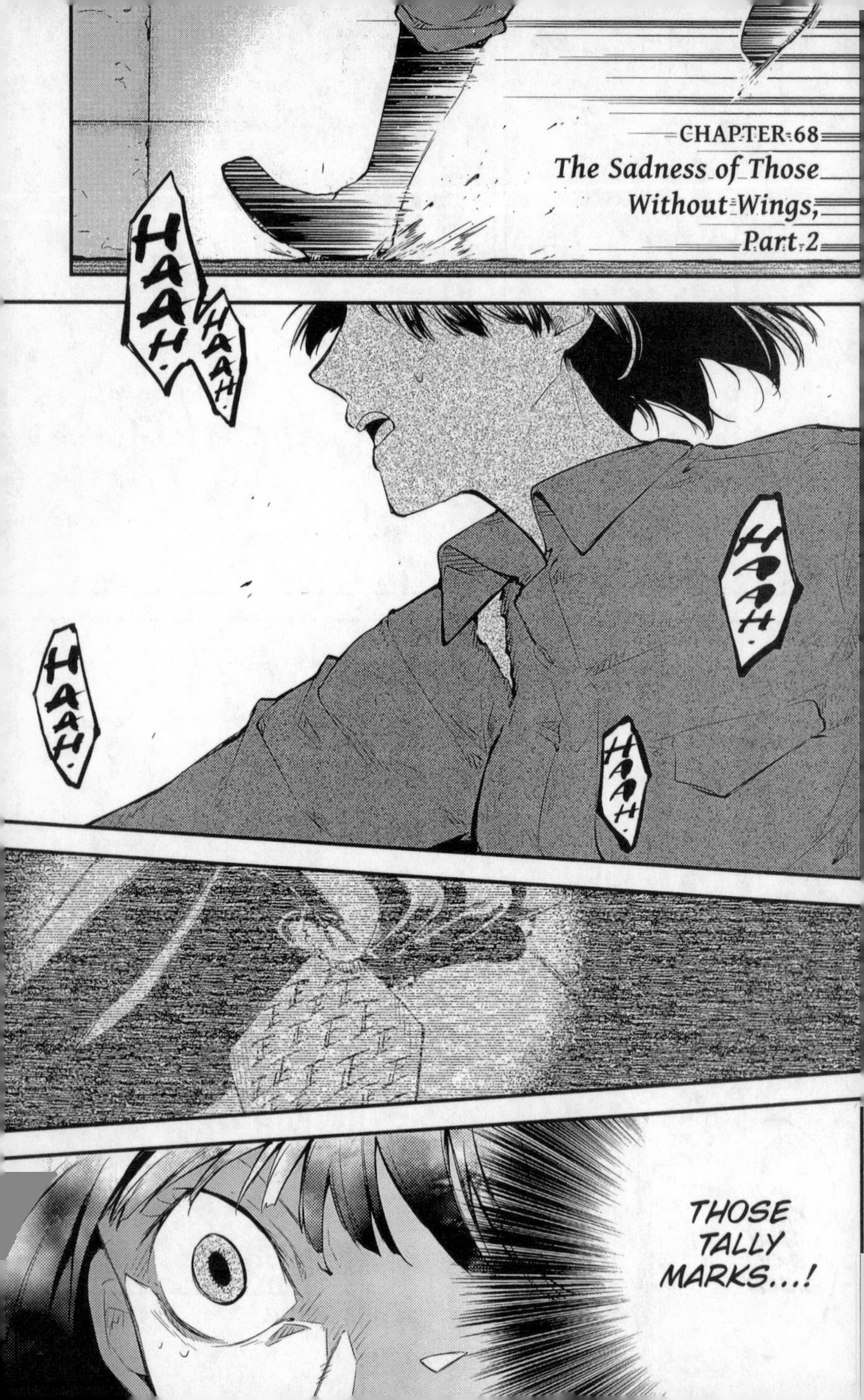
CHAPTER 68
The Sadness of Those Without Wings, Part 2
HAAH. HAAH.
HAAH.
HAAH.
HAAH.
THOSE TALLY MARKS...!

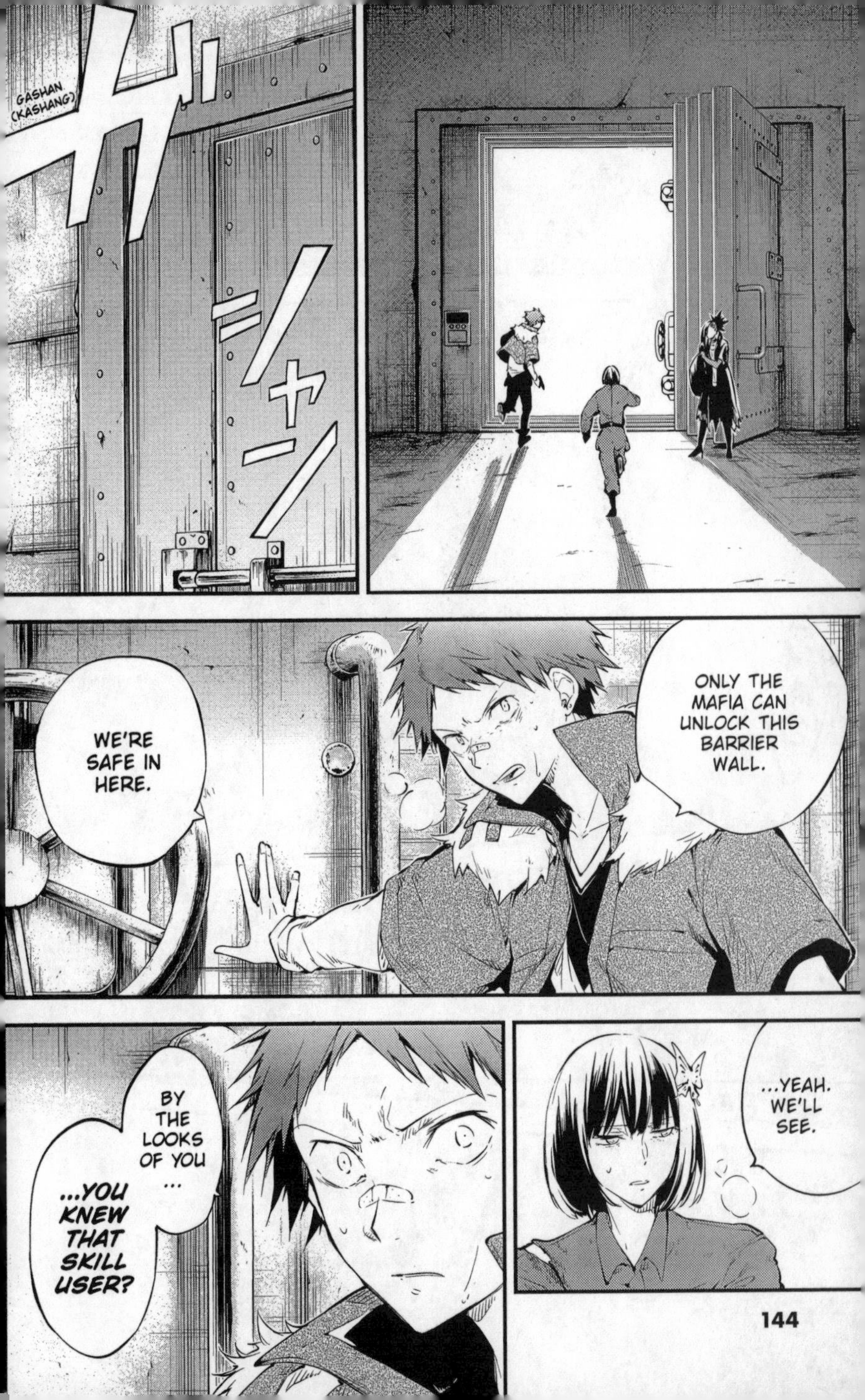
GASHAN (KASHANG)
ONLY THE MAFIA CAN UNLOCK THIS BARRIER WALL.
WE'RE SAFE IN HERE.
...YEAH. WE'LL SEE.
BY THE LOOKS OF YOU ...
...YOU KNEW THAT SKILL USER?

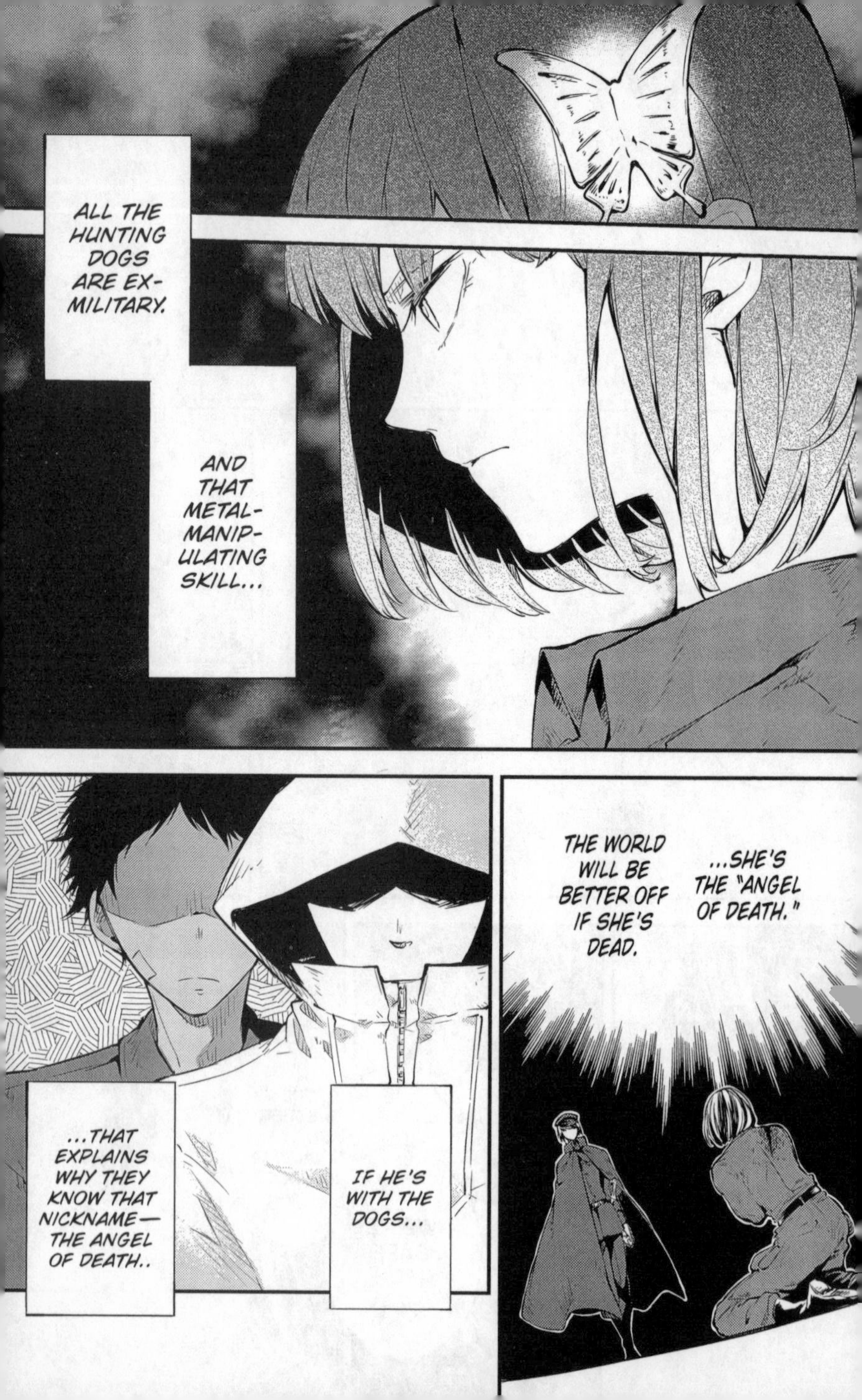
ALL THE HUNTING DOGS ARE EX-MILITARY.
AND THAT METAL-MANIPULATING SKILL...
...SHE'S THE "ANGEL OF DEATH."
THE WORLD WILL BE BETTER OFF IF SHE'S DEAD.
IF HE'S WITH THE DOGS...
...THAT EXPLAINS WHY THEY KNOW THAT NICKNAME—THE ANGEL OF DEATH..

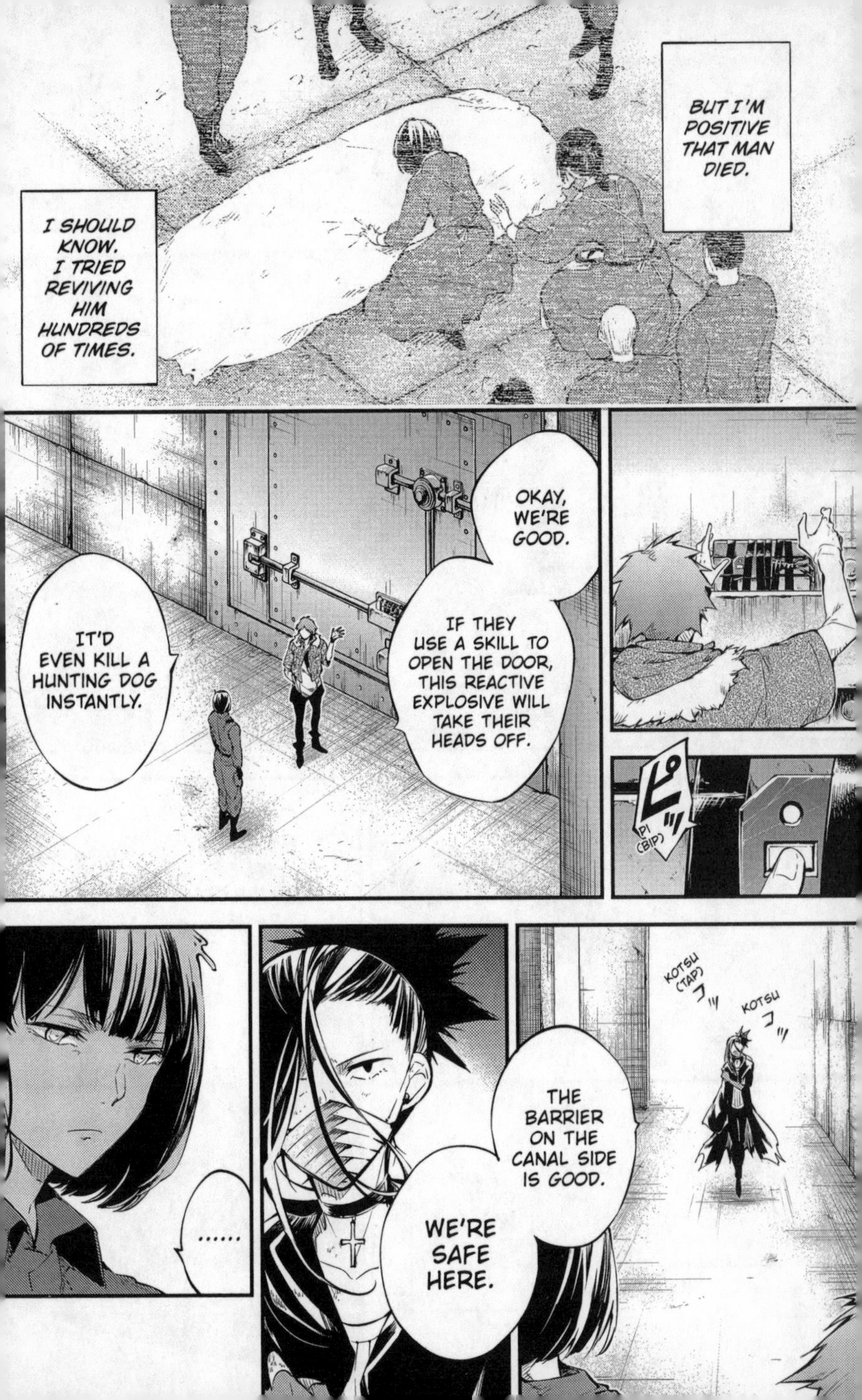
BUT I'M POSITIVE THAT MAN DIED.
I SHOULD KNOW. I TRIED REVIVING HIM HUNDREDS OF TIMES.
ピッ
PI (BIP)
OKAY, WE'RE GOOD.
IF THEY USE A SKILL TO OPEN THE DOOR, THIS REACTIVE EXPLOSIVE WILL TAKE THEIR HEADS OFF.
IT'D EVEN KILL A HUNTING DOG INSTANTLY.
KOTSU (TAP)
KOTSU
THE BARRIER ON THE CANAL SIDE IS GOOD.
WE'RE SAFE HERE.
......

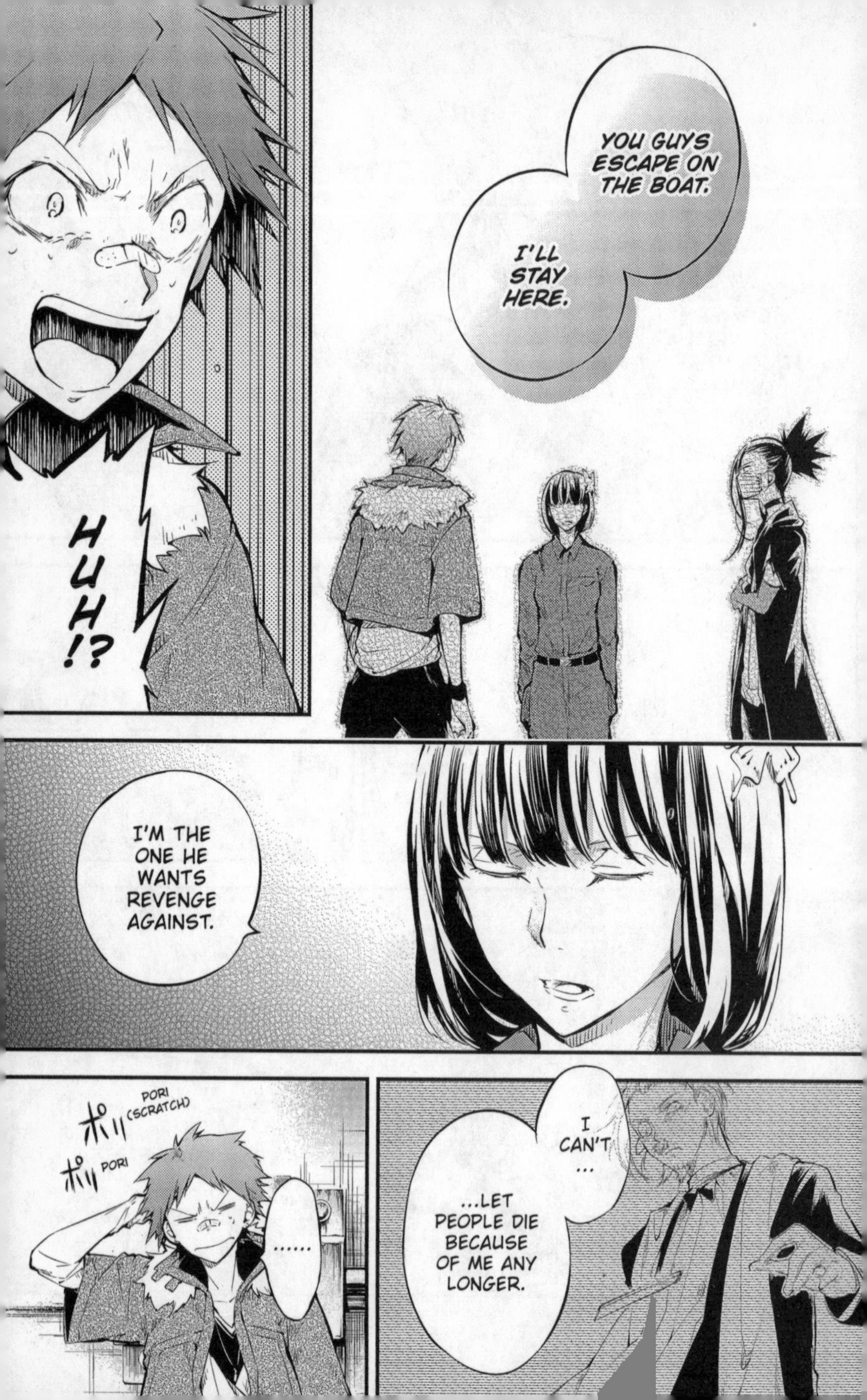
YOU GUYS ESCAPE ON THE BOAT.
I'LL STAY HERE.
HUH!?
I'M THE ONE HE WANTS REVENGE AGAINST.
I CAN'T...
...LET PEOPLE DIE BECAUSE OF ME ANY LONGER.
ポリ PORI (SCRATCH)
ポリ PORI
......

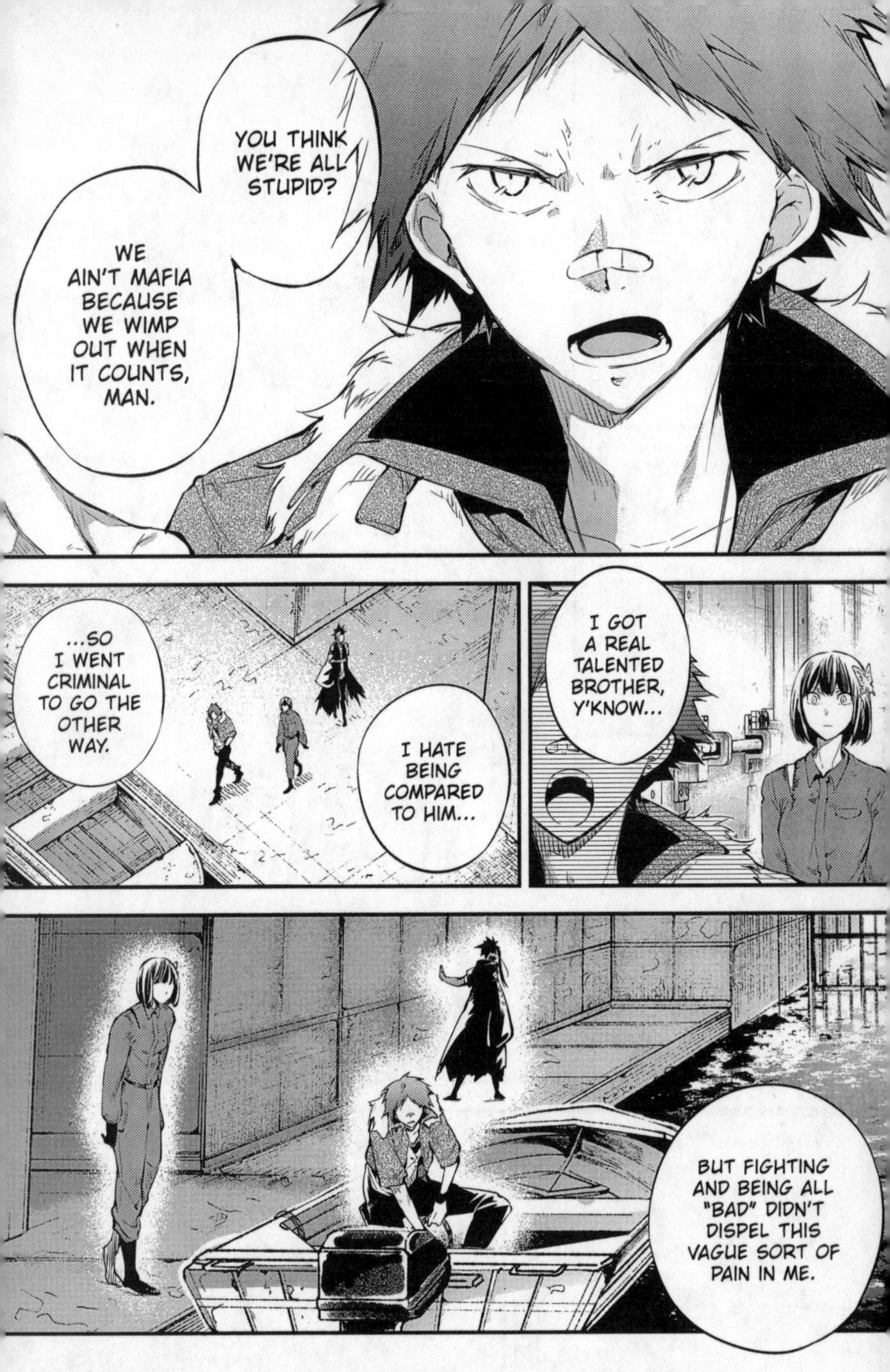
YOU THINK WE'RE ALL STUPID?
WE AIN'T MAFIA BECAUSE WE WIMP OUT WHEN IT COUNTS, MAN.
I GOT A REAL TALENTED BROTHER, Y'KNOW...
I HATE BEING COMPARED TO HIM...
...SO I WENT CRIMINAL TO GO THE OTHER WAY.
BUT FIGHTING AND BEING ALL "BAD" DIDN'T DISPEL THIS VAGUE SORT OF PAIN IN ME.

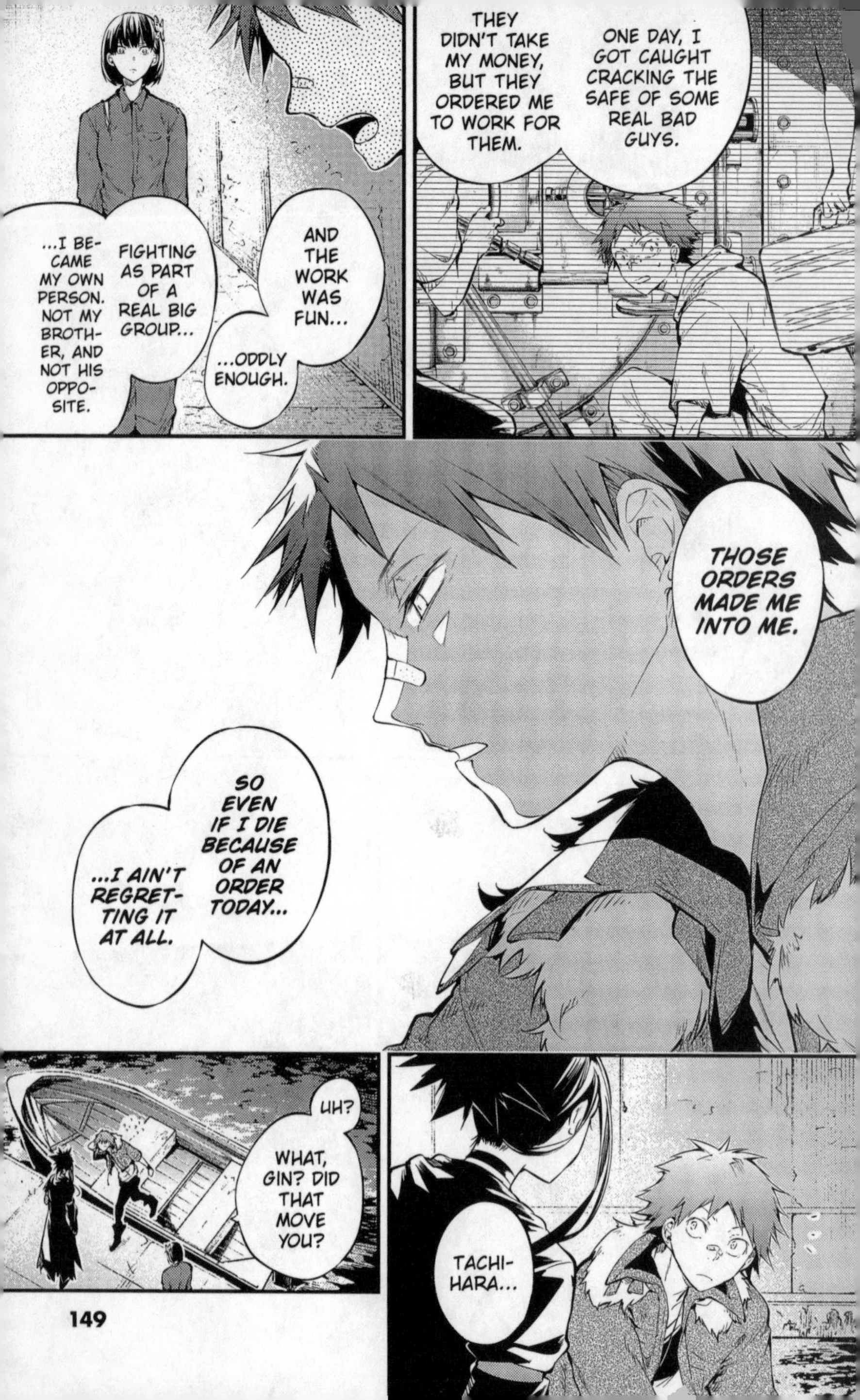
ONE DAY, I GOT CAUGHT CRACKING THE SAFE OF SOME REAL BAD GUYS.
THEY DIDN'T TAKE MY MONEY, BUT THEY ORDERED ME TO WORK FOR THEM.
AND THE WORK WAS FUN...
...ODDLY ENOUGH.
FIGHTING AS PART OF A REAL BIG GROUP...
...I BECAME MY OWN PERSON. NOT MY BROTHER, AND NOT HIS OPPOSITE.
THOSE ORDERS MADE ME INTO ME.
SO EVEN IF I DIE BECAUSE OF AN ORDER TODAY...
...I AIN'T REGRETTING IT AT ALL.
TACHIHARA...
UH?
WHAT, GIN? DID THAT MOVE YOU?

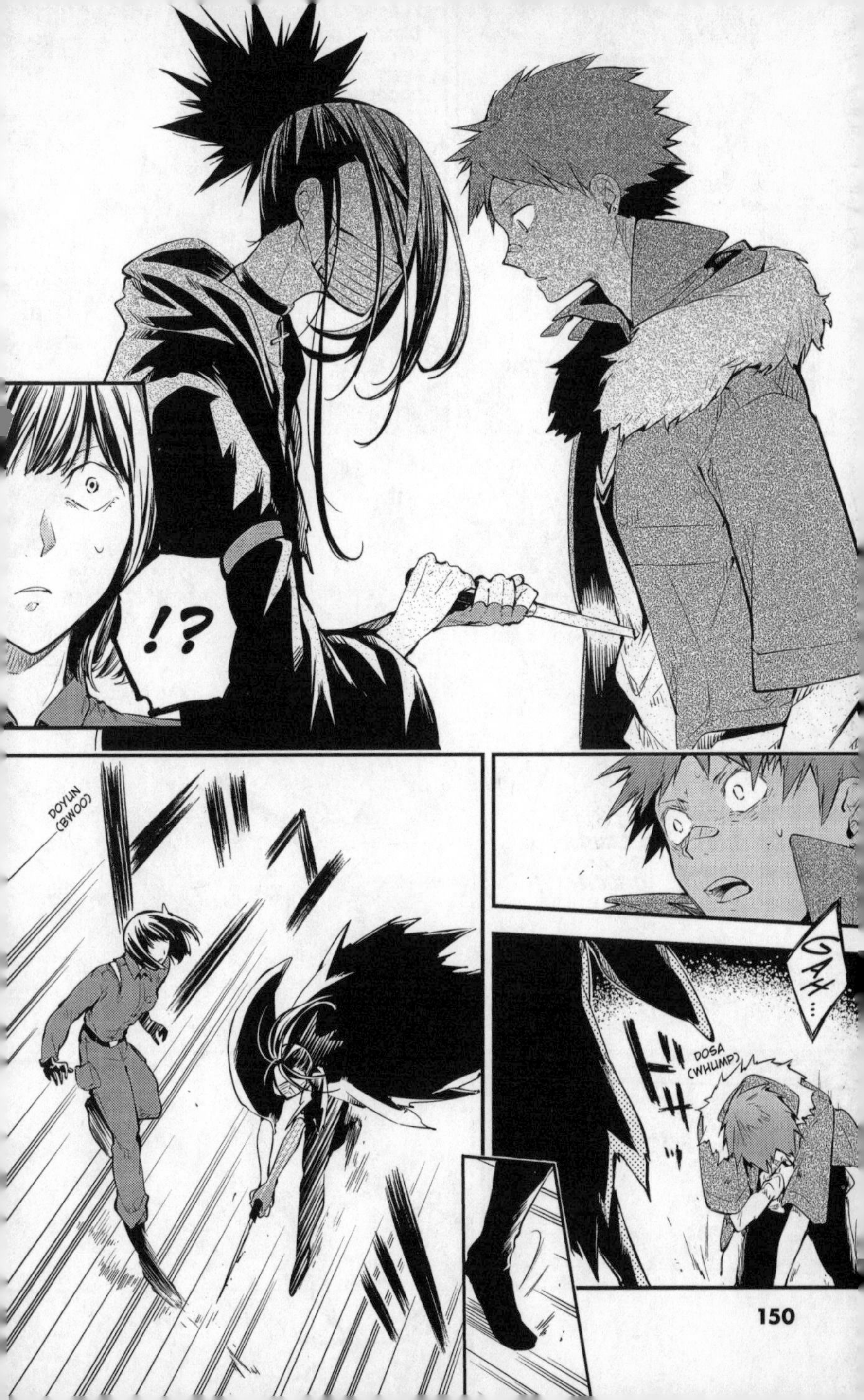
!?
GAX...
DOSA (WHUMP)
DOYUN (BWOO)

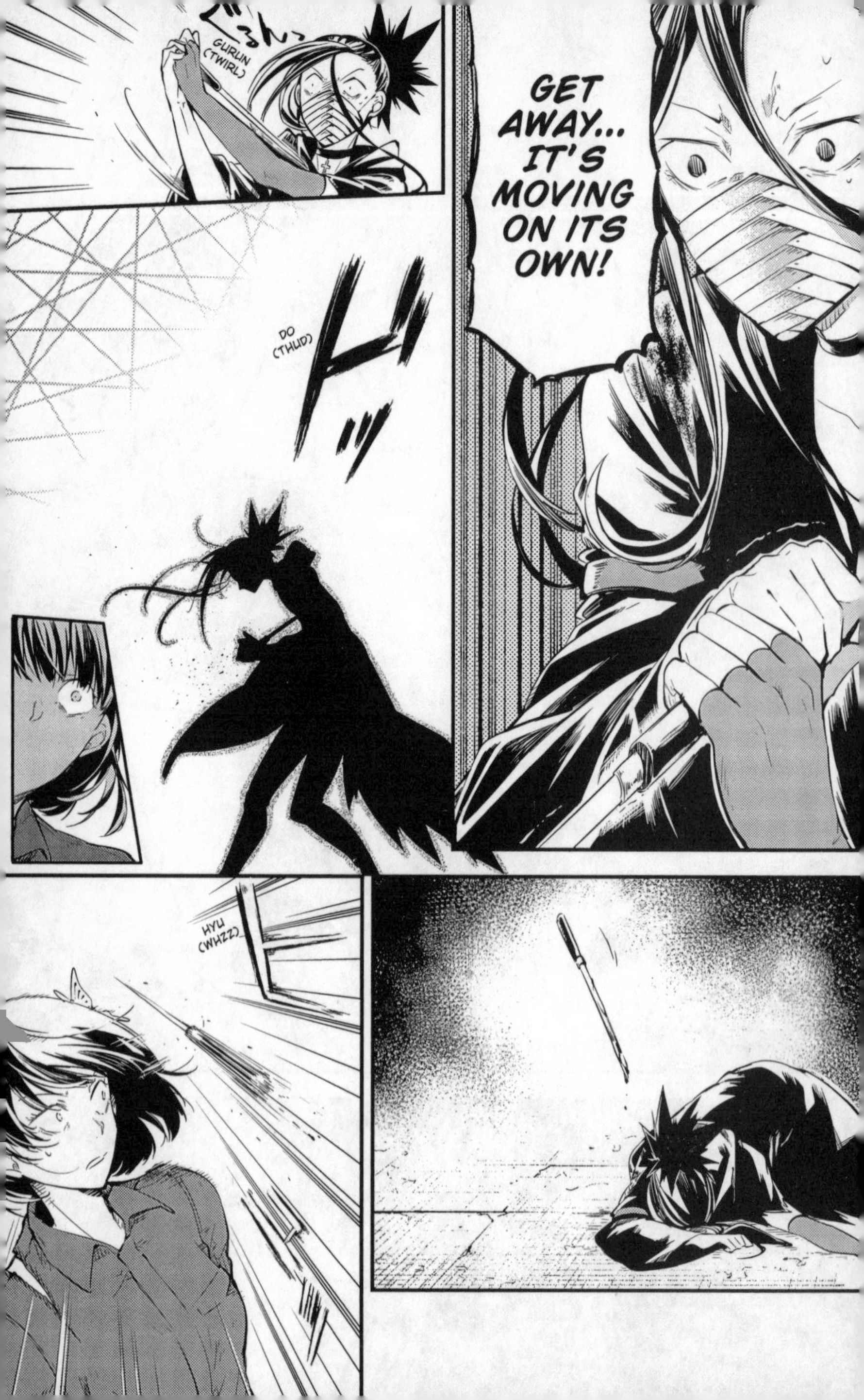
GET AWAY... IT'S MOVING ON ITS OWN!
GURUN (TWIRL)
DO (THUD)
HYU (WHZZ)

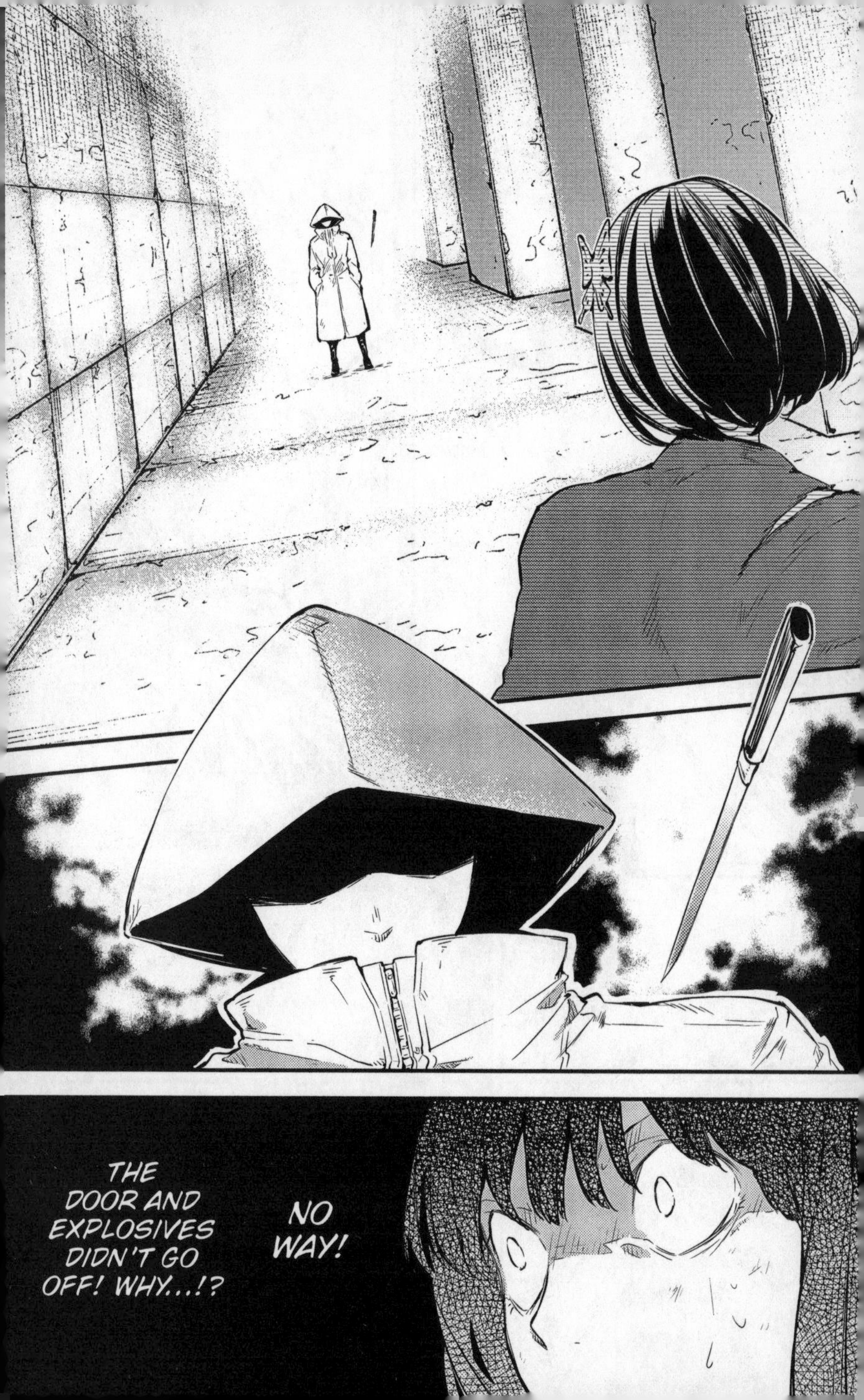
NO WAY!
THE DOOR AND EXPLOSIVES DIDN'T GO OFF! WHY...!?

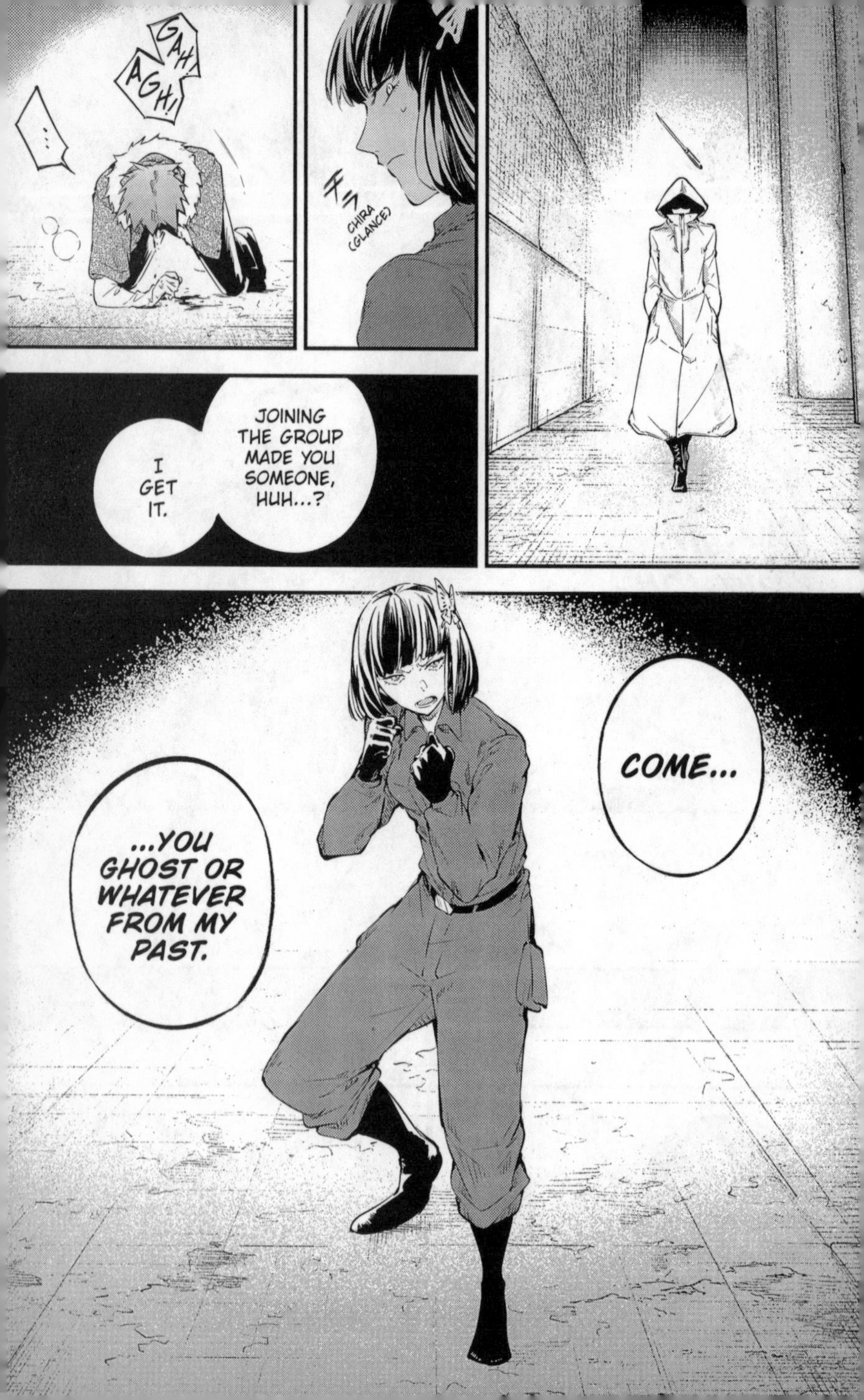

チラ
CHIRA (GLANCE)
GAH!
AGH!
...
JOINING THE GROUP MADE YOU SOMEONE, HUH...?
I GET IT.
COME...
...YOU GHOST OR WHATEVER FROM MY PAST.

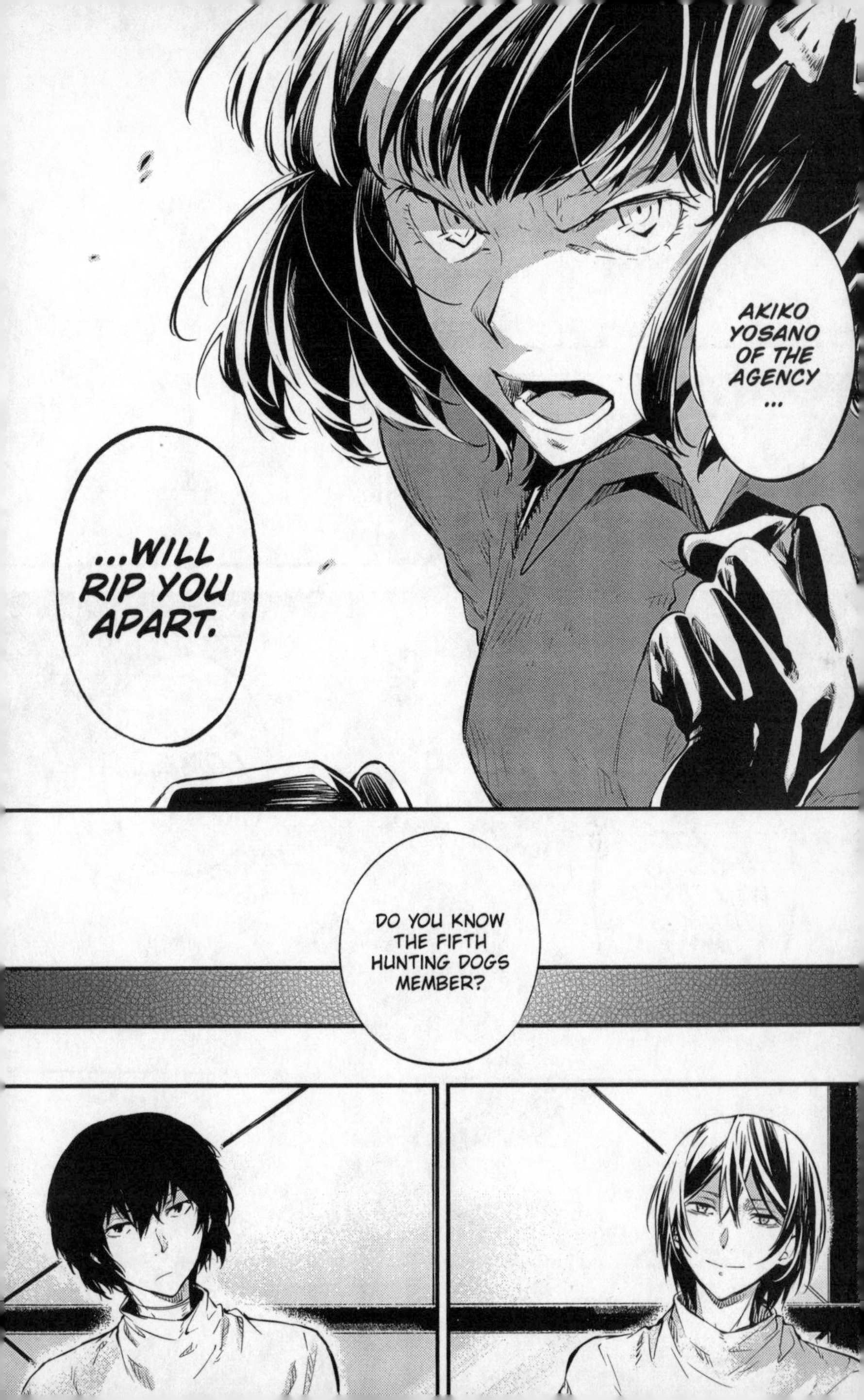
AKIKO YOSANO OF THE AGENCY ...
...WILL RIP YOU APART.
DO YOU KNOW THE FIFTH HUNTING DOGS MEMBER?

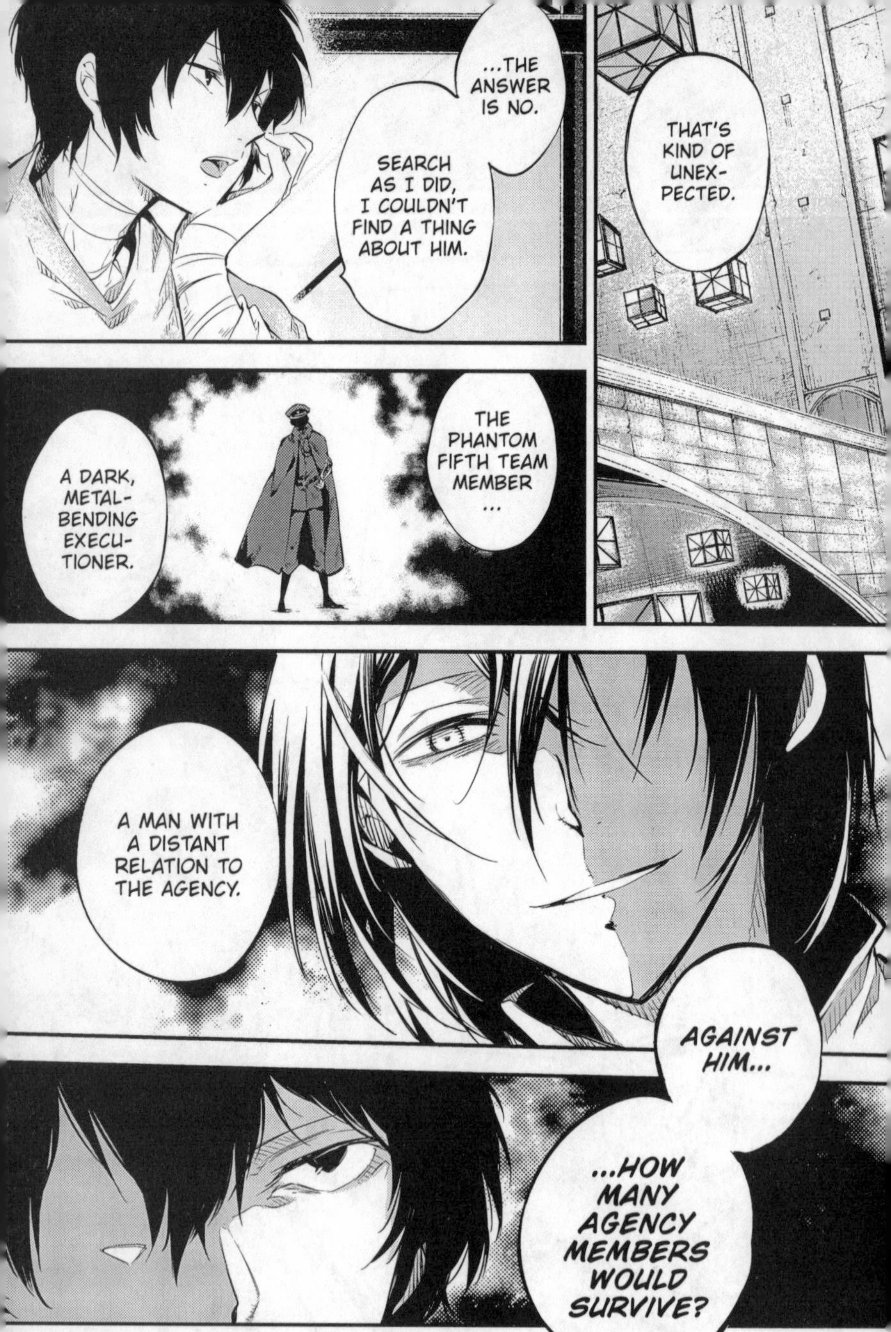
THAT'S KIND OF UNEXPECTED.
...THE ANSWER IS NO.
SEARCH AS I DID, I COULDN'T FIND A THING ABOUT HIM.
THE PHANTOM FIFTH TEAM MEMBER ...
A DARK, METAL-BENDING EXECUTIONER.
A MAN WITH A DISTANT RELATION TO THE AGENCY.
AGAINST HIM...
...HOW MANY AGENCY MEMBERS WOULD SURVIVE?

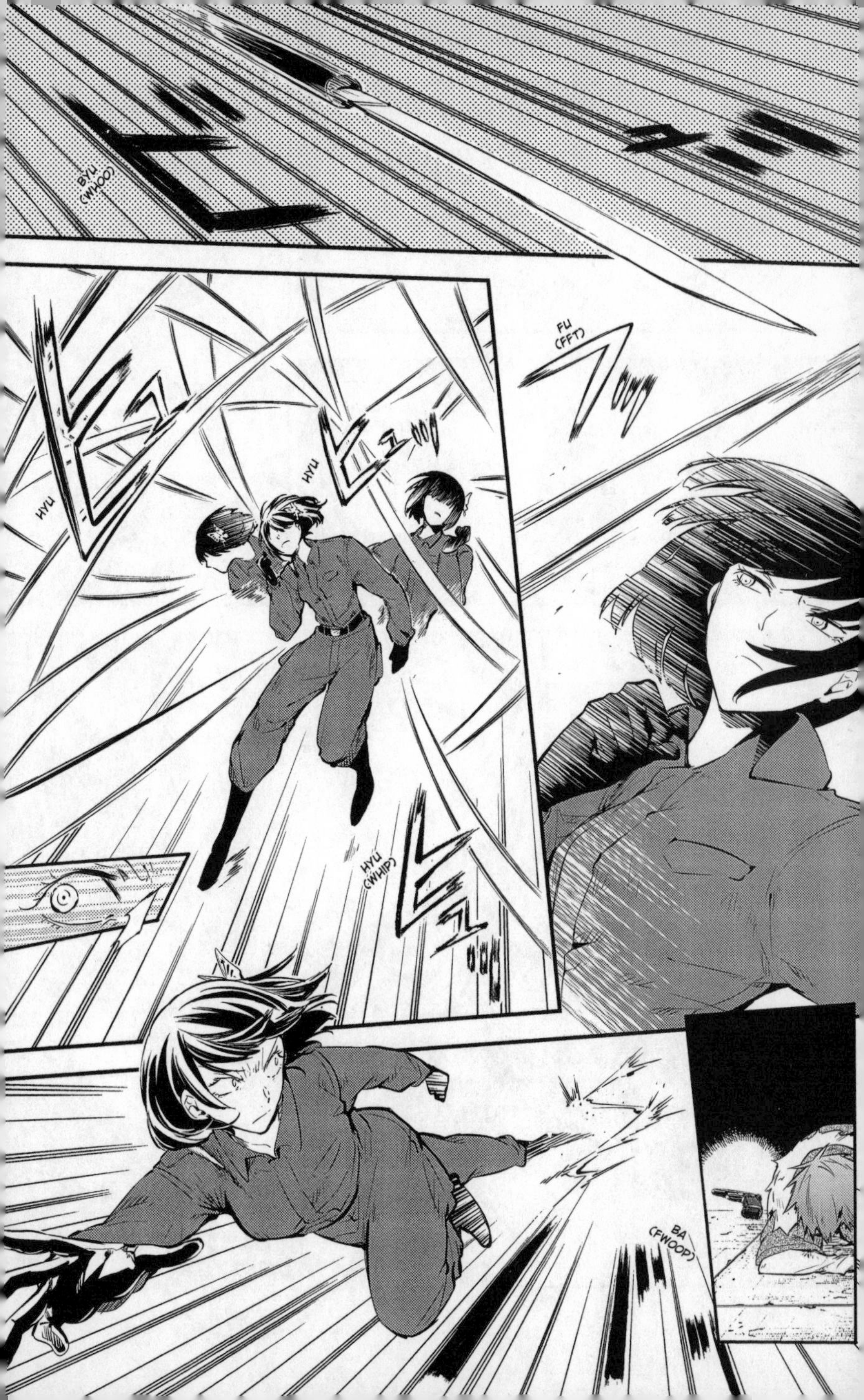
BYU (WHOO)
FU (FFT)
HYU
HYU
HYU (WHIP)
BA (FWOOP)

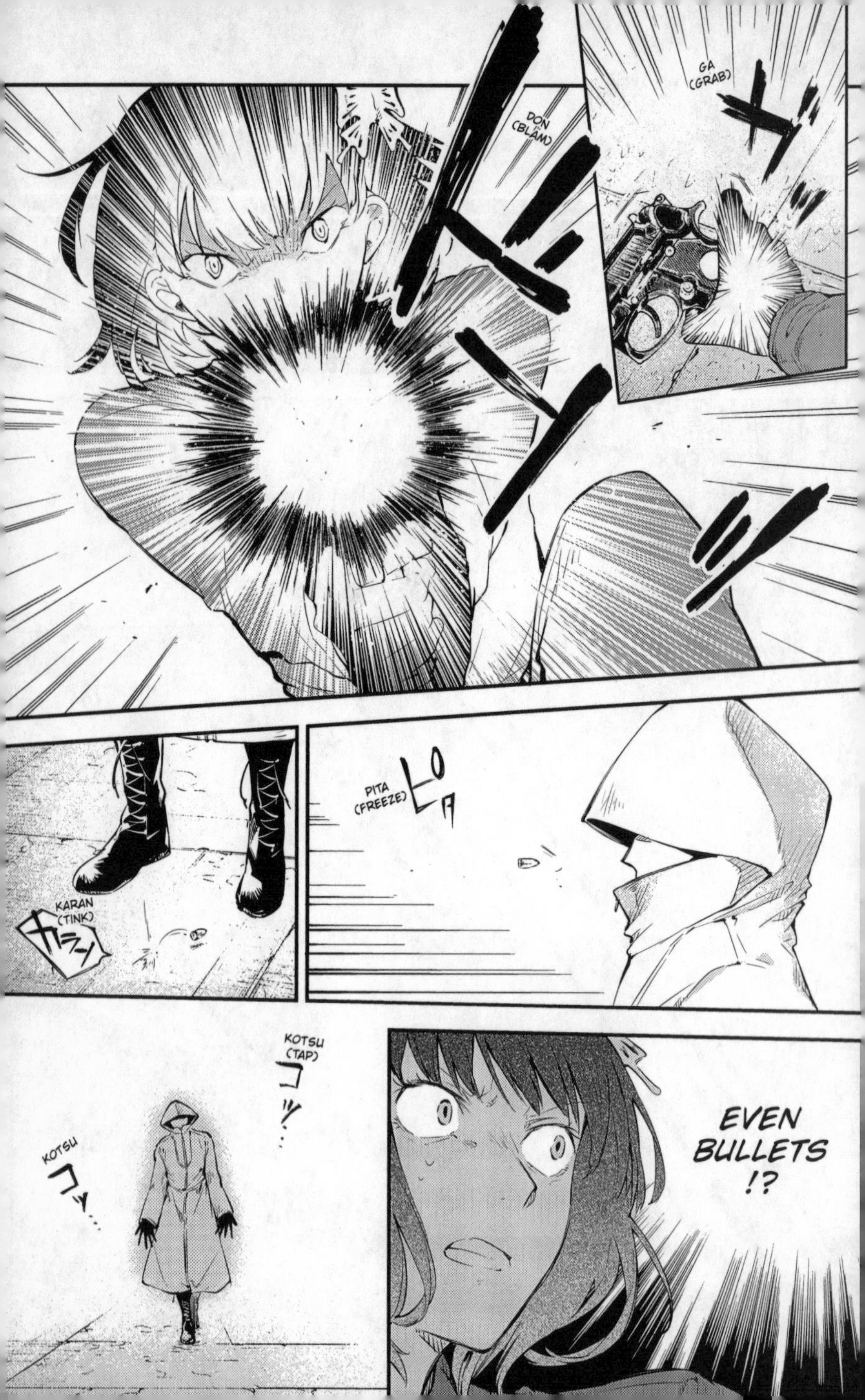
GA (GRAB)
DON (BLAM)
PITA (FREEZE)
KARAN (TINK)
EVEN BULLETS !?
KOTSU (TAP)
KOTSU

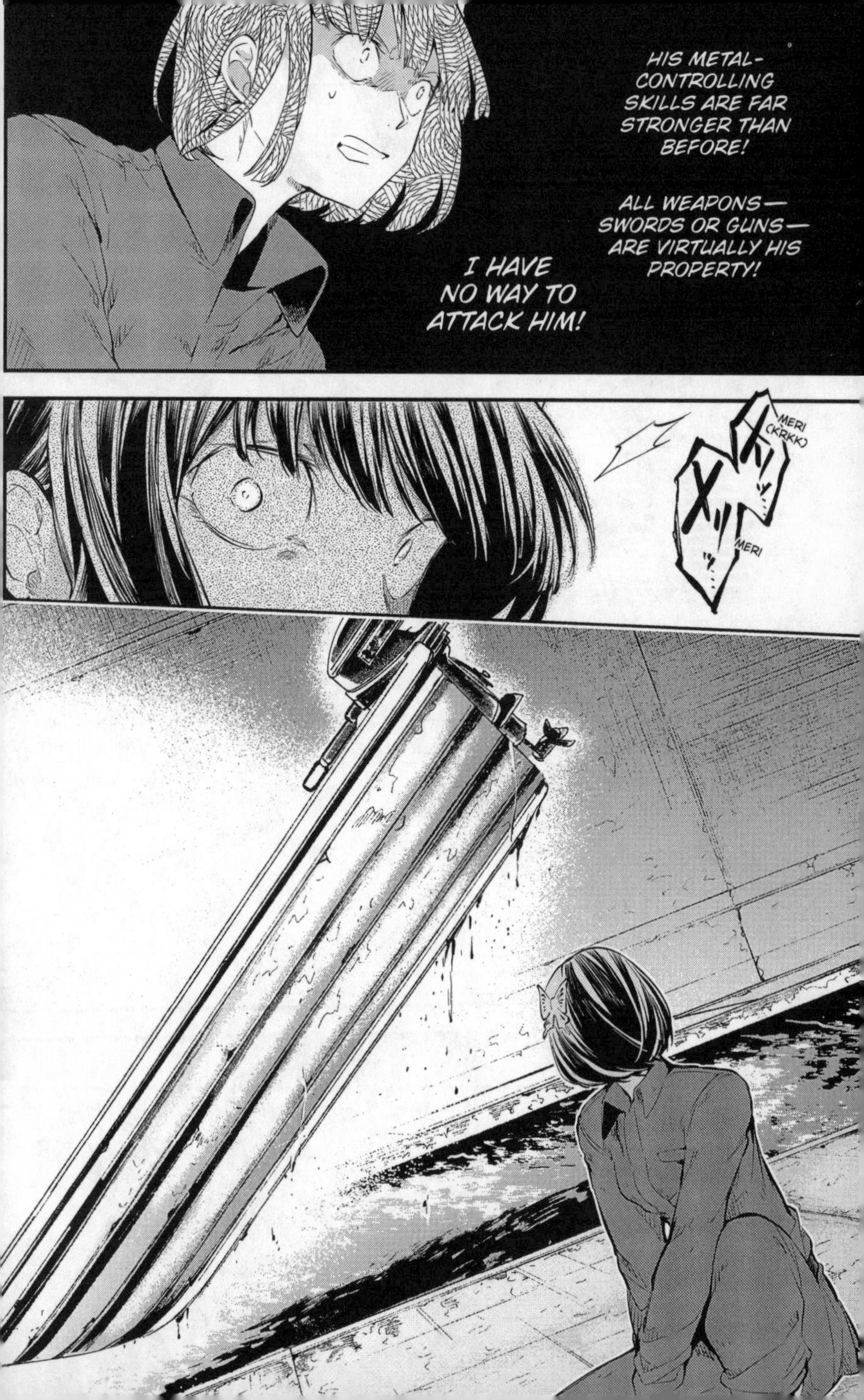
HIS METAL-CONTROLLING SKILLS ARE FAR STRONGER THAN BEFORE!
ALL WEAPONS—SWORDS OR GUNS—ARE VIRTUALLY HIS PROPERTY!
I HAVE NO WAY TO ATTACK HIM!
MERI (KRKK)
MERI

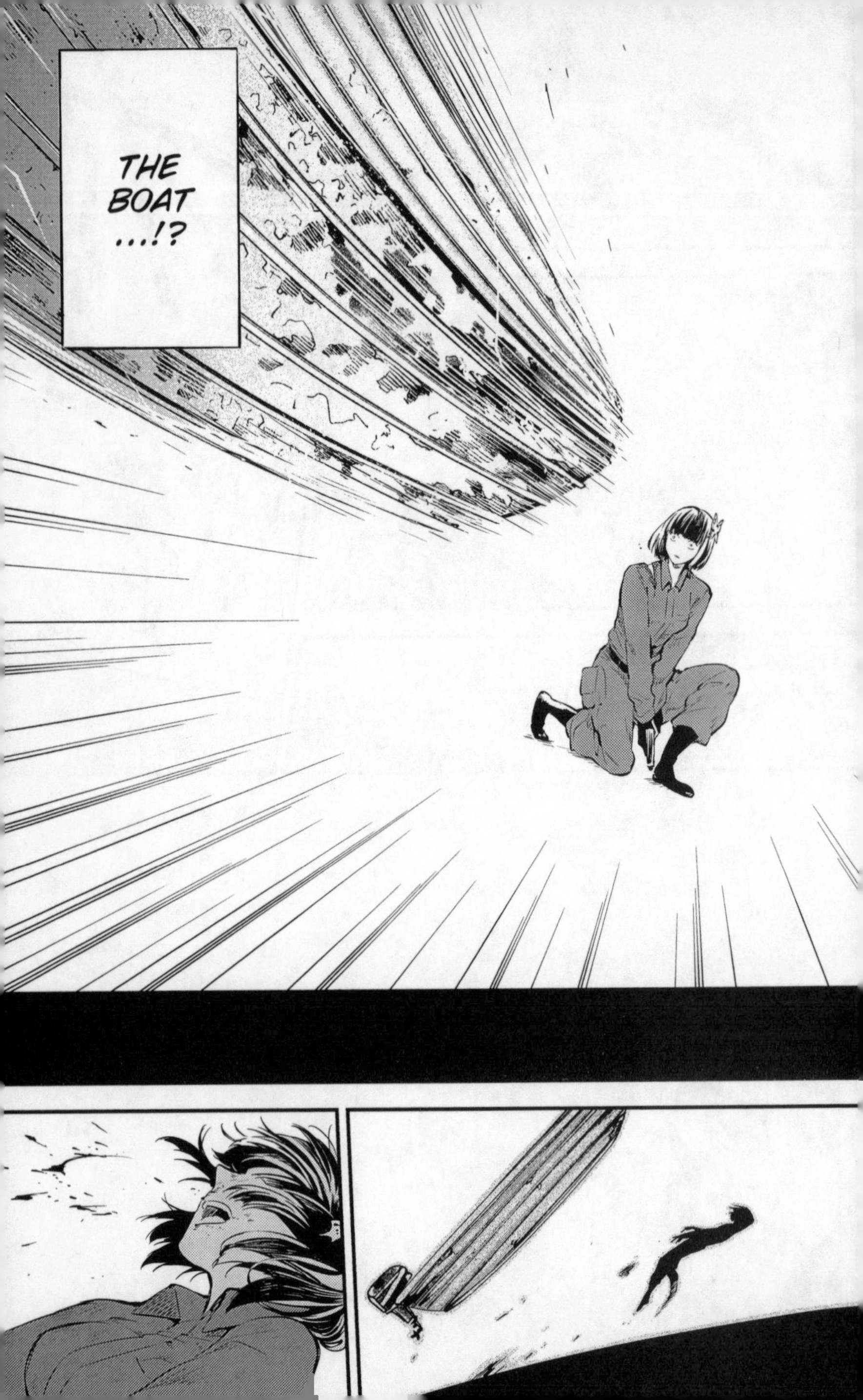
THE BOAT ...!?

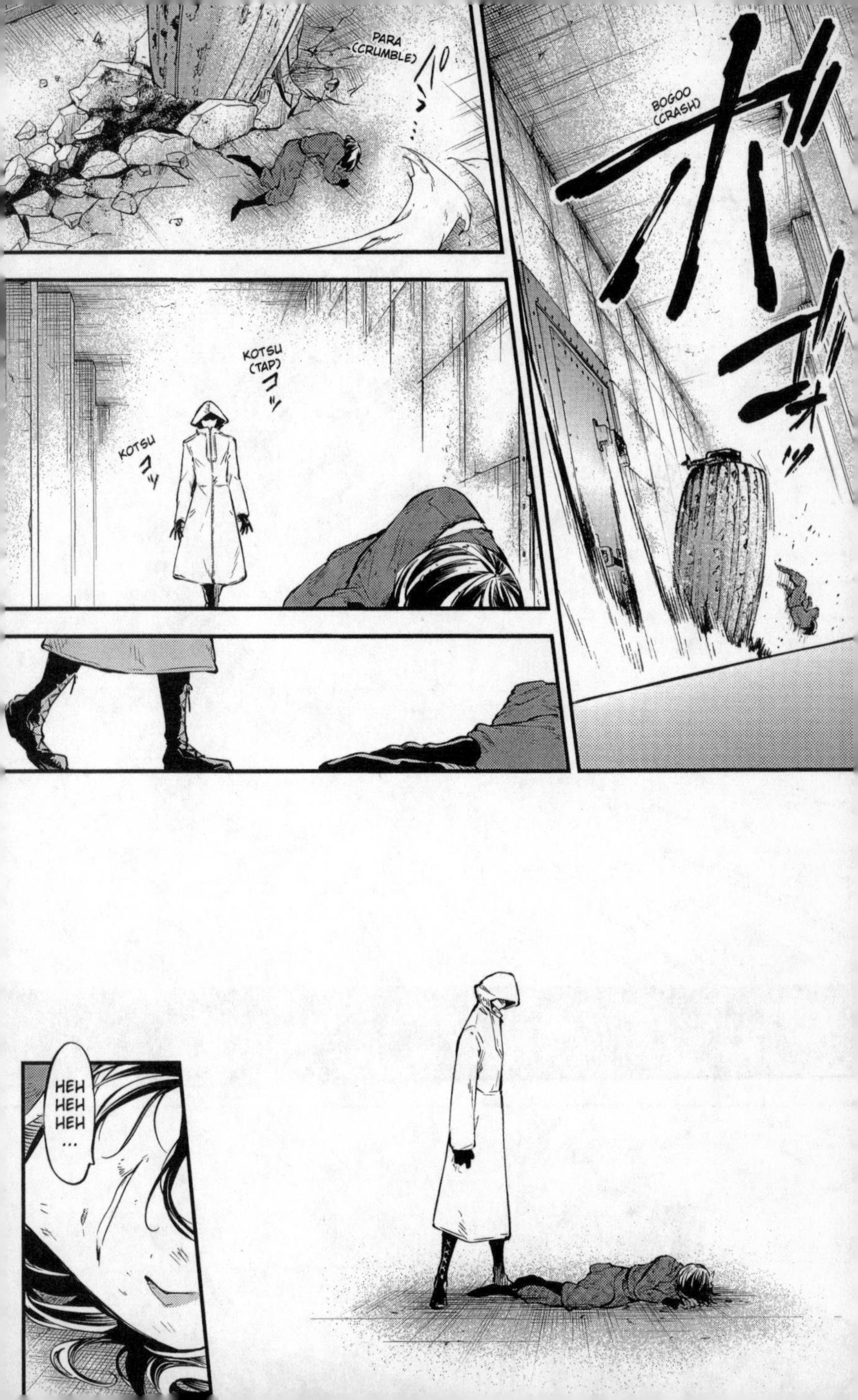
BOGOO (CRASH)
PARA (CRUMBLE)
KOTSU (TAP)
KOTSU
HEH HEH HEH ...

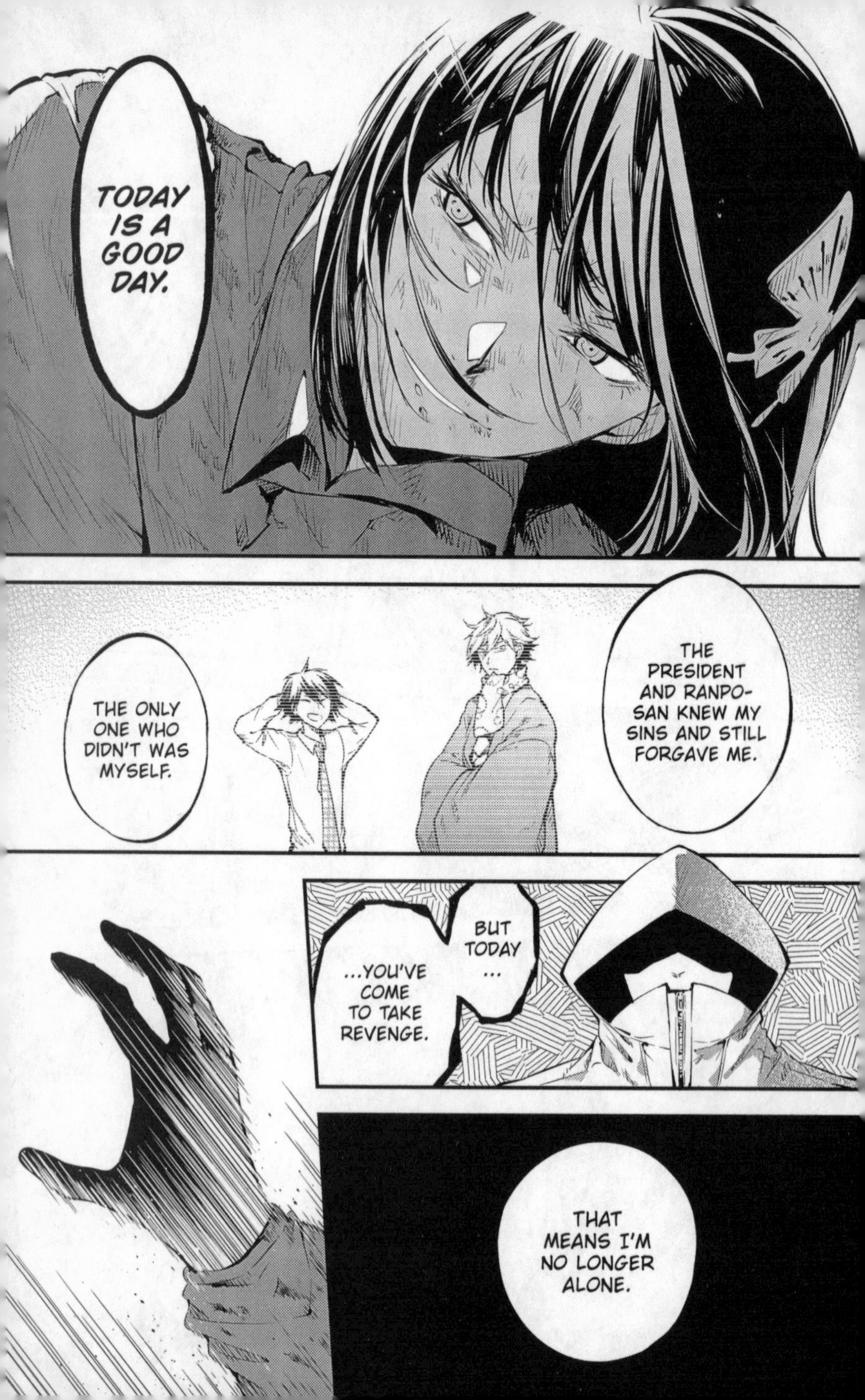
TODAY IS A GOOD DAY.
THE PRESIDENT AND RANPO-SAN KNEW MY SINS AND STILL FORGAVE ME.
THE ONLY ONE WHO DIDN'T WAS MYSELF.
BUT TODAY ...
...YOU'VE COME TO TAKE REVENGE.
THAT MEANS I'M NO LONGER ALONE.

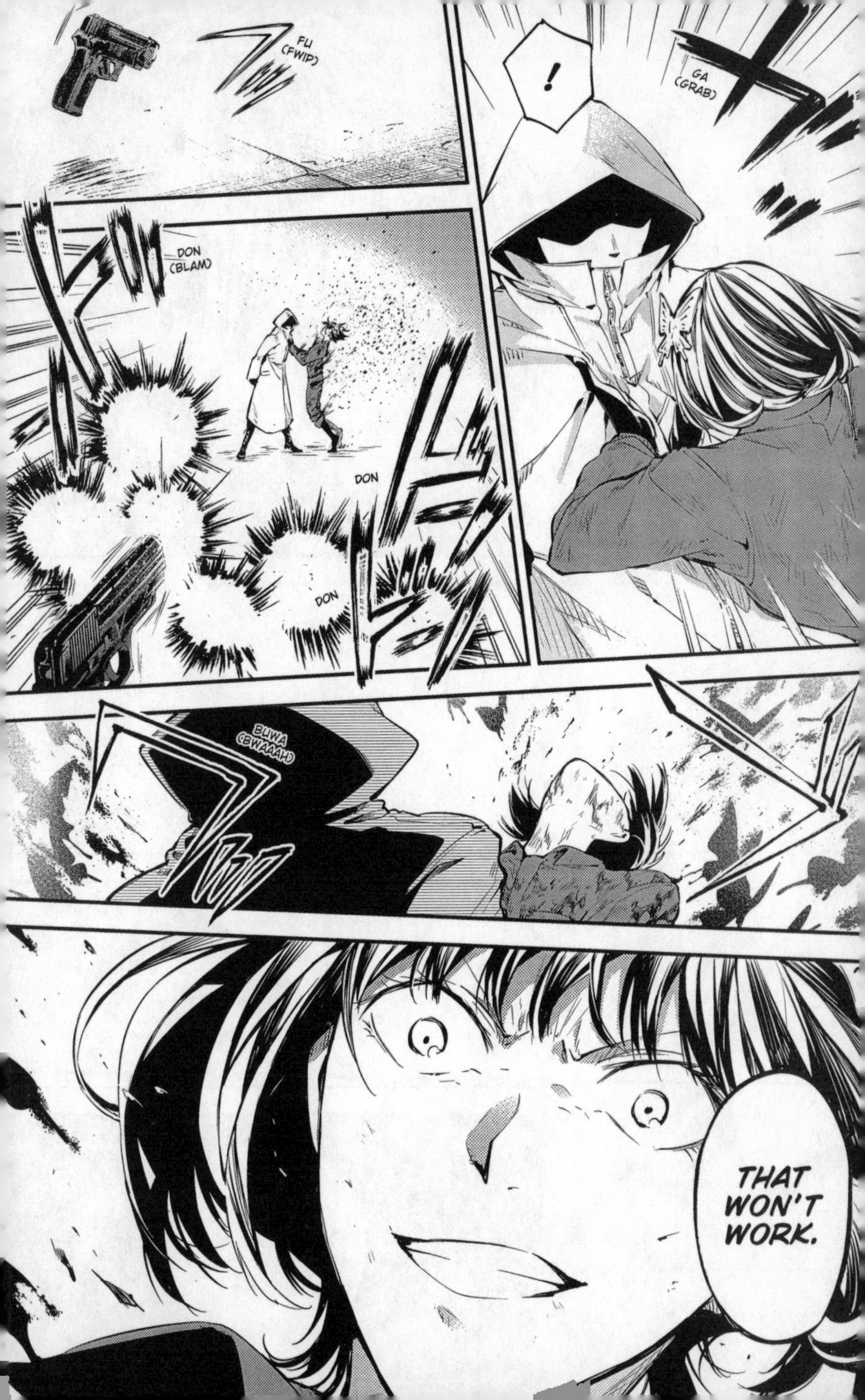
!
GA (GRAB)
FU (FWIP)
DON (BLAM)
DON
DON
BUWA (BWAAAH)
THAT WON'T WORK.

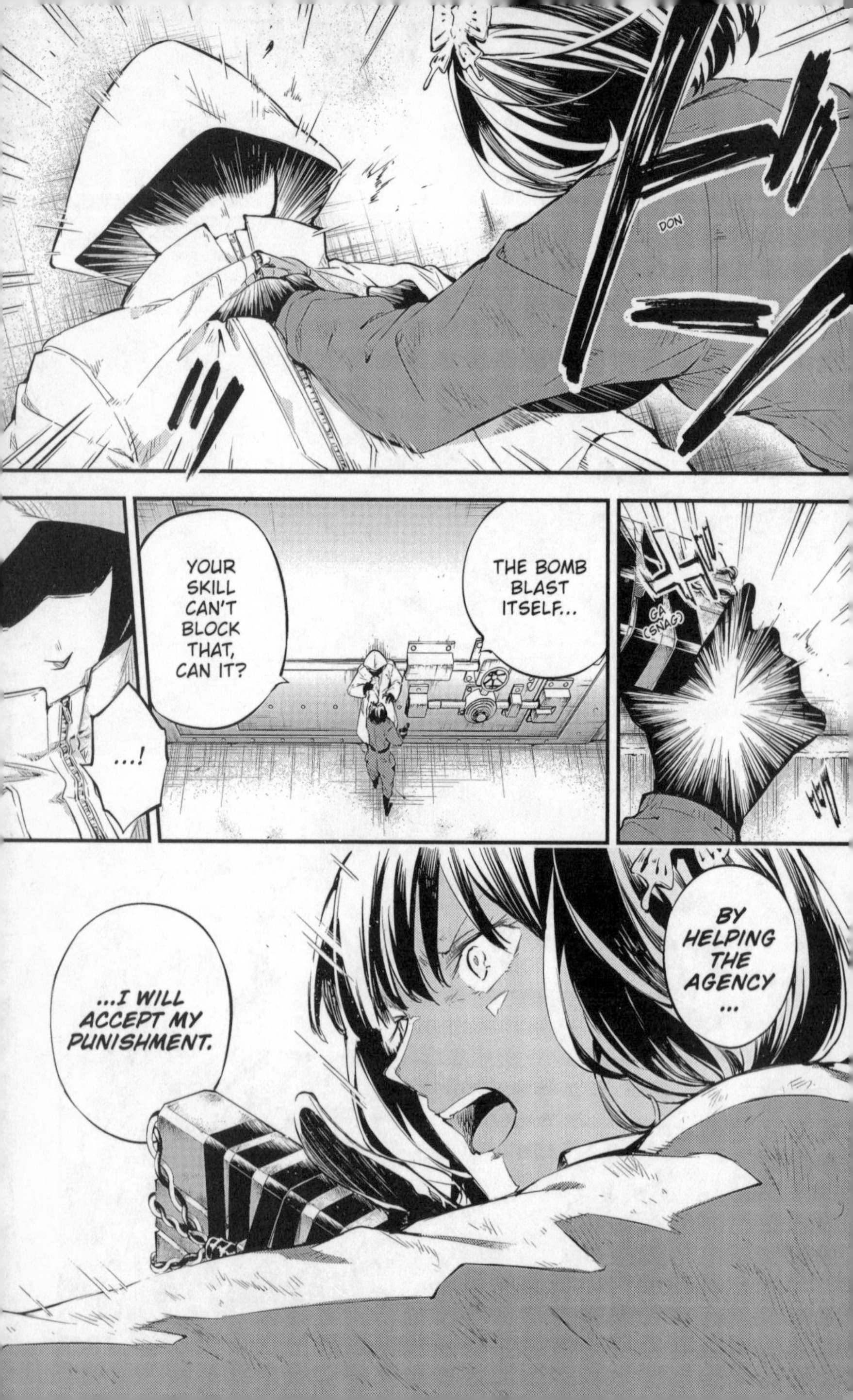
DON
GA (SNAG)
THE BOMB BLAST ITSELF...
YOUR SKILL CAN'T BLOCK THAT, CAN IT?
...!
BY HELPING THE AGENCY...
...I WILL ACCEPT MY PUNISHMENT.

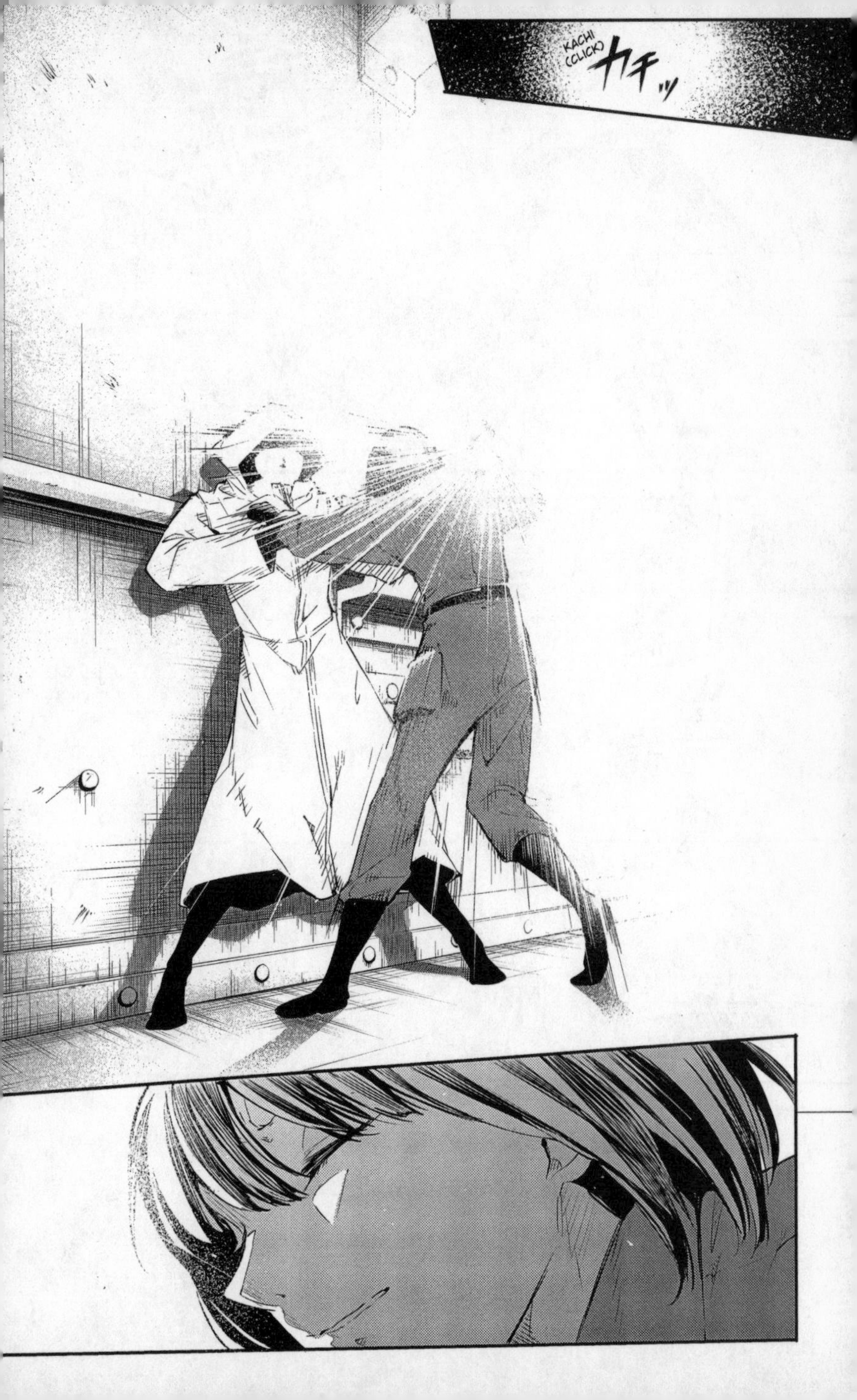
KACHI (CLICK)
カチッ

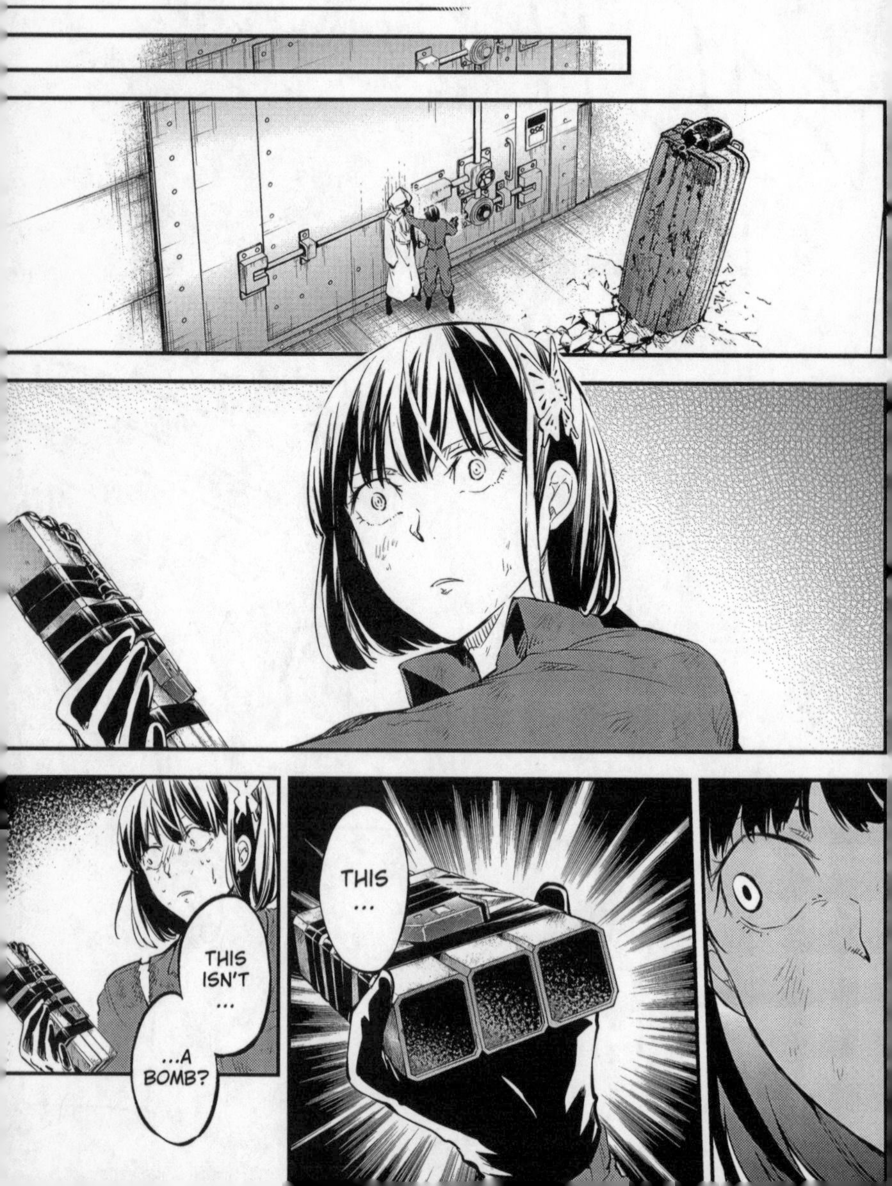
THIS ...
THIS ISN'T ...
...A BOMB?

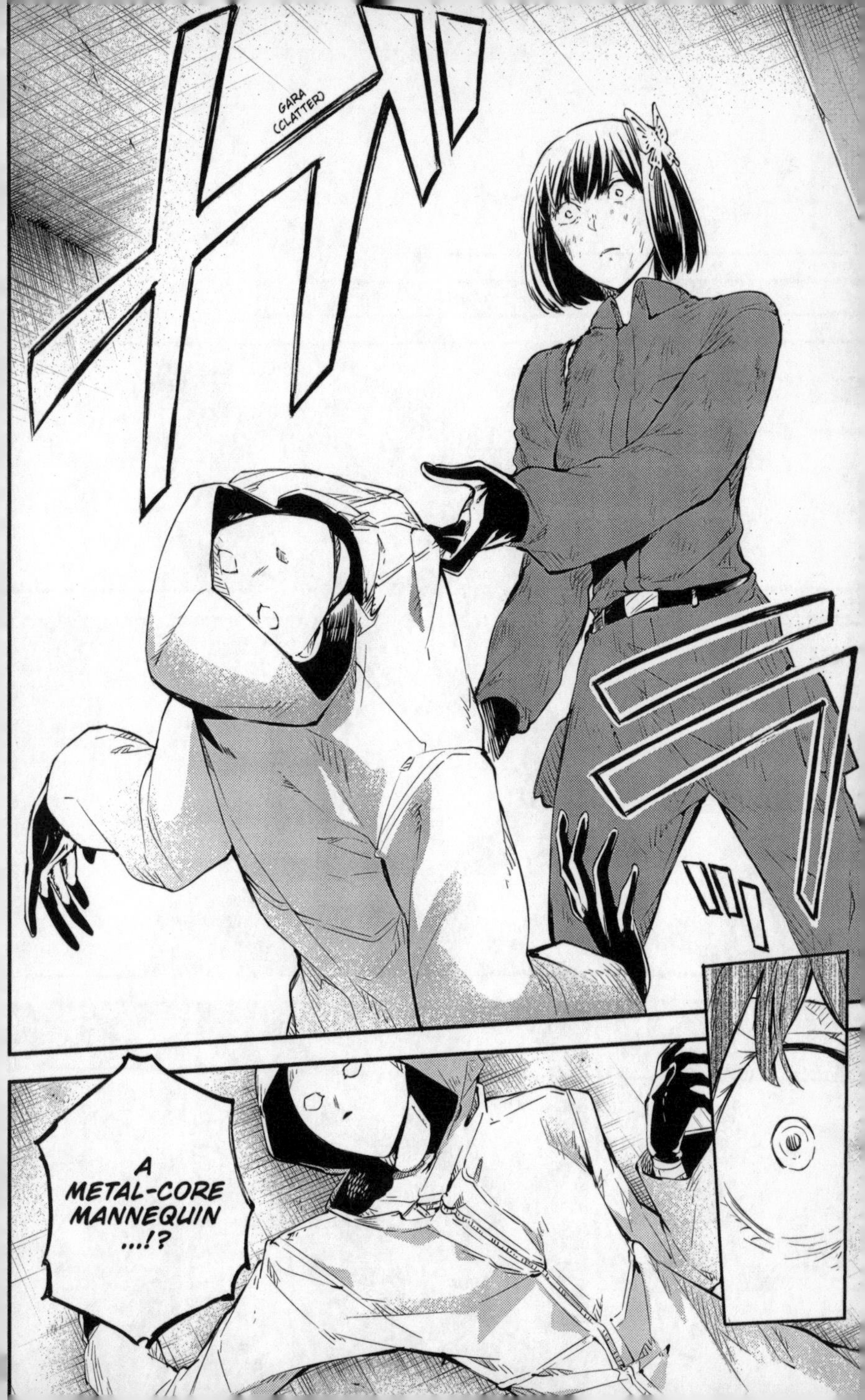
GARA (CLATTER)
A METAL-CORE MANNEQUIN ...!?

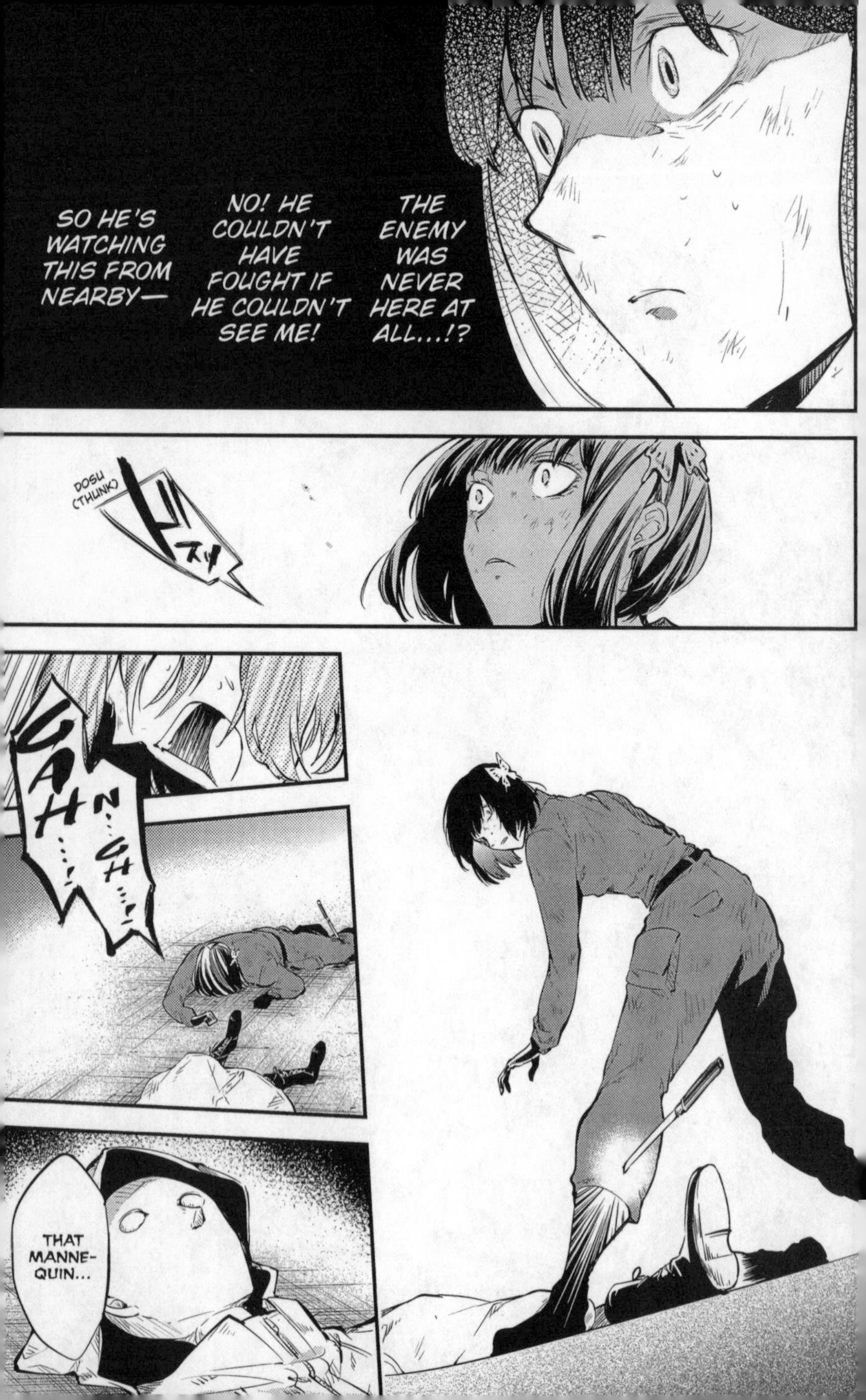
THE ENEMY WAS NEVER HERE AT ALL...!?
NO! HE COULDN'T HAVE FOUGHT IF HE COULDN'T SEE ME!
SO HE'S WATCHING THIS FROM NEARBY—
DOSU (THUNK)
ドスッ
N...GH...!
UAH...!
THAT MANNE-QUIN...

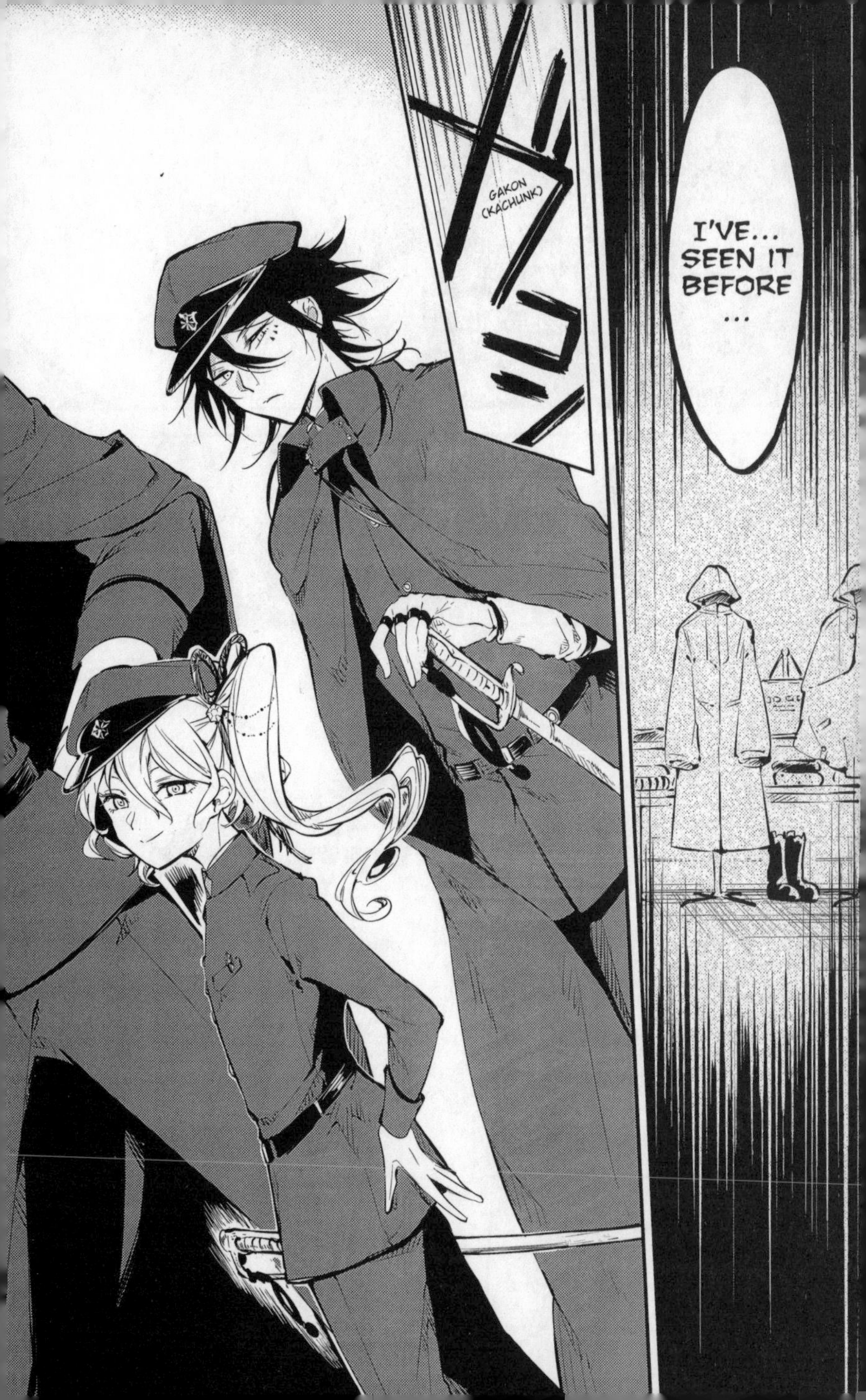
I'VE... SEEN IT BEFORE ...
GAKON (KACHUNK)

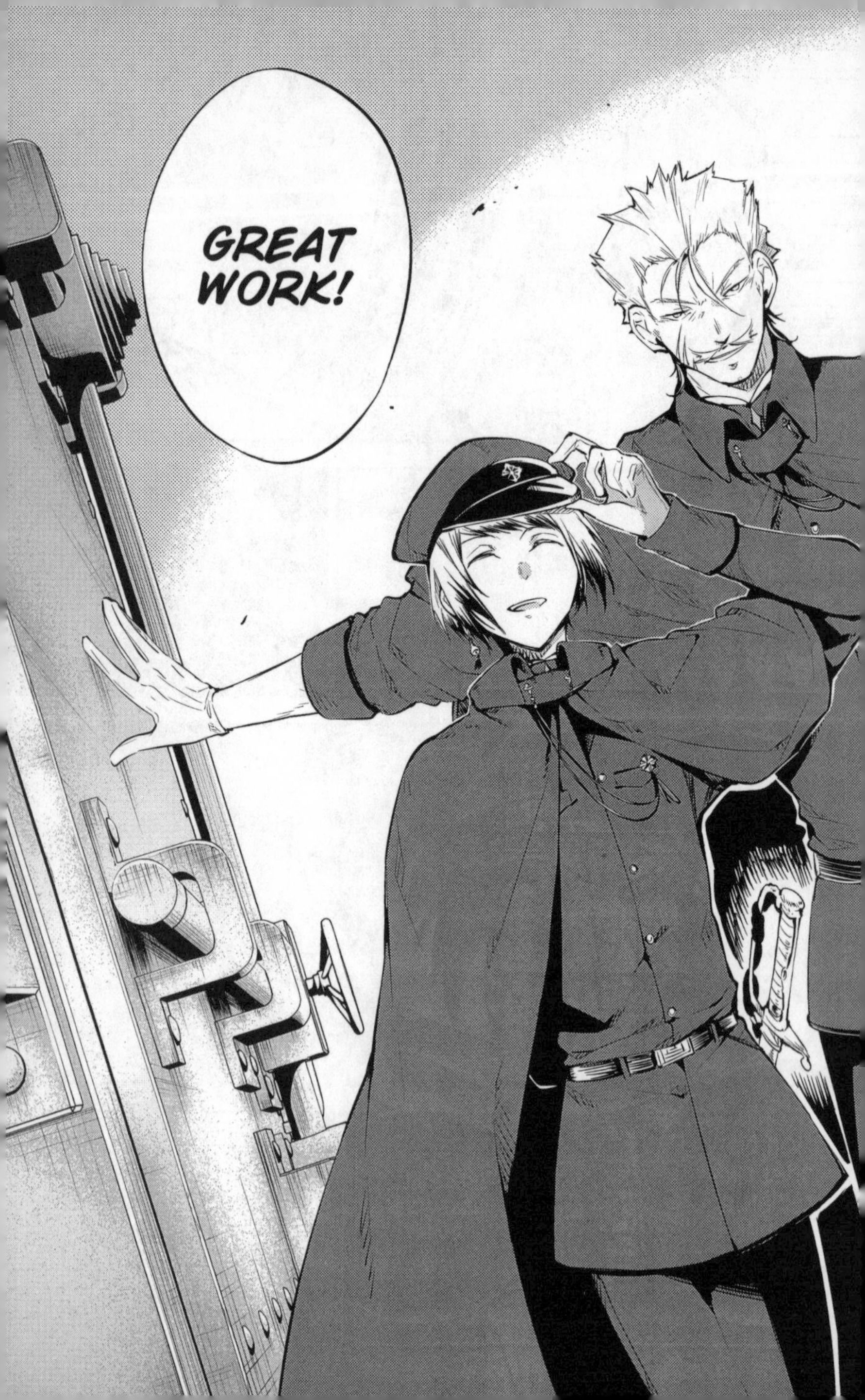
GREAT WORK!

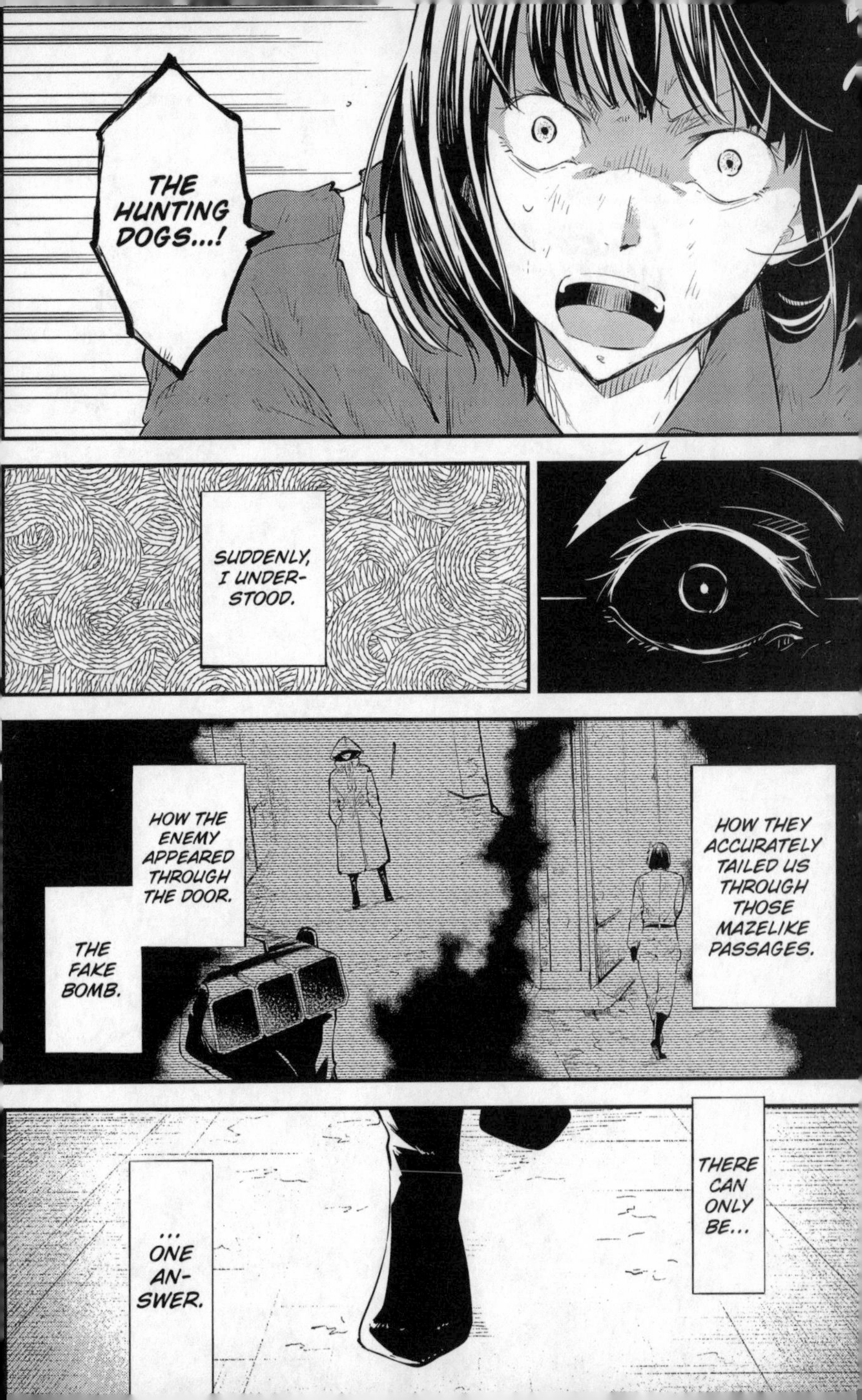
THE HUNTING DOGS...!
SUDDENLY, I UNDERSTOOD.
HOW THEY ACCURATELY TAILED US THROUGH THOSE MAZELIKE PASSAGES.
HOW THE ENEMY APPEARED THROUGH THE DOOR.
THE FAKE BOMB.
THERE CAN ONLY BE...
...ONE ANSWER.

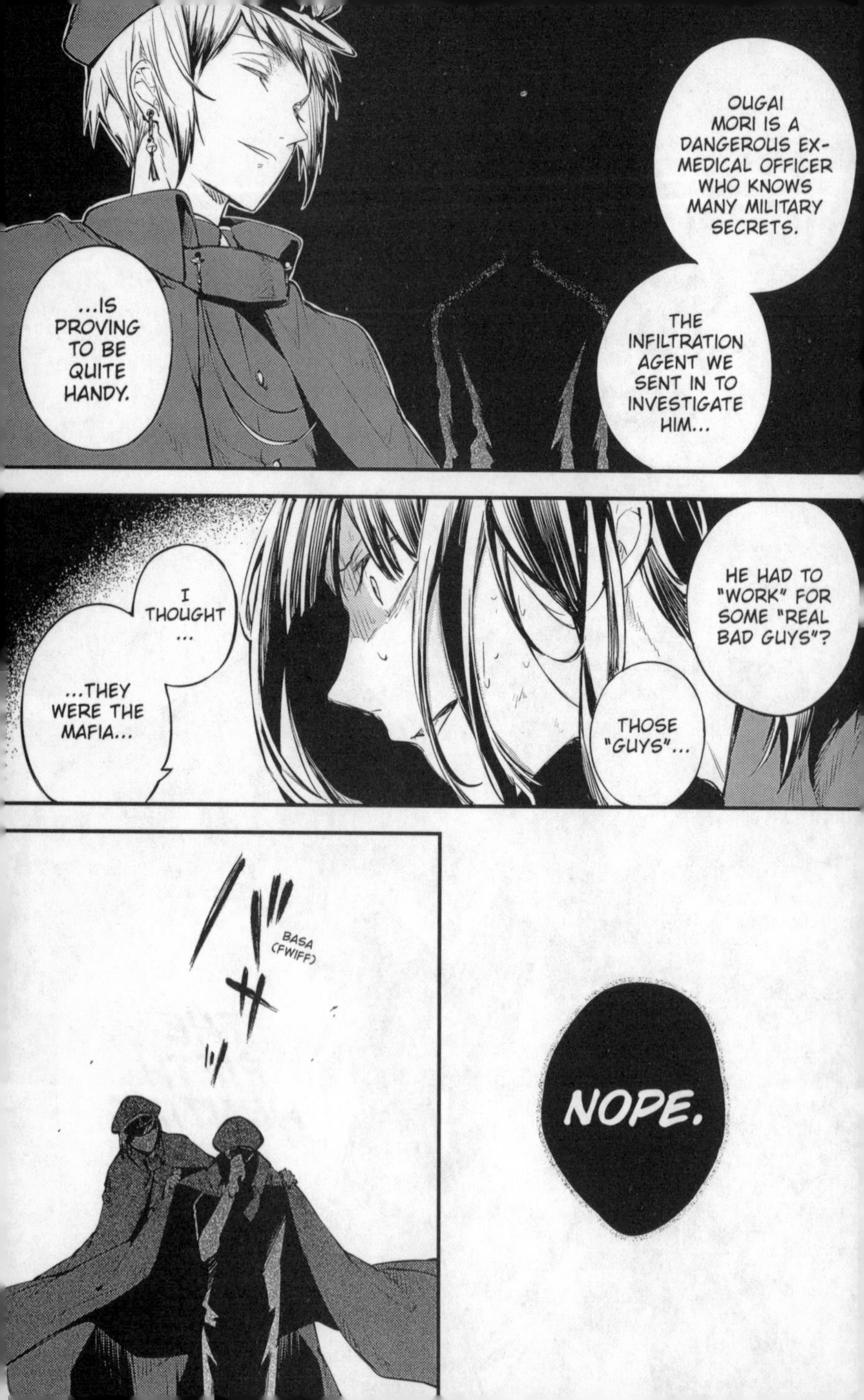
OUGAI MORI IS A DANGEROUS EX-MEDICAL OFFICER WHO KNOWS MANY MILITARY SECRETS.
THE INFILTRATION AGENT WE SENT IN TO INVESTIGATE HIM...
...IS PROVING TO BE QUITE HANDY.
HE HAD TO "WORK" FOR SOME "REAL BAD GUYS"?
THOSE "GUYS"...
I THOUGHT ...
...THEY WERE THE MAFIA...
NOPE.
BASA (FWIFF)

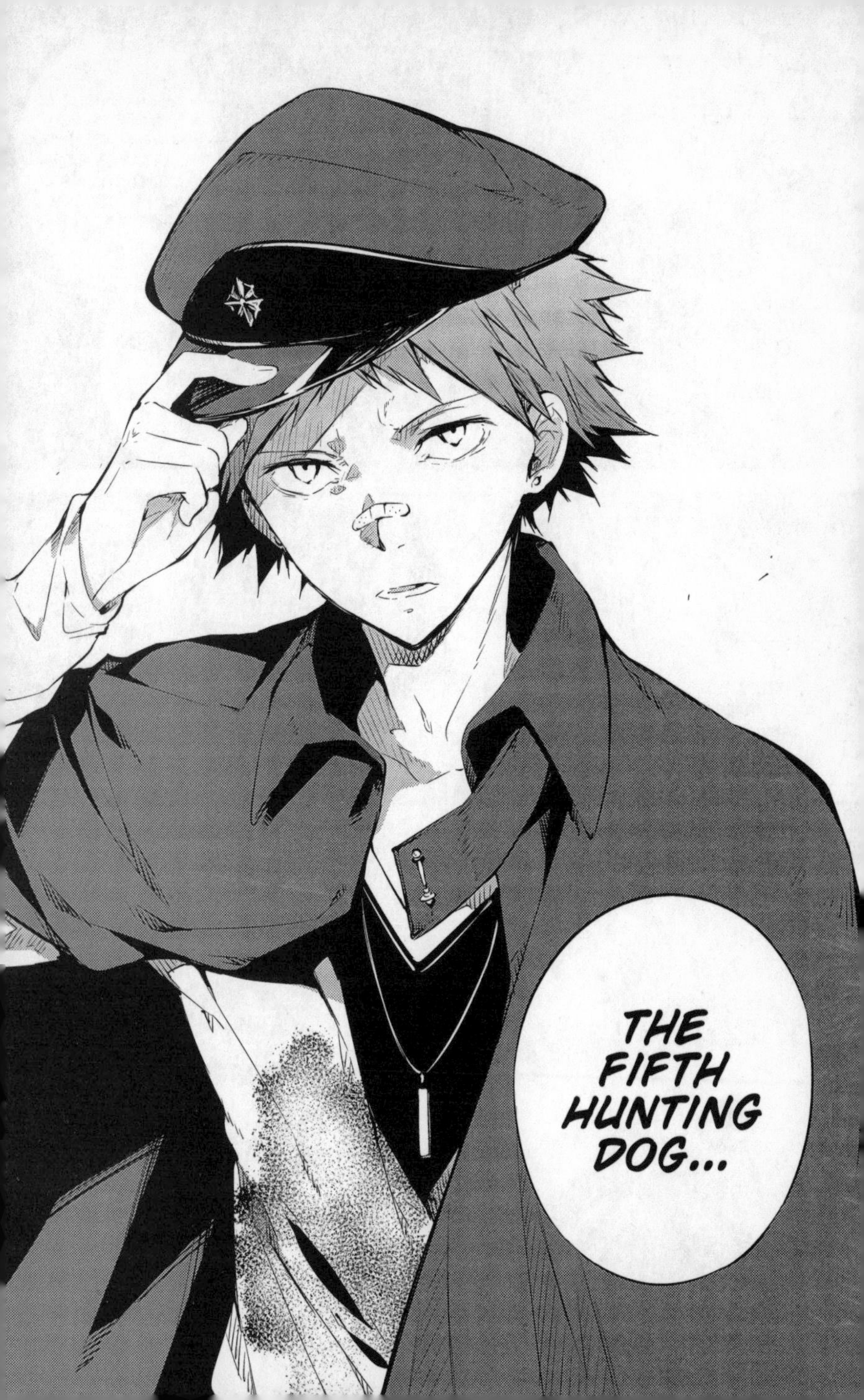
THE FIFTH HUNTING DOG...

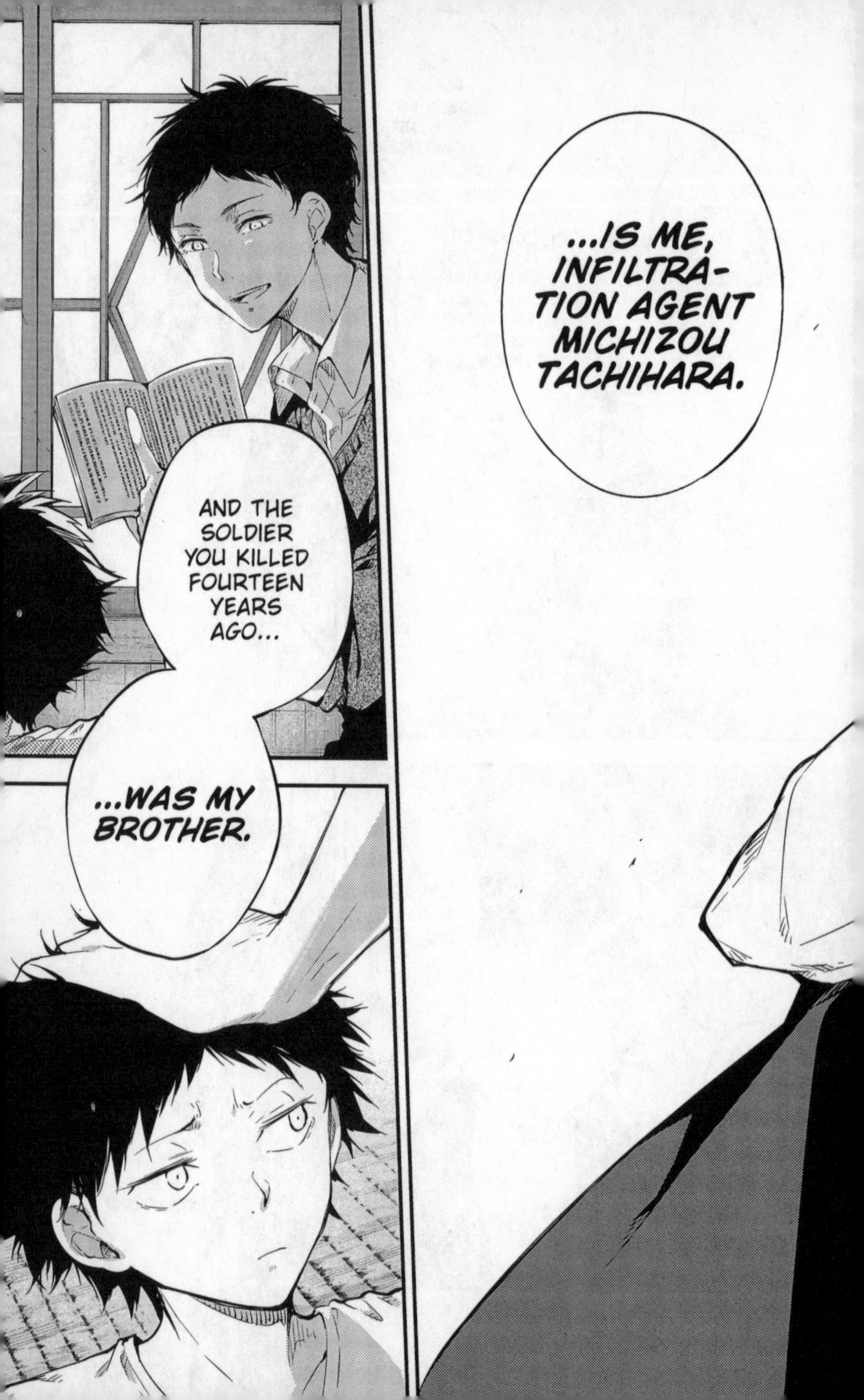
...IS ME, INFILTRATION AGENT MICHIZOU TACHIHARA.
AND THE SOLDIER YOU KILLED FOURTEEN YEARS AGO...
...WAS MY BROTHER.

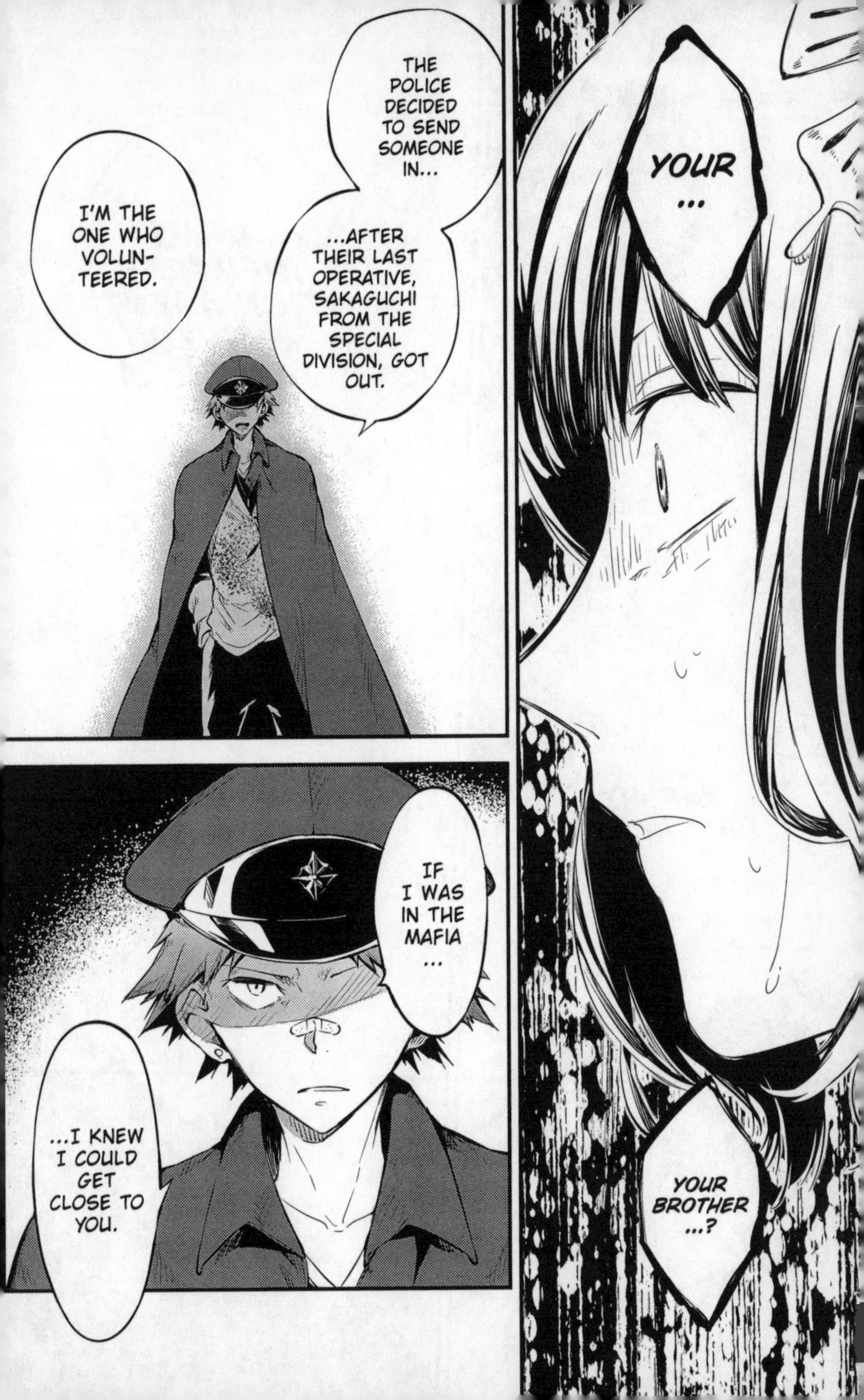
YOUR ...
YOUR BROTHER ...?
THE POLICE DECIDED TO SEND SOMEONE IN...
...AFTER THEIR LAST OPERATIVE, SAKAGUCHI FROM THE SPECIAL DIVISION, GOT OUT.
I'M THE ONE WHO VOLUN-TEERED.
IF I WAS IN THE MAFIA ...
...I KNEW I COULD GET CLOSE TO YOU.

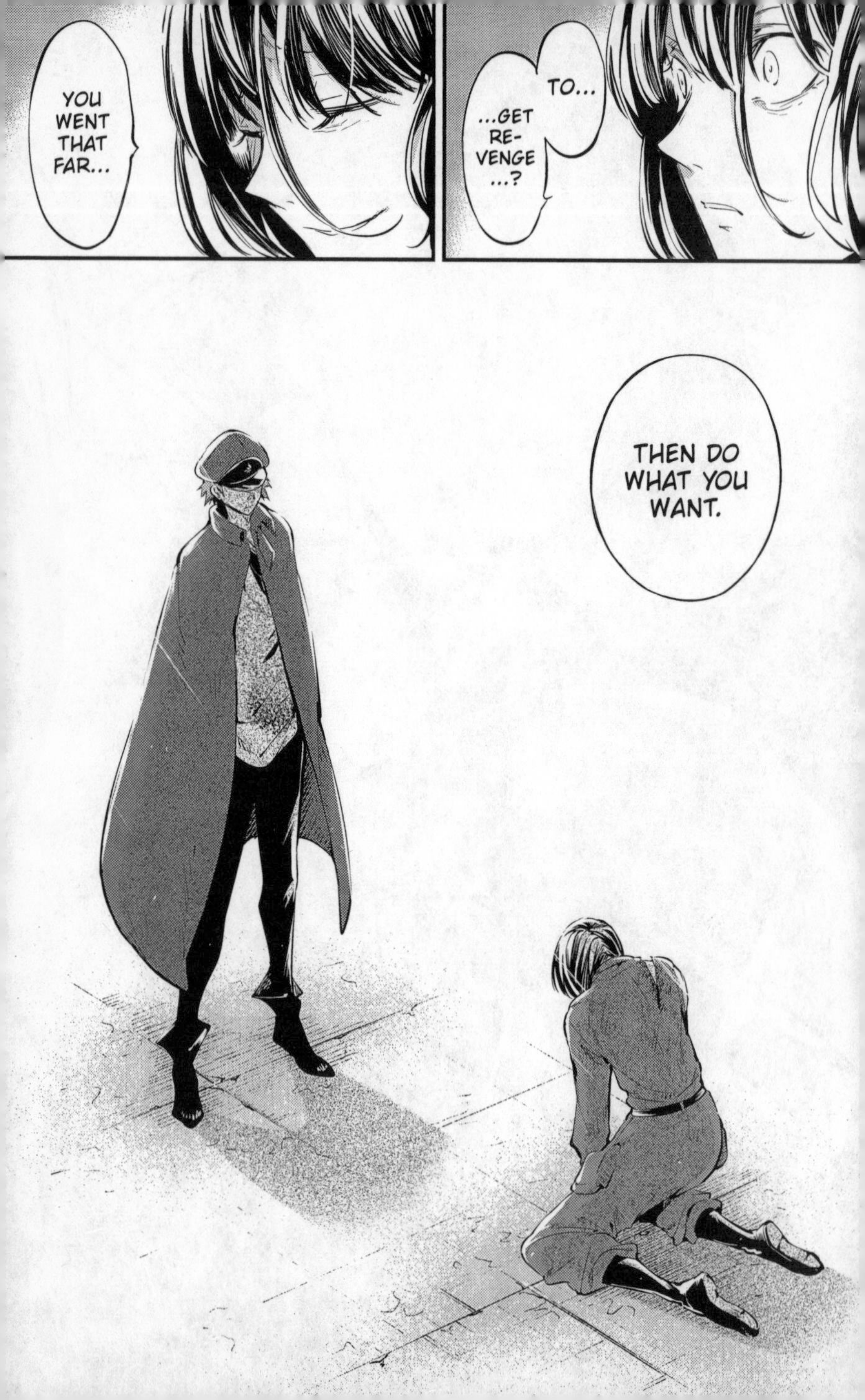
TO... ...GET RE-VENGE ...?
YOU WENT THAT FAR...
THEN DO WHAT YOU WANT.

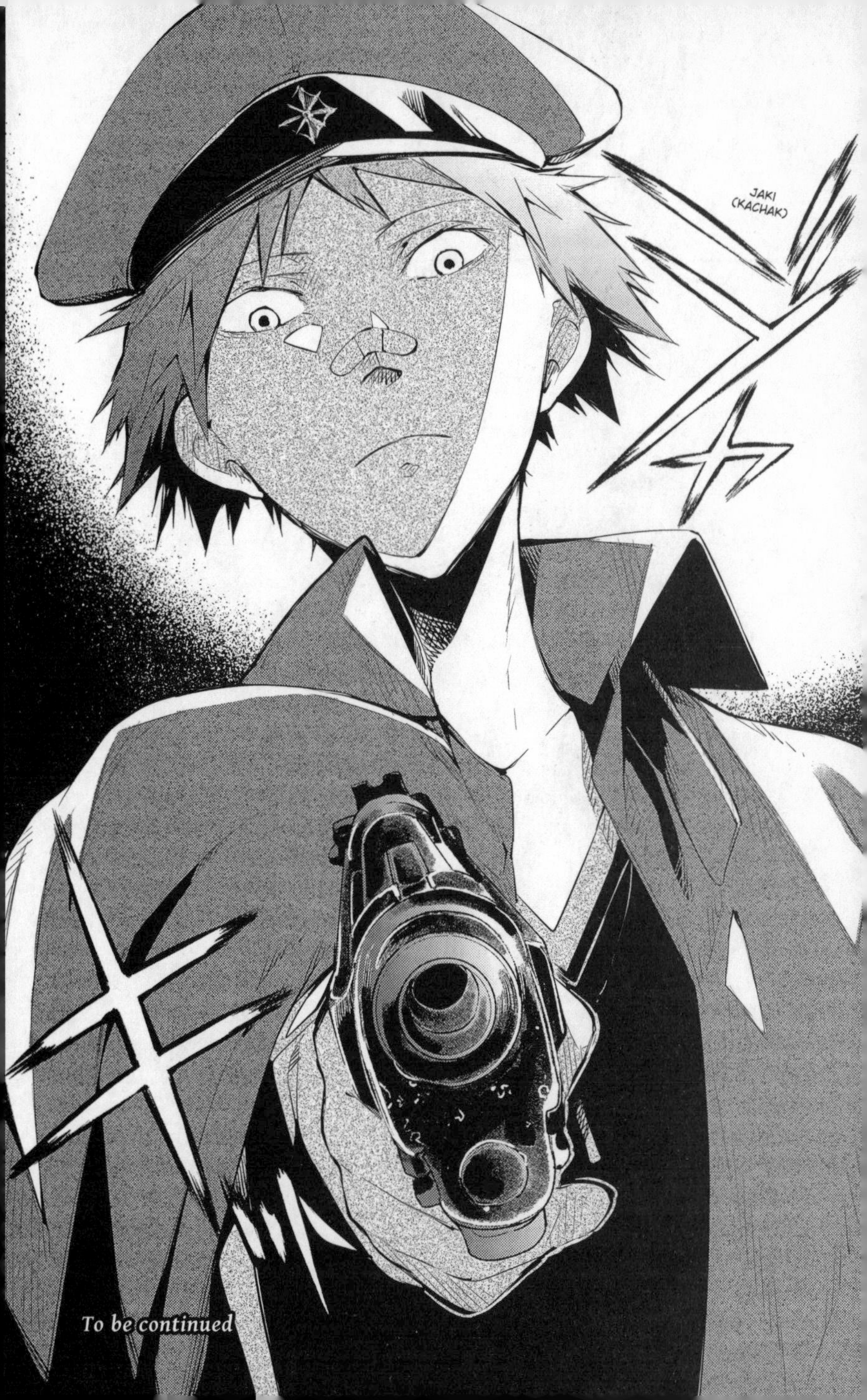
JAKI
(KACHAK)
To be continued

Translation Notes

Page 65
The character for **correct**, with five strokes, is used as a numerical tally in Asia.

Page 78
Routed is a translation of *zenmetsu*, which uses the characters for "complete destruction." While in common usage, it typically refers to total annihilation, its military definition only indicates the majority of a force being unable to continue fighting.

Page 138
In the original Japanese, Hirotsu is using terms from kabuki theater. **Dramatic entrance** is a loose translation of the term *hanamichi*, a special stage in kabuki used for entrances, exits, climactic scenes, and focused moments. **Buffoon** is *douke*, a comedic sidekick character archetype.

BUNGO STRAY DOGS

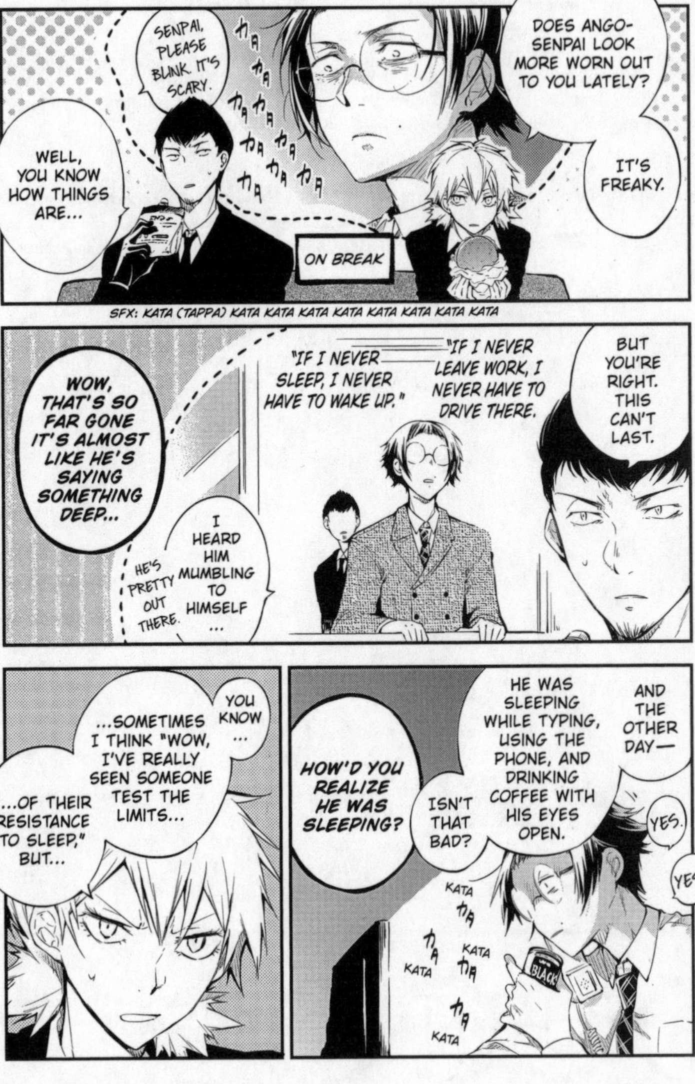
DOES ANGO-SENPAI LOOK MORE WORN OUT TO YOU LATELY?
IT'S FREAKY.
SENPAI, PLEASE BLINK. IT'S SCARY.
WELL, YOU KNOW HOW THINGS ARE...
ON BREAK
SFX: KATA (TAPPA) KATA KATA KATA KATA KATA KATA KATA KATA
BUT YOU'RE RIGHT. THIS CAN'T LAST.
"IF I NEVER LEAVE WORK, I NEVER HAVE TO DRIVE THERE.
"IF I NEVER SLEEP, I NEVER HAVE TO WAKE UP."
WOW, THAT'S SO FAR GONE IT'S ALMOST LIKE HE'S SAYING SOMETHING DEEP...
I HEARD HIM MUMBLING TO HIMSELF...
HE'S PRETTY OUT THERE.
AND THE OTHER DAY—
HE WAS SLEEPING WHILE TYPING, USING THE PHONE, AND DRINKING COFFEE WITH HIS EYES OPEN.
YES.
YES.
ISN'T THAT BAD?
HOW'D YOU REALIZE HE WAS SLEEPING?
KATA
KATA
KATA
KATA
BLACK
YOU KNOW...
...SOMETIMES I THINK "WOW, I'VE REALLY SEEN SOMEONE TEST THE LIMITS...
"...OF THEIR RESISTANCE TO SLEEP," BUT...

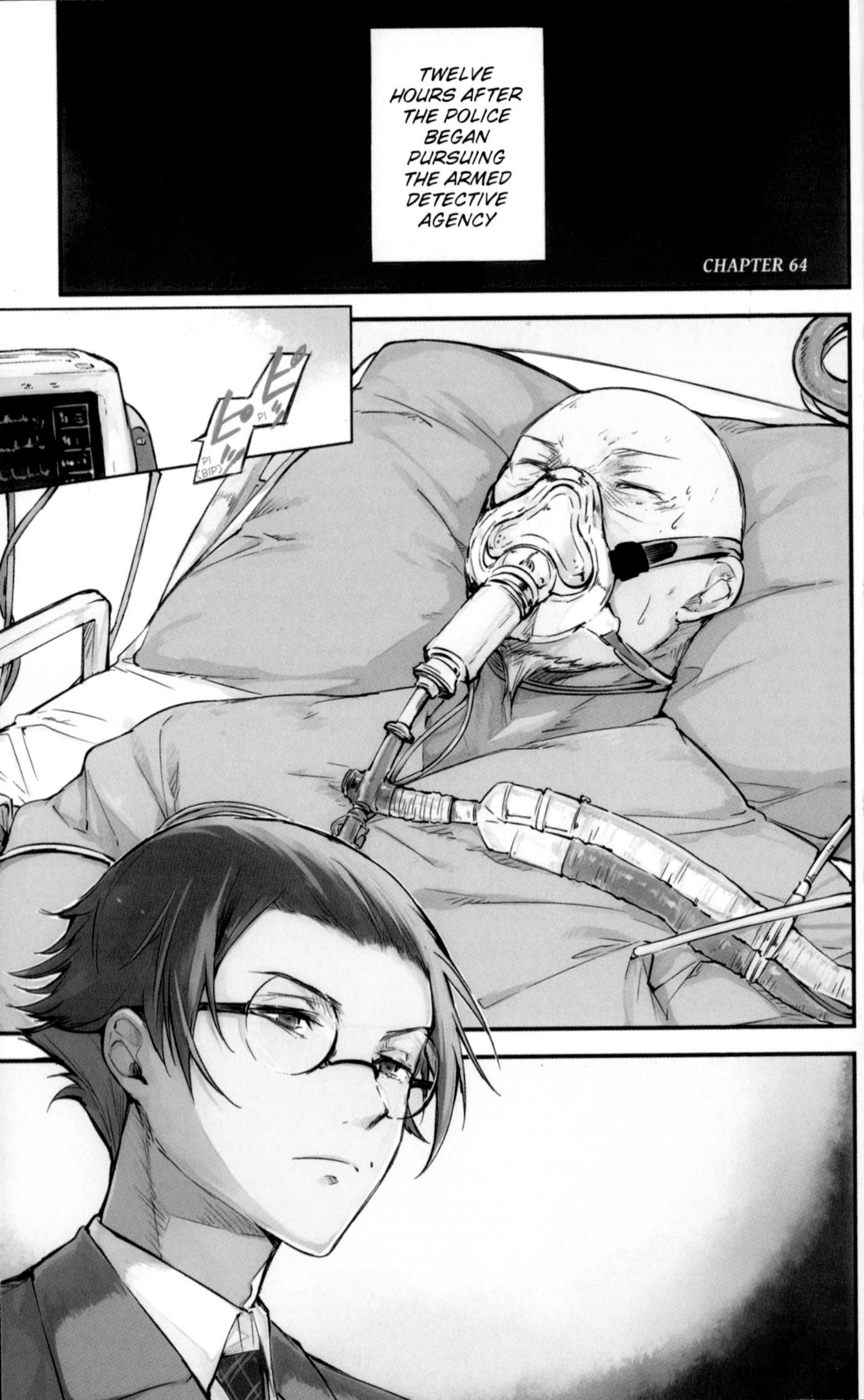
TWELVE HOURS AFTER THE POLICE BEGAN PURSUING THE ARMED DETECTIVE AGENCY
CHAPTER 64
PI PI (BIP)

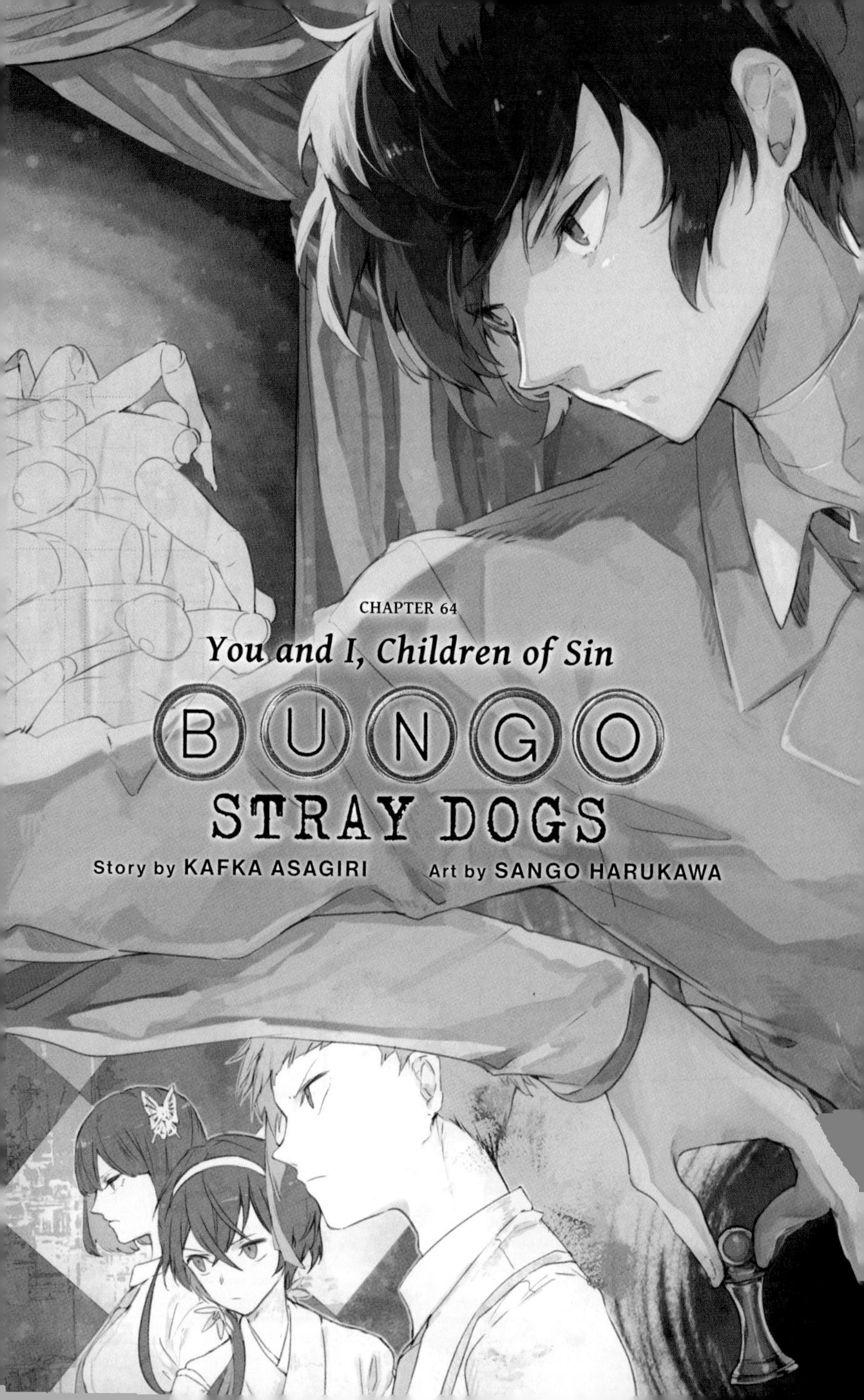
CHAPTER 64
You and I, Children of Sin
BUNGO
STRAY DOGS
Story by KAFKA ASAGIRI
Art by SANGO HARUKAWA

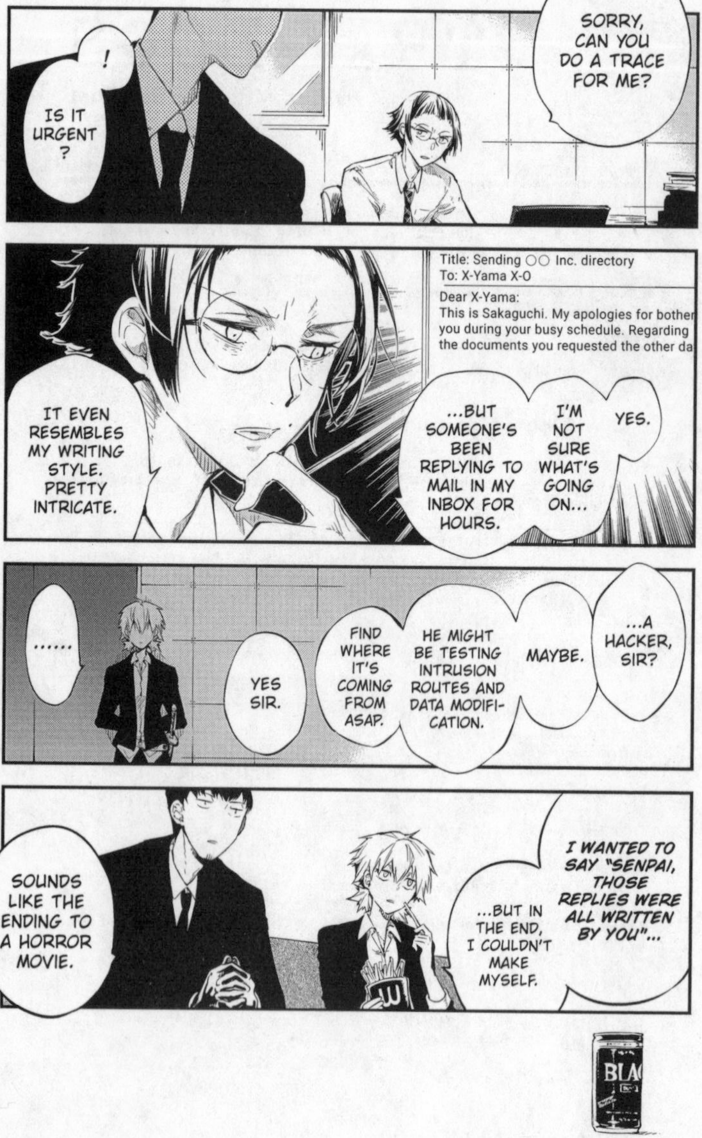
SORRY, CAN YOU DO A TRACE FOR ME?
!
IS IT URGENT?
Title: Sending ○○ Inc. directory
To: X-Yama X-O
Dear X-Yama:
This is Sakaguchi. My apologies for bother you during your busy schedule. Regarding the documents you requested the other da
YES.
I'M NOT SURE WHAT'S GOING ON...
...BUT SOMEONE'S BEEN REPLYING TO MAIL IN MY INBOX FOR HOURS.
IT EVEN RESEMBLES MY WRITING STYLE. PRETTY INTRICATE.
...A HACKER, SIR?
MAYBE.
HE MIGHT BE TESTING INTRUSION ROUTES AND DATA MODIFI-CATION.
FIND WHERE IT'S COMING FROM ASAP.
YES SIR.
......
I WANTED TO SAY "SENPAI, THOSE REPLIES WERE ALL WRITTEN BY YOU"...
...BUT IN THE END, I COULDN'T MAKE MYSELF.
SOUNDS LIKE THE ENDING TO A HORROR MOVIE.
BLAC

BUNGO
STRAY DOGS

Story: Kafka Asagiri   Art: Sango Harukawa

Translation: Kevin Gifford   †   Lettering: Bianca Pistillo

BUNGO STRAY DOGS Volume 16
©Kafka Asagiri 2018
©Sango Harukawa 2018
First published in Japan in 2018 by KADOKAWA CORPORATION, Tokyo.
English translation rights arranged with KADOKAWA CORPORATION, Tokyo through TUTTLE-MORI AGENCY, INC., Tokyo.

English translation © 2020 by Yen Press, LLC

Yen Press
150 West 30th Street, 19th Floor
New York, NY 10001

Visit us at yenpress.com
facebook.com/yenpress
twitter.com/yenpress
yenpress.tumblr.com
instagram.com/yenpress

First Yen Press Edition: October 2020

Yen Press is an imprint of Yen Press, LLC.
The Yen Press name and logo are trademarks of Yen Press, LLC.

The publisher is not responsible for websites (or their content) that are not owned by the publisher.

Library of Congress Control Number: 2016956681

ISBNs: 978-1-9753-5924-9 (paperback)
       978-1-9753-5925-6 (ebook)

10 9 8 7 6 5 4 3 2 1

BVG

Printed in the United States of America